Kate

THE
COLLECTED
ESSAYS
and Occasional Writings of
KATHERINE
ANNE
PORTER

1890 – 1980

Books by Katherine Anne Porter

FLOWERING JUDAS

KATHERINE ANNE PORTER'S
FRENCH SONG BOOK

PALE HORSE, PALE RIDER

THE LEANING TOWER

THE DAYS BEFORE

SHIP OF FOOLS

THE COLLECTED STORIES
OF KATHERINE ANNE PORTER

A CHRISTMAS STORY

THE COLLECTED ESSAYS
AND OCCASIONAL WRITINGS
OF KATHERINE ANNE PORTER

THE NEVER-ENDING WRONG

THE COLLECTED ESSAYS

and Occasional Writings of

KATHERINE ANNE PORTER

HOUGHTON MIFFLIN / SEYMOUR LAWRENCE

Boston

*The publishers wish to express
profound appreciation to
Robert A. Beach, Jr.,
George Core, William Humphrey,
Rhea Johnson, and Glenway Wescott
for their help and guidance
in the preparation of this volume.*

For information about permission to reproduce
selections from this book, write to
Permissions, Houghton Mifflin Company,
2 Park Street, Boston, Massachusetts 02108.

Library of Congress Cataloging-in-Publication Data

Porter, Katherine Anne, 1890–1980
The collected essays and occasional writings
of Katherine Anne Porter.
p.   cm.
Reprint. Originally published: New York :
Delacorte Press, 1970.
ISBN 0–395–53362–7
I. Title.
PS3531.0752A6   1990   90–30034
814'.52 — dc20   CIP

Printed in the United States of America

BP 10 9 8 7 6 5 4 3 2 1

The quotation on page 290 is from "The Journal of My
Other Self," by Rainer Maria Rilke. Translated by
M. D. Herter Norton and John Linton. Published by
W. W. Norton & Company, Inc.

Acknowledgments

Grateful acknowledgment is made to the following in whose pages these essays first appeared.

Encounter: for "A Wreath for the Gamekeeper", 1960.

New York Times Book Review: for "Max Beerbohm", October 22, 1950; "Eleanor Clark", April 13, 1952; and "Dylan Thomas", November 20, 1955, October 13, 1957, and February 2, 1958.

The Nation: for "The Winged Skull", July 17, 1943; "Pull Dick, Pull Devil", October 13, 1945; "A Letter to the Editor", May 24, 1947; and "Miss Porter Adds a Comment", March 6, 1943.

The Washington Post Company: for "On Modern Fiction" published in *Book Week.* Copyright © 1965 The Washington Post Company. Used by permission.

Mademoiselle: for "St. Augustine and the Bullfight"; "Letters to a Nephew"; "A Defense of Circe"; and "After a Long Journey."

Ladies Home Journal: for "A Little Incident in the Rue de L'Odeon", August 1964 and "Jacqueline Kennedy", March 1964.

Village Voice: for "A Letter to the Editor"; "Romany Marie"; and "Joe Gould".

Westwood, California *Daily:* for "On Communism in Hollywood", 1947.

Institute of International Education: for "Remarks on the Agenda" delivered at the IIE Conference on the Arts and Exchange of Persons, 1956.

Yale Review: for "A Letter to the Editor", 1961 and "Noon Wine: The Sources", 1956.

The Washington Post: for "A Letter to the Editor", October 21, 1961. Used by permission.

Proceedings of the American Academy of Arts and Letters: for "Speech of Acceptance", Copyright © 1968, American Academy of Arts and Letters.

Sewanee Review: for "Ole Woman River", Vol. LXVII, No. 4, 1959 and "A Sprig of Mint for Allen", Vol. LXXIV, No. 3, 1966.

Shenandoah: for "On First Meeting T. S. Eliot", 1961.

Esprit: for "Flannery O'Connor at Home", 1964.

The Southern Review: for "From the Notebooks", Summer 1965, Vol. I, No. 3.

Accent: for "Affectation of Praehiminincies", 1942.

Partisan Review: for "A Goat for Azazel", May–June 1940.

Doubleday & Company, Inc.: for "Notes on Life and Death of A Hero"; Introduction from "The Itching Parrot" by José Joaquim Fernandez de Lazardi, Copyright © 1942 by Doubleday & Company, Inc. Used by permission.

New Directions: for "Notes on Writing", 1941.

Harper's Magazine: for "November in Windham", November 1950 and "Measures for Song and Dance", May 1950.

From the Foreword to
The Days Before

It is my hope that the reader will find in this collection of papers written throughout my thirty years as published writer, the shape, direction, and connective tissue of a continuous, central interest and preoccupation of a lifetime.

They represent the exact opposite of my fiction, in that they were written nearly all by request, with limitations of space, a date fixed for finishing, on a chosen subject or theme, as well as with the certainty that they would be published. I wrote as well as I could at any given moment under a variety of pressures, and said what I meant as nearly as I could come to it: so as they stand, the pieces are really parts of a journal of my thinking and feeling. Then too, they served to get me a living, such as it was, so that I might be able to write my stories in their own time and way. My stories had to be accepted and published exactly as they were written: that rule has never once been broken. There was no one, whose advice I respected, whose help I would not have been glad to get, and many times did get, on almost any of these articles. I have written, re-written, and revised them. My stories, on the other hand, are written in one draft, and if short enough, at one sitting. In fact, this book would seem to represent the other half of a double life: but not in truth. It is all one thing. The two ways of working helped and supported each other: I needed both.

Rue Jacob, Paris   K.A.P.
25 July 1952

To E. Barrett Prettyman, Jr.
Faithful friend, able and
fearless counselor, gifted writer,
and joyful company, who has guided me
through a rain-forest in these
past rather terrible years.
Yet we can laugh together
and we know what to laugh at.

CONTENTS

CRITICAL

PERSONAL AND PARTICULAR

BIOGRAPHICAL

COTTON MATHER

MEXICAN

ON WRITING

POEMS

Practice an art for love
and the happiness of your life—
you will find it outlasts
almost everything but breath!

Yours,
Katherine Anne Porter

1958

(Printed in *Vignettes*, Vol. 4, The
Sophomore Class of Thomas A. Edison
High School, Tulsa, Oklahoma, 1959)

CRITICAL

On a Criticism of
Thomas Hardy

The Bishop of Wakefield, after reading Thomas Hardy's latest (and as it proved, his last) novel, *Jude the Obscure,* threw it in the fire, or said he did. It was a warm midsummer, and Hardy suggested that the bishop may have been speaking figuratively, heresy and bonfires being traditionally associated in his mind, or that he may have gone to the kitchen stove. The bishop wrote to the papers that he had burned the book, in any case, and he wrote also to a local M.P. who caused the horrid work to be withdrawn from the public library, promising besides to examine any other novels by Mr. Hardy carefully before allowing them to circulate among the bishop's flock. It was a good day's work, added to the protests of the reviewers for the press, and twenty-five years of snubbing and nagging from the professional moralists of his time; Thomas Hardy resigned as novelist for good. As in the case of the criticism presently to be noted, the attack on his book included also an attack on his personal character, and the bishop's action wounded Thomas Hardy. He seems to have remarked in effect "that if the bishop could have known him as he was, he would have found a man whose personal conduct, views of morality, and of vital facts of religion, hardly differed from his own."

This is an indirect quotation by his second wife, devoted apologist and biographer, and it exposes almost to the point of pathos the basic, unteachable charity of Hardy's mind. Of all evil emotions generated in the snake-pit of human nature, theological hatred is perhaps the most savage, being based on intellectual concepts and disguised in the highest spiritual motives. And what could rouse this hatred in a theologian like the sight of a moral, virtuous, well-conducted man who presumed to agree with him in the "vital facts of religion," at the same time refusing to sign the articles of faith? It was long ago agreed among the Inquisitors that these are the dangerous men.

The bishop threw the book in the fire in 1896. In 1928, Mrs. Hardy was happy to record that another "eminent clergyman of the church" had advised any priest preparing to become a village rector to make first a good retreat and then a careful study of Thomas Hardy's novels. "From Thomas Hardy," concluded this amiable man, "he would learn the essential dignity of country people and what deep and passionate interest belongs to every individual life. You cannot treat them in the mass: each single soul is to be the object of your special and peculiar prayer."

Aside from the marginal note on the social point of view which made it necessary thus to warn prospective rectors that country people were also human entities, each possessed of a soul important, however rural, to God, and the extraordinary fact that an agnostic novelist could teach them what the church and their own hearts could not, it is worth noting again that churchmen differ even as the laymen on questions of morality, and can preach opposing doctrine from the same text. The history of these differences, indeed, is largely the calamitous history of institutional religion. In 1934, a layman turned preacher almost like a character in a Hardy novel, runs true to his later form by siding with the bishop. Since his spectacular conversion to the theology and politics of the Church of England, Mr. T. S. Eliot's great gifts as a critic have been deflected into channels where they do not flow with their old splendor and depth. More and more his literary judgments have assumed the tone of lay sermons by a parochial visitor, and his newer style is perhaps at its most typical in his criticism of Thomas Hardy:

> The work of the late Thomas Hardy represents an interesting example of a powerful personality uncurbed by any institutional attachment or by submission to any objective beliefs; unhampered by any ideas, or even by what sometimes acts as a partial restraint upon inferior writers, the desire to please a large public. He seems to me to have written as nearly for the sake of "self-expression" as a man well can, and the self which he had to express does not strike me as a particularly wholesome or edifying matter of communication. He was indifferent even to

the prescripts of good writing: he wrote sometimes overpoweringly well, but always very carelessly; at times his style touches sublimity without ever having passed through the stage of being good. In consequence of his self-absorption, he makes a great deal of landscape; for landscape is a passive creature which lends itself to an author's mood. Landscape is fitted, too, for the purpose of an author who is interested not at all in men's minds, but only in their emotions, and perhaps only in men as vehicles for emotions.

After some useful general reflections on the moral undesirability of extreme emotionalism, meant as a rebuke to Hardy and to which we shall return briefly later, Mr. Eliot proceeds:

> I was [in a previous lecture] . . . concerned with illustrating the limit-ing and crippling effect of a separation from tradition and orthodoxy upon certain writers whom I nevertheless hold up for admiration for what they have attempted against great obstacles. Here I am concerned with the intrusion of the *diabolic* into modern literature in consequence of the same lamentable state of affairs. . . . I am afraid that even if you can entertain the notion of a positive power for evil working through human agency, you may still have a very inaccurate notion of what Evil is, and will find it difficult to believe that it may operate through men of genius of the most excellent character. I doubt whether what I am saying can convey very much to anyone for whom the doctrine of Original Sin is not a very real and tremendous thing.

Granting the premises with extreme reservations, Thomas Hardy was a visible proof of the validity of this disturbing doctrine. He had received early religious training in the Established Church, and by precept and example in a household of the most sincere piety, and of the most ag-gressive respectability. He remarked once, that of all the names he had been called, such as agnostic (which tag he adopted later, ruefully), atheist, immoralist, pessimist, and so on, a properly fitting one had been overlooked altogether: "churchy." He had once meant to be a parson. His relations with the church of his childhood had been of the homely, intimate, almost filial sort. His grandfather, his father, his uncle, all apt in music, had been for forty years the mainstay of the village choir. He felt at home in the place, as to its customs, feasts, services. He had a great love for the ancient churches, and as a young architect his aesthetic sense was outraged by the fashionable and silly "restorations" amounting to systematic destruction which overtook some of the loveliest examples of medieval church architecture in England during the nineteenth cen-tury. His devotion to the past, and to the history and character of his native Wessex, became at times a kind of antiquarian fustiness. His personal morals were irreproachable, he had an almost queasy sense of the awful and permanent effects of wrongdoing on the human soul and destiny. Most of his novels deal with these consequences; his most stupendous tragedies are the result of one false step on the part of his hero or heroine. Genius aside, he had all the makings of a good, honest, churchgoing country squire; but the worm of original sin was settled in his mind, of all fatal places; and his mind led him out of the tradition of orthodoxy into another tradition of equal antiquity, equal importance, equal seriousness, a body of opinion running parallel throughout history to the body of law in church and state: the great tradition of dissent. He went, perhaps not so much by choice as by compulsion of *belief*, with the Inquirers rather than the Believers. His mind, not the greatest, certainly not the most flexible, but a good, candid, strong mind, asked simply the oldest, most terrifying questions, and the traditional, orthodox answers of the church did not satisfy it. It is easy to see how this, from the churchly point of view, is diabolic. But the yawning abyss between question and answer remains the same, and until this abyss is closed, the dissent will remain, persistent, obdurate, a kind of church itself, with its leaders, teachers, saints, martyrs, heroes; a thorn in the flesh of orthodoxy, but I think not necessarily of the Devil on that account, unless the intellect and all its questions are really from the Devil, as the Eden myth states explicitly, as the church seems to teach, and Mr. Eliot tends to confirm.

There is a great deal to examine in the paragraphs quoted above, but two words in their context illustrate perfectly the unbridgeable abyss between Hardy's question and Mr. Eliot's answer. One is, of course, the word *diabolic*. The other is *edifying*. That struck and held my eye in a maze, for a moment. With no disrespect I hope to conventional piety, may I venture that in the regions of art, as of religion, edification is not the highest form of intellectual or spiritual experience. It is a happy truth that Hardy's novels are really not edifying. The mental and emotional states roused and maintained in the reader of *The Mayor of Casterbridge* or *The Return of the Native* are considerably richer, invoked out of deeper sources in the whole human consciousness, more substantially nourishing, than this lukewarm word can express. A novel by Thomas Hardy can be a chastening experience, an appalling one, there is great and sober pleasure to be got out of those novels, the mind can be disturbed and the heart made extremely uneasy, but the complacency of edification is absent, as it is apt to be from any true tragedy.

Mr. Eliot includes Lawrence and Joyce in his list of literary men of "diabolic" tendencies. Deploring Lawrence's "untrained" mind, he adds: "A trained mind like that of Mr. Joyce is always aware of what master it is serving. . . ."

Untrained minds have always been a nuisance to the military police of orthodoxy. God-intoxicated mystics and untidy saints with only a white blaze of divine love where their minds should have been, are perpetually creating almost as much disorder within the law as outside it. To have a trained mind is no guarantee at all that the possessor is going to walk infallibly in the path of virtue, though he hardly fails in the letter of the law. St. Joan of Arc and St. Francis in their own ways have had something to say about that. The combination of a trained mind and incorruptible virtue is ideal, and therefore rare: St. Thomas More is the first name that occurs to me as example. Hardy's mind, which had rejected the conclusions though not the ethical discipline of organized religion (and he knew that its ethical system in essentials is older than Christianity), was not altogether an untrained one, and like all true Dissenters, he knew the master he was serving: his conscience. He had the mathematical certainties of music and architecture, and the daily, hourly training of a serious artist laboring at his problems over a period of more than half a century. That he was unhampered by ideas is therefore highly improbable. He wrote a few fine poems among a large number of poor ones. He wrote fifteen novels, of which a round half-dozen are well the equal of any novel in the English language; even if this is not to say he is the equal of Flaubert or of Dostoievsky. His notebooks testify to a constant preoccupation with ideas, not all of them his own, naturally, for he inherited them from a very respectable race of thinkers, sound in heterodoxy.

He had got out of the very air of the nineteenth century something from Lucian, something from Leonardo, something from Erasmus, from Montaigne, from Voltaire, from the Encyclopaedists, and there were some powerful nineteenth century Inquirers, too, of whom we need only mention Darwin, perhaps. Scientific experiment leads first to skepticism; but we have seen in our time, how, pursued to the verge of the infinite, it sometimes leads back again to a form of mysticism. There is at the heart of the universe a riddle no man can solve, and in the end, God may be the answer. But this is fetching up at a great distance still from orthodoxy, and still must be suspect in that quarter. Grant that the idea of God is the most splendid single act of the creative human imagination, and that all his multiple faces and attributes correspond to some need and satisfy some deep desire in mankind; still, for the Inquirers, it is impossible not to conclude that this mystical concept has been harnessed rudely to machinery of the most mundane sort, and has been made to serve the ends of an organization which, ruling under divine guidance, has ruled very little better, and in some respects, worse, than certain rather mediocre but frankly manmade systems of government. And it has often lent its support to the worst evils in secular government, fighting consistently on the side of the heavy artillery. And it has seemed at times not to know the difference between Good and Evil, but to get them hopelessly confused with legalistic right and wrong; justifying the most cynical expedients of worldly government by a high morality; and committing the most savage crimes against human life for the love of God. When you consider the political career of the church in the light of its professed origins and purposes, perhaps Original Sin *is* the answer. But Hardy preferred to remove the argument simply to another ground. As to himself, in his personal life, he had a Franciscan tenderness in regard to children, animals, laborers, the poor, the mad, the insulted and injured. He suffered horror and indignation at human injustice, more especially at the kind committed by entrenched authority and power upon the helpless. In middle age he remembered and recorded an early shock he received on hearing that, in his neighborhood, a young boy, a farm laborer, was found dead of sheer starvation in the fruitful field he had worked to cultivate. When he was planning *The Dynasts*, he wrote in his notebook: "The human race is to be shown as one great net-work or tissue which quivers in every part when one point is shaken, like a spider's web if touched." For Hardy, the death of that boy was a blow that set the whole great web trembling; and all mankind received a lasting wound. Here was a human fate for which human acts were responsible, and it would not serve Hardy at all to put the blame on Original Sin, or the inscrutable decrees of Divine Providence, or any other of the manifold devices for not letting oneself be too uncomfortable at the spectacle of merely human suffering. He was painfully uncomfortable all his life, and his discomfort was not for himself—he was an extraordinarily selfless sort of man—but the pervasiveness of what he considered senseless and unnecessary human misery. Out of the strange simplicity of his own unworldliness he could write at the age of 78: "As to pessimism, my motto is, first correctly diagnose the complaint—in this case human ills—and ascertain the cause: then set about finding a remedy if one exists. The motto or practise of the optimists is: Blind the eyes to the real malady, and use empirical panaceas to suppress the symptoms." Reasonableness: the use of the human intelligence directed toward the best human solution of human ills; such, if you please, was the unedifying proposal of this diabolic soul.

He himself in his few remarks on public and practical affairs had always been very reasonable. War, he believed, was an abomination, but it recurred again and again, apparently an incurable ill. He had no theories to advance, but wished merely that those who made wars would admit the real motives; aside from the waste and destruction, which he viewed with purely humane feelings, he objected to the immoralities of statecraft and religion in the matter. He was opposed to capital punishment on the simple grounds that no man has the right to take away the life of another. But he believed it acted as a material deterrent to crime, and if the judges would admit that it was social expediency, with no foundation in true morality, that was another matter. On the Irish question he was acute and explicit in expressing his view in this direction. "Though he did not enter it here [in his notebook] Hardy . . . said of Home Rule that it was a staring dilemma, of which good policy and good philanthropy were the huge horns. Policy for England required that it should not be granted; humanity to Ireland that it should. Neither Liberals nor Conservatives would honestly own up to this opposition between two moralities, but speciously insisted that humanity and policy were both on one side—of course their own." At another time he complained that most of the philosophers began on the theory that the earth had been designed as a comfortable place for man. He could no more accept this theory than he could the theological notion that the world was a testing ground for the soul of man in preparation for eternity, and that his sufferings were part of a "divine" plan, or indeed, so far as the personal fate of mankind was concerned, of any plan at all. He did believe with a great deal of common sense that man could make the earth a more endurable place for himself if he would, but he also realized that human nature is not grounded in common sense, that there is a deep place in it where the mind does not go, where the blind monsters sleep and wake, war among themselves, and feed upon death.

" As soon as the knife kill thing come out "

He did believe that there is "a power that rules the world," though he did not name it, nor could he accept the names that had been given it, or any explanation of its motives. He could only watch its operations, and to me it seems he concluded that both malevolence and benevolence originated in the mind of man, and the warring forces were within him alone; such plan as existed in regard to him he had created for himself, his Good and his Evil were alike the mysterious inventions of his own mind; and why this was so, Hardy could not pretend to say. He knew there was an element in human nature not subject to mathematical equation or the water-tight theories of dogma, and this intransigent, measureless force, divided against itself, in conflict alike with its own system of laws and the unknown laws of the universe, was the real theme of Hardy's novels; a genuinely tragic theme in the grand manner, of sufficient weight and shapelessness to try the powers of any artist. Generally so reluctant to admit any influence, Hardy admits to a study of the Greek dramatists, and with his curious sense of proportion, he decided that the Wessex countryside was also the dwelling place of the spirit of tragedy; that the histories of certain obscure persons in that limited locality bore a strong family resemblance to those of the great, the ancient, and the legendary. Mr. Eliot finds Hardy's beloved Wessex a "stage setting," such as the Anglo-Saxon heart loves, and Hardy's Wessex farmers "period peasants pleasing to the metropolitan imagination." Hardy was Anglo-Saxon and Norman; that landscape was in his blood. Those period peasants were people he had known all his life, and I think that in this passage Mr. Eliot simply speaks as a man of the town, like those young rectors who need to be reminded of the individual dignity and importance of the country people. Further, taking all the Hardy characters in a lump, he finds in them only blind animal emotionalism, and remarks: ". . . strong passion is only interesting or significant in strong men; those who abandon themselves without resistance to excitements which tend to deprive them of reason become merely instruments of feeling and lose their humanity; and unless there is moral resistance and conflict there is no meaning." True in part: and to disagree in detail would lead to an endless discussion of *what* exactly constitutes interest in the work of a writer; *what* gives importance to his characters, their intrinsic value as human beings, or the value their creator is able to give them by his own imaginative view of them.

Hardy seems almost to agree with Mr. Eliot for once: "The best tragedy—highest tragedy in short—is that of the WORTHY encompassed by the INEVITABLE. The tragedies of immoral and worthless people are not of the best." My own judgment is that Hardy's characters are in every way superior to those of Mr. Eliot, and for precisely the reason the two writers are agreed upon. Hardy's people suffer the tragedy of being, Mr. Eliot's of not-being. The strange creatures inhabiting the wasteland of Mr. Eliot's particular scene are for the most part immoral and worthless, the apeneck Sweeneys, the Grishkins, and all. . . . They have for us precisely the fascination the poet has endowed them with, and they also have great significance: they are the sinister chorus of the poet's own tragedy, they represent the sum of the poet's vision of human beings without God and without faith, a world of horror surrounding this soul thirsting for faith in God. E. M. Forster has remarked that *The Waste Land* is a poem of real horror, the tragedy of the rains that came too late—or perhaps, never came at all. For how else can one explain the self-absorbed despair of Eliot's point of view, even in religion? That uncontrolled emotion of loathing for his fellow pilgrims in this mortal life? Was there not one soul worth tender treatment, not one good man interesting enough to the poet to inhabit his tragic scene? It is a curious paradox. Hardy feels no contempt for his characters at all; he writes of them as objectively as if they existed by themselves, they are never the background, the chorus, for the drama of his own experience. Beside Eliot's wasteland, with its inhuman beings, Hardy's Wessex seems an airy, familiar place, his characters at least have living blood in them, and though Mr. Eliot complains that Hardy was not interested in the minds of men, still their headpieces are not deliberately stuffed with straw by their creator.

Hardy's characters are full of moral conflicts and of decisions arrived at by mental processes, certainly. Jude, Gabriel Oak, Clym Yeobright, above all, Henchard, are men who have decisions to make, and if they do not make them entirely on the plane of reason, it is because Hardy was interested most in that hairline dividing the rational from the instinctive, the opposition, we might call it, between nature, and second nature; that is, between instinct and the habits of thought fixed upon the individual by his education and his environment. Such characters of his as are led by their emotions come to tragedy; he seems to say that following the emotions blindly leads to disaster. Romantic miscalculation of the possibilities of life, of love, of the situation; of refusing to reason their way out of their predicament; these are the causes of disaster in Hardy's novels. Angel Clare is a man of the highest principles, trained in belief, religion, observance of moral law. His failure to understand the real nature of Christianity makes a monster of him at the great crisis of his life. The Mayor of Casterbridge spends the balance of his life in atonement and reparation for a brutal wrong committed in drunkenness and anger; his past overtakes and destroys him. Hardy had an observing eye, a remembering mind; he did not need the Greeks to teach him that the Furies do arrive punctually, and that neither act, nor will, nor intention will serve to deflect a man's destiny from him, once he has taken the step which decides it.

A word about that style which Mr. Eliot condemns as touching "sublimity without ever having passed through the stage of being good." Hardy has often been called by critics who love him, the good simple man of no ideas, the careless workman of genius who never learned to write, who cared nothing for the way of saying a thing.

His own testimony is that he cared a great deal for *what* he said: "My art is to intensify the expression of things, as is done by Crivelli, Bellini, etc., so that the heart and inner meaning is made vividly visible." Again: "The Realities to be the true realities of life, hitherto called abstractions. The old material realities to be placed behind the former, as shadowy accessories." His notebooks are dry, reluctant, unmethodical; he seems to have spent his time and energies in actual labor at his task rather than theorizing about it, but he remarks once: "Looking around on a well-selected shelf of fiction, how few stories of any length does one recognize as well told from beginning to end! The first half of this story, the last half of that, the middle of another . . . the modern art of narration is yet in its infancy." He made few notes on technical procedure, but one or two are valuable as a clue to his directions: "A story must be exceptional enough to justify its telling. We tale tellers are all Ancient Mariners, and none of us is warranted in stopping Wedding Guests . . . unless he has something more unusual to relate than the ordinary experiences of every average man and woman." Again: "The whole secret of fiction and drama—in the constructional part—lies in the adjustment of things unusual to things eternal and universal. The writer who knows exactly how exceptional, and how non-exceptional, his events should be made, possesses the key to the art."

So much for theory. Not much about the importance of style, the care for the word, the just and perfect construction of a paragraph. But Hardy was not a careless writer. The difference between his first and last editions proves this, in matters of style aside from his painful reconstruction of his manuscripts mutilated for serial publication. He wrote and wrote again, and he never found it easy. He lacked elegance, he never learned the trick of the whip-lash phrase, the complicated lariat twirling of the professed stylists. His prose lumbers along, it jogs, it creaks, it hesitates, it is as dull as certain long passages in the Tolstoy of *War and Peace*, for example. That celebrated first scene on Egdon Heath, in *The Return of the Native*. Who does not remember it? And in actual rereading, what could be duller? What could be more labored than his introduction of the widow Yeobright at the heath fire among the dancers, or more unconvincing than the fears of the timid boy that the assembly are literally raising the Devil? Except for this in my memory of that episode, as in dozens of others in many of Hardy's novels, I have seen it, I was there. When I read it, it almost disappears from view, and afterward comes back, phraseless, living in its somber clearness, as Hardy meant it to do. I feel certain. This to my view is the chief quality of good prose as distinguished from poetry. By his own testimony, he limited his territory by choice, set boundaries to his material, focused his point of view like a burning glass down on a definite aspect of things. He practiced a stringent discipline, severely excised and eliminated all that seemed to him not useful or appropriate to his plan. In the end his work was the sum of his experience, he arrived at his particular true testimony; along the way, sometimes, many times, he wrote sublimely.

the Furies do arrive punctually 1940

A Wreath
for the Gamekeeper

The dubious Crusade is over, anybody can buy the book now in hard-cover or paperback, expurgated or unexpurgated, in drugstores and rail-way stations as well as in the bookshops, and 'twas a famous victory for something or other, let's wait and see. Let us remark as we enter the next phase that we may hope this episode in the history of our system of literary censorship will mark the end of one of our most curious native customs—calling upon the police and the post office officials to act as literary critics in addition to all their other heavy duties. It is not right nor humane and I hope this is the end of it; it is enough to drive good men out of those services altogether.

When I first read *Lady Chatterley's Lover,* thirty years ago, I thought it a dreary, sad performance with some passages of unintentional hilari-ous low comedy, one scene at least simply beyond belief in a book writ-ten with such inflamed apostolic solemnity, which I shall return to later; and I wondered then at all the huzza and hullabaloo about suppressing it. I realize how there were at least two reasons for it—first, Lawrence himself, who possessed to the last degree the quality of high visibility; and second, the rise to power of a demagoguery of political and social censorship by unparalleled ignoramuses in all things, including the arts, which they regarded as the expression of peculiarly dangerous forms of immorality. These people founded organizations for the suppression of Vice, and to them nearly everything *was* Vice, and other societies for the promotion of Virtue, some of them very dubious, and their enthusiasms took some weird and dangerous directions. Prohibition was their major triumph, with its main result of helping organized crime to become big business; but the arts, and especially literature, became the object of a morbid purblind interest to those strange beings who knew nothing about any art, but knew well what they feared and hated.

It is time to take another look at this question of censorship and protest which has been debated intermittently ever since I can remember. Being a child of my time, naturally I was to be found protesting: I was all for freedom of speech, of action, of belief, of choice, in every department of human life; and for authors all this was to be comprehended in the single perfect right to express their thoughts without reserve, write anything they chose, with publishers to publish and booksellers to sell it, and the vast public gloriously at liberty to buy and read it by the tens of thousands.

It was a noble experiment, no doubt, an attempt to bring a root idea of liberty to flower; but in practice it soon showed serious defects and abuses, for the same reason that prohibition of alcohol could not be made to work: gangsters and crooks took over the business of supplying the human demand for intoxication and obscenity, which hitherto had been in the hand of respectable elements who regulated it and kept it more or less in its place; but it still is a market that never fails no matter who runs it. (I have often wondered what were the feelings of the old-line pious prohibitionists when they discovered that their most powerful allies in the fight to maintain prohibition were the bootleggers.)

Publishers were certainly as quick to take advantage of the golden moment as the gangsters, and it did not take many of them very long to discover that the one best way to sell a book with "daring" passages was to get it banned in Boston, or excluded from the United States mails. Certain authors, not far behind the publishers, discovered that if they could write books the publisher could advertise as in peril from the censor, all the better. Sure enough, the censor would rise to the bait, crack down in a way that would be front-page news, the alarm would go out to all fellow writers and assorted lovers of liberty that one of the guild was being abused in his basic human rights guaranteed by our Constitution, by those hyenas in Boston or the Post Office. The wave of publicity was on, and the sales went up. Like too many such precariously balanced schemes, it was wonderful while it lasted, but it carried the seeds of its own decay. Yet those were the days when people really turned out and paraded with flags and placards, provocative songs and slogans, openly inviting arrest and quite often succeeding in being hauled off to the police station in triumph, there to sit in a cell perfectly certain that somebody was going to show up and bail them out before night.

Writers—I was often one of them—did not always confine their aid to freedom of the word, though that was their main concern. They would sometimes find themselves in the oddest company, defending strange causes and weirdly biased viewpoints on the grounds that they most badly wanted defense. But we also championed recklessly the most awful wormy little books we none of us would have given shelf room, and more than once it came over us in mid-parade that this was no downtrodden citizen being deprived of his rights, but a low cynic cashing in on our high-minded application of democratic principles. I suppose for a good many of us, all this must just be chalked up to Experience. After some time, I found myself asking, "Why should I defend a worthless book just because it has a few dirty words in it? Let it disappear of itself and the sooner the better."

No one comes to that state of mind quickly, and it is dangerous ground to come to at all, I suppose, but one comes at last. My change of view began with the first publication in 1928 of *Lady Chatterley's Lover.* He has become, this lover of Lady Chatterley's, as sinister in his effect on the minds of critics as that of Quint himself on the children and the governess in *The Turn of the Screw.* I do not know quite what role Lady Chatterley should play to Quint-Mellors. She is not wicked, as Miss Jessel is; she is merely a moral imbecile. She is not intense, imaginative, and dazzled like the governess, she is stupid; and it is useless to go on with the comparison, for she is not the center of the critics' attention as the Gamekeeper is, she has not that baneful fascination for them that he has. But there is one quality both books have in common and they both succeed in casting the same spell on plain reader and critic alike: the air of evil which shrouds them both, the sense of a situation of foregone and destined failure, to which there can be no outcome except despair. Only, the Lawrence book is sadder, because Lawrence was a badly flawed, lesser artist than James. He did not really know what he was doing, or if he did, pretended to be doing something else; and his blood-chilling anatomy of the activities of the rutting season between two rather dull persons comes with all the more force because the relations are precisely not between the vengeful seeking dead and living beings, but between the living themselves who seem to me deader than any ghost.

Yet for the past several months there has been a steady flood of extremely well-managed publicity in defense of Lawrence's motives and the purity of his novel, into which not only critics, but newspaper and magazine reporters, editorial writers, ministers of various religious beliefs, women's clubs, the police, postal authorities, and educators have been drawn, clamorously. I do not object to censorship being so loudly defeated again for the present. I merely do not approve of the way it was done. Though there were at this time no parades, I believe, we have seen such unanimity and solidarity of opinion among American critics, and many of them of our first order, as I do not remember to have seen before. What are we to think of them, falling in like this with this fraudulent crusade of raising an old tired Cause out of its tomb? For this is no longer just a book, and it never was a work of literature worth all this attention. It is no longer a Cause, if it ever was, but a publicity device and a well-worn one by now, calculated to rouse a salacious itch of curiosity in the prospective customer. This is such standard procedure by now it seems unnecessary to mention it. Yet these hard-headed, experienced literary men were trapped into it once more, and lent a strong hand to it. There is something touching, if misguided, in this finespirited show of manly solidarity, this full-throated chorus in defense of Lawrence's vocabulary and the nobility of his intentions. I have never questioned either; I wish only to say that I think that from start to finish he was about as wrong as can be on the whole subject of sex, and that he wrote a very laboriously bad book to prove it. The critics who have been carried away by a generous desire to promote freedom of speech, and give a black eye to prudes and nannies overlook sometimes—and in a work of literature this should not be overlooked, at least not by men whose profession it is to criticize literature—that purity, nobility of intention, and apostolic fervor are good in themselves at times, but at others they depend on context, and in this instance they are simply not enough. Whoever says they are, and tries to persuade the public to accept a book for what it is not, a work of good art, is making a grave mistake, if he means to go on writing criticism.

As for the original uproar, Lawrence began it himself, as he nearly always did, loudly and bitterly on the defensive, throwing out each book in turn as if he were an early Christian throwing himself to the lions. "Anybody who calls my novel a dirty, sexual novel is a liar." Further: "It'll infuriate mean people; but it will surely soothe decent ones." The Readers' Subscription (an American book club) in its brochure offering the book, carries on the tone boldly: "Now, at long last, a courageous American publisher is making available the unexpurgated version of *Lady Chatterly's Lover*—exactly as the author meant it to be seen by the intelligent, sensitive reader." No, this kind of left-handed flattery won't quite do: it is the obverse of the form of blackmail used by publishers and critics to choke their ambiguous wares down our throats. They say in effect, "If you disapprove of this book, you are proved to be (1) illiterate, (2) insensitive, (3) unintelligent, (4) low-minded, (5) 'mean,' (6) a hypocrite, (7) a prude, and other unattractive things." I happen to have known quite a number of decent persons, not too unintelligent or insensitive, with some love and understanding of the arts, who were revolted by the book; and I do not propose to sit down under this kind of bullying.

Archibald MacLeish regards it as "pure" and a work of high literary merit. He has a few reservations as to the whole with which I heartily agree so far as they go; yet even Mr. MacLeish begins trailing his coat, daring us at our own risk to deny that the book is "one of the most important works of the century, or to express an opinion about the literature of our own time or about the spiritual history that literature expresses without making his peace in one way or another with D. H. Lawrence and with this work."

Without in the least making my peace with D. H. Lawrence or with this work, I wish to say why I disagree profoundly with the above judgments, and also with the following:

Harvey Breit: "The language and the incidents or scenes in question are deeply moving and very beautiful—Lawrence was concerned how love, how a relationship between a man and a woman can be most touching and beautiful, but only if it is uninhibited and total." This is wildly romantic and does credit to Mr. Breit's feelings but there can be no such thing as a total relationship between two human beings—to begin with, what is total in such a changing, uncertain, limited state? and if there could be, just how would the persons involved know when they had reached it? Judging from certain things he wrote and said on this subject, I think Lawrence would have been the first to protest at even an attempt to create such a condition. He demanded the right to invade anybody, but he was noticeably queasy when anyone took a similar liberty with him.

Edmund Wilson: "The most inspiring book I have seen in a long time . . . one of his bestwritten . . . one of his most vigorous and brilliant. . . ."

This reminds me that I helped parade with banners in California in defense of Mr. Wilson's *Memoirs of Hecate County*—a misguided act of guild loyalty and personal admiration I cannot really regret, so far as friendship is concerned. But otherwise the whole episode was deplorably unnecessary. My preference has not changed for his magnificent *To the Finland Station* and for almost any of his criticisms and essays on literary and public affairs.

Jacques Barzun: "I have no hesitation in saying that I do not consider Lawrence's novel pornographic." I agree with this admirably prudent statement, and again when Mr. Barzun notes Lawrence's ruling passion for reforming everything and everybody in sight. My quarrel with the book is that it really is not pornographic—the great wild, free-wheeling Spirit of Pornography has here been hitched to a rumbling little domestic cart and trundled off to chapel, its ears pinned back and its mouth washed out with soap.

Mr. Schorer, who contributes the preface, even brings in Yeats to defend this tiresome book. Yeats, bless his memory, when he talked bawdy, knew what he was saying and why. He enjoyed the flavor of gamey words on his tongue, and never deceived himself for one moment as to the nature of that enjoyment; he never got really interestingly dirty until age had somewhat cooled the ardors of his flesh, thus doubling his pleasure in the thoughts of it in the most profane sense. Mr. Schorer reprints part of a letter from Yeats, written years ago, to Mrs. Shakespear: "These two lovers the gamekeeper and his employer's wife each separated from their class by their love and fate are poignant in their loneliness; the coarse language of the one accepted by both becomes a forlorn poetry, uniting their solitudes, something ancient and humble and terrible."

This comes as a breath of fresh air upon a fetid topic. Yeats reached acutely into the muddlement and brings up the simple facts: the real disaster for the lady and the gamekeeper is that they face perpetual exile from their own proper backgrounds and society. Stale, pointless, unhappy as both their lives were before, due to their own deficiencies of character, it would seem yet now they face, once the sexual furor is past, an utter aimlessness in life shocking to think about. Further, Yeats notes an important point I have not seen mentioned before—only one of the lovers uses the coarse language, the other merely accepts it. The gamekeeper talks his dirt and the lady listens, but never once answers in kind. If she had, the gamekeeper would no doubt have been deeply scandalized.

Yet the language needs those words, they have a definite use and value and they should not be used carelessly or imprecisely. My contention is that obscenity is real, is necessary as expression, a safety valve against the almost intolerable pressures and strains of relationship between men and women, and not only between men and women but between any human being and his unmanageable world. If we distort, warp, abuse this language which is the seamy side of the noble language of religion and love, indeed the necessary defensive expression of insult toward the sexual partner and contempt and even hatred of the insoluble stubborn mystery of sex itself which causes us such fleeting joy and such cureless suffering, what have we left for a way of expressing the luxury of obscenity which, for an enormous majority of men, by their own testimony, is half the pleasure of the sexual act?

I would not object, then, to D. H. Lawrence's obscenity if it were really that. I object to his misuse and perversions of obscenity, his wrongheaded denial of its true nature and meaning. Instead of writing straight, healthy obscenity, he makes it sickly sentimental, embarrassingly so, and I find that obscene sentimentality is as hard to bear as any other kind. I object to this pious attempt to purify and canonize obscenity, to castrate the Roaring Boy, to take the low comedy out of sex. We cannot and should not try to hallow these words because they are not hallowed and were never meant to be. The attempt to make pure, tender, sensitive, washed-in-the-blood-of-the-lamb words out of words whose whole intention, function, place in our language is meant to be exactly the opposite is sentimentality, and of a very low order. Our language is rich and full and I daresay there is a word to express every shade of meaning and feeling a human being is capable of, if we are not too lazy to look for it; or if we do not substitute one word for another, such as calling a nasty word— meant to be nasty, we need it that way—"pure," and a pure word "nasty." This is an unpardonable tampering with definitions, and, in Lawrence, I think it comes of a very deep grained fear and distrust of sex itself; he was never easy on that subject, could not come to terms with it for anything. Perhaps it was a long hangover from his Chapel piety, a violent revulsion from the inane gibberish of some of the hymns. He wrote once with deep tenderness about his early Chapel memories and said that the word "Galilee" had magic for him, and that his favorite hymn was this:

> *Each gentle dove, and sighing bough,*
> *That makes the eve so dear to me,*
> *Has something far diviner now,*
> *That takes me back to Galilee.*
> *Oh Galilee, sweet Galilee,*
> *Where Jesus loved so well to be,*
> *Oh Galilee, sweet Galilee,*
> *Come sing again thy songs to me.*

His first encounter with dirty words, as he knew them to be, must have brought a shocking sense of guilt, especially as they no doubt gave him great secret pleasure; and to the end of his life he was engaged in the hopeless attempt to wash away that sense of guilt by denying the reality of its cause. He never arrived at the sunny truth so fearlessly acknowledged by Yeats, that "Love has pitched his mansion in the place of excrement"; but Yeats had already learned, long before, in his own experience that love has many mansions and only one of them is pitched there—a very important one that should be lived in very boldly and in hot blood at its own right seasons; but to deny its nature is to vulgarize it indeed. My own belief is this, that anything at all a man and a woman wish to do or say in their sexual relations, their lovemaking, or call it what you please, is exactly their own business and nobody else's. But let them keep it to themselves unless they wish to appear ridiculous at best, at worst debased and even criminal. For sex resembles many other acts which may in themselves be harmless, yet when committed in certain circumstances may be not only a sin, but a crime against human life itself, human feelings, human rights—I do not say against ethics, morality, sense of honor (in a discussion of the motives not of the author perhaps, but of the characters in this novel, such words are nearly meaningless), but a never-ending wrong against those elements in the human imagination which were capable of such concepts in the first place. If they need the violent stimulation of obscene acrobatics, ugly words, pornographic pictures, or even low music—there is a Negro jazz trumpeter who blows, it is said, a famous aphrodisiac noise—I can think of no argument against it, unless it might be thought a pity their nervous systems are so benumbed they need to be jolted and shocked into pleasure. Sex shouldn't be that kind of hard work, nor should it, as this book promises, lead to such a dull future. For nowhere in this sad history can you see anything but a long, dull gray monotonous chain of days, lightened now and then by a sexual bout. I can't hear any music, or poetry; or the voices of friends, or children. There is no wine, no food, no sleep nor refreshment, no laughter, no rest nor quiet—no love. I remember then that this is the fevered daydream of a dying man sitting under his umbrella pines in Italy indulging his sexual fantasies. For Lawrence is a Romantic turned wrong side out, and like Swift's recently flayed woman, it does alter his appearance for the worse—and his visions are easy, dreamlike, not subject to any real interruptions and interferences—for like children they see the Others as the Enemy—a mixture of morning dew and mingled body-secretions, a boy imagining a female partner who is nothing but one yielding, faceless, voiceless organ of consent.

An organ, and he finally bestows on those quarters his accolade of approval in the language and tone of praise he might give to a specially succulent scrap of glandular meat fresh from the butcher's. "Tha's a tasty bit of tripe, th'art," he says in effect, if not in just those words. And adds (these *are* his words), "Tha'rt real, even a bit of a bitch." Why a bitch is more real than other forms of life he does not explain. Climbing on his lap, she confirms his diagnosis by whispering, "Kiss me!"

Lawrence was a very gifted, distraught man who continually over-reached himself in an effort to combine all the authorities of artist, prophet, messiah, leader, censor, and mentor, by use of an unstable and inappropriate medium, the novel. His poetry and painting aside, he should be considered first as a writer of prose, and as a novelist. If a novelist is going to be so opinionated and obstinate and crazed on so many subjects he will need to be a Tolstoy, not a Lawrence. Only Tolstoy could be so furiously and fiercely wrong. He can nearly persuade you by sheer overwhelming velocity of will to agree with him.

Tolstoy once said—as reported by Gorky in his little memoir of Tolstoy—that in effect (I have the book in the house, but cannot find it now) the truth about women was so hideous he dared not tell it, except when his grave was dug and ready for him. He would run to it—or was it to his coffin?—tell the truth about women, and then pull the lid, or was it the clods, over his head. . . .

It's a marvelous picture. Tolstoy was merely roaring in the frenzy roused in him in face of his wife's terrible, relentless adoration; her shameless fertility, her unbearable fidelity, the shocking series of jealous revenges she took upon him for his hardness of heart and wickedness to her, the whole mystery of her oppressive femaleness. He did not know the truth about women, not even about that one who was the curse of his life. He did not know the truth about himself. This is not surprising, for no one does know the truth, either about himself or about anyone else, and all recorded human acts and words are open testimony to our endless efforts to know each other, and our failure to do so. I am only saying that it takes Homer or Sophocles or Dante or Chaucer or Shakespeare, or, at rather a distance, Tolstoy, to silence us, to force us to listen and almost to believe in their version of things, lulled or exalted or outraged into a brief acceptance. Lawrence has no grandeur in wrath or arrogance in love; he buzzes and darts like a wasp, irritable and irritating, hovering and bedeviling with a kind of insectlike persistence—he nags, in a word, and that is intolerable from anyone but surely unpardonable in an artist.

This tendency to nag, to disguise poorly as fiction a political, sociological tract, leads Lawrence, especially in this book, into some scenes on the grisly comic-order; they remind me of certain passages in *The Grapes of Wrath*, and pretty much on the same level, regarded as literature. Yet Steinbeck's genius for bathos never exceeded a certain scene by Lawrence which I have never heard mentioned by anyone, in talk or in print, by any critic however admiring—certainly, I have not heard all the talk or seen all the print on this subject—but I sympathize with this omission for I hardly know where to begin with it. It is the unbelievably grotesque episode of this besotted couple weaving flowers in each other's pubic hair, hanging bouquets and wreaths in other strategic bodily spots, making feeble little dirty jokes, inventing double-meaning nicknames for their sexual organs, and altogether, though God knows it is of an imbecilic harmlessness, and is meant in all solemn God's-earnestness to illustrate true passion at lyric play, I for one feel that I have overheard talk and witnessed acts never meant for me to hear or witness. The act itself I could not regard as shocking or in any way offensive except for its lack of reserve and privacy. Lovemaking surely must be, for human beings at our present state of development, one of the more private enterprises. Who would want a witness to that entire self-abandonment and helplessness? So it is best in such a case for the intruder to tip-toe away quietly, and say nothing. I hold that this is not prudery nor hypocrisy; I still believe in the validity of simple respect and regard for the dark secret things of life—that they should be inviolable, and guarded by the two who take part, and that no other presence should be invited. Let us go on with the scene in question. The lovers are in his gamekeeper's lodge, it is raining, the impulsive woman takes off to the woods, stark naked except for a pair of rubbers, lifting her heavy breasts to the rain (she is constitutionally overweight), and doing eurythmic movements she had learned long ago in Dresden. The gamekeeper is so exalted by this spectacle he takes out after her, faunlike, trips her up, and they splash about together in the rilling rainwater. . . . It could, I suppose, be funnier, but I cannot think how. And somewhere in these extended passages the gamekeeper pauses to give his lady a lecture on the working class and its dullness due to the industrial system. He blames everything on the mechanized life "out there," and his complaint recurs with variations: "Though it's a shame, what's been done to people these last hundred years: man turned into nothing but labour-insects, and all their manhood taken away, and all their real life." Hadn't Lawrence got any notion of what had been done to such people the hundred years before the last, and the hundred before that, and so on, back to the beginning?

Yet both the lovers did accept the standards of her world in appearances at least; over and over she observes that her gamekeeper is really quite elegant or self-possessed or looks "like a gentleman," and is pleased to think that she could introduce him anywhere. He observes the same thing of himself from time to time in an oblique way—he is holding his own among them, even now and again putting them down. Here are glimpses of Lady Chatterley sizing up Mellors on their first meeting: "He was a man in dark green velveteen and gaiters . . . the old style, with a red face and red moustache and distant eyes. . . ." And later, she noted that "he breathed rather quickly, through parted lips," while pushing his invalid employer's wheelchair uphill. "He was rather frail, really. Curiously full of vitality, but a little frail and quenched." Earlier she has been described as "a soft, ruddy, country-looking girl, inclined to freckles, with big blue eyes, and curling hair, and a soft voice and rather strong, female loins"; in fact, "she was too feminine to be quite smart."

Essentially, these are fairly apt descriptions of Lawrence and Frieda Lawrence, as one would need only to have seen photographs to recognize. This is useful only because the artist's life is always his material and it seems pointless to look for hidden clues when they are so obviously on the surface. Lawrence the man and Lawrence the artist are more than usually inseparable: he is everywhere, and everywhere the same, in his letters, his criticism, his poetry, his painting, the uneasy, suffering, vociferous man who wanted to be All-in-All in all things, but never discovered what the All is, or if it exists indeed. This will to omniscience is most clearly seen in *Lady Chatterley's Lover*. In the entire series of sexual scenes, growing in heat and intensity quite naturally, with the language not coarsening particularly, it could not be coarser than it began, there is only more of it, with the man showing off his prowess as he perceives his success—all this is exposed from the point of view of the woman. Lawrence constantly described what the man *did*, but tells us with great authority what the woman *felt*. Of course, he cannot possibly know—it is like a textbook of instructions to a woman as to how she *should* feel in such a situation. That is not his territory, and he has no business there. This shameless, incessant, nosy kind of poaching on the woman's nature as if determined to leave her no place of her own is what I find peculiarly repellent. The best he can ever do is to gather at second-hand, by hearsay, from women, in these matters; and though he had the benefit no doubt of some quite valid confidences and instruction from women entirely honest with him, it still just looks pretty fraudulent; somehow he shouldn't pretend he is the woman in the affair, too, as well as the man. It shows the obsessional nature of his self-centeredness; he gives the nightmarish impression of the bisexual snail squeezed into its narrow house making love to itself—my notion of something altogether undesirable even in the lowest possible forms of life. We have seen in his writings his hatred and distrust of women—of the female principle, that is; with some of its exemplars he managed to get along passably—shown in his perpetual exasperated admonition to woman to be what he wants her to be, without any regard to what she possibly may be—to stop having any will or mind or indeed any existence of her own except what he allows her. He will dole out to her the kind of sex he thinks is good for her, and allow her just the amount of satisfaction in it he wishes her to have—not much. Even Lady Chatterley's ration seems more in the head than in the womb.

Yet, where can it end? The gamekeeper, in spite of a certain fragility of appearance, seems to be the fighting-cock sort, wiry and tough enough, and he certainly runs through a very creditable repertory of sexual styles and moods. Yet he is a man of physical limitations like any other. Lady Chatterley is the largish, slow-moving, solid sort, and we know by her deeds and her words she is not worn down by an active mind. Such a woman often wears extremely well, physically. How long will it be before that enterprising man exhausts himself trying to be everything in that affair, both man and woman too, while she has nothing to do but be passive and enjoy whatever he wants her to have in the way he wants her to have it? It seems to me a hopelessly one-sided arrangement, it places all responsibility on him, and he will be the loser. Such a woman could use up half a dozen such men, and it is plain already that she will shortly be looking for another man; I give him two years at the rate he is going, if sex is really all he has to offer her, or all she is able to accept. For if sex alone is what she must have, she will not abide with him.

Jean Cocteau has told somewhere a terrible story of a priest in a hotel, who hearing the death-rattle of a man in the next room, mistook it for animal noises of a successful intercourse and knocked censoriously on the wall. We should all be very careful not to make the same mistake.

Lawrence, who was prickly as a hedgehog where his own privacies were concerned, cannot in his mischievous curiosity allow to a woman even the privacy of her excremental functions. He has to tell her in so many words just where her private organs are located, what they are good for, and how praiseworthy he finds the whole arrangement. Nothing will do for him but to try to crawl into her skin; finding that impossible, at last he admits unwillingly a fact you would think a sensible person would have been born knowing, or would have learned very early: that we *are* separate, each a unique entity, strangers by birth, that our envelopes are meant as the perfect device for keeping us separate. We are meant to share, not to devour each other; no one can claim the privilege of two lives, his own and another's.

Mr. Schorer in his preface hails the work as "a great hymn to marriage." That, I should say, it is not, above all. No matter what the protagonists think they are up to, this is the story of an "affair," and a thoroughly disreputable one, based on the treachery of a woman to her husband who has been made impotent by wounds received in war; and by the mean trickery of a man of low origins out to prove he is as good as, or better than, the next man. Mr. Schorer also accepts and elucidates for us Lawrence's favorite, most pathetic fallacy. He writes:

> The pathos of Lawrence's novel arises from the tragedy of modern society. What is tragic is that we cannot feel our tragedy. We have grown slowly into a confusion of these terms, these two forms of power, and in confusing them we have left almost no room for the free creative functions of the man or woman who, lucky souls, possess "integrity of self." The force of this novel probably lies in the degree of intensity with which his indictment of the world and the consequent solitude of his lovers suggest such larger meanings.

If Mr. Schorer means to say—he sometimes expresses himself a little cloudily—that the modern industrial world, Lawrence's pet nightmare, has destroyed, among a number of other things, some ancient harmony once existing between the sexes which Lawrence proposes to restore by uttering of short words during the sexual act, I must merely remind him that all history is against his theory. The world itself, as well as the relationship between men and women, has not "grown into confusion." We have never had anything else, or anything much better; all human life since recorded time has been a terrible struggle from confusion to confusion to more confusion, and Lawrence, aided by his small but vociferous congregation—for there remain in his doctrine and manner the style of the parochial messiah, the Chapel preacher's threats and cajolements— has done nothing but add his own peculiar mystifications to the subject.

One trouble with him, always, and it shows more plainly than ever in this book, is that he wanted to play all the roles, be everywhere and everybody at once. He wished to be the godhead in his dreary rigamarole of primitive religion as in *The Plumed Serpent,* but must be the passive female too. Until he tires of it, and comes up with a fresh set of rules for everybody. Mr. Schorer cites a passage from a letter Lawrence wrote to someone when his feelings were changing. "The leader-cum-follower relationship is a bore," he decided, "and the new relationship will be some sort of tenderness, sensitive, between men and men, and between men and women." He gets a good deal of himself into these few words. First, when he is tired of the game he has invented and taught as a religion, everybody must drop it. Second, he seems not to have observed that tenderness is not a new relationship between persons who love one another. Third, he said between men and men, and men and women. He did not say between women and women, for his view of women is utterly baleful, and he has expressed it ferociously over and over. Women must be kept apart, for they contaminate each other. They are to be redeemed one by one through the sexual offices of a man, who seems to have no other function in her life, nor she in his. One of the great enlightenments of Lady Chatterley after her experience of the sentimental obscenities of her gamekeeper is to see other women clearly, women sexually less lucky than she, and to realize that they are all horrible! She can't get away fast enough, and back to the embraces of her fancy man-and-yet and-yet-

True marriage? Love, even? Even really good sex-as-such? It seems a very sad, shabby sort of thing to have to settle for, poor woman. I suppose she deserves anything she gets, really, but her just deserts are none of our affair. The pair are so plainly headed, not for tragedy, but just a dusty limbo, their fate interests us as a kind of curiosity. It is true that her youth was robbed by her husband's fate in the war. I think he was worse robbed, even with no way out, yet nobody seems to feel sorry for him. He is shown as having very dull ideas with conversation to match, but he is not more dull than the gamekeeper, who forgets that the lady's aristocratic husband was not born impotent, as Lawrence insists by way of his dubious hero, all upper class men were. At this point Lawrence's confusion of ideas and feelings, the pull and haul between his characters who go their own dreary way in spite of him, and the ideas he is trying to express through them, become pretty nearly complete. It would take another book to thread out and analyze the contradictions and blind alleys into which the reader is led.

Huizinga, on page 199 of his book, *The Waning of the Middle Ages*, tells of the erotic religious visions of a late medieval monk, and adds: "The description of his numerous visions is characterised at the same time by an excess of sexual imagination and by the absence of all genuine emotion." Lawrence used to preach frantically that people must get sex out of their heads and back where it belongs; and never learned that sex lives in all our parts, and must have the freedom of the whole being—to run easily in the blood and nerves and cells, adding its glow of life to everything it touches. The ineptitudes of these awful little love-scenes seem heart-breaking—that a man of such gifts should have lived so long and learned no more about love than that!

Reflections on Willa Cather

I never knew her at all, nor anyone who did know her; do not to this day. When I was a young writer in New York I knew she was there, and sometimes wished that by some charming chance I might meet up with her; but I never did, and it did not occur to me to seek her out. I had never felt that my condition of beginning authorship gave me a natural claim on the attention of writers I admired, such as Henry James and W. B. Yeats. Some proper instinct told me that all of any importance they had to say to me was in their printed pages, mine to use as I could. Still it would have been nice to have seen them, just to remember how they looked. There are three or four great ones, gone now, that I feel, too late, I should not have missed. Willa Cather was one of them.

There exist large numbers of critical estimates of her work, appreciations; perhaps even a memoir or two, giving glimpses of her personal history—I have never read one. She was not, in the popular crutch-word to describe almost any kind of sensation, "exciting"; so far as I know, nobody, not even one of the Freudian school of critics, ever sat up nights with a textbook in one hand and her works in the other, reading between the lines to discover how much sexual autobiography could be mined out of her stories. I remember only one photograph—Steichen's—made in middle life, showing a plain smiling woman, her arms crossed easily over a girl scout sort of white blouse, with a ragged part in her hair. She seemed, as the French say, "well seated" and not very outgoing. Even the earnestly amiable, finely shaped eyes, the left one faintly askew, were in some mysterious way not expressive, lacking as they did altogether that look of strangeness which a strange vision is supposed to give to the eye of any real artist, and very often does. One doesn't have to be a genius absolutely to get this look, it is often quite enough merely to believe one is a genius; and to have had the wild vision only once is enough—the afterlight stays, even if, in such case, it is phosphorescence instead of living fire.

Well, Miss Cather looks awfully like somebody's big sister, or maiden aunt, both of which she was. No genius ever looked less like one, according to the romantic popular view, unless it was her idol, Flaubert, whose photographs could pass easily for those of any paunchy country squire indifferent to his appearance. Like him, none of her genius was in her looks, only in her works. Flaubert was a good son, adoring uncle of a niece, devoted to his friends, contemptuous of the mediocre, obstinate in his preferences, fiercely jealous of his privacy, unyielding to the death in his literary principles and not in the slightest concerned with what was fashionable. No wonder she loved him. She had been rebuffed a little at first, not by his astronomical standards in art—none could be too high for her—but by a certain coldness of heart in him. She soon got over that; it became for her only another facet of his nobility of mind.

Very early she had learned to reverence that indispensable faculty of aspiration of the human mind toward perfection called, in morals and the arts, nobility. She was born to the idea and brought up in it: first in a comfortable farmhouse in Virginia, and later, the eldest of seven children, in a little crowded ranch house in Nebraska. She had, as many American country people did have in those times and places, literate parents and grandparents, soundly educated and deeply read, educated, if not always at schools, always at their own firesides. Two such, her grandmothers, taught her from her infancy. Her sister, Mrs. Auld, in Palo Alto, California, told it like this:

"She mothered us all, took care of us, and there was a lot to do in such a big family. She learned Greek and Latin from our grandmothers before she ever got to go to school. She used to go, after we lived in Red Cloud, to read Latin and Greek with a little old man who kept a general store down the road. In the evenings for entertainment—there was nowhere to go, you know, almost nothing to see or hear—she entertained us, it was good as a theater for us! She told us long stories, some she made up herself, and some were her versions of legends and fairy tales she had read; she taught us Greek mythology this way, Homer, and tales from the Old Testament. We were all story tellers," said her sister, "all of us wanted to be the one to tell the stories, but she was the one who told them. And we loved to listen all of us to her, when maybe we would not have listened to each other."

She was not the first nor the last American writer to be formed in this system of home education; at one time it was the customary education for daughters, many of them never got to school at all or expected to; but they were capable of educating their grandchildren, as this little history shows. To her last day Willa Cather was the true child of her plain-living, provincial farming people, with their aristocratic ways of feeling and thinking; poor, but not poverty-stricken for a moment; rock-based in character, a character shaped in an old school of good manners, good morals, and the unchallenged assumption that classic culture was their birthright; the belief that knowledge of great art and great thought was a good in itself not to be missed for anything; she subscribed to it all with her whole heart, and in herself there was the vein of iron she had inherited from a long line of people who had helped to break wildernesses and to found a new nation in such faiths. When you think of the whole unbelievable history, how did anything like this survive? Yet it did, and this life is one of the proofs.

I have not much interest in anyone's personal history after the tenth year, not even my own. Whatever one was going to be was all prepared for before that. The rest is merely confirmation, extension, development. Childhood is the fiery furnace in which we are melted down to essentials and that essential shaped for good. While I have been reading again Willa Cather's essays and occasional papers, and thinking about her, I remembered a sentence from the diaries of Anne Frank, who died in the concentration camp in Bergen-Belsen just before she was sixteen years old. At less than fifteen, she wrote: "I have had a lot of sorrow, but who hasn't, at my age?"

In Miss Cather's superb little essay on Katherine Mansfield, she speaks of childhood and family life: "I doubt whether any contemporary writer has made one feel more keenly the many kinds of personal relations which exist in an everyday 'happy family' who are merely going on with their daily lives, with no crises or shocks or bewildering complications. . . . Yet every individual in that household (even the children) is clinging passionately to his individual soul, is in terror of losing it in the general family flavor . . . the mere struggle to have anything of one's own, to be oneself at all, creates an element of strain which keeps everybody almost at breaking point.

". . . Even in harmonious families there is this double life . . . the one we can observe in our neighbor's household, and, underneath, another—secret and passionate and intense—which is the real life that stamps the faces and gives character to the voices of our friends. Always in his mind each member is escaping, running away, trying to break the net which circumstances and his own affections have woven about him. One realizes that human relationships are the tragic necessity of human life; that they can never be wholly satisfactory, that every ego is half the time greedily seeking them, and half the time pulling away from them."

This is masterly and water-clear and autobiography enough for me: my mind goes with tenderness to the lonely slow-moving girl who happened to be an artist coming back from reading Latin and Greek with the old storekeeper, helping with the housework, then sitting by the fireplace to talk down an assertive brood of brothers and sisters, practicing her art on them, refusing to be lost among them—the longest-winged one who would fly free at last.

I am not much given to reading about authors, or not until I have read what they have to say for themselves. I found Willa Cather's books for myself, early, and felt no need for intermediaries between me and them. My reading went on for a good many years, one by one as they appeared: *O Pioneers!*; *The Song of the Lark*; *My Ántonia*; *Youth and the Bright Medusa*; *Death Comes for the Archbishop*; *Obscure Destinies*; just these, and no others, I do not know why, and never anything since, until I read her notebooks about two years ago. Those early readings began in Texas, just before World War I, before ever I left home; they ended in Paris, twenty years later, after the longest kind of journey.

With her first book I was reading also Henry James, W. B. Yeats, Joseph Conrad, my introduction to "modern" literature, for I was brought up on solid reading, too, well aged. About the same time I read Gertrude Stein's *Tender Buttons*, for sale at a little bookshop with a shoeshine stand outside; inside you could find magazines, books, newspapers in half-a-dozen languages, avant-garde and radical and experimental; this in a Texas coast town of less than ten thousand population but very polyglot and full of world travelers. I could make little headway polyglot? libretto?

with Miss Stein beyond the title. It was plain that she meant "tender buds" and I wondered why she did not say so. It was the beginning of my quarrel with a certain school of "modern" writing in which poverty of feeling and idea were disguised, but not well enough, in tricky techniques and disordered syntax. A year or two after *Tender Buttons* I was reading Joyce's *Dubliners,* and maybe only a young beginning writer of that time, with some preparation of mind by the great literature of the past, could know what a revelation that small collection of matchless stories could be. It was not a shock, but a revelation, a further unfolding of the deep world of the imagination. I had never heard of Joyce. By the pure chance of my roving curiosity, I picked up a copy of the book at that little shoeshine bookstore. It was a great day.

By the time I reached Paris, I had done my long apprenticeship, published a small book of my own, and had gone like a house afire through everything "new"—that word meant something peculiar to the times— absolutely everything "new" that was being published; also in music; also painting. I considered almost any painting with the varnish still wet, the artist standing by, so to speak, as more interesting than anything done even the year before. But some of the painters were Klee, Juan Gris, Modigliani. . . . I couldn't listen to music happily if it wasn't hot from the composer's brain, preferably conducted or played by himself. Still, some of the music was Stravinsky's and Béla Bartók's and Poulenc's. I was converted to the harpsichord by the first New York recital of Wanda Landowska. In the theater I preferred dress rehearsals, or even just rehearsals, to the finished performance; I was mad about the ballet and took lessons off and on with a Russian for two years; I even wrote a ballet libretto way back in 1920 for a young Mexican painter and scene designer who gave the whole thing to Pavlova, who danced it in many countries but not in New York, because the scenery was done on paper, was inflammable and she was not allowed to use it in New York. I saw photographs, however, and I must say they did not look in the least like anything I had provided for in the libretto. It was most unsatisfactory.

What has this to do with Willa Cather? A great deal. I had had time to grow up, to consider, to look again, to begin finding my way a little through the inordinate clutter and noise of my immediate day, in which very literally everything in the world was being pulled apart, torn up, turned wrong side out and upside down; almost no frontiers left unat-

yes she I def... dress rehearsal

tacked, governments and currencies falling; even the very sexes seemed to be changing back and forth and multiplying weird, unclassifiable genders. And every day, in the arts, as in schemes of government and organized crime, there was, there had to be, something New.

Alas, or thank God, depending on the way you feel about it, there comes that day when today's New begins to look a little like yesterday's New, and then more and more so; you begin to suffer slightly from a sense of sameness or repetition: that painting, that statue, that music, that kind of writing, that way of thinking and feeling, that revolution, that political doctrine—is it really New? The answer is simply no, and if you are really in a perverse belligerent mood, you may add a half-truth—no, and it never was. Looking around at the debris, you ask has newness merely for its own sake any virtue? And you find that all along you had held and wound in your hand through the maze an unbreakable cord on which one by one, hardly knowing it, you had strung your life's treasures; it was as if they had come of themselves, while you were seeking and choosing and picking up and tossing away again, down all sorts of by-paths and up strange stairs and into queer corners; and there they were, things old and new, the things you loved first and those you loved last, all together and yours, and no longer old or new, but outside of time and beyond the reach of change, even your own; for that part of your life they belong to was in some sense made by them; if they went, all that part of your life would be mutilated, unrecognizable. While you hold and wind that cord with its slowly accumulating, weightless, unaccountable riches, the maze seems a straight road; you look back through all the fury you have come through, when it seemed so much, and so dismayingly, destruction, and so much just the pervasively trivial, stupid, or malignant-dwarfish tricks: fur-lined cups as sculpture, symphonies written for kitchen batteries, experiments on language very similar to the later Nazi surgical experiments of cutting and uniting human nerve ends never meant to touch each other: so many perversities crowding in so close you could hardly see beyond them. Yet look, you shared it, you were part of it, you even added to the confusion, so busy being new yourself. The fury and waste and clamor was, after all, just what you had thought it was in the first place, even if you had lost sight of it later—life, in a word, and great glory came of it, and splendid things that will go on living cleared of all the rubbish thrown up around their creation. Things you would have once thought incompatible to eternity take their right places in peace, in proper scale and order, in your mind—in your blood. They become that marrow in your bones where the blood is renewed.

I had liked best of all Willa Cather's two collections of short stories. They live still with morning freshness in my memory, their clearness, warmth of feeling, calmness of intelligence, an ample human view of things; in short the sense of an artist at work in whom one could have complete confidence: not even the prose attracted my attention from what the writer was saying—really saying, and not just in the words. Also I remember well my deeper impression of reserve—a reserve that was personal because it was a matter of temperament, the grain of the mind; yet conscious too, and practiced deliberately: almost a method, a technique, but not assumed. It was instead a manifesting, proceeding from the moral nature of the artist, morality extended to aesthetics—not aesthetics as morality but simply a development of both faculties along with all the others until the whole being was indivisibly one, the imagination and its expression fused and fixed.

A magnificent state, no doubt, at which to arrive; but it should be the final one, and Miss Cather seemed to be there almost from the first. What was it? For I began to have an image of her as a kind of lighthouse, or even a promontory, some changeless phenomenon of art or nature or both. I have a peculiar antipathy to thinking of anyone I know in symbols or mythical characters and this finally quietly alienated me from her, from her very fine books, from any feeling that she was a living, working artist in our time. It is hard to explain, for it was a question of tone, of implication, and what else? Finally, after a great while, I decided that Miss Cather's reserve amounted to a deliberate withholding of some vital part of herself as artist; not as if she had hidden herself at the center of her mystery but was still there to be disclosed at last; no, she had absented herself willfully.

I was quite wrong of course. She is exactly at the center of her own mystery, where she belongs. My immoderate reading of our two or three invaluably afflicted giants of contemporary literature, and their abject army of camp followers and imitators, had blurred temporarily my perception of that thin line separating self-revealment from self-exhibition. Miss Cather had never any intention of using fiction or any other form of writing as a device for showing herself off. She was not Paul in travesty, nor the opera singer in "The Diamond Mine," nor that girl with the clear eyes who became an actress: above all, not the Lost Lady. Of course she was all of them. How not? She made all of them out of herself, where else could they have taken on life?

Her natural lack of picturesqueness was also a good protective coloring: it saved her from the invasive prying of hangers-on: and no "school" formed in her name. The young writers did not swarm over her with flattery, manuscripts in hand, meaning to use her for all she was worth; publishers did not waylay her with seductions the instant her first little book appeared; all S. S. McClure could think of to do for her, after he published *The Troll Garden*, was to offer her a job as one of his editors on *McClure's Magazine*, where she worked hard for six mortal years before it seems to have occurred to her that she was not being a writer, after all, which was what she had started out for. So she quit her job, and the next year, more or less, published *Alexander's Bridge*, of which she afterward repented, for reasons that were to last her a lifetime. The scene, London, was strange and delightful to her; she was trying to make a novel out of some interesting people in what seemed to her exotic situations, instead of out of something she really knew about with more than the top of her mind. "London is supposed to be more engaging than, let us say, Gopher Prairie," she remarks, "even if the writer knows Gopher Prairie very well and London very casually."

She realized at once that *Alexander's Bridge* was a mistake, her wrong turning, which could not be retraced too instantly and entirely. It was a very pretty success, and could have been her finish, except that she happened to be Willa Cather. For years she still found people who liked that book, but they couldn't fool her. She knew what she had done. So she left New York and went to Arizona for six months, not for repentance but for refreshment, and found there a source that was to refresh her for years to come. Let her tell of her private apocalypse in her own words: "I did no writing down there, but I recovered from the conventional editorial point of view."

She then began to write a book for herself—*O Pioneers!*—and it was "a different process altogether. Here there was no arranging or 'inventing'; everything was spontaneous and took its own place, right or wrong. This was like taking a ride through a familiar country on a horse that knew the way, on a fine morning when you felt like riding. The other was like riding in a park, with someone not altogether congenial, to whom you had to be talking all the time."

What are we to think? For certainly here is a genius who simply will not cater to our tastes for drama, who refuses to play the role in any way we have been accustomed to seeing it played. She wrote with immense sympathy about Stephen Crane: "There is every evidence that he was a reticent and unhelpful man, with no warmhearted love of giving out opinions." If she had said "personal confidences" she could as well have been writing about herself. But she was really writing about Stephen Crane and stuck to her subject. Herself, she gave out quite a lot of opinions, not all of them warmhearted, in the course of two short little books, the second a partial reprint of the first. You hardly realize how many and how firm and how cogent while reading her fine pure direct prose, hearing through it a level, well-tempered voice saying very good, sensible right things with complete authority—things not in fashion but close to here and now and always, not like a teacher or a mother—like an artist—until, after you have closed the book, her point of view begins to accumulate and take shape in your mind.

Freud had happened: but Miss Cather continued to cite the old Hebrew prophets, the Greek dramatists, Goethe, Shakespeare, Dante, Tolstoy, Flaubert, and such for the deeper truths of human nature, both good and evil. She loved Shelley, Wordsworth, Walter Pater, without any reference to their public standing at the time. In her essay, "The Novel Demeublé," she had the inspired notion to bring together for purposes of comparison Balzac and Prosper Merimée; she preferred Merimée on the ground quite simply that he was the better artist: you have to sort out Balzac's meanings from a great dusty warehouse of misplaced vain matter—furniture, in a word. Once got at, they are as vital as ever. But Merimée is as vital, and you cannot cut one sentence without loss from his stories. The perfect answer to the gross power of the one, the too-finished delicacy of the other was, of course, Flaubert.

Stravinsky had happened; but she went on being dead in love with Wagner, Beethoven, Schubert, Gluck, especially *Orpheus*, and almost any opera. She was music-mad, and even Ravel's *La Valse* enchanted her; perhaps also even certain later music, but she has not mentioned it in these papers.

The Nude had Descended the Staircase with an epoch-shaking tread but she remained faithful to Puvis de Chavannes, whose wall paintings in the Panthéon of the legend of St. Genevieve inspired the form and tone of *Death Comes for the Archbishop*. She longed to tell old stories as simply as that, as deeply centered in the core of experience without extraneous detail as in the lives of the saints in *The Golden Legend.* She loved Courbet, Rembrandt, Millet and the sixteenth-century Dutch and Flemish painters, with their "warmly furnished interiors" but always with a square window open to the wide gray sea, where the masts of the great Dutch fleets were setting out to "ply quietly on all the waters of the globe. . . ."

Joyce had happened: or perhaps we should say, *Ulysses,* for the work has now fairly absorbed the man we knew. I believe that this is true of all artists of the first order. They are not magnified in their work, they disappear in it, consumed by it. That subterranean upheaval of language caused not even the barest tremor in Miss Cather's firm, lucid sentences. There is good internal evidence that she read a great deal of contemporary literature, contemporary over a stretch of fifty years, and think what contemporaries they were—from Tolstoy and Hardy and James and Chekhov to Gide and Proust and Joyce and Lawrence and Virginia Woolf, to Sherwood Anderson and Theodore Dreiser: the first names that come to mind. There was a regiment of them; it was as rich and fruitfully disturbing a period as literature has to show for several centuries. And it did make an enormous change. Miss Cather held firmly to what she had found for herself, did her own work in her own way as all the others were doing each in his unique way, and did help greatly to save and reassert and illustrate the validity of certain great and dangerously threatened principles of art. Without too much fuss, too—and is quietly disappearing into her work altogether, as we might expect.

Mr. Maxwell Geismar wrote a book about her and some others, called *The Last of the Provincials.* Not having read it I do not know his argument; but he has a case: she is a provincial; and I hope not the last. She was a good artist, and all true art is provincial in the most realistic sense: of the very time and place of its making, out of human beings who are so particularly limited by their situation, whose faces and names are real and whose lives begin each one at an individual unique center. Indeed, Willa Cather was as provincial as Hawthorne or Flaubert or Turgenev, as little concerned with aesthetics and as much with morals as Tolstoy, as obstinately reserved as Melville. In fact she always reminds me of very good literary company, of the particularly admirable masters who formed her youthful tastes, her thinking and feeling.

She is a curiously immovable shape, monumental, virtue itself in her art and a symbol of virtue—like certain churches, in fact, or exemplary women, revered and neglected. Yet like these again, she has her faithful friends and true believers, even so to speak her lovers, and they last a lifetime, and after: the only kind of bond she would recognize or require or respect.

1952

"It Is Hard to
Stand in the Middle"

E. P.: CANTO XIII (*Kung*)

In Mexico, many years ago, Hart Crane and I were reading again *Pavannes and Divisions*, and at some dogmatic statement in the text Crane suddenly burst out: "I'm tired of Ezra Pound!" And I asked him: "Well, who else is there?" He thought a few seconds and said: "It's true there's nobody like him, nobody to take his place." This was the truth for us then, and it is still the truth for many of us who came up, were educated, you might say, in contemporary literature, not at schools at all but by five writers: Henry James, James Joyce, W. B. Yeats, T. S. Eliot, and Ezra Pound. The beginning artist is educated by whoever helps him to learn how to work his own vein, who helps him to fix his standards, and who gives him courage. I believe I can speak for a whole generation of writers who acknowledge that these five men were in just this way, the great educators of their time.

The temptation in writing about *The Letters of Ezra Pound: 1907–1941* is to get down to individual letters, to quote endlessly, to lapse into gossip, to go into long dissertations on the state of society; the strange confusions of the human mind; music, sculpture, painting, war, economics; the menace of the American university; the weakness of having a private life; and finally the hell on earth it is to be at once a poet and a man of perfect judgment in all matters relating to art in a world of the deaf, dumb, and blind, of nitwits, numbskulls, and outright villains. One might go on for hours and pages citing instances, comparing letters, tracing change and development from year to year, noting enthusiasms turning into abhorrence, admirations into contempt, splendid altruistic plans to foster the arts falling into ruin because almost nobody would help, and following the frantic pattern of the poet's relations with his assortment of friends, for such I suppose they must be called. Friendship with Pound seems to have been a very uncertain state.

It would all be false, and misleading from the main road. These letters are the most revealing documents I have read since those of Boswell or Jane Carlyle, but how differently revealing. For where nearly all letters we know are attempts to express personal feeling, to give private news, to entertain; or set-pieces on a subject, but still meant for one reader; these letters as published contain hardly one paragraph which does not relate in one way or another to one sole theme—the arts. Almost nothing about the weather, or how the writer is feeling that day; and a magnificent disregard for how the reader is feeling, except now and then: to William Carlos Williams, 1909, "I hope to God you have no feelings. If you have, burn this *before* reading." He then launches into a scarifying analysis of his dear friend's latest poetry.

There are very few landscapes; very little about health. The poet is married, a marriage that now has lasted nearly thirty-five years, so there must have been some sort of family life, but the reader would hardly guess it. Now and then he remarks on the difficulty of paying rent, but you understand at once that the difficulties of paying rent and being an artist are closely connected. He mentions once or twice that he is aging a trifle, or feels tired, but he is tired of fighting people who fight art, or he feels too old to take on a certain job of work. Once he mentions kittens in a letter to William Carlos Williams, but I feel sure he meant something else; it must have been a code.* To his father he writes literary gossip, and remarks that he is playing tennis that afternoon. To his mother he mentions the marriage of Hilda Doolittle and Richard Aldington, and later writes to her, "I am profoundly pained to hear that you prefer Marie Corelli to Stendhal, but I cannot help it." He remembers Yeats's father on an elephant at Coney Island; but that was Jack Yeats, after all, a painter—otherwise one knows he might have sat on an elephant all day without a glance from Pound.

* W. B. Yeats told how Ezra Pound carried food scraps in his pockets for the hungry street cats who had so many enemies. Yeats doubted he really liked cats, though. "He never nurses the café cat," he observed. Of course not. The café cat was safe and comfortable.

No, this was not the point. Ezra Pound detested the "private life," denied that he ever had one, and despised those who were weak enough to need one. He was a warrior who lived on the battlefield, a place of contention and confusion, where a man shows all sides of himself without taking much thought for appearances. His own individual being is all the time tucked safely away within him, guiding his thoughts and feelings, as well as, at a long remove, his acts and words.

How right he was in so many things. The ferocious urge of his energy, his belief in himself with all his fears, his longing to be part of the world and his time, his curious lack of judgment of things outside his real interest now appear in these letters, and it is the truest document I have seen of that falling world between 1850 and 1950. We have been falling for a century or more, and Ezra Pound came along just at the right time to see what was happening.

He was a man concerned with public questions: specifically at first the question of the arts, the place of the artist in society, and he had a fanatical desire to force entire populations to respect art even if they could not understand it. (Indeed, he demanded reverence without understanding, for he sincerely did not believe that art was for the multitude. Whatever was too much praised he distrusted—even to the works of Sophocles. This is the inconsistency of his attitude all the way through: the attempt to force poetry upon people whom he believed not fitted to understand it.)

He believed himself to be the most patient soul alive, but he was not patient, he was tenacious, quite another thing. He was blowing up in wrath regularly from the very start, but he did not give up. He did not give up because he was incapable of abandoning a faith so furious it had the quality of religious fanaticism.

Witness his running fight, beginning in 1912, with Harriet Monroe, who controlled *Poetry; Poetry* was Pound's one hope in this country for a good number of years, so, some of the time, and at great cost to his nervous system, he controlled Miss Monroe. His exasperation with that innocent, unteachable, hard-trying woman came to the point where he was all the same as beating her over the head with a baseball bat. I should like to see the other side of this correspondence: her patience, or whatever it was, and her ability to absorb punishment, were equal to her inability to change her ways.

When Miss Monroe got really frightened at some of the things he sent her, he wrote: "Don't print anything of mine you think will kill the review, but . . . the public can go to the devil. It is the public's function to prevent the artist's expression by hook or by crook. . . . Given my head I'd stop any periodical in a week, only we are bound to run five years anyhow, we're in such a beautiful position to save the public's soul by punching its face that it seems a crime not to do so."

So it went for twenty-four long years, one of the most sustained literary wars on record, and yet it is hard to see what they would have done without each other. Harriet Monroe was his one instrument in this country, and continually she broke in his hands. She had some very genteel notions about language, and a schoolgirl taste for pretty verses that rhymed nicely and expressed delicate feelings, preferably about nature. ("No, most emphatically I will not ask Eliot to write down to any audience whatever," Pound wrote her in 1914. "I daresay my instinct was sound enough when I volunteered to quit the magazine a year ago. Neither will I send you Eliot's address in order that he may be insulted.") Bloody, Harriet's head undoubtedly was, but she would not let him go, and he would have been outraged if she had.

When after long years and in her old age, she tried at last to give up *Poetry*, to escape into private life with her family, he wrote: "The intelligence of the nation more important than the comfort or life of any one individual or the bodily life of a whole generation." That is truly the public spirit, the Roman senator speaking. Why did he take the trouble? For he adds, in contempt: "It is difficult enough to give the god damn amoeba a nervous system." Still, she had done her bit and could go, but she had no right to allow *Poetry* to die "merely because you have a sister in Cheefoo. . . ."

Pound was one of the most opinionated and unselfish men who ever lived, and he made friends and enemies everywhere by the simple exercise of the classic American constitutional right of free speech. His speech was free to outrageous license. He was completely reckless about making enemies. His so-called anti-Semitism was, hardly anyone has noted, only equaled by his anti-Christianism. It is true he hated most in the Catholic faith the elements of Judaism. It comes down squarely to antimonotheism, which I have always believed was the real root of the difficulty between Judaism and the West. Pound felt himself to be in

the direct line of Mediterranean civilization, rooted in Greece. Mono-
theism is simply not natural to the thought of such people and there are
more of them than one might think without having looked into the
question a little. Pound believed, rightly or wrongly, that Christianity
was a debased cult composed of too many irreconcilable elements, and as
the central power of this cult, he hated Catholicism worse than he did
Judaism, and for many more reasons.

He was not a historian, and apparently did not know that religion
flows from a single source, and that all are by now mingled and interre-
lated. Yet he did quote some things from ancient Chinese thought that
are purely Christian in the sense that Christianity teaches the same
ethics and morality, and so do the Jews, no matter from what earlier
religion either of them derived it. So he was reckless and bitter and badly
informed, but said what he thought, and in religious matters, in this
period perhaps the most irreligious the world has ever known, it is still
dangerous enough to be frank on that subject. "Anti-Semite" is a stupid,
reprehensible word in that it does not mean what it says, for not only
Semitic peoples have taught the doctrine of the One God, and Anti-
Semite is used now largely for purposes of moral blackmail by irresponsible people.

Pound's lapses, his mistakes—and this would include his politics—
occur when he deals with things outside his real interest, which was always art, literature, poetry. He was a lover of the sublime, and a seeker
after perfection, a true poet, of the kind born in a hair shirt—a God-sent
disturber of the peace in the arts, the one department of human life
where peace is fatal. There was no peace in that urgent, overstimulated
mind, where everything was jumbled together at once, a storehouse of
treasure too rich ever to be sorted out by one man in one lifetime. And it
was treasure.

It held exasperation, too; and related to the exasperation, but going
deeper, are the cursing, and the backwoods spelling, and the deliberate
illiteracy—at first humorous, high animal spirits, youthfully charming.
They become obsessional, exaggerated, the tone of near-panic, the voice
of Pound's deep fears. His fears were well founded; he was hard beset in
a world of real and powerful enemies. I heard a stowaway on a boat once,
cursing and shouting threats in that same monotonous, strained, desperate voice; in the end his captors only put him in the brig for the voyage.
The artist Pound knew had become a kind of stowaway in society.

With the same kind of energy and obsessional faith Pound collided with the Douglas theory of social credit. He himself appears to have a basic principle of thought about economics: "Debt is slavery." Ernestine Evans said she heard it on a gramophone record that got stuck, and Pound's voice repeated steadily at least fifty times: "Debt is slavery." She said the more often she heard it the more sense it made. This technique of repetition, in this case accidental, is known to the spreaders of lies. Maybe, though, it would be useful to repeat now and again a simple basic fact like that. "Debt is slavery." But for Pound even the Douglas plan was immediately drawn into the service of the arts.

Often in these letters there is in Pound a kind of socks-down, shirttail-out gracelessness which many will take delightedly for his true Americanism. In these moments he was a lout, and that is international. But he wore his loutishness with a difference. It is in his judgments, and his earlier judgments were much better than his later: though his pronouncements even on those he most admires run up and down like a panicky stock market. It is always praise or dispraise precisely according to what they have done in that present moment, and he is indignant when they do not always sit down quietly under it. He thundered not with just the voice of Jove, he *was* Jove. His judgments were indeed fallible, but his faith in them was not. "It isn't as if I were set in a groove. I read any number of masters, and recognize any number of kinds of excellence. But I'm sick to loathing of people who don't care for the master-work, who set out as artists with no intention of producing it, who make no effort toward the best, who are content with publicity and the praise of reviewers." He loathed rightly in this case, if ever a man did, yet so often simply in arrogant temper. His perfect assurance that he knew a work of art when he saw one, and his bent toward all kinds of excellence, led him into some lamentable errors which time little by little may correct.

As critic he was at his very best in the teacher-pupil relationship, when he had a manuscript under his eye to pull apart and put together again, or in simply stating the deep changeless principles of the highest art, relating them to each other and to their time and society. As one of the great poets of his time, his advice was unfathomably good and right in these things, and they are not outdated, and they cannot be unless the standard is simply thrown out.

Pound understood the nature of greatness: not that it voluntarily separates itself from the mass but that by its very being it is separate because it is higher. Greatness in art is like any other greatness: in religious experience, in love, it is great because it is beyond the reach of the ordinary, and cannot be judged by the ordinary, nor be accountable to it. The instant it is diluted, popularized, and misunderstood by the fashionable mind, it is no longer greatness, but window dressing, interior decorating, another way of cutting a sleeve. . . . Ezra Pound understood this simple law of natural being perfectly, and it is what redeems every fault and mitigates every failure and softens to the outraged ear of the mind and heart all that shouting and bullying and senseless obscenity—makes one respect all those wild hopeful choices of hopeless talents.

There is a doctrine that we should be patient in times of darkness and decline: but darkness and decline are the very things to fight, they are man-made, and can be unmade by man also. I am glad Pound was not patient in that sense, but obstinate and tenacious and obsessed and enraged. When you read these letters you will see what good sound reasons he had to be, if he was to make any headway against the obsessed tenacious inertia of his particular time. Most of the things and the kind of people he fought are still sitting about running things, fat and smug. That is true. And a great many of the talents he tried to foster came to nothing. Fighting the dark is a very unfashionable occupation now; but it is not altogether dead, and will survive and live again largely because of his life and example.

1950

The Art of
Katherine Mansfield

This past fourteenth of October [1937] would have been Katherine Mansfield's forty-ninth birthday. This year is the fifteenth since her death. During her life she had a fabulous prestige among young writers in England and America. Her readers were not numerous but they were devoted. It must be a round dozen years since I have read any of her stories; reading them again in the collected edition, I am certain she deserved her fame, and I wonder why it was not greater.

Of late I find my interest diverted somewhat from her achievement as artist to the enigma of her personal history. Actually there is little in her work to justify this, since the work itself can stand alone without clues or notes as to its origins in her experience; a paper chase for autobiographical data in these stories may be interesting in itself, but it adds nothing to the value of the stories. They exist in their own right. Yet I find it impossible to make these few notes without a certain preoccupation with her personal life of constant flight and search with her perpetual longing for certainties and repose; her beginnings in New Zealand; going to London to find the kind of place and the kind of people she wanted; her life there first as musician and then as writer; the many influences upon her mind and emotions of her friends and enemies—who in effect seem to have been interchangeable; her prolonged struggle with tuberculosis; her insoluble religious dilemma; her mysterious loss of faith in her own gifts and faculties; the disastrous failure of her forces at thirty-three, and the slowly engulfing despair that brought her finally to die at Fontainebleau.

These things are of first importance in a study which is yet to be done of the causes of Katherine Mansfield's own sense of failure in her work and in her life, but they do little to explain the work itself, which is superb. This misplaced emphasis of my attention I owe perhaps to her literary executor,* who has edited and published her letters and journals with a kind of merciless insistence, a professional anxiety for her fame on what seems to be the wrong grounds, and from which in any case his personal relation to her might have excused him for a time. Katherine Mansfield's work is the important fact about her, and she is in danger of the worst fate that an artist can suffer—to be overwhelmed by her own legend, to have her work neglected for an interest in her "personality."

There are eighty-eight stories in the collected edition, fifteen of which, her last, were left unfinished. The matter for regret is in these fifteen stories. Some of her best work is in them. She had been developing steadily, along a straight and fairly narrow path, working faithfully toward depth and concentration. Her handling of her material was firmer, her style had reached the flexibility of high tension and control, she had all her prime virtues and was shedding her faults, but her work had improved strictly in kind and not in difference. It is the same quick, ironic, perceptive mind, the same (very sensual) emotional nature, at work here from beginning to end.

In her the homely humility of the good craftsman toward his medium deepened slowly into a fatal self-distrust, and she set up for herself a standard of impossible perfection. It seems to have been on the grounds of the morality of art and not aesthetics that she began to desire a change in her own nature, who would have had quite literally to be born again to change. But the point is, she believed (or was persuaded that she believed) she could achieve a spiritual and mental rebirth by the practice of certain disciplines and the study of esoteric doctrines. She was innately religious, but she had no point of reference, theologically speaking; she was unable to accept her traditional religion, and she did finally, by what appears to have been an act of the will against all her grain, adopt means to make her fatal experiment in purification. As her health failed, her fears grew, her religious impulse wasted itself in an anxious straining toward some unknown infinite source of strength, of energy-

* John Middleton Murry, her husband.

renewing power, from which she might at the cost of single-hearted invocation find some fulfillment of true being beyond her flawed mortal nature. Now for her help and counsel in this weighty matter she had all about her, at different periods, the advice and influence of John Middleton Murry, A. R. Orage, D. H. Lawrence, and, through Orage, Gurdjieff.

Katherine Mansfield has been called a mystic, and perhaps she was, but in the severe hierarchy of mysticism her rank cannot be very high. André Maurois only yesterday wrote of her "pure feminine mysticism." Such as it was, her mysticism was not particularly feminine, nor any purer than the mysticism of D. H. Lawrence; and that was very impure matter indeed. The secret of her powers did not lie in this domain of her mind, and that is the puzzle: that such a good artist could so have misjudged herself, her own capacities and directions. In that rather loosely defined and changing "group" of variously gifted persons with whom Katherine Mansfield was associated through nearly all her working years, Lawrence was the prophet, and the idol of John Middleton Murry. They all were nervously irritable, self-conscious, and groping, each bent on painting his own portrait (The Young Man as Genius), and Katherine Mansfield's nerves suffered too from the teaching and the preaching and the quarreling and the strange vocabulary of perverted ecstasy that threw a pall over any true joy of living.

She possessed, for it is in her work, a real gaiety and a natural sense of comedy; there were many sides to her that made her able to perceive and convey in her stories a sense of human beings living on many planes at once, with all the elements justly ordered and in right proportion. This is a great gift, and she was the only one among them who had it, or at least the only one able to express it. Lawrence, whose disciple she was not, was unjust to her as he was to no one else, and that is saying a good deal. He did his part to undermine her, and to his shame, for personal rather than other reasons. His long maudlin relationship with John Middleton Murry was the source of his malignance toward her.

Mr. Murry's words in praise of her are too characteristic of the time and the special point of view to be ignored. Even today he can write that "her art was of a peculiarly instinctive kind." I confess I cannot understand the use of this word. That she was born with the potentialities of an artist, perhaps? I judge her work to have been to a great degree a matter of intelligent use of her faculties, a conscious practice of a hard-won craftsmanship, a triumph of discipline over the unruly circumstances and confusions of her personal life and over certain destructive elements in her own nature. She was deliberate in her choice of material and in her methods of using it, her technical resources grew continually, she cleared away all easy effects and tricky turns of phrase; and such mastership is not gained by letting the instincts have it all their own way.

Again Mr. Murry, in his preface to the stories: "She accepted life . . . she gave herself . . . to life, to love . . . she loved life, with all its beauty and pain . . . she responded to life more completely than any writer I have known except D. H. Lawrence. . . ."

Life, love, beauty, pain, acceptance, response, these are great words and they should mean something, and their meaning depends upon their exact application and reference. Whose life? What kind of love? What sort of beauty? Pain from what cause? And so on. It was this kind of explicitness that Katherine Mansfield possessed and was able to use, when she was at her best and strongest. She was magnificent in her objective view of things, her real sensitiveness to climate, mental or physical, her genuinely first-rate equipment in the matter of the five senses, and my guess, based on the evidence of her stories, is that she by no means accepted everything, either abstractly or in detail, and that whatever her vague love of something called Life may have been, there was as much to hate as to love in her individual living. Mistakenly she fought in herself those very elements that combined to form her main virtue: a certain grim, quiet ruthlessness of judgment, an unsparing and sometimes cruel eye, a natural malicious wit, an intelligent humor; and beyond all she had a burning, indignant heart that was capable of great compassion. Read "The Woman at the Store," or "A Birthday," and "The Child-Who-Was-Tired," one of the most terrible of stories; read "The Fly," and then read "Millie," or "The Life of Ma Parker." With fine objectivity she bares a moment of experience, real experience, in the life of some one human being; she states no belief, gives no motives, airs no theories, but simply presents to the reader a situation, a place, and a character, and there it is; and the emotional content is present as implicitly as the germ is in the grain of wheat.

Katherine Mansfield has a reputation for an almost finicking delicacy. She was delicate as a surgeon's scalpel is delicate. Her choice of words was sure, a matter of good judgment and a good ear. Delicate? Read, in

"A Married Man's Story," the passage describing the prostitute who has been beaten, coming into the shop of the evil little chemist for his famous "pick-me-up." Or such a scene as the fat man spitting over the balcony in "Violet"; or the seduction of Miss Moss in "Pictures." "An Indiscreet Journey" is a story of a young pair of lovers, set with the delicacy of sober knowledge against the desolate and brutalized scene of, not war, but a small village where there has been fighting, and the soldiers in the place are young Frenchmen, and the inn is "really a barn, set out with dilapidated tables and chairs." There are a few stories which she fails to bring off, quite, and these because she falls dangerously near to triviality or a sentimental wistfulness, of which she had more than a streak in certain moments and which she feared and fought in herself. But these are few, and far outweighed by her best stories, which are many. Her celebrated "Prelude" and "At the Bay," "The Doll's House," "The Daughters of the Late Colonel" keep their freshness and curious timelessness. Here is not her view of life but her many views of many kinds of lives, and there is no sign of even a tacit acquiescence in these sufferings, these conflicts, these evils deep-rooted in human nature. Mr. Murry writes of her adjusting herself to life as a flower, etc.; there is an elegiac poesy in this thought, but—and remember I am judging by her pages here under my eye—I see no sign that she ever adjusted herself to anything or anybody, except at an angle where she could get exactly the slant and the light she needed for the spectacle.

She had, then, all her clues; she had won her knowledge honestly, and she turned away from what she knew to pursue some untenable theory of personal salvation under a most dubious teacher. "I fail in my personal life," she wrote in her journal, and this sense of failure infected her life as artist, which is also personal. Her decision to go to Fontainebleau was no whim, no accident. She had long been under the influence of Orage, her first publisher and her devoted friend, and he was the chief disciple of Gurdjieff in England. In her last finished story, "The Canary," a deep parable of her confusion and despair, occurs the hopeless phrase: "Perhaps it does not so much matter what one loves in this world. But love something one must." It seems to me that St. Augustine knew the real truth of the matter: "It doth make a difference whence cometh a man's joy."

"The Canary" was finished in July, 1922. "In the October following she deliberately abandoned writing for a time and went into retirement at Fontainebleau, where she died suddenly and unexpectedly on the night of January 9, 1923." And so joined that ghostly company of unfulfilled, unhappy English artists who died and are buried in strange lands.

1937

Orpheus in Purgatory

On his fiftieth birthday, "What a bore, what futility!" Rilke wrote to a friend about all the flowers and messages and visitors. ". . . Naturally, if one looks at it justly, there was something dear in it, but where is the love that does not make more trouble?"

It is hardly possible to exaggerate the lovelessness in which most people live, men or women: wanting love, unable to give it, or inspire it, unable to keep it if they get it, not knowing how to treat it, lacking the humility, or the very love itself that could teach them how to love: it is the painfullest thing in human life, and, since love is purely a creation of the human imagination, it is merely perhaps the most important of all the examples of how the imagination continually outruns the creature it inhabits. . . . Having imagined love, we are condemned to its perpetual disappointment; or so it seems.

"You know Rilke . . . you know how he is and how much he means to me. . . . You have never asked how it will end. . . . I . . . have not asked that question either, and perhaps that was wrong of me, I have been happy with him in the present . . . because of his noble and lofty spirit . . . because of his inexhaustible kindness. Every time I saw him was a gift of God to me. And I thought that if some day he had to withdraw, and be quite alone with his work, then I should be alone again . . . far away from him, not hearing from him any more but guarding his holy image in my heart. I should almost forbid myself to think of him."

This is Magda von Hattingberg, Rilke's Benvenuta (The Welcome One), writing to her sister when her curious association, whatever its real nature, with Rainer Maria Rilke was drawing to its close in 1914. It had been brief: two months of letters, three of living together; and strange: for by this account, the obvious conditions of such a relationship seem never to have existed. They traveled openly together for those three months, to Paris, to Berlin, Munich, Venice, besides visits to houses and castles of his friends. Yet Benvenuta says plainly (and she does wrap some plain things in the sustained fanatic rapture of her style) that when they parted forever they kissed for the first and last time. This statement comes as rather an anticlimax after the heroic if fevered effort of an apparently healthy, all-too-feminine young woman to grow wings for her god, devoted as he was to angels.

One hardly knows where to place *Rilke and Benvenuta* in the clutter of letters, memoirs, critical studies, and biographies so steadily accumulating around Rilke's name. As much hysterical nonsense has been written about him as about D. H. Lawrence, if that is possible. Like Lawrence, his personal attractiveness drew to him the parasitic kind of adorers who insist on feeding on the artist himself instead of on his work: who make mystification of the mysterious, and scandals instead of legends. But Rilke was luckier than Lawrence in this: that he also had many faithful good friends who anxiously and constantly for long years succeeded in defending and helping him, almost in spite of himself. For he demanded, and would have, and would content himself with nothing less than, the humanly impossible in all human relationships. As relatives, friends, publishers now dole out mangled fragments of his literary estate, the secret of their long enchantment with him seems lost, for a temperament rather less than enchanting is being revealed little by little. His afterlife of fame is very similar to his former life in his restless, painful flesh: the perpetual unsatisfied guest, the helpless dependent, the alienated genius seeking silence and solitude to work out his destiny— Paul Valéry was shocked at the inhumanity of an "existence so separated . . . in such an abuse of the intimacy with silence, so much license given to one's dreams . . ." the continuing stranger who claimed the veneration due to the poet, that is to say, prophet, priest, seer, one set apart by his tremendous mission. In the meantime: "One lives so badly one always comes into the present unready, unfit, and distraught for everything . . . only the ten days after Ruth's (his daughter's) birth, I think, did I live without the smallest waste; finding reality as indescribable, even to the smallest detail, as it doubtless always is." This to his wife in 1907.

By 1914 he had not yet discovered the truths of reality, indeed, it was not his goal; but after seven years of search and flight, of homelessness and poverty, added to his double sense of failure as human being and as poet—for the two warring beings were never to be reconciled in him—he was ready, or hoped he was ready, for "a more human and natural footing in life," and Magda von Hattingberg seemed to be the one who could provide it for him. She wrote him first, as women so often did, an adoring letter; he hastened to answer it, and thirty-five long years later, she publishes some of his letters—very interesting letters, too—some of hers, passages from her diary, some very valuable transcriptions of conversations they had, and for the rest, a rhapsodical, high-flung, far-fetched romance which for style is an extraordinary blend of Marianna Alcoforado and The Duchess. . . .

In the best German Romantic tradition of the 1840's, not only all nature, and all society, but heaven itself, are tender accomplices in this transcendent episode. Nature especially assists with manifestations symbolically appropriate: the rains, the snows, the fogs, the sunshine, flowers of spring, arrive punctually; the moon is always obligingly full to witness a high encounter. They travel through enchanted landscapes like spirits in a dream, they even sit up all night outdoors somewhere at a crisis, she sleeps on his shoulder and the dawn finds them there, weary, a little stiff in their bones, but with exaltation undiminished. It is absurd, no other word for it. For the heroine was a young, beautiful, professional concert pianist, and too often, especially in the castles and drawing rooms, it is as if she played out her dream-romance on a grand piano, her costume always perfect, the moment perfect, the high-born spectators always on hand and attentive, the cultural ambience of the purest edelweiss.

But the fact that she has made herself so easy a target does not mean that she can be dismissed so easily. E. M. Butler, in her *Rilke*, tells her story in a few lines, and does not mention her name but quotes a letter from Rilke about her, written shortly after he had broken with her, broken with a decision and finality which shows plainly how dangerous to his future he considered her. For he was incapable of the kind of love she gave, and humanly wished to have from him; he could not endure the burden of her adoring warmth and energy and naturalness. After admitting that for years he had tried to flatter himself that his failures in love and in friendship had been the fault of others, that each in turn had violated, injured, wronged him, he writes: "I have entirely altered my opinion now after these last months of suffering. This time I have been obliged to recognize the fact that no one can help me, no one at all. And even if he (she) should come with the best and most loving of hearts, and should prove his worth to the very stars . . . keeping his regard for me pure and untroubled, however often I broke the ray of his spirit with the cloudiness and density of my submarine world I would yet (I know it now) find the means to strip him of the fulness of his ever-renewed assistance, and to enclose him in a loveless vacuum, so that his useless succor would rot and wither and die a terrible death."

It is pleasant to know that none of this happened to his tenderly nick-named Benvenuta; she had to a triumphant degree the womanly knack of starving gracefully on the thinnest ration of love, and yet at last spreads her own feast—a strange feast, but her food—out of that famine.

Only once had he succeeded in almost frightening her off. He was admiring some fantastic doll figure, and she protested that the virtue of a toy was in its effect on a child, and she could not imagine an innocent, healthy little girl not being repelled by this monster. Rilke proceeded to rip to shreds her notions of childish innocence, and to explain to her at length the innate corruptness of toys—and quoted also at length from his fierce essay against dolls, published shortly afterwards. She had unknow-ingly touched him on the quick: his mother had dressed him as a girl, and had given him dolls to play with.

The faithful and patient Princess Marie of Thurn and Taxis witnessed not only this love affair at one point, but many others with many other women. She was disconcerted, she wrote in her journal, at the attraction women had for Rilke. Rilke was equally disconcerted many times at the attraction he had for them: it seemed to him that what a man did only for God, a woman did always for a man. For a while he could imper-sonate a man, imitate his functions passably—provided the woman was infatuated enough, and most often she was, for women, of all sorts, and for all sorts of reasons, are flattered by the attentions of genius—even he could deceive himself into a plausible enough feeling, or a belief that he felt, or was capable of feeling, a natural, spontaneous sexual desire. But nothing of this could last: in no time at all he was faced with the terrible alternative: to go on with a eunuchlike sniffing and fumbling, or flight—flight in almost any direction, to any goal, even into another trap of womanly tenderness and incomprehension.

He depended in all faith, and with good reason too, on the tenderness and sympathy of women: all of them high-minded, romantic, some of them very gifted, many nobly born and rich: but alas, seekers after a man-god rather than the God in man. By the simplest means, and without any method except that provided by the natural duplicity of his need to be adored and taken care of, Rilke wove his web about them for good. This web was the Word—the Word multiplied, an endless spinning of high, poetic, noble words, flowing easily as a melody carrying with it painless didactic counsel, and if they had not been so flattered, they might have read as we do now the warning between the lines: This is what I have to give, ask for nothing more.

He flattered the soul, or the intellect, or the heart, or all three at once; whatever the individual woman craved that words could supply, he gave her generously. There were more than enough words to go around. Not one of them had any real right to complain, for he was faithful to them all, and he paid them the highest compliment of never confusing one of them with another. . . . And he asked of them all the same thing—that they would save him for himself and from them.

1950

"The Laughing Heat
of the Sun"

Of all fine sights in the world to me, the best is that of an artist growing great, adding to his art with his years, as his life and his art are inseparable. Henry James's and W. B. Yeats's careers occur to mind first as spectacles in which I took delight, and Edith Sitwell, with *The Canticle of the Rose*, the collected volume of her work of more than thirty years, joins them. The true sign of this growth, in all alike, is the unfailing renewal, the freshness of every latest piece of work, the gradual, steady advance from phase to phase of increased power and direction, depth of feeling, and virtuosity, that laurel leaf added to technical mastery. Decade by decade, the familiar voice adds other notes to its range, a fuller tone, more sustained breath: an organic growth of the whole being.

Miss Sitwell's early work belonged to youth—it had the challenging note of natural arrogance, it was boldly experimental, inventive from a sense of adventure, full of high spirits and curiosity as to how many liberties the language would suffer to be taken without hitting back. There was sometimes also a certain artifice, the dew upon the rose turned out to be a crystal bead on a mother-of-pearl petal. Yet it was the work of a deft artificer, and a most ornamental rose, meant to amuse and charm, never intended to be mistaken for a natural flower.

It was the shimmer, the glancing light of this wit, this gaiety, one found so refreshing, for they were qualities markedly absent from the serious poetry of that long grim generation of censorious poets who were her contemporaries or later. Hardly anyone knew how to laugh, and those who did hardly dared to; it was no time for frivolity, and laughter was frivolous in such a murderous time. Miss Sitwell dared: she laughed outright whenever she felt like it, and the reader laughed too: for plainly this laughter was not levity nor frivolity, it was the spontaneous merriment of a vital spirit, full of natural courage and confidence. The idea of death, which has paralyzed the humanity of so many poets for more than a century, affected her very differently. In the old robust way, she set out to make hay while her sun still shone. One felt this quality in her then, one is reassured of it now: "My poems are hymns in praise of the glory of life," she writes without any shade of apology for such an antique point of view. This praise is as clear in the early "Trio for Two Cats and a Trombone," or "Hornpipe," as it is in "Still Falls the Rain," written during a night raid in 1940.

The glory of life—the force of the affirmative passion of love in this poet, the feeling for glory in her, are the ground-virtues of her art, twin qualities almost lost for the present in the arts as in all human existence; as in her youth it sharpened her wit and her comedy, in middle life her sensuous celebration of the noble five human senses, in age her spiritual perceptions. This is such a progression as makes life and art worth practicing.

Her early poetry was, for me, associated, for all its "modern" speed and strepitation, with the old courtly music of Lully, Rameau, Purcell, Monteverdi, that I loved and do love: festival music, meant to be played in theaters, at weddings, christenings, great crystal-lighted banquets; or in the open air, in sweet-smelling gardens and the light of the full moon, with the torches waving their banners under the trees—gay music, serious great music, one can trust one's joy in it.

So with Edith Sitwell's poetry in those days between two wars, and so it is still. I am tempted to pick out here and there a few lines from some of those early things, but they do not take well to it. They are in full flight, it would be like plucking feathers from a bird. Pretty feathers, but they do not sing. Every word, every syllable does its part toward the final effect—her country songs are fresh as country mornings; her kitchen songs are a welter of sooty pots, hard cold early light and tangle-haired sleepy girls fighting with early cook-fires that will not catch. The beggar maid is "that pink flower spike full of honey." Rain is rain in these poems, it rains on the page and you can smell it and feel it. There are "horses as fat as plums"—of course, I have seen them. When witches are on the prowl, one ". . . hears no sound but wind in trees; /One candle spills out thick gold coins, /Where quilted dark with tree shade joins." Who does not remember ". . . the navy-blue ghost of Mr. Belaker / The allegro Negro Cocktail shaker?" asking, at four in the morning, his violent, unanswerable question, "Why did the cock crow? Why am I lost?" "The gaiety of some" (of her poems) "masks darkness," writes Miss Sitwell.

Large numbers of the public felt lost, too. It all sounded horridly novel and they hated it. Miss Sitwell did not have an easy time of it. The story has been told by her brother Sir Osbert Sitwell in his memoirs, so we need not go into here. After all these years, Time having brought it about that Miss Sitwell is now being called "classic" by the younger generation, she being famous, a Doctor of Letters, at last she has time to sit down and explain what she was doing in those days and why, and what she meant by it.

She chooses many poems, those which caused the most disturbance when they were new; line by line, syllable by syllable, sometimes letter by letter, patiently she threads out meanings and makes a design of them. It makes good sense—that good sense the artist can always make of his intentions and methods after he has done the work. It is an endearing habit artists have, and I find nothing so enthralling as to hear or read a good artist telling how he does it. For practical purposes he might as well try to communicate his breath for our use. For example, Miss Sitwell chooses words not only for their meaning, but for sound, number of syllables, color, shape, texture, speed or slowness, thickness, thinness, weight, and for the shadow they cast upon the words near them. "Said King Pompey" is built on a scheme of R's for very good reasons. It is also "a poem about materialism and the triumphant dust."

Her introduction to *The Canticle* is good reading, and you can see, by the passages she cites, that whether or not it was so deliberate a thing as she now believes, she got her effects by just the means she says she did; a good deal more than most artists can prove. Beginning poets should be warned that this is not a ready-made technique, a bridge to anywhere. The live, inborn instinct for language, for the mother-tongue, must first be present, and whoever else has it to anywhere near this degree, will not get anything from Miss Sitwell except the pleasure of reading her poetry and an incitement to get on with his own work. This is about all that one artist can do for another, and it is really quite enough.

This poet's vision: "Seeing the immense design of the world, one image of wonder mirrored by another image of wonder—the pattern of fern and feather by the frost on the windowpane, the six rays of the snowflake mirrored in the rock-crystal's six-rayed eternity—seeing the pattern on the scaly legs of birds mirrored in the pattern of knot-grass, I asked myself, were those shapes molded by blindness? Are not these the correspondences, to quote a phrase of Swedenborg, whereby we speak with the angels?" Her theme: the eternal theme of saints and poets: the destiny of Man is to learn the nature of love and to seek spiritual rebirth. Her range of variations on this theme is endless. Every poem therefore is a love poem, even those towering songs of denunciation out of her counter-passion of hatred for the infamies of life and the willful wrong man does to the image of God in himself. So many peevish and obscene little writers of late have been compared to Swift I hesitate to set his name here even where I feel it is not out of place. In "Gold Coast Customs" I find for the first time in my contemporary reading a genius for invective as ferocious as Swift's own, invective in the high-striding authoritative style, the same admirable stateliness of wrath, the savage indignation of a just mind and generous heart outraged to the far edge of endurance. The mere natural murderousness of the human kind is evil enough, but her larger rejection is of "the terrible ideal of useless Suffering" symbolized by "Lazarus, the hero of death and the mud, taking the place in men's minds of the Hero of Life who was born in a stable."

This passage is from "Gold Coast Customs":

> But Lady Bamburgher's Shrunken Head
> Slum hovel, is full of the rat-eaten bones
> Of a fashionable god that lived not
> Ever, but still has bones to rot:
> A bloodless and an unborn thing
> That cannot wake, yet cannot sleep,
> That makes no sound, that cannot weep,
> That hears all, bears all, cannot move—
> It is buried so deep
> Like a shameful thing
> In that plague-spot heart, Death's last dust-heap.

Again: "Though Death has taken/And pig-like shaken/Rooted, and tossed/the rags of me—"

"At one time," writes Miss Sitwell, "I wrote of the world reduced to the Ape as mother, teacher, protector. But too, with poor Christopher

Smart, I blessed Jesus Christ with the Rose and his people, a nation of living sweetness. My time of experiment was over."

This was later, and there is still the vast middle section of the work, the rages, the revolts, the burning noon of drunkenness on sensuous sound and image, the exaltation of the pagan myth, the earth's fertility; the bold richness of the roving imagination taking every land and every sea, every far-off and legendary place, every dream and every nightmare of the blood, every response of every human sense for its own. In this part, I find my own favorites are all, one way or another, songs of mourning: "Colonel Fantock"; "Elegy on Dead Fashion"; "Three Rustic Elegies"—"O perfumed nosegay brought for noseless death!" She acknowledges his power over the suffering flesh, the betrayed heart: but he can plant only carrion which belongs to his kingdom of the dust; Christ the Golden Wheat sows Himself perpetually for our perpetual resurrection. Rarely in the poetry of our time is noseless death stared down so boldly.

"After 'Gold Coast Customs,' " writes Miss Sitwell, "I wrote no poetry for several years, with the exception of a long poem called 'Romance,' and one poem in which I was finding my way. Then after a year of war, I began to write again—of the state of the world, of the terrible rain" (of bombs). During this long pause, she made the transition from the short, violently accented line, to a long curving line, a changed tone and pace. Of the late poems, the first one begins:

> I who was once a golden woman like those who walk,
> In the dark heavens—but am now grown old
> And sit by the fire, and see the fire grow cold,
> Watch the dark fields for a rebirth of faith and of wonder.

Again, in "Tattered Serenade":

> These are the nations of the Dead, their million-year-old
> Rags about them—these, the eternally cold,
> Misery's worlds, with Hunger, their long sun
> Shut in by polar worlds of ice, known to no other,
> Without a name, without a brother,
> Though their skin shows that they yet are men.

In these later poems, without exception tragic, a treasure of distilled tragic experience, the mysterious earthly rapture is mingled with a strain of pure, Evangelical Christianity, raised to the apocalyptic vision. Here, rightly, are some of the most wonderful (wonderful, and I know the meaning of that word) love songs in the English language: "Anne Boleyn's Song"; "Green Song"; "The Poet Laments the Coming of Old Age"; "Mary Stuart to James Bothwell"; and here begins the sustained use of the fire symbols, of gold the color of fire, the sun, the sun's flame, the gold of wheat, of lions' manes, of foxes' pelts, of Judas' hair, fire of the hearth, molten gold, gold seed, the gold of corn, golden cheeks, golden eyelids; "the great gold planets, spangling the wide air," "gold-bearded thunders"—a crescendo of rapture in celebration of fire after the ice-locked years of war when fire carried only death. As every symbol has many meanings, and is corruption or purification according to its relationships, so the sun, "the first lover of the earth," has been harnessed by man to his bloody purposes, and must be restored as the lover, as the giver of life:

> And I who stood in the grave-clothes of my flesh
> Unutterably spotted with the world's woes,
> Cry, "I am Fire. See, I am the bright gold
> That shines like a flaming fire in the night—the gold-trained planet,
> The laughing heat of the Sun that was born from darkness."

In "The Song of the Cold," the cold which is the symbol of poverty, death, the hardened human heart, there is the final speech of marrow-frozen grief: "I will cry to the Spring to give me the birds' and the serpents' speech,/That I may weep for those who die of the cold—" but "The Canticle of the Rose" says:

> The Rose upon the wall
> Cries—"I am the voice of Fire:
> And in me grows
> The pomegranate splendor of Death, the ruby, garnet, almandine
> Dews: Christ's wounds in me shine!"

This is the true flowering branch springing fresh from the old, unkillable roots of English poetry, with the range, variety, depth, fearlessness, the passion and elegance of great art.

1949

On Christopher Sykes

(a review of Character and Situation,
*six stories by Christopher Sykes,
with an introduction by Evelyn Waugh)*

The dust jacket carries a statement that Christopher Sykes' talent resembles that of Harold Nicholson. Let the reader be warned that this is a very debatable opinion. In this collection of short stories I was not once even faintly reminded of Mr. Nicholson's "Some People" for example. The only resemblances are, that this book is about some people, too, and the scenes are "exotic," which we may suppose means any scene the reader has not visited.

Mr. Evelyn Waugh's introduction has all the bright bounciness of a snake-oil vendor, or of someone selling packaged breakfast food on the radio. He gives us one of those intimate portraits which befog the subject with details. Rashly he fixes the date of Mr. Sykes' birth, 1907, as "perhaps the last year in which a good Englishman could be born." The Welfare State and other public calamities then blighted the British Isles, and British "manhood was struck hard and mysteriously." A great pity if true. These are strong words. He makes a great point of Mr. Sykes' Roman Catholic origin and upbringing, which naturally give him a superior moral and philosophical outlook; he dresses carelessly because he was educated by the Benedictines. In conversation he is apt to talk about what interests him whether it interests his hearer or not. That is not a pretty habit, no matter how sound one's theology is.

He is not the stuffy literary type, either; man of action in war or peace, world traveler and a keen observer of the goings-on of those who live in foreign parts. Yet he "contrives somehow, somewhere out of sight, to do a reasonable amount of conscientious research and literary composition." Mr. Waugh does not tell us what a reasonable amount of work is, for a

64

writer who respects his medium and even perhaps his reader. Mr. Sykes "amassed the experiences that were to fit him to be a writer. He did not take a course in 'Creative Writing': he lived. . . ."

Conscientious research and experiences do not fit one to be a writer; no amount of conscientious living helps either; and courses in creative writing are also just thrown away, unless one has the gift. Or not to be too serious about this sort of thing, let's call it the knack. And a man's moral and religious principles may be entirely irreproachable without adding one tittle to his ability to express them interestingly.

By now it must be clear that I got so wound up splitting hairs with Mr. Waugh, I began to fear I should never get to the stories; indeed it appeared he was doing his best to discourage me. After rebuking us for not having known all about Mr. Sykes and his work long ago, Mr. Waugh says endearingly: "Take him to your warm hearts. He is worthy of them."

Well, let's see.

About a century and a half ago, English literature settled down into a good solid tradition of the hard-working, steady, earnest hacks (Trollope to Wells to Bennett) with now and again a brilliant eruption of genius: Jane Austen, E. Brontë, Dickens, Hardy, Hopkins. They could produce in one small island such artists, so independent and so individual they might have belonged to different races, each using their common speech to create his unique language. There is a new sort sprung up in the past twenty-odd years. We should know, for we have been grappling them to our warm hearts all along, in platoons—the literate, carefully unliterary writer who, no matter how many books he has published, still gives the impression of clinging defensively to his semi-amateur status, just in case. He can always say it was a hobby, never a full-time job; a novel or short story is something you can shake out of your sleeve, and at times it is all too easy to believe that that is the way it was done. This is the kind of bad idea which always leads to worse. There are among these writers two main schools with infinite small deviations and branches: the Willful Fantastic who will tell you anything in a reasonable tone of voice, and the Romantic-Erotic-Religious, most of them Catholic, some of them converts, who have a message to convey. It is a pity that both Mr. Waugh and Mr. Sykes can manage to make religious doctrine and feeling so repellent to one's better nature. I shouldn't be surprised if they have driven hundreds of promising souls away from the very gates of the fold.

And they wrap the message sometimes in a gaudy coating of sex as such, or rather, sex as sin. You are never allowed to forget it for a minute.

Yet, different as the things they tell, and worth telling as some of it is, there is the strangest leveling process going on lately. For my own reasons I have read at least a dozen new books of fiction by as many British authors, and no matter what they had to say, the mere monotony of the styles, or style, caused them in no time to run all together in my memory, I could not tell one from the other, hardly Mr. Nicholson from Mr. Sykes. This leveling is a dire misfortune to English literature, and makes me inclined to accept Mr. Waugh's theory about that sudden blight on Britain. Only, he himself, supposedly of a vintage year, is one of the victims and so, to a less degree, is Mr. Sykes.

What this state of affairs requires is more warm hearts and sturdier talents among British novelists, and more cool heads among their critics and readers. Mr. Sykes slogs along with a manly competence, he can see a character in a situation and tell about it, sometimes very entertainingly, but it remains a made-up story, and I am unable to decide whether the final effect of shapelessness and vagueness has been carefully worked, or is it what it really seems to be, an inability to come to grips with his stuff? Does he really know and feel so little about other human beings? —and mind you, he knows what the correct sentiments and moral conclusions should be—or is he deliberately keeping himself free from attachments? As a religious, that may be all very well; as an artist, he is making a mistake.

The nearest he comes to a plausible being is his portrait of a vain aging author, in "The Interview." The most ironical situation is exposed in "My Brother and Me." But he is as tetchy about his religious dogma as a convert, and his monkish distrust of women leads him to set up some improbable figures of straw and wax, dressed in skirts, which he then slaps around so severely it becomes rather embarrassing to witness.

He is almost gentle with one young girl, in "The Interview," but still, she is a little stupid and insensitive: "They embraced with desperate mutual desire. . . . 'My father is a curious man,' she said, in the calm, inappropriate voice women can use suddenly on amorous occasions, unconcerned that this ordinary remark had been preceded by a near-equivalent of the carnal act of love and its dark mysteries." This is not a love-scene, it is an attack of writer's cramp caused by theology nudging his elbow. Still I do prefer Mr. Sykes' stony polysyllabic reserve to the kind of flux which ravaged some of our younger American writers in the past few years, and which now shows signs of disappearing.*

If you have enjoyed reading Graham Greene, or Henry Green, or the Waugh brothers, or William Sansom, or almost any one of a dozen, why then, you should not neglect Mr. Sykes, either. He may have something to say to you. Yet there are still the passion of love and the art of literature, and as a true believer in both, I should like to see another generation of writers come on who will know how to treat them both with the concern and the dignity they deserve.

1951

* 1970—What a hope!

Virginia Woolf

Leonard Woolf, in selecting and publishing the shorter writings of his wife, Virginia Woolf, has taken occasion to emphasize, again and again, her long painstaking ways of working, her habit of many revisions and rewritings, and her refusal to publish anything until she had brought it to its final state. The four volumes to appear in the nine years since her death will probably be the lot, Mr. Woolf tells us. There seems to remain a certain amount of unfinished manuscripts—unfinished in the sense that she had intended still to reconsider them and would not herself have published them in their present versions. One cannot respect enough the devoted care and love and superb literary judgment of the executor of this precious estate.

"In the previous volumes," Mr. Woolf writes in his foreword to the latest collection, *The Captain's Death Bed*, "I made no attempt to select essays in accordance with what I thought to be their merit or importance; I aimed at including in each volume some of all the various kinds of essay."

It is easy to agree with him when he finds "The essays in this volume are . . . no different in merit and achievement from those previously published." Indeed, I found old favorites and new wonders in each of the earlier collections, finding still others again in this: the celebrated "Mr. Bennett and Mrs. Brown"; "Memories of a Working Woman's Guild"; "The Novels of Turgenev"; "Oliver Goldsmith." She speaks a convincing good word for Ruskin, such was her independence of taste, for surely this word is the first Ruskin has received in many a long year. She does a really expert taxidermy job on Sir Walter Raleigh, poor man, though he certainly deserved it; does another on reviewing, so severe her husband feels he must modify it a little with a footnote.

The Captain's Death Bed contains in fact the same delicious things to read as always; apparently her second or third draft was as good as her ninth or fifteenth; her last would be a little different, but surely not much better writing, that is clear. Only she, the good artist, without self-indulgence, would have known how much nearer with each change she was getting to the heart of her thought. For an example of how near she could come to it, read the three and one-half pages called "Gas." It is about having a tooth out, in the same sense, as E. M. Forster once remarked, that *Moby Dick* is a novel about catching a whale.

Now it is to be supposed that with this final gathering up of her life's work the critics will begin their formal summings-up, analyses, exegeses; the various schools will attack or defend her; she will be "placed" here and there; Freud will be involved, if he has not been already; elegies will be written: Cyril Connolly has already shed a few morning tears, and advised us not to read her novels for at least another decade: she is too painfully near to our most disastrous memories.

It turns out merely that Mr. Connolly wishes us to neglect her because she reminds him of the thirties, which he, personally, cannot endure. A great many of us who have no grudges against either the twenties or the thirties will find this advice mystifying. And there is a whole generation springing up, ready to read what is offered, who know and care nothing for either of those decades. My advice must be exactly the opposite: read everything of Virginia Woolf's now, for she has something of enormous importance to say at this time, here, today; let her future take care of itself.

I cannot pretend to be coldly detached about her work, nor, even if I were able, would I be willing to write a purely literary criticism of it. It is thirty-five years since I read her first novel, *The Voyage Out.* She was one of the writers who touched the real life of my mind and feeling very deeply; I had from that book the same sense of some mysterious revelation of truth I had got in earliest youth from Laurence Sterne ("of all people!" jeers a Shandy-hating friend of mine), from Jane Austen, from Emily Brontë, from Henry James. I had grown up with these, and I went on growing with W. B. Yeats, the first short stories of James Joyce, the earliest novels of Virginia Woolf.

In the most personal way, all of these seemed and do seem to be my contemporaries; their various visions of reality, their worlds, merged for me into one vision, one world view that revealed to me little by little my familiar place. Living as I did in a world of readers devoted to solid, tried and true literature, in which unimpeachable moral grandeur and inarguable doctrine were set forth in balanced paragraphs, these writers were my own private discoveries. Reading as I did almost no contemporary criticism, talking to no one, still it did not occur to me that these were not great artists, who if only people could be persuaded to read them (even if by the light of Dr. Johnson or Dean Swift) they would be accepted as simply and joyously as I accepted them.

In some instances I was to have rude surprises. I could never understand the "revival" of Henry James; I had not heard that he was dead. Rather suddenly Jane Austen came back into fashionable favor; I had not dreamed she had ever been out of it.

In much the same way I have been amazed at the career of Virginia Woolf among the critics. To begin with, there has been very little notice except of the weekly review variety. Compared to the libraries of criticism published about Joyce, Lawrence, Eliot and all her other fellow artists of comparable stature, she has had little consideration. In 1925 she puzzled E. M. Forster, whose fountain pen disappeared when he was all prepared in his mind to write about her early novels.

Almost everything has been said, over and over, about Virginia Woolf's dazzling style, her brilliant humor, her extraordinary sensibility. She has been called neurotic, and hypersensitive. Her style has been compared to cobwebs with dew drops, rainbows, landscapes seen by moonlight, and other unsubstantial but showy stuff. She has been called a Phoenix, Muse, a Sybil, a Prophetess, in praise, or a Feminist, in dispraise. Her beauty and remarkable personality, her short way with fools and that glance of hers, which chilled many a young literary man with its expression of seeing casually through a millstone—all of this got in the way. It disturbed the judgment and drew the attention from the true point of interest.

Virginia Woolf was a great artist, one of the glories of our time, and she never published a line that was not worth reading. The least of her novels would have made the reputation of a lesser writer, the least of her critical writings compare more than favorably with the best criticism of the past half-century. In a long, sad period of fear, a world broken by wars, in which the artists have in the most lamentable way been the children of their time, knees knocking, teeth chattering, looking for personal salvation in the midst of world calamity, there appeared this artist, Virginia Woolf.

She was full of secular intelligence primed with the profane virtues, with her love not only of the world of all the arts created by the human imagination, but a love of life itself and of daily living, a spirit at once gay and severe, exacting and generous, a born artist and a sober craftsman; and she had no plan whatever for her personal salvation; or the personal salvation even of someone else; brought no doctrine; no dogma. Life, the life of this world, here and now, was a great mystery, no one could fathom it; and death was the end. In short, she was what the true believers always have called a heretic.

What she did, then, in the way of breaking up one of the oldest beliefs of mankind, is more important than the changes she made in the form of the novel. She wasn't even a heretic—she simply lived outside of dogmatic belief. She lived in the naturalness of her vocation. The world of the arts was her native territory; she ranged freely under her own sky, speaking her mother tongue fearlessly. She was at home in that place as much as anyone ever was.

1950

E. M. Forster

Dates memorable to me escape my mind, so I write them down on bits of paper. Bits of paper escape me, too; they love to hide themselves at the bottoms of large baskets of other papers marked "Miscellany." But E. M. Forster's volume of essays, called *Abinger Harvest*, until now my favorite book of his except *A Passage to India*, is never far from my reach, so by turning to a certain page in it, I am able to name exactly the time, the first and last time, that I ever saw Mr. Forster.

Mr. Forster sees so clearly the damage that Olympic Games, or any other form of commercialized, politicalized sport, does to everybody concerned I cannot help but hope that he sees through all those Cultural Fronts by now, too. We were nearly all of us taken in at least once. So it was one crowded, dusty evening, June 21, 1935, in Paris, that Mr. Forster appeared before a meeting of the International Congress of Writers. You can read about it in *Abinger Harvest*. I distrusted the whole thing for good reasons and attended only on the one evening when Mr. Forster was to speak. At that time, the Communists were busy dividing the whole world into two kinds of people: Fascist and Communist. They said you could tell Fascists by their abhorrence of culture, their racial prejudices, and their general inhumanity. This was true. But they said also that Communists were animated solely by a love of culture and the general good of their fellow man. Alas, this was not true.

But for great numbers of well-disposed persons, especially in France, England, and some of the Americas, it was dear, familiar talk and we fell for it like a ton of scrap iron. When I say, then, that the evening Mr. Forster spoke in Paris was dusty and crowded, it was literally true: but it also is a way of saying that Communists in numbers running a show anywhere always gave me this sense of suffocation; and heaven knows they were there, with their usual solidarity of effrontery, efficiency and dullness, all over the place making muddlement, as ubiquitous and inescapable as a plague of June bugs in Texas.

Yet there were on the program as window-dressing a convincing number of artists not Communists, others just political geldings by Communist standards, and a few honest but uncommitted sympathizers. Among these last I suppose they counted Mr. Forster, and he did manage to get in a kind word for communism on the ground that its intentions were good; a high compliment, all considered. He also defended a mediocre book in the defense of free speech and the right to publish; restated his humane, liberal political views, and predicted that he and all his kind, including Aldous Huxley, should expect to be swept away by the next war.

I heard nothing of this at the time. I had to wait and read it in *Abinger Harvest*. I think it was just after André Malraux—then as dogmatic in communism as he is now in some other faith—had leaped to the microphone barking like a fox to halt the applause for Julien Benda's speech, that a little slender man with a large forehead and a shy chin rose, was introduced and began to read his paper carefully prepared for this occasion. He paid no attention to the microphone, but wove back and forth, and from side to side, gently, and every time his face passed the mouthpiece I caught a high-voiced syllable or two, never a whole word, only a thin recurring sound like the wind down a chimney as Mr. Forster's pleasant good countenance advanced and retreated and returned. Then, surprisingly, once he came to a moment's pause before the instrument and there sounded into the hall clearly but wistfully a complete sentence: "I DO believe in liberty!"

The applause at the end was barely polite, but it covered the antics of that part of the audience near me; a whole pantomime of malignant ridicule, meaning that Mr. Forster and all his kind were already as extinct as the dodo. It was a discouraging moment.

Well, sixteen unbelievably long, painful years have passed, and it is very reassuring to observe that, far from having been swept away, Mr. Forster has been thriving in an admirable style—that is to say, his own style, spare, unportentous but serious, saying his say on any subject he chooses, as good a say as any we are likely to have for a long time; fearless but not aggressive; candid without cruelty; and with that beautiful, purely secular common sense which can hardly be distinguished in its more inspired moments from a saintly idealism.

Indeed, Mr. Forster is an artist who lives in that constant state of grace which comes of knowing who he is, where he lives, what he feels and thinks about his world. Virginia Woolf once wrote: "One advantage of having a settled code of morals is that you know exactly what to laugh at." She knew, and so does Mr. Forster. He pokes fun at things in themselves fatally without humor, things oppressive and fatal to human happiness: megalomania, solemn-godliness, pretentiousness, self-love, the meddlesome impulse which leads to the invasion and destruction of human rights. He disclaims a belief in Belief, meaning one can only suppose the kind of dogmatism promoted by meddlesomeness and the rest; come right down to it, I hardly know a writer with more beliefs than Mr. Forster; and all on the side of the angels.

Two Cheers for Democracy, a collection of his short writings on a tremendous range of subjects, is his first book since *Abinger Harvest*. It is an extension and enlargement of his thought, a record of the life and feelings of an artist who has been in himself an example of all he has defended from the first: the arts as a civilizing force, civilization itself as the true right aim of the human spirit, no matter what its failures may have been, above all, his unalterable belief in the first importance of the individual relationships between human beings founded on the reality of love—not in the mass, not between nations, nonsense!—but between one person and another. This is of course much more difficult than loving just everybody and everything, for each one must really do something about it, and show his faith in works. He manages to raise two mild cheers for poor old misprized, blasphemed, abused Democracy, who took an awful thrashing lately, but may recover; and he hopes to be able honestly some day to give three. He has long since earned his three cheers, and a tiger.

1951

Max Beerbohm

(*a review of* And Even Now,
essays by Max Beerbohm)

If your youth or even part of it was misspent in the twenties in this
country it is very likely that some of your more profitable hours were
passed reading certain things of Max Beerbohm's: essays, observations,
and "Zuleika Dobson." There he ever so presently was, a celebrated
member of the older literary generation, a man who knew the world in
the most desirably worldly way. He was a wit and his sayings went the
rounds. He did famously funny caricatures of other celebrated persons
and he wrote, oh, what charming good-tempered pieces about anything
that struck his interest.

He must have got pretty tired in those days of reading reviews about
his "mellow" style. It may have been this recurring word, or maybe his
self-caricature, or a stray photograph, but one did have in mind the image of a round, well-nourished, middling old gentleman—he was in fact
a perfect Methuselah, at least forty-five or fifty years old—carefully
garbed and groomed, chubby cheeked, hair thinning on top, who no
doubt did his writing seated, bland and kind as a pitcher of milk, at a
desk in his very exclusive London club.

It may well be asked what attraction such a specimen could have for
the brash young in a time when, in certain literary circles at least, even a
trace of good manners was looked upon as a moral weakness, if not proof
of positive reactionary political tendencies. It was possible that one saw
through his disguise, his toughness of mind and intransigent though restrained character.

He managed to get some very sharp things said through the mesh of
that excellent, disciplined way of writing. After thirty years these things

seem as sharp and even more timely. In "Servants" he shows some reasons why that race is disappearing rapidly and why he thinks it a good
thing. For those to whom Goethe is somewhat less than godlike, "Quia
Imperfectum" will take away the brackish taste of the recent American
Goethe orgy.

We are reminded, "In Homes Unblest," that not only after this latest
war were people beginning to live in converted hen houses and Quonset
huts—after World War I, the huts were more likely abandoned railway
carriages—and he could see clearly the slums under the gaudy paint.
"No. 2, The Pines" is an account of his early adoring visits to Swinburne,
the one time when the famous prose almost goes overboard, and Mr.
Beerbohm turns rhapsodic by propinquity.

"In a Point to Be Remembered by Eminent Men," however, he
makes amends with a fine parody of his earlier essay.

He described himself very well as a Tory-Anarchist, who anticipated
change with gloom, having seen very little of it that seemed to him for
the better. "The Mobled King," one of the best things in the book, is a
fine example of political and social views, implicit yet never named.
Then, too, here one finds again "William and Mary," which, no matter
what the author intended it to be, always seemed to me a superb short
story.

1950

Eleanor Clark

(*a review of* Rome and a Villa
by Eleanor Clark)

The subject of Miss Clark's book is Rome, that city which, like God, can be patient because it is eternal; she never departs from it. Her sense of proportion and order are phenomenal, and her mind radiates from and returns to this tremendous orbit of power without losing herself in that surge and seethe of human uproar we have agreed to call movements of history.

There is movement enough here, and this is history, no doubt about it. From the movement she brings us first to the ancient approach to the center of the world, we view it from the sixth century, the thirteenth, the eighteenth, and the day before yesterday, by foot and animal train, by coach, by rail, by air; we arrive in every sort of condition and state of mind. At the same time we see other people running away: St. Jerome, Luther, even Hawthorne—for you begin remembering, too; she evokes as well as says.

Since we are going to wander in a fog for weeks or months, anyway, we are started off on our long journey through time, space and event, in the Campidoglio, which "is at least in the middle"; the scene is crowded, as it is going to be always, but for myself, the first person I saw there was Cola di Rienzi, who gave himself flamboyant titles and aspired to a more than human power, beheaded and hanging by the heels; or is it another whom we have seen in our day?

We are from then on in the middle of wherever we are: among the fountains and urinals and wine barrels and coffee cups and the muddy but exhilarating flood of life; everybody is alive, whether they lived two thousand years ago visibly, or live now; the scene pulses with their presence; their doings are real. You are not shaken and pulled about by the elbow, but transported here, there, then yonder, as if conducted by a genie, one who knows where he is going and why.

This spot where the peasant mother of a murdered bandit, Giuliano, is screaming over his body, "Oh my blood!" is related to the one you just left, where a peasant mother is sitting in St. Peter's in great honor as with overwhelming grandeur of ceremony, her little daughter, Maria, murdered while defending her chastity, is being made a saint. Maria's statue will be in churches, and she will intercede in Heaven for sinners. Giuliano is only a hero, which means at least half a saint to his peasant adorers, and his legend is painted on all the carts in Sicily, where "all life is legend." Centuries jostle centuries, rubbing souls and knees and buttocks familiarly as is right and natural: Hadrian's villa in stone and marble and water, and Piranesi's opium-dream reconstruction of the ancient city.

We go again, not straight—for nothing is straight—but through mazes of time and avenues and aqueducts and catacombs, to the wonderful mosaic athletes from the baths of Caracalla, and the Sitting Boxer, Greek but not Olympic, "time-less naked man waiting for the next round" to the latest obscene caricature sculptures of athletes in Mussolini's vast sports field dedicated to the conquest of Abyssinia. Between these ancient "gorilla heroes, who represent the ultimate reduction of man to the strength of his own body, surely the most tragic state," and the muff-handed, jutting-jawed improbabilities of Fascist art, what happened? Rome does not say; time takes care of all. Two tyrants, both names synonyms for infamy: yet under one, great art could flourish, and under the other, only its willful parody. Even when the people of Italy wished to honor their new martyrs, the 335 hostages shot by the Germans in the Ardeatine caves, the monument they built "was bound to be false," and a dull, many-ton-weight slab of concrete was in effect the best they could do, "because there was not even any vocabulary left to do honor."

It was ruin, but then Rome is full of ruins, and there is in this book the sense, so often expressed by foreigners who visit or even live there, of the weight, the perpetual presence of antiquity, absolutely real as a hand on your arm, sometimes a stone on your heart or mind. "The past eats out of your plate there," a friend once said to me. And Miss Clark sees in the eyes of hundreds of cats who live in unique well-fed ease in their own small open city, "a living knowledge of Agrippa." Her account of the cats is delightful, for she treats them with respect, no less valid because it is matched to the scale of their dignity; and reading it, one is enlightened as to a certain elusive quality in her mind: not vague, it is a most positive thing, but difficult to define. The passage about the cats cleared it up.

She has a painter's or an architect's eye for scale, literally, as may be seen in her way of describing any building, window, statue, fountain. But morally, too, and intellectually, and there is above all some acutely measuring eye of that other power of the spirit. With her genius for attention, observation and recording, she sees with beautiful accuracy the differences between things, with a true sense and love of the grand, the tragic, the beautiful, she has that necessary sense of their opposites; and of the not-quite, and the would-be; she knows what is sentimental vulgarity, what the monstrous, and what perverted and deformed; and where all these things meet and mingle and what the nature of the meeting is and why they are necessary to each other.

I feel strangely to praise a good artist for qualities one might expect to be taken for granted at a certain level of being; it is a little like being called "honest." But this faculty of discrimination is extremely highly developed in Miss Clark, and the great distinction and worth of this book is based firmly on it. It is in the immensely bold use of language; she is not afraid of it, she picks up a word where she finds it and uses it to her purpose; language, like the broken statuary in the Vatican cellars, is lying around in a bad state of dismemberment, with just a feeble attempt to sort out certain kinds of words from the other kinds, Miss Clark, an American novelist and short-story writer, does all this magnificently.

The one Roman poet—and late, he died in 1863—Belli, reminds one instantly in Miss Clark's translations of Villon, in the free-swinging vernacular, the ferocious realism, the brawling laugh, the bitter-good nature: and love, too, love of the poor, of life itself; and hope, a fighting kind of hope. He is a great discovery, and she has done a deeply perceptive study of his work related to his life, his beliefs, his genius and his place in literature. Yet like Virgil's faith in the empire, his faith in the people died in his hands: and like Virgil, he wanted what he had written celebrating it destroyed. Yet neither of them destroyed their work themselves: and so they were saved; Belli's work consists of two thousand sonnets, not one published before his death.

This whole book is the distillation of a deep personal experience; it is autobiography in the truest sense, in terms of what outward impact set the inner life in motion toward its true relation to the world: the story of the search for what is truly one's own, and the ability to recognize it when found, and to be faithful in love of it. "Rome, being one continuity, requires wholeness, and instills it; we bring to it in ideas disgust, in feelings failure, in art something like a splintered windshield. So we are both enthralled and for a long time in mortal conflict with it." Then: "There is a moment and a place where one might consider retreating from the world."

This place is the church of Quattro Santi Coronati, and the moment of decision occurred there. It is in the Roman Journal II, and if you skip a little you are in danger of missing it. After the nearly mortal conflict came peace, rapture—there is even an angel in it.

What is the mystical experience but reconciliation with, and a taking to yourself the strength of your higher power?

Then: "Whatever matters or happens, you have touched the quietness there is in all Rome, that has been built into it not only by monks and such, but by many others too, poets, and wonderers, building into their city from their solitudes this solid element, like the stone of its columns, its other permanence. They have walked there, thought, prayed, moved slowly in some small circle till they died and their faces perhaps in stone on the church floors were slowly trodden away, leaving a communal indestructible glory that informs even the marble and the gold . . . the angel accompanies you up the road a little way."

1952

The Wingéd Skull

(*a review of* This Is Lorence:
A Narrative of the Reverend Laurence Sterne,
by Lodwick Hartley)

Did the chaise break down under the broiling sun in a treeless waste near Toulouse, as Sterne wrote in a letter to his banker, or was it much earlier and more amusing, near Lyons, as he says in *Tristram Shandy,* or were there two accidents? And why did he say in that book he decided to dash to France so suddenly it never entered his mind that England and France were at war, when plainly he had planned it long before, and had to get leave from his Bishop and ask for a safe conduct from Mr. Pitt? To say nothing of a twenty-pound loan from Mr. David Garrick. Did he really get into bed with that long procession of shadowy ladies, from Catherine Fourmentelle early to Eliza Draper late, or did he just think and talk and write about it and make a great display of sentiment and then back out more or less gracefully at the right, or wrong, moment? Exactly how diabolic were those nightlong frolics at Skelton Castle with his old friend Hall-Stevenson and the other demoniacs, squires and parsons as they mostly were? Were they imitating feebly the goings-on of the Medmenham Monks, from which now and then John Wilkes strayed over to Skelton? Did he actually leave his mother to die in the workhouse (Byron thought so, and many before him and since), or did he care for her last days? Was his wife's belief, for a time, that she was the Queen of Bohemia due to his neglect and infidelities, or was it a strain of paranoia in that ill-starred mind? Was his mother really low Irish as he said, or member of a respectable Lancashire family? Just how deeply in love is a man who writes, through the years, substantially the same letters to a series of women, sometimes keeping copies for himself? Just where does truth end and fiction begin in Sterne's account of himself in *Tristram Shandy* and *The Sentimental Journey?*

Mr. Hartley wrestles manfully with these and a hundred other trivial or dubious or off-color questions of Laurence Sterne's career with a discretion and strait regard for the records that might surprise his subject, who, being a novelist, was hampered by no such scruples. An immense amount of devoted study and trained research appears to have gone into this fairly short book, which handles with ease a baffling complexity of detail and carries the story along swiftly and with concentration on several planes at once. It is only the tone I find a little troublesome at times; such a balancing of the evidence for and against, such a leveling down of both the good and the evil in the history of Sterne, almost succeeds in smoothing the man away. There is a smack of prudishness at times, small biased hints of moral disapproval dragged in by the ears as if under some compulsion not the author's own. Mr. Hartley confesses that one of his aims was to make the book palatable to the lay, or general, reader in the hope that this mysterious being may be encouraged to seek out *Tristram Shandy* and read it for himself. I never saw a general reader, but I am convinced he exists, so many books are written for him. It is a mistake, just the same; general reader should not be pampered in any such way; Laurence Sterne should not be arranged to advantage or disadvantage for his view; he should be made to take his chances along with the rest of us, not only with the available truths of life but also with the very best work the author can do. For this book, in spite of its placating foreword, will be a stiff introduction indeed to a reader who does not already know something of the period.

For one who knows *Tristram Shandy, This Is Lorence* may bring to mind again how melancholy a cloud lies over all the recorded life of Laurence Sterne, even his triumphs and frolics, and how clear and merry the light shed by *Tristram Shandy*. That book contains more living, breathing people you can see and hear, whose garments have texture between your finger and thumb, whose flesh is knit firmly to their bones, who walk about their affairs with audible footsteps, than any other one novel in the world, I do believe. Uncle Toby, Corporal Trim, Yorick and Mrs. Yorick, the Widow Wadman, Bridget, Dr. Slop, Susannah, Obadiah, the infant Tristram hovering between breeches and tunics, all live in one house with floorboards under their boot soles, a roof over their heads, the fires burning and giving off real smoke, cooking smells coming from the kitchen, real weather outside and air blowing through the windows. When Dr. Slop cuts his thumb real blood issues from it, and everybody has a navel and his proper distribution of vital organs. One hangs around the place like an enchanted ghost, all eyes and ears for fear of missing something. The story roams apparently at random all over creation, following the living thoughts of these human beings in their infinitely varied experiences, memories, points of view. Sparks of association flash in showers at the slightest collision of temperaments. Every word spoken gets its instant response in the hearer; they are all intensely interested in each other and everything else under heaven all the time. Little clashes of wills lead to the most complicated roundabouts of personal history, anecdotes, opinion; a mere gesture is enough to set up a whole new train of thought and deed in these people, who live and go about their affairs every instant, not just at moments chosen by the author when it suits his convenience. Meanwhile, steadily, like time passing visibly before your eyes, Uncle Toby's unbroken devoted occupation with his campaigns, and the building of his fortified town, go on, accompanied by the most remarkable theories of military strategy and a running comment on the science of warfare, full of deep and sly satire. The celebrated comic improprieties go on too, a running fire of double talk punctuated by episodes such as that of the hot chestnut, the Abbess and the Novice who divided the sinful words which move a balky mule, the courtship of the Widow Wadman, the accidental circumcision of the newly born Tristram. It all has the most illusive air of having been dropped upon the paper by a flying pen which never stopped long enough for the author to read what he had written. Sterne drew on a page a few little graphs of his progress in *Tristram Shandy*; they are amusing but also accurate. That lightness was achieved with the intensity and painstakingness of a spider spinning its web, during those twenty obscure years as parson, along with the farming, and the philandering, and the wife driven distracted with jealousy, and the breaking blood vessels in his lungs, and the rows among his large family connection, and the local politics and the jollifications at Skelton Hall and the hunting and the August racing season at York.

Then his life work was published, a book or so at a time, and he went up modestly to London in the wake of Squire Crofts, a local worthy who paid the expenses of the trip, and there found scandalous fashionable success and enjoyed it enormously. Dr. Johnson thought his sermons "froth," Oliver Goldsmith found him dull, the Bishop of Gloucester called him "an irrecoverable scoundrel," but Sir Joshua Reynolds painted his portrait, David Garrick carried him into the orbit of the theater, the extremely mixed society around the Duke of York found him fascinating, for there was nothing they liked better than the cloven hoof peeping from beneath a cassock; he was in the dear tradition of the worldly abbé, and could write it all down, besides. Religion in any formal sense, and I greatly doubt any sense at all, he had not, and with some relief he ceased to feign it. He took some pains to be cultivated by respectable society, but what he loved best among even that was the fringe of wealthy young rakehells and their desperate sports. The rest is flight from death and pursuit of fame and pleasure: he "met" most of the great of his time, but his happiest days seem to have been a few weeks (when he had already the look of a dancing skeleton) of rioting around Paris with John Wilkes, interrupted, alas, by another blood vessel breaking at the height of the fun. As for women, to whom he gave so much attention, and who responded infallibly in their various ways, there is no fathoming his feelings or his motives. He appears to have squandered his whole available fund of human love upon his daughter Lydia, a headless, flighty creature ruled by her mother; judged by her story, she was the fine flower of all the weaknesses of every branch of all his families, a notably faulty lot. Even the highfalutin' affair with Eliza Draper died, as all his fancies died, of his own weariness with his own role in them.

Mr. Hartley makes all the ladies rather duller than they may have been, even, but his wife must be admitted as a total loss. She was a homely woman whose husband made cruel caricatures of her, and wrote to a friend that he grew more sick and tired of her every day. She loved pleasure too, and had had a dull dog's life of it for years. She was delighted to get to France, and her ruses, and stratagems to be allowed to stay on there, with her daughter and without her husband, would have been pitiable if they had not succeeded. But they did. Sterne died in lodgings in London with the nurse and landlady present, and a footman sent to inquire after him by John Crauford of Errol, who was giving a dinner to Garrick, Lord Ossory, David Hume, the Earl of March, Lord Roxburgh, the Duke of Grafton, and Mr. James, husband of Anne—the gay and good-hearted, who visited Sterne almost constantly in his last days. The footman reported to the waiting guests: "He was just a-dying . . . he said: now it is come. He put up his hand as if to stop a blow, and died in a minute."

His friends were saddened, but went on with their dinner. His wife and daughter and Eliza Draper were severally bitterly inconvenienced by his death. This and much more is in the book, but where is the real Laurence Sterne, the one who wrote *Tristram Shandy?* That wingéd skull seems to have made his getaway again, taking his main secret with him.

1943

On Modern Fiction

(Book Week Symposium)

As to the argument that "We have no titans among us anymore," etc., it is a little early to pronounce judgment, and I should first have to know who says so; for a good many persons pronouncing final judgments and assigning exact seat numbers in the literary hierarchy are quite simply incapable of recognizing even talent when they see it, much less genius, and the old sport of picking the winners too often comes out like those tip-sheets uninstructed people buy at horse-races. . . . All I can say for my choice is that it *is* my choice and as I have loved and admired titans of the arts from all ages of the past, so maybe I have chosen a titan or two here, but I make no claims other than that these writers I have named are first among my contemporaries and the recent past that I choose for a long and honorable life in the story of our literature.

It is rather a strange list of writers supposed to represent American literature that omits* the names of Peter Taylor, William Humphrey, George Garrett, Walter Clemons, Andrew Lytle, James Agee, Eudora Welty, Glenway Wescott, Caroline Gordon, Allen Tate, each a first-rate artist in exactly his own style and character, living in his own mysterious gift, on his own ancestral grounds, speaking his mother tongue: if you ignore these writers, it is somewhat like leaving out the spinal column when making a man. . . . I confess I am surprised at some of the choices on the list. If David Stacton, why not Tillie Olsen, with her strong steadfast talent? If Ken Kesey, why not Donald Stewart? This sort of thing could go on and on; you will see that I distrust this list, it looks very "loaded" to me. And the dates, 1945–1965, manage to exclude a

* As the list sent me for this symposium omitted the names above.

novel or two that most surely belong to this time, though published a few years earlier. Caroline Gordon's *None Shall Look Back* is a masterpiece, out of print now, probably because her scene is the South during the Civil War, and she knows and tells things that are not acceptable now when Southern history is being rewritten or reconstructed to the fancy of those who took no part in it. I am glad someone remembered John Barth: a one-book man so far as I know, *The Sot-Weed Factor,* but a gaudy, gorgeous burst of humor—real comedy—American style, in our best tradition. When I selected my titles I had to leave out many favorites coming more or less within the time limits, but belonging to our literature not just yesterday, nor today, but for many tomorrows, or so I can only hope. Here they are, for they belong here: Allen Tate, *The Fathers;* Robert Penn Warren, *All the King's Men;* Eudora Welty, anything except perhaps *The Ponder Heart*—that is, *Curtain of Green, The Wide Net, Golden Apples;* Flannery O'Connor, *The Violent Bear It Away;* Glenway Wescott, *The Pilgrim Hawk, Apartment in Athens;* Andrew Lytle, *The Velvet Horn;* James Purdy, *Color of Darkness;* Truman Capote, *The House of Flowers* and other stories; J. F. Powers, all his short stories and these are the first that occur to memory, so I trust my memory: Favorites—"Lions, Harts, Leaping Does"; "Prince of Darkness."

For what it is worth, let me add my admiration in prose fiction for many years past on which my judgment of present fiction is founded, no doubt: E. M. Forster, *A Passage to India;* Richard Hughes, *High Wind in Jamaica;* Ford Madox Ford, *The Good Soldier;* Virginia Woolf, *To The Lighthouse;* James Joyce, *Portrait of the Artist as a Young Man; Dubliners;* Ernest Hemingway, *Big Two-Hearted River,* the first in mind of many books I have enjoyed and believed in in my time. This taste again was I am sure formed by my love of the works of the eighteenth-century novelists, on to our own time beginning with *Moll Flanders* and coming on through to Jane Austen and Emily Brontë, and Dickens and Hardy and James and Hawthorne and Melville, taking in our Mark Twain on the way. And you can't think how it annoys me to see the New Ignorami of criticism refer to Mark Twain merely as *Twain,* as if that were his real name; I get tired of explaining that Mark Twain is a term in navigation, meaningless unless used in full, but, then, I am long weary of explaining to the same set that no witch was ever burned in New England or anywhere else in America, and even no Negro except among the New England Puritans in the seventeenth century: where burning at the stake was a punishment reserved strictly for Negro slaves. The Southerners did not begin burning Negroes until the 1870s or thereabout, during that "Reconstruction." If these questions seem somewhat unrelated to our subject, which I take to be American Literature, perhaps only an American of the old breed, descended from those Englishmen who took this country not only away from the Indians, but from the French, the Dutch and the British as well, can feel the importance of remembering our past and our origins, of relating our history to our customs, our arts to our lives and the things we have loved and fought for. If you look over this list, incomplete as it is, you will see that there is a line of march, unbroken and continuous and I believe due to go on for a good while.

In spite of past, present, and future hell!

1965

PERSONAL
AND
PARTICULAR

St. Augustine
and the Bullfight

Adventure. The word has become a little stale to me, because it has been applied too often to the dull physical exploits of professional "adventurers" who write books about it, if they know how to write; if not, they hire ghosts who quite often can't write either.

I don't read them, but rumors of them echo, and re-echo. The book business at least is full of heroes who spend their time, money and energy worrying other animals, manifestly their betters such as lions and tigers, to death in trackless jungles and deserts only to be crossed by the stoutest motorcar; or another feeds hooks to an inedible fish like the tarpon; another crosses the ocean on a raft, living on plankton and seaweed, why ever, I wonder? And always always, somebody is out climbing mountains, and writing books about it, which are read by quite millions of persons who feel, apparently, that the next best thing to going there yourself is to hear from somebody who went. And I have heard more than one young woman remark that, though she did not want to get married, still, she would like to have a baby, for the adventure: not lately though. That was a pose of the 1920s and very early '30s. Several of them did it, too, but I do not know of any who wrote a book about it—good for them.

W. B. Yeats remarked—I cannot find the passage now, so must say it in other words—that the unhappy man (unfortunate?) was one whose adventures outran his capacity for experience, capacity for experience being, I should say, roughly equal to the faculty for understanding what has happened to one. The difference then between mere adventure and a real experience might be this? That adventure is something you seek for pleasure, or even for profit, like a gold rush or invading a country; for the illusion of being more alive than ordinarily, the thing you will to occur; but experience is what really happens to you in the long run; the truth that finally overtakes you.

Adventure is sometimes fun, but not too often. Not if you can remember what really happened; all of it. It passes, seems to lead nowhere much, is something to tell friends to amuse them, maybe. "Once upon a time," I can hear myself saying, for I once said it, "I scaled a cliff in Boulder, Colorado, with my bare hands, and in Indian moccasins, bare-legged. And at nearly the top, after six hours of feeling for toe- and fingerholds, and the gayest feeling in the world that when I got to the top I should see something wonderful, something that sounded awfully like a bear growled out of a cave, and I scuttled down out of there in a hurry." This is a fact. I had never climbed a mountain in my life, never had the least wish to climb one. But there I was, for perfectly good reasons, in a hut on a mountainside in heavenly sunny though sometimes stormy weather, so I went out one morning and scaled a very minor cliff; alone, unsuitably clad, in the season when rattlesnakes are casting their skins; and if it was not a bear in that cave, it was some kind of unfriendly animal who growls at people; and this ridiculous escapade, which was nearly six hours of the hardest work I ever did in my life, toeholds and fingerholds on a cliff, put me to bed for just nine days with a complaint the local people called "muscle poisoning." I don't know exactly what they meant, but I do remember clearly that I could not turn over in bed without help and in great agony. And did it teach me anything? I think not, for three years later I was climbing a volcano in Mexico, that celebrated unpronounceably named volcano, Popocatepetl which everybody who comes near it climbs sooner or later; but was that any reason for me to climb it? No. And I was knocked out for weeks, and that finally did teach me: I am not supposed to go climbing things. Why did I not know in the first place? For me, this sort of thing must come under the head of Adventure.

I think it is pastime of rather an inferior sort; yet I have heard men tell yarns like this only a very little better: their mountains were higher, or their sea was wider, or their bear was bigger and noisier, or their cliff was steeper and taller, yet there was no point whatever to any of it except that it had happened. This is not enough. May it not be, perhaps, that experience, that is, the thing that happens to a person living from day to day, is anything at all that sinks in? is, without making any claims, a part of your growing and changing life? what it is that happens in your mind, your heart?

Adventure hardly ever seems to be that at the time it is happening: not under that name, at least. Adventure may be an afterthought, something that happens in the memory with imaginative trimmings if not downright lying, so that one should suppress it entirely, or go the whole way and make honest fiction of it. My own habit of writing fiction has provided a wholesome exercise to my natural, incurable tendency to try to wangle the sprawling mess of our existence in this bloody world into some kind of shape: almost any shape will do, just so it is recognizably made with human hands, one small proof the more of the validity and reality of the human imagination. But even within the most limited frame what utter confusion shall prevail if you cannot take hold firmly, and draw the exact line between what really happened, and what you have since imagined about it. Perhaps my soul will be saved after all in spite of myself because now and then I take some unmanageable, indigestible fact and turn it into fiction; cause things to happen with some kind of logic—my own logic, of course—and everything ends as I think it should end and no back talk, or very little, from anybody about it. Otherwise, and except for this safety device, I should be the greatest liar unhung. (When was the last time anybody was hanged for lying?) What is Truth? I often ask myself. Who knows?

A publisher asked me a great while ago to write a kind of autobiography, and I was delighted to begin; it sounded very easy when he said, "Just start, and tell everything you remember until now!" I wrote about a hundred pages before I realized, or admitted, the hideous booby trap into which I had fallen. First place, I remember quite a lot of stupid and boring things: there were other times when my life seemed merely an endurance test, or a quite mysterious but not very interesting and often monotonous effort at survival on the most primitive terms. There are dozens of things that might be entertaining but I have no intention of telling them, because they are nobody's business; and endless little gossipy incidents that might entertain indulgent friends for a minute, but in print they look as silly as they really are. Then, there are the tremendous, unmistakable, life-and-death crises, the scalding, the bone-breaking events, the lightnings that shatter the landscape of the soul—who would write that by request? No, that is for a secretly written manuscript to be left with your papers, and if your executor is a good friend, who has probably been brought up on St. Augustine's *Confessions,* he will read it with love and attention and gently burn it to ashes for your sake.

Yet I intend to write something about my life, here and now, and so far as I am able without one touch of fiction, and I hope to keep it as shapeless and unforeseen as the events of life itself from day to day. Yet, look! I have already betrayed my occupation, and dropped a clue in what would be the right place if this were fiction, by mentioning St. Augustine when I hadn't meant to until it came in its right place in life, not in art. Literary art, at least, is the business of setting human events to rights and giving them meanings that, in fact, they do not possess, or not obviously, or not the meanings the artist feels they should have—we do understand so little of what is really happening to us in any given moment. Only by remembering, comparing, waiting to know the consequences can we sometimes, in a flash of light, see what a certain event really meant, what it was trying to tell us. So this will be notes on a fateful thing that happened to me when I was young and did not know much about the world or about myself. I had been reading St. Augustine's *Confessions* since I was able to read at all, and I thought I had read every word, perhaps because I did know certain favorite passages by heart. But then, it was something like having read the Adventures of Gargantua by Rabelais when I was twelve and enjoying it; when I read it again at thirty-odd, I was astounded at how much I had overlooked in the earlier reading, and wondered what I thought I had seen there.

So it was with St. Augustine and my first bullfight. Looking back nearly thirty-five years on my earliest days in Mexico, it strikes me that, for a fairly serious young woman who was in the country for the express purpose of attending a Revolution, and studying Mayan people art, I fell in with a most lordly gang of fashionable international hoodlums. Of course I had Revolutionist friends and artist friends, and they were gay and easy and poor as I was. This other mob was different: they were French, Spanish, Italian, Polish, and they all had titles and good names: a duke, a count, a marquess, a baron, and they all were in some flashy money-getting enterprise like importing cognac wholesale, or selling sports cars to newly rich politicians; and they all drank like fish and played fast games like polo or tennis or jai alai; they haunted the wings of theaters, drove slick cars like maniacs, but expert maniacs, never missed a bullfight or a boxing match; all were reasonably young and they had ladies to match, mostly imported and all speaking French. These persons stalked pleasure as if it were big game—they took their fun exactly where they found it, and the way they liked it, and they worked themselves to exhaustion at it. A fast, tough, expensive, elegant, high low-life they led, for the ladies and gentlemen each in turn had other friends you would have had to see to believe; and from time to time, without being in any way involved or engaged, I ran with this crowd of shady characters and liked their company and ways very much. I don't like gloomy sinners, but the merry ones charm me. And one of them introduced me to Shelley. And Shelley, whom I knew in the most superficial way, who remained essentially a stranger to me to the very end, led me, without in the least ever knowing what he had done, into one of the most important and lasting experiences of my life.

He was British, a member of the poet's family; said to be authentic great-great-nephew; he was rich and willful, and had come to Mexico young and wild, and mad about horses, of course. Coldly mad—he bred them and raced them and sold them with the stony detachment and merciless appraisal of the true horse lover—they call it love, and it could be that: but he did not like them. "What is there to like about a horse but his good points? If he has a vice, shoot him or send him to the bullring; that is the only way to work a vice out of the breed!"

Once, during a riding trip while visiting a ranch, my host gave me a stallion to ride, who instantly took the bit in his teeth and bolted down a steep mountain trail. I managed to stick on, held an easy rein, and he finally ran himself to a standstill in an open field. My disgrace with Shelley was nearly complete. Why? Because the stallion was not a good horse. I should have refused to mount him. I said it was a question how to refuse the horse your host offered you—Shelley thought it no question at all. "A lady," he reminded me, "can always excuse herself gracefully from anything she doesn't wish to do." I said, "I wish that were really true," for the argument about the bullfight was already well started. But the peak of his disapproval of me, my motives, my temperament, my ideas, my ways, was reached when, to provide a diversion and end a dull discussion, I told him the truth: that I had liked being run away with, it had been fun and the kind of thing that had to happen unexpectedly, you couldn't arrange for it. I tried to convey to him my exhilaration, my pure joy when this half-broken, crazy beast took off down that trail with just a hoofhold between a cliff on one side and a thousand-foot drop on the other. He said merely that such utter frivolity surprised him in someone whom he had mistaken for a well-balanced, intelligent girl; and I remember thinking how revoltingly fatherly he sounded, exactly like my own father in his stuffier moments.

He was a stocky, red-faced, muscular man with broad shoulders, hard-jowled, with bright blue eyes glinting from puffy lids; his hair was a grizzled tan, and I guessed him about fifty years old, which seemed a great age to me then. But he mentioned that his Mexican wife had "died young" about three years before, and that his eldest son was only eleven years old. His whole appearance was so remarkably like the typical horsy, landed-gentry sort of Englishman one meets in books by Frenchmen or Americans, if this were fiction I should feel obliged to change his looks altogether, thus falling into one stereotype to avoid falling into another. However, so Shelley did look, and his clothes were magnificent and right beyond words, and never new-looking and never noticeable at all except one could not help observing sooner or later that he was beyond argument the best-dressed man in America, North or South; it was that kind of typical British inconspicuous good taste: he had it, superlatively. He was evidently leading a fairly rakish life, or trying to, but he was of a cast-iron conventionality even in that. We did not fall in love—far from it. We struck up a hands-off, quaint, farfetched, tetchy kind of friendship which consisted largely of good advice about worldly things from him, mingled with critical marginal notes on my character—a character of which I could not recognize a single trait; and if I said, helplessly, "But I am not in the least like that," he would answer, "Well, you should be!" or "Yes, you are, but you don't know it."

This man took me to my first bullfight. I'll tell you later how St. Augustine comes into it. It was the first bullfight of that season; Covadonga Day; April; clear, hot blue sky; and a long procession of women in flower-covered carriages; wearing their finest lace veils and highest combs and gauziest fans; but I shan't describe a bullfight. By now surely there is no excuse for anyone who can read or even hear or see not to know pretty well what goes on in a bullring. I shall say only that Sánchez Mejías and Rudolfo Gaona each killed a bull that day; but before the Grand March of the toreros, Hattie Weston rode her thoroughbred High School gelding into the ring to thunders of shouts and brassy music.

She was Shelley's idol. "Look at that girl, for God's sake," and his voice thickened with feeling, "the finest rider in the world," he said in his dogmatic way, and it is true I have not seen better since.

She was a fine buxom figure of a woman, a highly colored blonde with a sweet, childish face; probably forty years old, and perfectly rounded in all directions; a big round bust, and that is the word, there was nothing plural about it, just a fine, warm-looking bolster straight across her front from armpit to armpit; fine firm round hips—again, why the plural? It was an ample seat born to a sidesaddle, as solid and undivided as the bust, only more of it. She was tightly laced and her waist was small. She wore a hard-brimmed dark gray Spanish sailor hat, sitting straight and shallow over her large golden knot of hair; a light gray bolero and a darker gray riding skirt—not a Spanish woman's riding dress, nor yet a man's, but something tight and fit and formal and appropriate. And there she went, the most elegant woman in the saddle I have ever seen, graceful and composed in her perfect style, with her wonderful, lightly dancing, learned horse, black and glossy as shoe polish, perfectly under control—no, not under control at all, you might have thought, but just dancing and showing off his paces by himself for his own pleasure.

"She makes the bullfight seem like an anticlimax," said Shelley, tenderly.

I had not wanted to come to this bullfight. I had never intended to see a bullfight at all. I do not like the slaughtering of animals as sport. I am carnivorous, I love all the red juicy meats and all the fishes. Seeing animals killed for food on the farm in summers shocked and grieved me sincerely, but it did not cure my taste for flesh. My family for as far back as I know anything about them, only about 450 years, were the huntin', shootin', fishin' sort: their houses were arsenals and their dominion over the animal kingdom was complete and unchallenged. When I was older, my father remarked on my tiresome timidity, or was I just pretending to finer feelings than those of the society around me? He hardly knew which was the more tiresome. But that was perhaps only a personal matter. Morally, if I wished to eat meat I should be able to kill the animal— otherwise it appeared that I was willing to nourish myself on other people's sins? For he supposed I considered it a sin. Otherwise why bother about it? Or was it just something unpleasant I wished to avoid? Maintaining my own purity—and a very doubtful kind of purity he found it, too—at the expense of the guilt of others? Altogether, my father managed to make a very sticky question of it, and for some years at intervals I made it a matter of conscience to kill an animal or bird, something I intended to eat. I gave myself and the beasts some horrible times, through fright and awkwardness, and to my shame, nothing cured me of my taste for flesh. All forms of cruelty offend me bitterly, and this repugnance is inborn, absolutely impervious to any arguments, or even insults, at which the red-blooded lovers of blood sports are very expert; they don't admire me at all, any more than I admire them. . . . Ah, me, the contradictions, the paradoxes! I was once perfectly capable of keeping a calf for a pet until he outgrew the yard in the country and had to be sent to the pastures. His subsequent fate I leave you to guess. Yes, it is all revoltingly sentimental and, worse than that, confused. My defense is that no matter whatever else this world seemed to promise me, never once did it promise to be simple.

So, for a great tangle of emotional reasons I had no intention of going to a bullfight. But Shelley was so persistently unpleasant about my cowardice, as he called it flatly, I just wasn't able to take the thrashing any longer. Partly, too, it was his natural snobbery: smart people of the world did not have such feelings; it was to him a peculiarly provincial if not downright Quakerish attitude. "I have some Quaker ancestors," I told him. "How absurd of you!" he said, and really meant it.

The bullfight question kept popping up and had a way of spoiling other occasions that should have been delightful. Shelley was one of those men, of whose company I feel sometimes that I have had more than my fair share, who simply do not know how to drop a subject, or abandon a position once they have declared it. Constitutionally incapable of admitting defeat, or even its possibility, even when he had not the faintest shadow of right to expect a victory—for why should he make a contest of my refusal to go to a bullfight?—he would start an argument during the theater intermissions, at the fronton, at a street fair, on a stroll in the Alameda, at a good restaurant over coffee and brandy; there was no occasion so pleasant that he could not shatter it with his favorite gambit: "If you would only see one, you'd get over this nonsense."

So there I was, at the bullfight, with cold hands, trembling innerly, with painful tinglings in the wrists and collarbone: yet my excitement was not altogether painful; and in my happiness at Hattie Weston's performance I was calmed and off guard when the heavy barred gate to the corral burst open and the first bull charged through. The bulls were from the Duke of Veragua's* ranch, as enormous and brave and handsome as any I ever saw afterward. (This is not a short story, so I don't have to maintain any suspense.) This first bull was a beautiful monster of brute courage: his hide was a fine pattern of black and white, much enhanced by the goad with fluttering green ribbons stabbed into his shoulder as he entered the ring; this in turn furnished an interesting design in thin rivulets of blood, the enlivening touch of scarlet in his sober color scheme, with highly aesthetic effect.

He rushed at the waiting horse, blindfolded in one eye and standing at the proper angle for the convenience of his horns, the picador making only the smallest pretense of staving him off, and disemboweled the horse with one sweep of his head. The horse trod in his own guts. It happens at least once every bullfight. I could not pretend not to have expected it; but I had not been able to imagine it. I sat back and covered my eyes. Shelley, very deliberately and as inconspicuously as he could, took both my wrists and held my hands down on my knees. I shut my eyes and turned my face away, away from the arena, away from him, but not before I had seen in his eyes a look of real, acute concern and almost loving anxiety for me—he really believed that my feelings were the sign of a grave flaw of character, or at least an unbecoming, unworthy weakness that he was determined to overcome in me. He couldn't shoot me, alas, or turn me over to the bullring; he had to deal with me in human terms, and he did it according to his lights. His voice was hoarse and fierce: "Don't you dare come here and then do this! You must face it!"

Part of his fury was shame, no doubt, at being seen with a girl who would behave in such a pawky way. But at this point he was, of course, right. Only he had been wrong before to nag me into this, and I was altogether wrong to have let him persuade me. Or so I felt then. "You have got to face this!" By then he was right; and I did look and I did face it, though not for years and years.

During those years I saw perhaps a hundred bullfights, all in Mexico City, with the finest bulls from Spain and the greatest bullfighters—but not with Shelley—never again with Shelley, for we were not comfortable together after that day. Our odd, mismatched sort of friendship declined and neither made any effort to revive it. There was bloodguilt between us, we shared an evil secret, a hateful revelation. He hated what he had

* Lineal descendant of Christopher Columbus.

revealed in me to himself, and I hated what he had revealed to me about myself, and each of us for entirely opposite reasons; but there was nothing more to say or do, and we stopped seeing each other.

I took to the bullfights with my Mexican and Indian friends. I sat with them in the cafés where the bullfighters appeared; more than once went at two o'clock in the morning with a crowd to see the bulls brought into the city; I visited the corral back of the ring where they could be seen before the corrida. Always, of course, I was in the company of impassioned adorers of the sport, with their special vocabulary and mannerisms and contempt for all others who did not belong to their charmed and chosen cult. Quite literally there were those among them I never heard speak of anything else; and I heard then all that can be said—the topic is limited, after all, like any other—in love and praise of bullfighting. But it can be tiresome, too. And I did not really live in that world, so narrow and so trivial, so cruel and so unconscious; I was a mere visitor. There was something deeply, irreparably wrong with my being there at all, something against the grain of my life; except for this (and here was the falseness I had finally to uncover): I loved the spectacle of the bullfights, I was drunk on it, I was in a strange, wild dream from which I did not want to be awakened. I was now drawn irresistibly to the bullring as before I had been drawn to the race tracks and the polo fields at home. But this had death in it, and it was the death in it that I loved. . . . And I was bitterly ashamed of this evil in me, and believed it to be in me only—no one had fallen so far into cruelty as this! These bullfight buffs I truly believed did not know what they were doing—but I did, and I knew better because I had once known better; so that spiritual pride got in and did its deadly work, too. How could I face the cold fact that at heart I was just a killer, like any other, that some deep corner of my soul consented not just willingly but with rapture? I still clung obstinately to my flattering view of myself as a unique case, as a humane, blood-avoiding civilized being, somehow a fallen angel, perhaps? Just the same, what was I doing there? And why was I beginning secretly to abhor Shelley as if he had done me a great injury, when in fact he had done me the terrible and dangerous favor of helping me to find myself out?

In the meantime I was reading St. Augustine; and if Shelley had helped me find myself out, St. Augustine helped me find myself again. I read for the first time then his story of a friend of his, a young man from the provinces who came to Rome and was taken up by the gang of clever, wellborn young hoodlums Augustine then ran with; and this young man, also wellborn but severely brought up, refused to go with the crowd to the gladiatorial combat; he was opposed to them on the simple grounds that they were cruel and criminal. His friends naturally ridiculed such dowdy sentiments; they nagged him slyly, bedeviled him openly, and, of course, finally some part of him consented—but only to a degree. He would go with them, he said, but he would not watch the games. And he did not, until the time for the first slaughter, when the howling of the crowd brought him to his feet, staring: and afterward he was more bloodthirsty than any.

Why, of course: oh, it might be a commonplace of human nature, it might be it could happen to anyone! I longed to be free of my uniqueness, to be a fellow-sinner at least with someone: I could not bear my guilt alone—and here was this student, this boy at Rome in the fourth century, somebody I felt I knew well on sight, who had been weak enough to be led into adventure but strong enough to turn it into experience. For no matter how we both attempted to deceive ourselves, our acts had all the earmarks of adventure: violence of motive, events taking place at top speed, at sustained intensity, under powerful stimulus and a willful seeking for pure sensation; willful, I say, because I was not kidnapped and forced, after all, nor was that young friend of St. Augustine's. We both proceeded under the power of our own weakness. When the time came to kill the splendid black and white bull, I who had pitied him when he first came into the ring stood straining on tiptoe to see everything, yet almost blinded with excitement, and crying out when the crowd roared, and kissing Shelley on the cheekbone when he shook my elbow and shouted in the voice of one justified: "Didn't I tell you? Didn't I?"

1955

A Little Incident
in the Rue de l'Odéon

Last summer in Paris I went back to the place where Sylvia Beach had lived, to the empty bookshop, Shakespeare and Company, and the flat above, where she brought together for sociable evenings the most miscellaneous lot of people I saw; persons you were surprised to find on the same planet together, much less under the same roof.

The bookshop at 12 rue de l'Odéon has been closed ever since the German occupation, but her rooms have been kept piously intact by a faithful friend, more or less as she left them, except for a filmlike cobweb on the objects, a grayness in the air, for Sylvia is gone, and has taken her ghost with her. All sorts of things were there, her walls of books in every room, the bushels of papers, hundreds of photographs, portraits, odd bits of funny toys, even her flimsy scraps of underwear and stockings left to dry near the kitchen window; a coffee cup and a small coffeepot as she left them on the table; in her bedroom, her looking glass, her modest entirely incidental vanities, face powder, beauty cream, lipstick. . . .

Oh, no. She was not there. And someone had taken away the tiger skin from her bed—narrow as an army cot. If it was not a tiger, then some large savage cat with good markings; real fur.

I remember, spotted or streaked, a wild woodland touch shining out in the midst of the pure, spontaneous, persevering austerity of Sylvia's life; maybe a humorous hint of some hidden streak in Sylvia, this preacher's daughter of a Baltimore family, brought up in unexampled high-mindedness, gentle company and polite learning; this nervous, witty girl whose only expressed ambition in life was to have a bookshop of her own. Anywhere would do, but Paris for choice. God knows modesty could hardly take denser cover, and this she did at incredible expense of hard work and spare living and yet with the help of quite dozens of devoted souls one after the other; the financial and personal help of her two delightful sisters and the lifetime savings of her mother, a phoenix of a mother who consumed herself to ashes time and again in aid of her wild daughter.

For she was wild—a wild, free spirit if ever I saw one, fearless, untamed to the last, which is not the same as being reckless or prodigal, or wicked, or suicidal. She was not really afraid of anything human, a most awe-inspiring form of courage. She trusted her own tastes and instincts and went her own way; and almost everyone who came near her trusted her too. She laid her hands gently, irresistibly on hundreds of lives, and changed them for the better; she had second sight about what each person really needed.

James Joyce, his wife, his children, his fortunes, his diet, his eyesight, and his book *Ulysses* turned out to be the major project of her life; he was her unique darling, all his concerns were hers. One could want a rest cure after merely reading an account of her labors to get that book written in the first place, then printed and paid for and distributed even partially. Yet it was only one, if the most laborious and exhausting, of all her pastimes, concerned as she was solely with bringing artists together— writers preferred, any person with a degree of talent practicing or connected with the art of Literature, and in getting their work published and set before the eyes of the world. Painters and composers were a marginal interest. There was nothing diffused or shapeless in Sylvia's purpose; that bizarre assortment of creatures shared a common center— they were artists or were trying to be. Otherwise many of them had only Sylvia in common. She had introduced many of them to each other.

We know now from many published memoirs what Ford Madox Ford thought of Hemingway, what Hemingway thought of Ford and F. Scott Fitzgerald, how William Carlos Williams felt about Paris Literary Life, how Bryher felt herself a stranger to everyone but Sylvia. They seemed to be agreed about her, she was a touchstone.

She was a thin, twiggy sort of woman, quick-tongued, quick-minded and light on her feet. Her nerves were as tight as a tuned-up fiddle string and she had now and then attacks of migraine that stopped her in her tracks before she spun herself to death, just in the usual run of her days.

When I first saw her, in the early spring of 1932, her hair was still the color of roasted chestnut shells, her light golden brown eyes with greenish glints in them were marvelously benign, acutely attentive, and they sparkled upon one rather than beamed, as gentle eyes are supposed to do. She was not pretty, never had been, never had tried to be; she was attractive, a center of interest, a delightful presence not accountable to any of the familiar attributes of charm. Her power was in the unconscious, natural radiation of her intense energy and concentration upon those beings and arts she loved.

Sylvia loved her hundreds of friends, and they all loved her—many of whom loved almost no one else except perhaps himself—apparently without jealousy, each one sure of his special cell in the vast honeycomb of her heart; sure of his welcome in her shop with its exhilarating air of something pretty wonderful going on at top speed. Her genius was for friendship; her besetting virtue, generosity, an all-covering charity in its true sense; and courage that reassured even Hemingway, the distrustful, the wary, the unloving, who sized people up on sight, who couldn't be easy until he had somehow got the upper hand. Half an hour after he was first in her shop, Hemingway was sitting there with a sock and shoe laid aside, showing Sylvia the still-painful scars of his war wounds got in Italy. He told her the doctors thought he would die and he was baptized there in the hospital. Sylvia wrote in her memoirs, "Baptized or not—and I am going to say this whether Hemingway shoots me or not—I have always felt he was a deeply religious man."

Hemingway tried to educate her in boxing, wrestling, any kind of manly sport, but it seemed to remain to Sylvia mere reeling and writhing and fainting in coils; but Hemingway and Hadley his wife, and Bumby the Baby, and Sylvia and Adrienne Monnier, her good friend, all together at a boxing match must have been one of the sights of Paris. Sylvia tells it with her special sense of comedy, very acute, and with tenderness. Hemingway rather turns out to be the hero of her book, helping to bootleg copies of *Ulysses* into the United States, shooting German snipers off her roof on the day the American army entered Paris; being shown in fact as the man he wished and tried to be. . . .

As I say, Sylvia's friends did not always love each other even for her sake, nor could anyone but Sylvia expect them to, yet it is plain that she did. At parties especially, or in her shop, she had a way, figuratively, of taking two of her friends, strangers to each other, by the napes of their necks and cracking their heads together, saying in effect always, and at times in so many words, "My dears, you *must* love one another," and she could cite the best of reasons for this hope, compounding her error by describing them in turn as being of the highest rank and quality each in his own field.

Usually the strangers would give each other a straight, skeptical stare, exchange a few mumbling words under her expectant, fostering eyes; and the instant she went on to other greetings and exchanges, they faced about from each other and drifted away. There may have been some later friendships growing from this method, but I don't know of any; it never made one for me, nor, I may say, the other way about.

It was in Sylvia's shop that I saw Ernest Hemingway for the first and last time. If this sounds portentous now, it is only because of all that has happened since to make of him a tragic figure. Then he was still the *beau garçon* who loved blood sports, the dark-haired, sunburned muscle boy of American literature; the war hero with scars to show for it; the unalloyed male who had licked Style to a standstill. He had exactly the right attitude toward words like "glory" and so on. It was not particularly impressive: I preferred Joyce and Yeats and Henry James, and I had seen all the bullfights and done all the hunting I wanted in Mexico before I ever came to Paris. He seemed to me then to be the walking exemplar of the stylish literary attitudes of his time; he may have been, but I see now how very good he was; he paid heavily, as such men do, for their right to live on beyond the fashion they helped to make, to play out to the end not the role wished on them by their public, but the destiny they cannot escape because there was a moment in their lives when they chose that destiny.

It was such a little incident, and so random and rather comic at the time, and Sylvia and I laughed over it again years later, the last time I saw her in New York.

I had dropped into Sylvia's shop looking for something to read, just at early dark on a cold, rainy winter evening, maybe in 1934, I am not sure. We were standing under the light at the big round table piled up with books, talking; and I was just saying good-bye when the door burst open, and Hemingway unmistakably Ernest stood before us, looking just like the snapshots of him then being everywhere published—tall, bulky, broadfaced (his season of boyish slenderness was short), cropped black moustache, watchful eyes, all reassuringly there.

He wore a streaming old raincoat and a drenched floppy rain hat pulled over his eyebrows. Sylvia ran to him calling like a bird, both arms out; they embraced in a manly sort of way (quite a feat, sizes and sexes considered), then Sylvia turned to me with that ominous apostolic sweetness in her eyes.

Still holding one of Hemingway's hands, she reached at arm's length for mine. "Katherine Anne Porter," she said, pronouncing the names in full, "this is Ernest Hemingway . . . Ernest, this is Katherine Anne, and I want the two best modern American writers to know each other!"

Our hands were not joined.

"Modern" was a talismanic word then, but this time the magic failed. At that instant the telephone rang in the back room, Sylvia flew to answer, calling back to us merrily, merrily, "Now you two just get acquainted, and I'll be right back." Hemingway and I stood and gazed unwinkingly at each other with poker faces for all of ten seconds, in silence. Hemingway then turned in one wide swing and hurled himself into the rainy darkness as he had hurled himself out of it, and that was all. I am sorry if you are disappointed. All personal lack of sympathy and attraction aside, and they were real in us both, it must have been galling to this most famous young man to have his name pronounced in the same breath as writer with someone he had never heard of, and a woman at that. I nearly felt sorry for him.

Sylvia seemed mystified that her hero had vanished. "Where did he go?" "I don't know." "What did he say?" she asked, still wondering, I had to tell her: "Nothing, not a word. Not even good-bye." She continued to think this very strange; I didn't, and don't.

1964

A Letter to
Sylvia Beach

(on the death of Adrienne Monnier)

Roxbury Road,
Southbury, Connecticut
6 February 1956

Dear Sylvia:

Please tell me about Adrienne, if you feel you can. The *Souvenir* reached me here in the country day before yesterday, and in spite of all my shocks of the past six months, many losses by death of family and old friends, it was still a shock, there is no way of accepting without painful instinctive regret the death of anyone dear to us. Adrienne—you and Adrienne, for I thought of you together, even though you were both so distinct as individuals and friends in my mind—was a beautiful living being in my memory, though you were nearer to me; and I did have that pathetic fallacy of thinking of us all as immortal, or enough so for our purposes—we could never hear of each other's death!

How good of you to send me the *Souvenir;* I read in it, and a whole space of life comes back to me: that little pavilion and garden at 70 bis rue Notre Dame des Champs, with you and Adrienne at dinner there, and such good talk! And your flat above 12 rue de l'Odéon, the parties there, the sparkle of life in *everybody* present, which you two could always bring out. And your wonderful books that I loved to roam around among, the best place I knew in Paris. . . . Do you remember that dark rainy afternoon, almost evening, when Ernest Hemingway came in streaming rain from a big coat, you introduced us and then went to the back room to answer the telephone, and when you got back, Ernest was gone. He had just stood there looking across the big table at me with no particular expression on his face, I looked back, we never said one word to each other, and all at once he simply turned and bolted forth into the weather, and I have never seen him since. I am sure we have not been avoiding each other, it was just no doubt the right thing to happen. And Adrienne with her firmness and calmness and humorous wit, in her long gray beguine's dress and her clear eyes that could undoubtedly see through millstones, told such delicious things about her childhood. I remember best about how she and her sister Marie always wept when their parents took them to hear *Melisande*. "From the first notes, we would begin to shed tears, and to sniff and sob, with people around us hissing at us for silence. We could not help it, and we wept just the same, every time. That music was '*si mystérieusement . . . émouvante!*' "

And now we shed tears for her, whose life was so mysteriously moving, its motives coming from such depths of feeling and intelligence they were hardly fathomable (except to you and to her nearest friends) but always to be believed in and loved: I knew well what she meant, I could guess the sources of her power. Bless her memory. . . . Sylvia darling, the last time we saw each other was in the general confusion which seems always to attend my life in New York. I wish I could see you now, on this quiet hill in the country, all so tranquil and with time for everything. Or better in 12 rue d l'Odéon . . . but really, anywhere would do. Please let me know where you will be, what your plans are if you expect to change. With my same affection and remembrance and friendly love

Katherine Anne

What was the date of her death?

1956

Letters to a Nephew

AUTHOR'S NOTE: *Letter One was written to my nephew, Paul Porter, who had spent four years in Europe in World War II, and was at the time of this letter in the University of California, Los Angeles. I was on a tour reading my stories and speaking. The "Winkie" referred to is a California friend of us both, at that time completely enslaved by a houseful of cats and a dog. Dorothy is Paul's sister.*

Purdue University
West Lafayette, Indiana
5 June 1948

Dear Paul:

You send so much news I hardly know where to begin, but I expect family carryings-on first, as always. It could be the hospital's fault that Dorothy had her baby on the bathroom floor, but it is strictly Dorothy's to give a helpless infant such a dowdy name. Even Charlotte Susan would not be so bad—not so good either—as a hidden, secret name never to be uttered, and something more becoming for everyday use. Even so, it could have been Brenda or Sandra or Barbra or Debra*—as J. F. Powers mentioned when writing me that he had named his little daughter for me—a solid bread-and-butter sort of name. Suzy is a pretty nickname, but they'll probably call our poor child Charlie or Lottie. Well, let's not be troubled.

Winkie wrote a large post card entirely taken up with the history of her dachl who had a bad cold and was rapidly losing interest in things. She (Winkie) gave her (the dachl) a spoonful of the Old Forester bourbon I left with her (Winkie), adding casually that Anne, her sister, had just called from Oregon to say she (Anne) was engaged. I know how Winkie feels about the relative importance of such events. The dachl got well, which was the main point.

. . . .

You mentioned that, in the midst of your recent drunken revelries, such a change from the chaste rule of the armed forces, you have "rediscovered Sex—the Foul Kind." Dear me, what other kind is there? You must tell me more at once. Of course, Times do change and vocabularies change, too, but in *my* time there was among certain advanced spirits a determined effort to identify—or at least confuse—Sex with love; that is, to disprove the old theological doctrine that sex took place entirely be-

* Especially Barbra and Debra—vulgar misspellings of good names.

low the belt, and love entirely above it. Somewhere in the region of the heart, and if you worked at it, it could sometimes get as high as the brain. Never the twain could meet, of course, unless you were a moral acrobat, which was reprehensible. As I say, the young pioneers set out to disprove this dirty doctrine in two different directions, or schools: First, the most popular, that sex is *all*, just plain sex undiluted by any piffling notions about spiritual overtones, or even just romantic glow—a good hearty low roll in the hay without getting "involved" was the best, perhaps the only, purifying thing in life. The extremists went so far as to say, and claim, they practiced wallows only with total strangers, so that no slag of personal attachment could get into the pure gold of sex. Hence a lot of young women taking up with Italian bootleggers and Brooklyn gangsters, and getting smacked in the eye more than once. Hence brash young men taking up with high-yellow girls in Harlem, getting their pockets picked and a dose of clap.

Then of course, not to give only the gloomy side, there were those of this school who picked up with strangers, and wallowed so successfully that in a few days, or weeks, or months, they were setting the alarm clock together to keep an early date at the marriage bureau.

The second school still believed in love: love that began perhaps in the heart, all tender feelings and warm hopes, worked itself up to the head in a community of ideas, and finally got round to exploring the cellar, but only incidentally. That is to say, True Love included Sex, naturally, but it got its innings only after careful preparation in the higher departments of life. Some of these fanatics actually waited until they were married to sleep together, but this was considered very dangerous, because sometimes, when everything else was perfect, sex the louse would be tried and found wanting. It was, therefore, much more sensible to have a few rehearsals beforehand.

Fire, fire, fire, fire!

Sorry, I just said that to catch your attention, so we can get on to the next paragraph.

But it seemed to me, as time blundered on, that the Foul Sex school was winning because it simply seemed to be more fun. At least in general the male sort preferred it. They seemed to be a touch schizophrenic on that topic, though it is only fair to say the young women had some strange reservations, too. I have heard more than one of that long-vanished generation of liberated young women say she didn't want to marry, but would like to have a baby, just for the experience. A few of them did it, too. A great error, as they realized quickly. The men remained a touch divided between behavior suitable to the vanguard, and certain old-fashioned notions about relations between the sexes. They went on rather furtively dividing girls into the kind they respected, and the other kind. I confess I translated this as meaning the kind they didn't want to sleep with, and the other kind. Also, through some natural perversity of the male, they clung to the notion that they should marry the kind they respect, on the grounds (in other days at least, and I suspect even now) that a woman fit to be a wife and mother should never have any fun thataway. Look at all these horrible little books giving advice on technical procedures and assuring all parties that bed can be wonderful if only the subjects can get rid of their inhibitions and practice a bag of new tricks. I have never read one—the table of contents in the advertisements throw me off, somehow. Their outmoded point of view no doubt has something to do with a certain snobbishness, too, for often the other kind are ladies of inferior caste. Be all this as it may, it still leaves a great deal unaccounted for. I don't know a lot about the subject—only through some experience and a great deal of observation; can't expect you to trust me when I confess I never read a book about it.

Well, I noticed at last that the True Love school got divorces almost as often as the Foul Sex school, only the Foul Sexers didn't get so bruised because they had known all along that nothing lasts, while the true lovers were left holding a sackful of broken ideals. I know well the words have changed, but not, alas, the notions. I should not waste my time mourning, and indeed, I do not. Each generation must get on the same old merry-go-round, only disguised in a fresh coat of paint.

There is a third school, to which I long adhered, though now I should say the question is academic. This is the Stroke of Lightning (*coup de foudre*) or "love at first sight and the hell with theories" school. In this, one beholds (and the circumstances may be of the most ordinary, the time any hour, the place anywhere, the only fixed rule being that it must happen with absolute suddenness, when one is thinking of something, almost anything else); an Object irrevocably becomes a Subject—in my case, of course, male—which is instantly transfigured with a light of such blinding brilliance all natural attributes disappear and are replaced by those usually associated with archangels at least. They are beautiful, flawless in temperament, witty, intelligent, charming, of such infinite grace, sympathy, and courage, I always wondered how they could have come from such absurdly inappropriate families. I notice I have fallen into the plural in describing this paragon. It is just as well. The meeting between us is like an exchange of signals with lightning, they also seeing in me whatever improbable qualities they wish me to have.

It is a disaster, in fact. We are in love and while it lasts—

It is no good going into details, for while it lasts there simply aren't any. And when it is over, it is over. And when I have recovered from the shock, and sorted out the damage and put my mangled life in order, I can then begin to remember what really happened. It is probably the silliest kind of love there is, but I'm glad I had it. I'm glad there were times when I saw human beings at their best, for I don't think by any means that I lent them all their radiance . . . it was there ready to be brought out by someone who loved them. It is still there, it may have shone out again if they were ever loved like that again. It is just that I knew them better than anyone else for a little while, they showed me a different face because they knew I could really see it—and no matter what came of it, I remember and I never deny what I saw.

If you ask me where they are now, whatever became of them, I must simply say that I think that question entirely beyond the point. Lightning makes the most familiar landscape wild, strange, and beautiful, and it passes. It was all my fault, though. If one ever treats a man as if he were an archangel, he can't ever, possibly, consent to being treated like a human being again. He cannot do it, it's nonsense to expect it. It begins to look as if I had never wanted it.

And why should I treat him (them) like that in the first place? Because that is the way I felt. Not any too sensible, is it?

. . . .

Now it is only four days until I must be on the road again, but only for two days' work and then I shall stop in the Missouri University Sorority House until time for the big show in Kansas. Then another short rest and on to Seattle, Nebraska, Indiana—the North and Middle West seem like foreign lands to me, in a way that France or Mexico never did. After all the stylish literary communism of New York and the West Coast, these people are quite innocently, you might say almost unconsciously, Fascist or Nazi—

I resist all three as you know; and I say the most incendiary things, and everybody applauds and comes around to tell me I am saying exactly what people need to hear, and to keep it up. Most of the disturbance on the West Coast is made by people who think they are Communists, but at least they always know what they are up to: but these Midwesterners are Nazis or Fascists (same thing really, only one speaks German and the other Italian), and it comes over me uneasily that they think I am talking about somebody else, never about them. Even when I describe their ways and works, and quote their views back at them, they believe they are all good democratic Republicans; they *still* applaud, and may just demur a shade or two: "Well, I didn't go all the way with you about the Mundt Bill," or "I do think we ought to do something about all those Communists"—and I try once more to explain that I want to do something about the Communists and the Nazis and the Fascists, to say nothing of Franco Spain, but the Mundt Bill is not the way, and the whole talk goes up in smoke. The population here is largely German, the university crawls with them, and they worry day and night about the poor Hungry Germans—"Suppose they DID follow Hitler, is that their fault? Don't they get hungry just like anybody else? Aren't they human beings?" The only answer I can think of, which is much too wicked to say, and is only partly true besides, is that of late I have not found that being human is any great recommendation. So I haven't said it, and I hope I never shall. I have always admired the way the French hate the *sales Boches* steadily and for good reasons and without foaming at the mouth, without screaming for revenge, but without any intention ever to let them get the upper hand again. Nobody can tell them anything new about the Germans as regards France, and, OH, I hope they'll remember until Judgment Day!

Your description of the spider in the bathtub was delicious, and all your fantasy about Marianne Moore sitting in the block of crystal; that is where she will land, bless her, or so I hope, where she can be seen clearly for a long time. The note you sent on *The Idiot* says a true thing about Dostoyevsky. It's easy to see now, too late, what damage was being done to all of us by his perverted kind of Christianity, which deplores and revels in, and gives a free hand to all of our evil instincts.

I agree with your teacher that you should read Milton and Keats now, which seems strange to me at your age, because I was mumbling around in them when I was ten years old, and had learned all of Shakespeare's sonnets by heart when I was twelve. Other times, other ways, as the saying is. What were you learning at the age of 12? Well, darling, you've been wronged and we'll have to make it up some way. Try to chink up all these dark crevices in your education while you are young and have time, soak up the riches of poetry and music while your heart and mind are tender and absorbent. It gives such joy—that is the real reason-to-be of all the arts, and please don't be intimidated by the kind of solemn culture vultures who try to take all the juice out of life. When they touch the arts, they leave grubby thumbprints. I think you would enjoy good criticism too—Eliot, Warren, John Crowe Ransom, Cleanth Brooks, Blackmur, Edmund Wilson . . . all for or against something or somebody of course, as I expect they should be. Critics are usually partisan, who isn't? It is as hard to find a neutral critic as it is a neutral country in time of war. I suppose if a critic were neutral, he wouldn't trouble to write anything.

Hope you get your scholarship, and am pleased to hear your finances are looking up. Yes (you see I am answering your letter nearly line by line), yes, Hemingway is beginning to show up badly now, but go back to the period of his flourishment, and find out why nearly all those Paris-based writers in the '20s were so discouraged and so soft and bitter, and so suicidal. Yes, it's a dull nasty book about a dull thin state of mind, in spite of all the pumped-up bloodlust, which is revolting—Wolfe, Anderson, Dreiser set the examples, then G. Stein's Frivolity all belonged to that Let's Not Think crowd, yet none of them could really feel, either. Yet we did have Eliot, Yeats, and Ransom all in the world at once, and Joyce and Faulkner. But they didn't run in a pack.

Remind me again to read *Sadism and Masochism*. I'm sure it would take a man named Stekel to paw that topic over thoroughly.

Enough, darling. More later, but who knows when?

Tante

AUTHOR'S NOTE: *Nephew Paul, settled in New York, fifteen years later than the first letter, wrote not too seriously to his aunt, who was spending a year in Europe, that he was afflicted with an obstinate depression of spirits. This accounts for the general theme of this letter.*

Eden Hotel,
49 Via Ludovisi,
Rome, Italy,
23 March 1963

Paul Darling:

Your symptoms are fairly recognizable, having been studied, charted, and codified in several departments of life—medical, psychological, philosophical, and theological—and though they each give different theories, they agree it is a state to be avoided at all costs.

The old-fashioned medical word was melancholy (Italian, *malinconia*; much prettier), and your condition, if prolonged and increasing, is supposed to indicate a certain degree of insanity, though I believe that word is no longer used: they have a newer, more scientific, less drastic word for it now—but I forget.

Psychologically, I believe it is supposed to have something to do with emotional and other frustrations due to inhibited libido due in turn to I forget what (I gave up reading Freud in 1925, only the general drift of his thought remains, the awful vocabulary escapes me), but something just as fascinating, firmly based on our hidden, long-denied wayward sexual impulses which keep us all feeling like criminals, or at least sinners: a mixed-up state somewhere between the pain of an impacted wisdom tooth and a sense of original sin; soul and body at perpetual feud with each other, and both at war with the law and order of society.

I have nothing to say either for or against this theory. But I have been in your black mood many times for my own good reasons, and I can always tell when it is coming on by the fact that I don't want to wash. Ordinarily, I wash all the time just for the fun of it, like a tidy cat, feeling that cleanliness doesn't *have* to be next to godliness; it is an end and a pleasure and a good in itself. And all of a sudden I won't take a bath without beating myself over the head, so to speak. It doesn't last long.

What really interests me is the theological view. It is called accidia or acedia, that is, Despair, and it is one of the deadliest of the seven deadly sins. All despair is, of course, in its deepest nature, despair of God's mercy, and you can hardly do worse. It comes naturally from our incurable sense of original sin, which is of sexual origin, just as the Bible says more or less two thousand years before Freud "discovered" it; the words are different, but the meaning is the same. Originally it was an Oriental idea. I do not know what other people besides Jews and Christians base their ideas of sexual guilt upon, but it is most certainly pandemic; any halfway intelligent person does not need to be told this by the time he is 16 years old, and my feeling is that the best thing you can do is to say "God be merciful to me, a sinner," and try not to totter under your share of human perversity of thought and feeling. It is indeed a nuisance, but we are part of it.

This way of taking things gives me something to get my teeth into: I don't like blaming other people for failings I know well enough I have myself, or for the disasters, large and small, I have called down on my own head simply by—it is hard to say by just what means, they are so many. It has always been my boast-in-reverse that I never make the same mistake twice. I don't need to. There is a never-failing supply of new ones on hand, waiting. . . .

In its lighter form, and I hope fondly that your attack is on the light order, it amounts to an acute boredom; the extreme classic example is that of the Frenchman—I don't know why he was always a Frenchman when this was cited to me in my childhood—who hanged himself because he couldn't bear to put on his shoes another time. This seems to me to be more or less your fix at the moment, or was at the moment of your writing. You probably just need a change of sky, as the Italians say—maybe "an invite with gilded edges"—remember Auden's delightful poem with that line, oh, for an invite with gilded edges? It's really about being bored, or it could be, but it cheers up the reader no end. Well, you have had a good lot of these—isn't there someone near you, or just far enough away to make it seem like a change, to have you out for another of those merry weekends you have told me about? It is no cure, it is only a sleeping pill, but that can help, sometimes, by breaking a fixed mood.

Next morning, Sunday, 24th March . . . Cold weather here again, that is, for us: 44°-57°; New York, I notice, 36°-47°. All winter we have had cloudbursts, freezes, snowslides, mudslides, floods, and now earthquakes, but strangely, always somewhere else. Here, other events, other styles. An American opera singer, apparently a very fine singer and really beautiful, married, mother of four, gets herself shot to death right around the corner on Via Veneto by a big dull-looking German who was her manager. He also shot himself, but did not die until yesterday. Letters from him to her, the very loyal testimony of her husband, all sorts of evidence almost proved that she was really innocent and troubled and even persecuted, except, alas for appearances, she was killed around seven P.M. in her room, and was found wearing a red nightgown. I don't know, I really can't say . . . what would *you* think?

. . . .

A note from D. E. saying he was in hospital, but not which one; his latest letters have the tone of someone who has abandoned hope—not despair in the sense that we sometimes have it, as a cardinal sin if not actually the sin against the Holy Ghost, that is, collapsing morally with no real cause for it; no, his despair is that of one who knows at last and has to face the fact that he is not up to character—it might be hard for you to believe what promise he showed, what wit and natural shrewdness of eye, and what talent—all just gone down the drain in a trance of self-love and self-destructiveness. He is one man most certainly ruined by homosexuality that he never came to terms with; what I gather from the little he has said on that subject, his role was that of a hysterical perverse woman, as nearly as a man can imitate even that weakness in a woman; I have known as many, maybe more, hysterical men than I have women, and it doesn't always come of sexual frustrations. There are a lot of things more frustrating than sex, as I hope people will soon begin to find out again. But D. was living an awful parody of femaleness: his affairs always consisted of him making romantic scenes, being helpless, expecting to be waited on and pampered and indulged, and being in general such a nuisance that the other half of the sketch went on, one by one, evaporating into the horizon, just as real men do with real women who behave like that. Sooner or later. But D. has been all these years such a good faithful friend, and when he was in such a powerful highly paid place in ——— he helped me in every way he could, at every chance. I am uneasy about his condition; his letter was very melancholy.

. . . .

Let us get back to your attack of acedia. Thinking it over, I believe you are suffering from loneliness, which is a natural part of human life, but we need not suffer its extremest forms, or not always. You are at a summing-up sort of age: if you were married, you, and your wife, too, no doubt, would be trying to balance the books and find out just where everything had gone, or been stowed away—if you had children, you might say, as I heard your father say once in a temporary fit of summing up, "They're more trouble than they're worth!" Of course, that is nothing to what I heard MY father say: "If your mother had taken my advice, none of you would ever have been born!" But you aren't married and I suppose you have no children, and so you have no natural bonds and burdens to blame things on; your long association with N. seems to have been a very happy one, whatever it was and is, but obviously nothing you have built any part of your expectations upon. You have friends, delightful ones, I have, too, and fine faithful loving ones, all distant, centered elsewhere. I am distant from them, too, and not centered upon any one of them. . . . But I have got a life engagement, a work that has not been a substitute for other relations but has merely superseded them; I have something that will last me until I die, and my loneliness is only that of a naturally lonely person. I have never thought it a misfortune, but a part of my daily life most important to the work I do. Yet, there is no one I would call for in the hour of my death, and that I think is the final test of whether you are really alone or not. Have you someone?

I saw Fellini's 8½, and a wild fast noisy affair it is; not at all mysterious to anybody who trained in 1921 more or less with *Dr. Caligari*, and later with *Blood of a Poet* and so on. Nothing new, just an imaginative variation on a method which by now should be a classic if it's still around at all. I seem to remember I wrote you about the fat woman's dance on the beach before the little boys? It was a parody on Anita Ekberg's parody in *La Dolce Vita:* Only this woman was what Anita will be very soon if she doesn't look out, and I want you to pay special attention to her first appearance, coming up out of what looks like a cave, a great shapeless dark bundle with a shaggy mop, just the top of her head showing until she looks into the camera with the face of a dangerous wild beast. This is Fellini's favorite trick in the picture—having people walk into the camera with their faces hidden, then revealing themselves at close range, sometimes hideous, sometimes not.

. . . .

For some reason I have no interest in ballet, music, pictures (here, I mean, at present), I don't even go to the Etruscan Museum. I have been so tired all this time, and I haven't done anything except get some pretty clothes—I will find somebody to make outdoor snapshots in color to send you. I have some fine new shoes, so simple and subtly shaped, from Ferragamo, who is, you might say, the Gucci of footwear. One for walking, one for indoor dress. I am expecting a hat I bought by mail from Paris, I enclose the picture I ordered it by. The hatmaker is Jean Barthet, new to me, but they took my personal check in payment and wired they were sending it by air Friday, day before yesterday, so I am looking forward to wearing it with my splendid emerald-green Brittany Jacket suit (from Ricci), my new walking shoes, and so on. I don't seem even to miss music . . . a horrible little piece in this morning's paper about Ezra Pound, who tells the reporter his whole life has been a mistake, everything that he touched he damaged, he was wrong all the way, he will never finish the *Cantos*, he has nothing left but Gluttony and Laziness. . . . (Two more of the cardinal sins, in case you've lost track!) This strikes me cold, because age, real age, can play dreadful tricks on the mind and spirit; Gluttony I do not practice; in fact, I eat less and less; but is my lassitude just *laissez faire*, which translates nicely into Lazy. That worries me, I shall put myself on a sterner regime. . . . I want to work, I am suffering from the impossibility of getting my mail answered—my girl Friday works more and more, but the stack rises and rises, so I am going to send out hundreds of change-of-address notices, so everything except your letters and Ann's and my sister's and, of course, my agents and publishers and everybody connected with the business which they run for me—and themselves—now, will be deflected to Atlantic Monthly [Press]. There it will be opened, read, weeded out, and just those from a list I have given them will be sent on. It's a drastic step, but I'll never have another free day if I don't do this. . . . My mind is painfully distracted by all the hundreds of things irrelevant to anything I am doing, and it must end. . . .

I think of Robert Frost and William Carlos Williams, dying old— good poets, honorable men, going away with dignity, in silence; and poor Ezra Pound, who was as good a poet as either, and a critic who helped a whole generation of writers to find out what they were doing, repudiating his whole life because he made a fool of himself politically. . . . He was prejudiced and had some ugly notions, but God, so had Robert Frost—I've heard him talk at cocktail parties. Opinionated old bullheaded bore, he could be. But a great poet and a good man. I think maybe the thing that killed Ezra Pound's spirit is knowing that he committed treason, which is about the lowest crime there is—and he didn't even have sense enough to know it was treason until he was told. . . . That is enough, I suppose. But it is such a pity.

S. was simply ecstatic with rage at the [1963] National Book Award, though I had tried my best to prepare him for it weeks before. I told him exactly why I would not be given it, and I even made a hopeful guess that [J.F.] Powers would be. And I am happy. I am now trying to explain to S. why I am not going to be given any more awards, grants, prizes in that country, probably in my whole life: Too many people who have resented me for years are getting into the act.* And I myself think I have had my share of love and praise and fine criticism, and must expect

* Note varied honors since then—so much for prophecy.

a reaction, especially when I hit a million-dollar jackpot, as I have: the kind of people who hate my writing, and my reputation, are joined by the people who hate my having that money—it makes quite a mob. I find it exhilarating, probably because I know that no thing, nobody can harm me, or take away what I have!

That is not the heroic stance, and I don't intend to be heroic. I intend to be at ease in Zion from this time on out . . . I am going to get the use of my time, energies, and money firmly into my own hands, and get to work again.* Otherwise I'll really be sick, not just a mild attack of flu. I have an Italian doctor who looks like a rather young Julius Caesar, who went over my chest and midriff, same old routine, and said, "Flu, and a kick-up of diverticulae," and I said, "But I took a whole row of flu shots just before leaving Washington last fall." He smiled like the tiger coming out of the Colosseum after a nice warm lunch of Christians, and said, "They don't work. You were just lucky." I had told him I hadn't had flu for four years, since I took the yearly shots. . . . Well, there went another dear delusion. Then he said—this was on the third round, when I was able to go to the office and really be listened to and poked in the midriff—"Yes, you have bronchitis; yes, the lungs are distended; yes, there is a certain amount of damage. . . ." Then he gazed at me almost tenderly, I mean with real *caritas*, human sympathy, and said in a nice conversational tone: "You do know, don't you, that what you have is incurable; you will be better, and worse, and better, and worse, with now and then an acute attack, and your condition just depends on the way you take care of yourself, eat properly, sleep, live as well as you can. . . ."

I said, "I have lived with this all these years, and I have never lived well until now, I have never been able to care for myself, really! And look how long I have lived! Well, what an amiable sort of incurable trouble to have . . . I don't mind at all."

He gave me a few little pellets to swallow, just to make it official, I suppose, between doctor and patient, then said, as we shook hands, "Don't take medicines—you don't need them." I said, "What about this cough?" "It will go away if you will rest a few days. Drink fruit juices and tea and coffee and red wine, plenty of everything . . . and grilled meats, beef and lamb."

I went away happy as a lark. . . . The blessed man has freed me from

* Another reckless prophecy.

doctors. Now I don't have to have any more until that day they round me up and try to put tubes in my nose and feed me in the veins, and on that day I want you or Ann to be present to say, "Let my pore ole good ole aunt alone. Keep your busy hands off her! She knows what she's doing!" I want to be let die in peace and quiet, with a good shot in the arm to speed me onward. Now you see that that is done, you hear me?

. . . .

But oh, how I wish I could be there to go to see *our* Siobhan Mc-Kenna and all of them in *The Playboy of the Western World*. I must have told you, didn't I, how, on my first wild dash into the wilder world, out of that preposterous first marriage, I went to Chicago and got a job as extra in the moom-pitchers, and a lot of silly things happened, but the only thing I really remember that was mine and should have happened to me, was I went to see *The Playboy of the Western World* with the original Abbey Players, Frank Fay as the Boy, Sarah Allgood as the Widow Quinn, and Synge's own darling and affianced bride, Maire (pronounced Moira) O'Neill, as Pegeen Mike herself. And I am certain nobody has come along until now that could play that role as well. . . . Tell me how it was, and maybe it will come here, but in general I find moving-picture programs looking dull—I don't go to see, of course.

. . . .

Just to think that Chekhov and Synge lived at nearly the same time, two of the best playwrights—THE best—of the world before or since for a hundred years or more: and if I had the money, I would found a theater to play *only* Chekhov and Synge, turn and turn about, season after season, with the right companies, Russian and Irish to begin with, until they had trained a generation in the art—and maybe it would help to cure the public of the mange of Tennessee Williams, Beckett, Genêt, Giono, Albee—you name your list! Darling, wouldn't that be a lovely act of civic virtue? We'd intersperse, now and then, one of Yeats's one-act magic plays. And maybe for variety bring over a French company to play a series of Molière's comedies. Well, it would be fun, wouldn't it? If I get my hands on that money, I'll DO it.

Darling, I must stop this. I have tons of letters to answer, but I like doing this. You are not in such a sunken state as you think if you can still go by and swim and then eat and bathe in scented water like an ancient Pompeian; and *The Guns of August* is a very lively bedfellow. I know. My favorite books this last year were: *Guns of August; George*, by that fine actor? Williams?; *The Blue Nile; Renoir, My Father,* Dwight Mac-Donald's *Against the American Grain.* No fiction. Except *Morte d'Urban.* All right, Mr. Porter, from now on you are just Paul to me, not Cole; did you know he is a collateral relative, and not too far off, either? But I don't fancy we'll ever be kissing cousins, or even calling! Love as always

Aunt Katherine Anne

Dylan Thomas

(*a review of* Dylan Thomas in America
by *John Malcolm Brinnin*)

John Malcolm Brinnin has described this personal memoir of his friend and fellow-poet, Dylan Thomas, as an act of exorcism, and the reader will easily understand why, as he reads on; but I take it also as a very honorable attempt to set his share of the record straight, at a time when the events he writes about are so near and bitter a memory to him. Dylan Thomas died two years ago [November 9th] in a New York hospital of brain lesions caused by alcoholism.

Certain English newspaper critics were very quick to say that we, the Americans, had in our usual thoughtless way destroyed a great poet by tempting him with our easy money to work himself to death traveling about exhibiting himself. It was not easy money, to begin with, and after he was here the poet confessed that he hated his public readings and suffered fearful anxieties on account of them. But he needed money desperately and this was something he could do well. It is perhaps true that he came here out of despair, in his poverty and distraction. This may have been the jumping-off place, but there was going to be one soon, anywhere at all—time was closing in on him; he was probably as well-off here as he would have been anywhere at that exact time, for the simple reason that he was not going to be well-off anywhere ever again.

But obviously he did not know this, and Mr. Brinnin's idea of bringing him to this country, to arrange for him a transcontinental poetry-reading tour, and to manage his financial affairs for the time being, resulted in one of those fateful events which leaves moral and emotional wreckage, an almost incurable sense of wrong and bitterness and frustration in all those concerned in it. Yet as so often happens, the thing began for such good reasons, in such charming high hopes on Brinnin's part, at least good faith, good motives, and splendid practical prospects all around.

There was quite simply nothing visibly wrong with the plan; Thomas confessed he had been longing for years to come to America, but nothing had happened to put him in the way of it. Brinnin, himself a fine poet, was in a position as director of programs for the Poetry Center to be positively helpful. Dylan Thomas was at the top of his fame, he had achieved what turned out to be his life work, and though his first youthful poetic fervor had passed, he appeared to be in a cycle of change for further development; yet, as all artists do at that time, he feared a waning of his powers. He needed a radical change by way of rest and refreshment; and he would make enough money to go back to Wales to his fishing village, his wife and three extraordinarily beautiful children and go on writing poetry.

This book is the story of disgrace and disaster and death that came of all these hopes and plans. For the poet the end was death, tragic yet sordid, in a strange uproar of conflicting claims and feelings, from the most oddly assorted lot of people; with hospital discipline and medical science and the few steadfast friends keeping vigil hardly able to stem the rush of rage and hysteria and melodrama of visitors to his bedside; and all around the cloud of scandal and outrageous gossip floated like dirty smoke in anybody's ears, leaving its gritty deposit in the memory. But the dying of the silent figure at the center of this disturbance, already wrapped in darkness, has its own majesty, and Brinnin never loses sight of this reality in the clutter of mean detail.

No man can be explained by his personal history, least of all a poet. Dylan Thomas' life was formed by his temperament, his genius, in relation—in collision—with his particular human situation. As Brinnin discovered in his saddest days, a drunken poet is not more interesting than any other drunken man behaving badly and stupidly. His daily, personal life in fact was no better than that of tens of thousands of dull alcoholics who never wrote a line of poetry. His poetry made the difference, and that is all the difference in this world. All his splendor and virtue are in this poetry—the terrors and follies of his short life here below may very well be put away and forgotten. He wrote his own epitaph, as a poet should: "This was not everlasting death, but a death of days; this was a sleep with no heart. We bury the dead, said the voice that heard my heart, the brief, and the everlasting."

1955

(*a review of* Leftover Life to Kill
by Caitlin Thomas)

"I added that I loved him still, and perhaps later . . . so reluctant is love to part with any part of itself. Or should I say so tenacious is a bitch of her carrion meat." This is one of the milder tones of this book which Caitlin Thomas promised to write, telling her side of the story, in her foreword to John Malcolm Brinnin's memoir, *Dylan Thomas in America*. She felt bitterly injured then, and one might have expected a counterattack. But time has worked its changes, and, while her hatreds of others and fierce repudiation of almost every human relationship is as hot as ever (except for a few chosen ones who indulge her moods), her rage, as W. B. Yeats once described it, is now like a knife turned against itself. Subjective, self-centered to the last degree, she tells nothing that contradicts or falsifies Mr. Brinnin's story, nor the stories of others, even the wildest rumors that flew about. This is quite simply another story, from her own valid point of view, and a more painful one than any I have known.

On one plane it is a melancholy account of her furious attempts to waste and spoil her life out of a mingling of revenge against, and remorse for, her dead husband. It is a memoir, an apology, an accusation against God, the devil, life and death alike; a show-off temper tantrum with a vocabulary of self-hatred and abuse of others that often goes far beyond the merely outrageous. It is a losing battle to free herself from a medieval sense of guilt in an almost medieval ferocity of language: "I sought filthily to purge the blood-thronging devils out by using the devil's own filthier still instruments." These instruments seem to have been the husbands of her neighbors during the first year or two of her widowhood, if I make out the time, first in Laugharne, where Dylan Thomas' family still live, and then on the island of Elba, with her younger son, Colm, the witness of her disorders.

She describes her daily life and habits as "buckets of squalor and feck-lessness." And though one feels that she does pile it on at times, I dare-say by any standards things were grubby and wretched, even sordid. She confesses, or rather boasts, that this was so, and it was as if she were determined to trample herself into the mud. Her husband, who thought women fit only for bed and board, betrayed her as masculine matter of course, but demanded of her the most rigid fidelity—not even a sidelong glance permitted. She therefore had two separate affairs on the island where she had once visited with her husband, both of them in the very room they had occupied together.

Both men were highly ineligible—one nearly as young as her eldest son, the other her middle-aged landlord, with a wife in the same house. She describes the young one as enchantingly beautiful and charming, the older as a paragon of manly virtue; yet I got the impression that the one was stupid as a pot, and the other really vicious. She lived in sloth and lethargy, in dirt and drunkenness; she describes herself as "stinking" for want of a bath. The old lover slaps her around for jealousy and orders her out of the house more than once as if she were a sluttish servant, a tramp or a beggar; and she refuses to go and will take any amount of abuse because she has no other place to go. She was a woman noted for her beauty in the grand style, and even this grace and treasure she treated with the utmost disrespect, as if she could not despise and de-stroy herself brutally enough.

Why? It is a true mystery, and to her as much as to any one. One might think it came about because of her fatal collision in love, her marriage to a poet who had a secret he could not share with her or with anyone, whose obstinate impervious genius exasperated her, and whose final escape into death was taken by her as a bitter personal wrong; but all this seems to have been only the final provocation to a spirit blindly rebellious from the beginning.

She says of her disasters: "By such devilish devices, you'd swear there was somebody behind it with the lowest intentions; my rindy fruit of bitterness, already installed since childhood, though I can trace no evi-dence of suppression," had tainted everything. She has always had this rage and panic in her, though she does not plead the shabby excuse of an unhappy, mistreated childhood. She says further: "My bitterness is not an abstract substance, it is solid as a Christmas cake. I can cut it in slices and hand it around and there is still plenty left for tomorrow." Wrath can be a great healing power when put to use in some direction or other —but this seems to be going nowhere. She rages that no one loves her, no one needs her, and that all she ever needed was love: and goes on to relate some bloodchilling incidents of what she did to several unfortunates who mistakenly took her at her word.

One has trouble following the line of this story because it is like a wild fever chart without the guiding squares on the background. The disorderly sentences and the relentless violence of the style become at times as dull as dullness itself. In her writing, as apparently in her several other diffused talents, Mrs. Thomas is untrained and wildly runaway. She has no more control over her thoughts and method than she has over her emotions and behavior. I feel that she must be a wonderful talker and she might be a splendid writer if she had not such contempt for any and all disciplines. There are many passages of power and feeling as expressive as the most knowledgeable art could make them, and they seem accidental, though they may have been done in full consciousness. It is possible, for Mrs. Thomas regrets that she is not a spontaneous person, and that this book cost her heavy labor and suffering. We may well believe it.

So far as the actual events of her life go this is not an interesting or a particularly unusual story. There are too many women with ambitions beyond their talents, experiences beyond their capacity, with romantic daydreams of glory and fame as the center of attention—we have many of their sad histories.

If they happen to marry men of gifts or even genius, they inevitably stubbornly refuse to play their natural role of second fiddle. But this one, Caitlin Thomas, passes all bounds; her war was with her god, hand-to-hand, like Lucifer's; she would be damned rather than take second place, and again, would be damned on her own terms. So this pathetic and apparently pointless escapade on Elba ends as it must; she takes away again the same despair that she brought with her.

Yet this book has a good reason to be and a beauty of its own. It is not only about dingy love affairs and senseless hatreds. It is a long lament, the heart-moving lykewake dirge that the widow Caitlin Thomas set down and brought back from her funerary island where she went to perform the antique rituals of tearing her hair and befouling her flesh in mourning. Sometimes she screams like a banshee; she howls and curses and blasphemes like a lost soul; even, though not often, she weeps like a woman. There is something grand and legendary in this self-punishing grief, a true note of wild primitive poetry which runs through the book, a theme with numberless variations, a refrain repeated and repeated to the hundredth return, as if there could never be an end to memory and to tears.

Beginning tenderly as a lullaby over the newly dead, not yet changed beyond recognition: "The same endearing childish hair," the tone changes to raptures of rebellion, to bitter, ugly memories, to resentment, to terrible grudges and remorse, to homely, dearly treasured things, to a nightmare vision of the rotting body in the grave and her ghoulish descent into the earth to feed again upon his corruptible part. It is a curiously impressive performance, and I could wish to see it isolated from the rest of the story, for I feel that this is what she really wished to say.

Yet—strange woman—after all this; after going back to that island where she had once been with her love, and there in search of a cure she had done all that she could to degrade and humiliate herself in all the ways that would most surely put her love and her marriage to shame, and offend most deeply the ghost of her husband, she says quite suddenly and flatly: "I was not even sure I ever loved Dylan."

After a short coda, the story closes, or rather, comes to a pause, on a note of sentimental collapse into total bathos of nursery rhyme and rather tardy maternal tenderness. And yet, and yet! There is a paradox of a hopeful kind in this whole muddle; it is a true chronicle of despair, it is not shameless, but shameful, it is not irreparable, for there is almost nothing one can do to be disgraced at present. Getting this book down on paper must have been a good, hard, steady, galling job of work—that in itself is a good sign of returning health and the sense of form. In spite of hell, the afflicted, unhappy woman got this work done, an act I don't doubt of positive therapeutic value. She says herself somewhere in this work that sooner or later one has to take hold and do plain hard work. I have always doubted that art could be used as a medicine for the artist's personal unhappiness or confusions. But this is not art, it is a huge loud clamor out of the depths, and sometimes as oppressive to read as if the raging woman was in the same room making daylight hideous with her unreason.

1957

(*a review of* Dylan Thomas: Letters to Vernon Watkins,
edited with an introduction by Vernon Watkins)

This collection of letters from Dylan Thomas to his best, earliest friend and fellow-poet, Vernon Watkins, is fresh and reassuring as a spring of water—a very lively spring to be sure, bubbling and leaping and running sometimes through muddy flats and stones and rubbish, but a true source, just the same; a good long look at the poet in the morning of his energies and gifts. So many persons have looked at Dylan Thomas through themselves, it is a change for the better to have Thomas looking at himself through a friend, a good, faithful, gifted friend who played it straight. Here are no perverse sexual motives, no wifely jealousy and rivalry, no literary hangers-on elbowing each other out of the reflected glory, no wistful would-be's hoping that a little of the genius would rub off on them if only they could get close enough. Oh, none of all that dreariness!

Besides the early gaiety in some of the letters and the hubbub of daily life lived quite literally from hand to mouth, and later family life and the almost constant shifting of domestic arrangements, the eternal grind of poverty, which oppressed him constantly for years, these pages record the growth of a poet into the mastery of his art, and that with the simplicity of a man with his sleeves rolled up, working. The excitement of this occupation carries all the accidents and mischances of living triumphantly up to a certain point, and then the signs of exhaustion, the hints and surmises of disaster to come, begin to oppress the reader's mind—or is it only because we know the end?

Though Watkins adds no word of his own except the most reserved introduction, the reserve of the man who does not need to explain anything to anybody, and a few very enlightening notes to some of the letters, and though he saved all of Thomas' letters, while apparently Thomas saved none of Watkins', yet the latter is the central figure in this history of a friendship, which for all we know was unique in both their lives; a long, faithful friendship in which Watkins was the touchstone. Several very important letters, he says, "disappeared" mysteriously as letters of persons who become celebrated have a way of doing.

He accuses no one, but regrets that he did not publish earlier while the collection was intact, and mentions that, rather tardily he has made copies of those still in his possession.

The dignity and restraint of Watkins in the face of the insoluble problem of how to guard your treasures from anonymous "collectors" is very impressive, but so is his entire character in this long-drawn-out trial of friendship. Their bond was poetry, the common topic between them which did not need to be defined—poetry, or rather, the making of poetry, the daily search for the word, getting it in the phrase, making it mean what it should mean and the best way of doing this; for they were both hard-working poets, and, in the end and in spite of all, nothing else.

It is strange, for those who know only the lamentable last years, to see Dylan Thomas treating anything or anybody with respect, but Watkins plainly had him convinced from the beginning, and I believe quite simply by his profound reserves of moral force, calm generosity, acute critical sense, besides a first-rate talent and a head start as a practicing poet who could teach Thomas a number of things he badly needed to know. Who could better instruct a Welsh poet than another Welsh poet? Each one liked the work of only two poets—his own and the other's. Far from being merely an amiable weakness, or narrowness (think of the vast reaches of poetry they agreed to ignore for the time being!) this mutual admiration was a source of strength to them both, and insured their unbroken attention to each other's words and feelings.

Then, besides, Thomas was by nature melancholy, living at odds with a world he never trusted, and how rightly; and he believed that Watkins was the only really happy person he knew, and for the only good reason, because he had come through everything and was safely out on the other side of the fears and horrors of life. All these circumstances, so formed and directed and given meaning by Watkins' own personal character, make up this lucky episode in both their lives.

For Thomas was the one always in trouble, one escapade after another, always needing to borrow money on the instant, asking for advice and quite often not taking it, making engagements for all sorts of occasions from tea "with toasted things" to Watkins' own wedding, and just not making it, by hair's breadth always.

He had a gorgeous sense of the comic whenever he could get his head above his troubles. Besides the constant discussion of poetry, the unbroken thread running through all the confusions and worries, his passing account of the events of his days fall on the page as freshly as talk; yet there is a certain reserve even in his bitter-merry letter about being stuck in Cornwall with a lady who speaks no language but Freud—nothing like the utter sprawl of his shameless confidences to others who have also published some of his letters.

This record begins in April, 1936, and ends December 29, 1952: that is, from youth to manhood, his whole life as poet, through marriage, fatherhood, part of the American adventure and the beginning of the end. He was enchanted with Caitlin: just after they were married he wrote to Watkins: "I think you'll like (her) very much, she looks like the princess on the top of a Christmas tree, or like a stage Wendy; but, for God's sake, don't tell her that." His children enchanted him: several of his best poems are written to or about his first son, Llewelyn, especially "This Side of the Truth."

His attachment to his family was touching, and another great poem, "Do Not Go Gentle into That Dark Night," was written to his father. His people were of small means, no education worth mentioning, of humble occupation, of no particular ability in any member except the poet, and full of that pious mediocrity which is the worst enemy not only of poets, but of all life itself. Yet it is plain they loved him dearly and did what they could for him.*

He was continually running back to them for shelter and comfort long after he was a famous poet and a husband and the father of two children and a third to come, and they shared their miseries; "I am so cold this morning I could sing an opera, all the parts, and do the orchestra with my asthma" (November 23, 1948). And on the 13th of December, same year, same place, same household: "All well, but poor and tired here."

What is left is the poetry, and his book of letters to a friend. Here is one dated February 1, 1939, that delights me almost more than any: "Dear Vernon: This is just to tell you that Caitlin and I have a son aged 48 hours. Its name is Llewelyn Thomas. It is red-faced, very angry and blue-eyed. Bit blue, bit green. Caitlin is well, and beautiful. I'm sorry

---

* NOTE. Mr. Vernon Watkins wrote me a pleasant letter about this, saying Dylan enjoyed telling stories about the hardships of his childhood, family ignorance, and so on. They were certainly not rich, and they were religious enough, but *not* illiterates— educated, respectable people, and most loving and tender parents. N.B. I sent this letter to *The New York Times* to be published. The editor did not return the letter, and published it changed to appear that the letter had been written to *The Times* instead of to me.

Yeats is dead. What a loss of the great poems he would write. Aged 73, he died in his prime. Caitlin's address—if you would like to send her a word—is Maternity Ward, Cornelia Hospital, Poole, Dorset. Our love to you. Dylan."

1958

A Defense of Circe

AUTHOR'S NOTE: *In this retelling of the Circe episode I have followed the old Butcher-Arnold translation, the first I ever knew, and it still has for me the wonder of early love and true poetry. I believe I have every translation into English of the Odyssey but I preferred this for my Defense.*

She was one of the immortals, a daughter of Helios; on her mother's side, granddaughter to the Almighty Ancient of Days, Oceanus. Of sunlight and sea water was her divine nature made, and her unique power as goddess was that she could reveal to men the truth about themselves by showing to each man himself in his true shape according to his inmost nature. For this she was rightly dreaded and feared; her very name was a word of terror.

She was a beautiful, sunny-tempered, merry-hearted young enchantress, living on her own island in a dappled forest glade, in her great high open hall of polished stone, with her four handmaidens, nymphs "born of the wells and of the woods and of the holy rivers, that flow forward into the salt sea." Tall, golden haired, serene, she walked up and down before her high loom, weaving her imperishable web of shining, airy splendid stuff such as goddesses weave. As she walked she sang in such a high clear sweet voice the sound carried through the halls and into the forest to the suspicious ears of the fearful men, that half of Odysseus' companions chosen by lot for the dangerous task of approaching and entering if possible the enchanted lair.

The proud and lofty-souled Eurylochus, near kinsman of Odysseus, was by his bad luck at the head of this foray or was supposed to be. He had not liked anything about his mission. Far from leading, he held back. But peril was everywhere—there roamed about the place savage mountain-bred lions and wolves, which gave our heroes a fresh turn. These boisterous veterans of the ten years' war over Helen (I follow Homer strictly) had gone through more than enough disaster lately, and almost anything could upset them. These frightful animals behaved in a way to confirm their worst fears: far from attacking the company, they came romping and fawning with a human gaze of entreaty in their eyes; unnerved at last, the heroes rushed upon the palace, shouting in voices tuned between fear and anger; when Circe instantly opened the great door and gently bade her uninvited guests welcome, they surged in heedlessly—except Eurylochus. He, guessing treason to lurk within, deserted promptly and ran back to the safety of Odysseus and the rest of the company on the shore near the long black ship, bawling like a calf all the way, of course; this dastardly act—dastardly even by ancient Greek heroic standards—has not been so generally condemned as it merits. But, he brought the terrible news they had been half-expecting. Odysseus, against the clamor and tears and lamentations of Eurylochus, who refused to show him the way back, cast upon his shoulder his silver-studded sword, and slung his bow about him and set out by himself to the rescue.

Odysseus was Pallas Athene's darling, she never failed him in battle or any manly exploit. She loved to swoop down like an eagle at the side of her hero in times of hurly-burly and uproar. There was nobody like her for putting on whatever shape was suitable to the occasion and appearing beside him upon the disordered scene with her powers in full play. He was, she told him, the only mortal who could almost match her for guile and subtle trickery—for that she loved him. But she took no interest in his erotic entanglements and at such times abandoned him to his troubles. Such trivialities were not her province— she left that sort of thing to Hermes, whose business and delight it was to interfere in the love between men and women and to sever and to separate; he was the messenger of the high gods in this matter; for, as the goddesses had cause to complain, the gods who made so free with mortal women were jealous of goddesses who loved mortal men; Calypso complained bitterly of this, and even Aphrodite, the very goddess of love herself, was not free from the reproaches of Zeus or the tamperings of Hermes.

So there was Hermes, the ambiguous and beautiful, a youth with the first down on his lip; in his golden sandals, carrying his wand, lurking in the forest to waylay Odysseus, to give him advice about Circe and to offer him the curious herb moly, more easily gathered by gods than by men, the one sure countermagic for men against the enchantments of women. Now all the gods were crafty, but they kept their word with their favored ones. Not Hermes—he was on all sides at once, stealing from anybody—Admetus' oxen, you remember, and the girdle of Aphrodite right off of her, that time he begot the monster on her; and other incidents besides. A thoroughly untidy if fascinating character, he was, in this instance, thoroughly reliable; his heart was in his work. Odysseus accepted the herb and the advice, and there was a wonderful fairness in him being thus armed, for Odysseus, often called divine, was not so; he was of the seed of Zeus but not a half-god; and it was not justice that he should encounter with merely mortal weapons the half-goddess Circe with her fearful power. Circe, said Hermes, once outmagicked by the herb, will invite Odysseus to become her lover. She will be very likely to amuse herself by making him "a dastard and unmanned" once she has got him stripped and in bed.

Odysseus, therefore, to avoid this fate worse than death, must force her to "swear a mighty oath by the blessed gods" that she will do no such thing, nor any other harm to him or his companions.

This gives us an oblique glimmer of truth about Circe; for these two methodically unreliable beings, strangely enough, never doubt for a moment that Circe can be trusted to honor her oath. It might reasonably be expected that she could not be relied upon any more than any of the other gods once they were set against one; but she could be trusted, it seems; they both knew it and set out cheerfully to take advantage of their knowledge.

Not even a god, having once formed a man, can make a swine of him. That is for him to choose. Circe's honeyed food with the lulling drug in it caused them to reveal themselves. The delicate-minded goddess touched them then with her wand, the wand of the transforming truth, and penned the groaning, grunting, weeping, bewildered creatures in the sty back of the hall. In the whole episode she showed one touch of witty malice, when she tossed them a handful of acorns and other victuals suitable to their new condition. No doubt she did it smilingly with her natural grace; what else should she have offered them at that moment? I think it was very good of her to go on feeding them at all. But then I am only human.

Then Odysseus with a darkly troubled heart called aloud at the great shining door, and the goddess like a rainbow made of sunlight and sea water welcomed him gently, and the drama was played out again, up to that point where she tapped him with her wand and said, "Go thy way now to the sty, couch thee there with the rest of thy company." The gods know each other on first sight but they do not always fathom each other's magic. Was Circe so blinded by Hermes' ambiguous herb she could not see she was dealing with a fox?

Hermes had advised Odysseus instantly to draw his sword upon her and threaten her with death. She was deathless, as Hermes must have known and Odysseus might have guessed; but he seems to have forgot this, so convincing was her manner and look of a mortal woman. She did then, instantly and flatteringly, exactly what Hermes had said she would do—she slipped down and clasped his knees and bewailed her fate in perfect form, and said the one thing most calculated to win his heart; she guessed that he was Odysseus and that he had a mind within him that could not be enchanted, and ended: "Nay come, put thy sword into the sheath, and thereafter let us go up into my bed, that meeting in love and sleep we may trust each other." Her tender, appropriate, womanly intentions were entirely misunderstood by Odysseus, experienced as he was in the ways of goddesses and women. He was irresistible to them all alike, except to Helen; he was the fate of women as Helen was the fate of men. He had married his dear mortal Penelope as a long second choice after half-goddess Helen, who refused him along with a phalanx of other suitors. Penelope had no rivals but goddesses ever after. In a way, he was tender to weakness with women, as men who really need them are apt to be; he wept upon them and pleaded and touched their hearts when he was getting ready to go. . . .

He showed unexpected firmness and severity with Circe, defended as he was by the moly; he accused her of all the evil Hermes had spoken against her, and required of her the mighty oath, which she swore at once; and kept.

And then— but this is all pure magic, this poem, the most enchanting thing ever dreamed of in the human imagination, how have I dared to touch it? And what is this passage that stops my heart with joy, as do so many others—the description of Calypso's island; the scene of recognition between Odysseus and Penelope; Argive Helen in tears before Telemachus, remembering Troy and wondering at herself, so shameless, so blinded by Aphrodite; and all the rest? It is a description of women casting purple and white linen coverlets on silver-studded chairs, with golden baskets and golden wine goblets and silver wine bowls on silver tables; and "a great fire beneath a mighty cauldron" to warm the water; and of the goddess herself bathing away weariness of the loved mortal body under her hands; and it celebrates the smoothness of olive oil on the skin, and of fine linen next the flesh, and of good cheer and comfort and sweet smells and savors . . . a song of praise and delight in the pure senses, fresh as the pearl rosy morning of that morning world. . . .

But Odysseus still grieved, could not eat, could not be at rest until she had restored his dear companions. So she took her wand and went out and drove them back into the hall, a herd of great pigs shedding human tears. Circe, compelled by countermagic to give them back their belying human shapes, was still a goddess, and in this moment she showed an easy, godlike magnanimity. While she anointed the unhappy beasts, they went on weeping; ancient Greek heroes spent a good part of their time lamenting, howling in anguish, bewailing their fates. They wept alike for joy or grief, tears like spring rain; for they lived in a world of mystery and they were its children—what is the strength and the skill of even the bravest and wisest man when matched against the gods, their inscrutable wills, their incomprehensible purposes? As they wept, first in pain and then in happiness, Circe restored them not merely to what they had been but taller, younger, more beautiful than they were born to be—the act of a creatrix, the pure aesthetic genius at play; and we must not be tempted to think of it drearily in our sad terms as an act of divine mercy and reparation, full of profound moral and theological meanings, such as: that the regenerated soul, after punishment and purification, rises in a perfection it could never know except through suffering. No. In this sunny high comedy there are profound meanings, some lovely truth almost lost to us but that still hovers glimmering at the farthest edge of consciousness, a nearly remembered dream of glory; and it is our fault and our utter loss if we tarnish the bright vision with our guilt-laden breath, our nightmare phantasies. . . .

The transformed warrior and the whole company, joined by still reluctant Eurylochus, stayed on cheerfully for a year as the guests of Circe. Odysseus shared her beautiful bed, in gentleness and candor, with that meeting in love and sleep and trust she had promised him. No one was in the least changed, no one learned anything by his experiences. They were not intent on building their characters or improving themselves; they were what they were and their concern was to fulfill their destinies.

Meantime they were in the earthly Elysian fields, feasting themselves on the abundant roast flesh and sweet red wine, lolling in perfumed baths and rolling in perfumed oil, sleeping soft and waking easy to another rosy-fingered dawn. The goddess sat among them taking her own nectar and ambrosia, or walked singing back and forth before her endless shining web. This life was suitable to her; but the men became bored, then satiated, then sickened with all this abundance and generosity, this light and grace, tenderness, freedom from care, godlike splendor—they could endure it no longer. They complained to Odysseus when she was not present, or so Odysseus told her, and it could very well be true, but the warriors spoke his secret thought too. Circe had borne him a son, the quarter-godling Telegonus; Odysseus remembered with longing Telemachus and Penelope and Ithaca his kingdom. He longed to be again in the hollow black ship breasting the wild sea; the time had come for him to go. So, by her fair bed at her knees, he wept and told her all his longing, and reminded her of her promise that she would send him and his companions safely on their way toward home. Search Homer as you may, it is clear that she made no such promise at any time—no hint of it in any of her flowing honeyed words.

Now one may ask, since she knew that the ambiguous Hermes had outcharmed her, why did she not, as some women or even some goddesses might have done, steal the herb and destroy it or cast a counterspell to annul it? Why did she not, as Calypso did later, make a towering scene, remind Odysseus that she had promised him nothing and then, with a smart tap of her wand, turn him into a fox to run his life away with those other wild creatures outside her walls?

The only answer I can give is, this is Circe, and this is Odysseus; when he says to her, "Now is my spirit eager to be gone," she replies at once, with gentle remoteness, "Odysseus of many devices, tarry ye now no longer in my house against your will," and breaks to him the dreadful news that he must at once perform another journey, to Hades, to seek out Theban Teiresias, the blind soothsayer, who will give him directions how to reach home. This broke his heart and he went and groveled and implored her to tell him who would guide him on his way—"no man ever yet sailed to hell in a black ship."

"Set up the mast and spread abroad the white sails and sit thee down," she told him, and promised to send the North Wind to waft his ship on its way. And she told him the ceremonies proper to one entering the place of the dead, the sacrifice of the black ram and the black ewe and the guarding of the blood from the voracious ghosts until Teiresias had spoken. Then things moved very swiftly and with great beauty and dignity. In the dawn Odysseus went through the hall waking his men; Circe gave him a mantle and doublet and "clad herself in a great shining robe . . . and put a veil upon her head." But the youngest lad, Elpenor, heavy with wine, was sleeping on the roof, and roused too suddenly, fell, and his neck was broken. The men, who had arrived mourning and in tears, now departed the same way, tearing their hair. The goddess made herself invisible and went ahead of them and fastened a black ram and a black ewe by the dark ship: "lightly passing us by," said Odysseus in wonder, "who may behold a god against his will, whether going to or fro?"

When they returned to the island to give Elpenor burial and quiet his uneasy spirit, while they were mourning and performing the rites, Circe came with her handmaids bringing "flesh and bread in plenty and dark red wine." She made them a noble speech of salutation: "Men overbold, who have gone alive into the house of Hades, to know death twice, while all men else die once for all. Nay come, eat ye meat and drink wine here all day long; and with the breaking of the day ye shall set sail, and myself I will show you the path and declare each thing, that ye may not suffer pain or hurt through any grievous ill-contrivance by sea or on the land."

As if she could! As if her divine amiability and fostering care could save these headstrong creatures from their ordained sufferings. But Odysseus was wise in his mortal wisdom: He knew that man cannot live as the gods do. His universal fate: birth, death, and the larger disasters, are from the gods; but within that circle he must work out his personal fate with or without their help. He saw his own inevitable end in the swarming, angry, uneasy, grieving shades of the dark underworld of death; but when later the lonely goddess Calypso offered him immortality he was not shaken. When she spoke jealously and contemptuously of Penelope's beauty he answered her in a speech that is the key to all his history, a mortal bent on mortality: "Myself I know it well, how wise Penelope is meaner to look upon than thou, in comeliness and stature. *But she is mortal and thou knowest not age or death.* [Note: my italics.] Yet even so, I wish and long day by day to see the day of my returning.

Yes, and if some god shall wreck me in the wine-dark deep, even so I will endure, with a heart within me patient of affliction. For already I have suffered full much, and much have I toiled in perils of waves and war; let this be added to the tales of these."

And there it is. But earlier, on the island of Circe, at the very last moment there was a memorable scene. After the ship and the men were supplied and ready, "then she took me by the hand," Odysseus remembered long afterward, "and led me apart from my dear company, and made me sit down and laid herself at my feet, and asked all my tale." He told everything about the journey to Hades, and she warned him again against the dangers to come, trying one last time to guide her wayward lover safely home. . . .

After this long night of good counsel and loving kindness, "anon came the golden-throned Dawn. Then the fair goddess took her way up the island. . . ."

This should be the end. But someone is certain to ask: "What about the unpleasant episode of Circe turning Scylla into a monster?" Ah, well —without troubling to deny, or even mention, that hideous rumor, Circe told Odysseus plainly that Scylla was born a monster. In view of what we know about Circe, I am entirely happy to believe her.

1954

Pull Dick,
Pull Devil

(a review of Saints and Strangers
by George F. Willison)

Artemus Ward said, "I believe we are descended from the Puritans, who
nobly fled from a land of despotism to a land of freedom, where they
could not only enjoy their own religion but prevent everybody else from
enjoying his." Ward was a fairly low humorist in a period of dowdy local
humor, but he managed to say that at a time when it badly needed
saying. You will find this note at the back of the book, with many others
that are just what notes should be, true marginalia, illuminating sparks
flying out from the main narrative, sly, witty, apropos, full of health and
purpose. Don't miss the notes; and you will also do well to take a look at
the selected bibliography, if for no other reason than that you will think
twice before rushing into an enterprise like this. In spite of the easy
reading, this is work of long-suffering scholarship. As a student of the
period, having read more than two thousand "items" on that and related
subjects, I assure you that when you have read it, you will know all you
need to know, now or ever, about that group of early American settlers
now called the Pilgrim Fathers, their lives and hazards in the Plymouth
Plantation.

Whatever else Mr. Willison does in his career of writing, teaching,
editing, it would be useful and heroic of him to abandon everything else
and devote his days to clearing up and putting in shape other murky,
demon-haunted spots in American history. As a nation we are in danger
of becoming myth-ridden to a point where our true story will be lost.

Rarely have I seen a handsomer job of imposing chronological order, narrative sequence, and the plain facts of the matter on utter chaos than in this book. It is a pattern for writing from documentation, and is the first completely understood, coherent account, in all its large importance and pettifogging, abject detail, that I have seen not written by a specialist for other specialists. The large importance takes care of itself: the story is told in terms of personal experience, of human relationships on every plane of society, event modifying event, character striking sparks from character; and the eternal conflicts and sympathies between religion, economics, and politics could hardly be more clearly and fairly presented.

These English emigrants from Holland by way of England were not, it seems, Puritans in the technical sense of the word. That title belonged to the later theocrats of Massachusetts Bay. The Pilgrims were not theocrats, either; they were Separatists in every sense: separated from other Christians by God's own election; separated from the mummeries and superstitions of the Church of England; separated from the things of this world, so far as they were able. This turned out to be the most difficult clause. They began with fairly definite notions of communal property interests, a ban on profits and usury, a more or less clear division between the secular and the religious office. So far so good; but during the long years of hardship in Holland that mere handful of not very imaginative or intelligent people had gone maggoty-minded with their troubles and the religious manias of their time, and had reached the benumbing conclusion that they were God's Chosen and nobody else at all was in His favor. In time they became so Elect they could no longer mingle with their fellow-men on any reasonable terms. They got so they could hardly endure each other, for they were all saints but no two in the least alike, and such uniqueness is more than the human soul can bear, the terrible spiritual pride of Chosenness brought to its dead end. They really had the effrontery to call themselves Saints. And their fellow-voyagers outside the Discipline they called Strangers.

Nothing could be less true than that they were looking for religious freedom in this country. This is a myth of later times; freedom of thought and of conscience as we regard it was abhorrent to the Pilgrims. They had religious freedom in Holland, but so had everybody else, and this was a condition intolerable to them. In England their activities were treasonable: in liberal Holland they were mere economic liabilities and social nuisances. During that time they must have learned that no religion has any real power without the support of the state. Their intention, they believed, was pure and unworldly: they were to restore the Golden Age of primitive Christian unity and simplicity of faith. That such an age had never existed made no difference—they would restore it. They needed for this great spiritual undertaking a new country, economic independence and stability, and a body politic of their own devising. They moved toward this goal slowly and painfully, making all the blunders and self-defeating errors of men divided in their minds. After years of the most hysterical quarreling and religious scandals among themselves, political ruses and stratagems never quite successful, a long drama of crosspurposes, cheats, double-dealings, ineptitudes, and false starts in their dealings with the merchant adventurers who were trying to make of them a profitable commercial enterprise, a company of 102 men, women, and a preposterous number of children set sail on the *Mayflower* in September, 1620.

Nobody had enough money or clothes or bedding or supplies of any sort. The Pilgrims, having been farmers or artisans, had decided to become fishermen, but they did not bring enough fishing gear even to supply fish during their periods of starvation. The farmers had not brought any agricultural implements to speak of, and had forgotten the first year's supply of seed corn. The artisans had not proper tools of their trades. The saltmaker on whom they depended for salt to cure the fish they were going to catch without any tackle couldn't, after all, make salt. He had only said he could. I have mentioned the large number of children. It may occur to more than one reader as he follows Mr. Willison through the almost unbelievable series of disasters that follow that the children might have managed things better.

Not all the Voyagers were Saints by a long shot, and that made trouble. Nearly half of them belonged to the category known to the Fathers as Strangers. These were for the most part well-meaning, fairly well-behaved persons who had been christened in the Church of England and like any decent churchman had never given the matter another thought. Even in mid-voyage the Saints began harassing and oppressing them into the Holy Discipline. The struggle was to go on for years, and Mr. Willison follows every step of it to the bitter end. For example, take the threatened mutiny on board the *Mayflower* just on the point of landing. Bradford tiptoes over this in his account, but Mr. Willison ferrets out the names and histories of the malcontents, and places the incident in its proper relation to the celebrated covenant drawn up by the Separatists and signed by all or nearly all on board. This agreement has been romantically described as the first charter of American freedom, which it was not, nor was ever meant to be. It was an instrument designed to bind to obedience the dissenting classes, represented by indentured servants, hired men, and a few of the more respectable Strangers who showed fight at the last uneasy moment.

Mr. Willison quotes from the records with splendid effect, turning on, now and then, in the midst of his own easy colloquial prose that noble Elizabethan English in which some very paltry aims and dubious sentiments and questionable motives were disguised in phrases that lift the heart in a momentary and largely misguided impulse of belief and sympathy. As for rebuke and fault-finding, downright slanging, there was never a better language for it. Everybody who could write at all had it at pen's point; they were as loquacious as the Greeks and censorious as Puritans, and it makes wonderful reading.

With all this admirable work, done with such human tenderness and natural good humor, with all the virtues of the book as history, Mr. Willison has succeeded brilliantly in every detail but one: he has not been able to make his Pilgrims attractive, either as saints or sinners. But if God Himself could not do this, or at least did not choose to do so, our historian may well be content with his achievement and his readers with him. For myself, they are no forefathers of mine, and I still feel about them as the Dutch did, and large numbers of their fellow-Englishmen, and most of their contemporaries in other regions who shared the furious labors of settling this country and founding this nation. Their virtues are simply not great enough to overbalance their disturbing lack of charm. And I wish I might never have to hear again that they brought the idea of political and religious freedom to this country. It got in in spite of them; and has had rough going ever since, which is the fault of all of us.

1945

The Flower of Flowers

Rose, O pure contradiction, bliss
To be the sleep of no one under so many eyelids.
RAINER MARIA RILKE: *Epitaph*

Its beginnings were obscure, like that of the human race whose history it was destined to adorn. The first rose was small as the palm of a small child's hand, with five flat petals in full bloom, curling in a little at the tips, the color red or white, perhaps even pink, and maybe sometimes streaked. It was a simple disk or wheel around a cup of perfume, a most intoxicating perfume, like that of no other flower. This perfume has been compared to that of many fruits: apricot, peach, melon; to animal substance: musk, ambergris; to honey (which has also many perfumes), to other flowers, to crushed leaves of the tea plant—this from China, naturally—and perhaps this is the secret of its appeal: it offers to the individual sense of smell whatever delights it most. For me, a rose smells like a rose, no one exactly like another, but still a rose and it reminds me of nothing else.

This rose grew everywhere in Africa and Asia, and it may have had many names, but they are lost.

This shall be a mere glimpse at some aspects of the life of the rose; it keeps the best company in the world, and the worst, and also the utterly mediocre: all with the same serenity, knowing one from the other; and all by name, but making, in the natural world, no difference between individuals, like any saint: which perhaps is a sign of its true greatness. In working miracles, as we shall see, it exercises the most scrupulous discrimination between one thing and another.

It was, and is, thorny by nature, for it detests the proximity of any other kind of plant, and serious botanists have deduced seriously that the rose was given its thorns as a weapon against other crowding vegetation. With such a perfume as it has, it needs more than thorns for its protection. It has no honey, yet even the bees and wasps who rob its generous pollen for food, get silly-drunk on the perfume, and may sometimes be seen swooping hilariously away at random, buzzing wildly and colliding with each other in air. For the sake of this perfume other great follies of extravagance have been committed. The Romans with their genius for gluttony devoured the roses of Egypt by the shipload, covering their beds and floors and banquet tables with petals; rose leaves dropped in their wine helped to prevent, or at least delay, drunkenness; heroes were crowned with them; and they were at last forced to bloom out of season by being grown in a network of hot water pipes.

The debasement of the rose may be said to have begun with this Roman invention of the hot house. After a long period in Europe when the rose fell into neglect, there came a gradual slow return in its popularity; and for the past century or so, in Europe and America, the rose has been cultivated extravagantly, crossbred almost out of recognition, growing all the time larger, showier. The American Beauty Rose—in the 1900's the rose of courtship, an expensive florist's item, hardly ever grown in good private gardens—in its hugeness, its coarse texture and vulgar color, its inordinate length of cane, still stands I believe as the dreariest example of what botanical experiment without wisdom or taste can do even to the rose. In other varieties it has been deprived of its thorns, one of its great beauties, and—surely this can never have been intended—its very perfume, the true meaning of the rose, has almost vanished. Yet they are all children of that precious first five-petaled rose which we call the Damask, the first recorded name of a rose.

It has been popularly supposed that the Crusaders brought the rose and the name back with them to Europe from Damascus, where they saw it for the first time. Rosarians argue back and forth, saying, *not* so, the Damask Rose was known in France and by that name many centuries before the Crusades. It is very likely, for the Christian penitential pilgrimages to Rome, to the tombs and shrines of saints, and to the Holy Sepulchre, had begun certainly as early as the eighth century. The most difficult and dangerous and meritorious of these pilgrimages was, of course, to the Holy Land, and the rose may very well have been among the dear loot in the returning pilgrim's scrip, along with water from the Jordan, bits of stone from the Sepulchre, fragments of the True Cross, Sacred Nails, and a few Thorns; and, judging by medieval European music, he had got a strange tune or two fixed in his head, also. We know that more than this came into Europe through long traffic and negotiation with the East, the great threatening power which encroached steadily upon the New World and above all, upon the new religion.

By the time of the troubadours, the rose was a familiar delight. In Richard Lion-heart's day, Raoul, Sire de Coucy, a famous poet, singer, soldier, nobleman, was writing poems full of nightingales, morning dew, roses, lilies, and love to his lady, the Dame de Fayel. He went with Richard on the Third Crusade, and was killed by the Saracens at the battle of St. Jean d'Acres, in 1191. The whole tone of his glittering little songs, their offhand ease of reference, makes it clear that roses and all those other charming things had long been the peculiar property of European poets. De Coucy names no species. "When the rose and lily are born," he sings blithely, knowing and caring nothing about Rosa Indica, Rosa Gallica, Rosa Centifolia, Eglantina; no, for the troubadour a rose was a rose. It was beautiful to look at, especially with morning dew on it, a lily nearby and a nightingale lurking in the shrubbery, all ready to impale his bosom on the thorn; it smelled sweet and reminded him of his lady, as well as of the Blessed Virgin, though never, of course, at the same moment. That would have been sacrilege, and the knight was nothing if not pious. Sacred and profane love in the Western World had by then taken their places at opposite poles, where they have remained to this day; the rose was the favorite symbol of them both.

Woman has been symbolized almost out of existence. To man, the myth maker, her true nature appears unfathomable, a dubious mystery at best. It was thought proper to becloud the riddle still further by referring to her in terms of something else vaguely, monstrously, or attractively resembling her, or at least her more important and obvious features. Therefore she was the earth, the moon, the sea, the planet Venus, certain stars, wells, lakes, mines, caves; besides such other works of nature as the fig, the pear, the pomegranate, the shell, the lily, wheat or any grain, Night or any kind of darkness, any seed pod at all; above all, once for all, the Rose.

The Rose. What could be more flattering? But wait. It was the flower of Venus, of Aurora, a talisman against witchcraft, and the emblem, when white, and suspended over a banquet table, of friendly confidence: one spoke and acted freely under the rose, for all present were bound to silence afterward. It was the flower of the Blessed Virgin, herself the Mystical Rose; symbol of the female genitals, and the Gothic disk of celestial color set in the brows of great cathedrals. For Christian mystics the five red petals stood for the five wounds of Christ; for the pagans, the blood of Venus who stepped on a thorn while hurrying to the aid of Narcissus. It is the most subtle and aristocratic of flowers, yet the most varied of all within its breed, most easily corruptible in form, most susceptible to the changes of soil and climate. It is the badge of kings, and the wreath to crown every year the French girl chosen by her village as the most virtuous: *La Rosière*. *Le Spectre de la Rose*: a perverted image. No young girl ever dreamed of her lover in the form of a rose. She is herself the rose. . . .

The rose gives its name to the prayer-beads themselves slipped millions of times a day all over the world between prayerful fingers: these beads are still sometimes made of the dried hardened paste of rose petals. The simple flower is beloved of kings and peasants, children, saints, artists, and prisoners, and then all those numberless devoted beings who grow them so faithfully in little plots of gardens everywhere. It is a fragile flower that can survive for seventy-five years draped over a rail fence in a deserted farm otherwise gone to jungle; it blooms by the natural exaltation of pure being in a tin, with its roots strangling it to death; yet it is by nature the grossest feeder among flowers. With very few exceptions among wild roses, they thrive best, any good gardener will tell you, in deep trenches bedded with aged cow manure. One famous grower of Old Roses (Francis E. Lester, *My Friend the Rose*, 1942) advises one to bury a big beef bone, cooked or raw, deep under the new plant, so that its growing roots may in time descend, embrace and feed slowly upon this decayed animal stuff in the private darkness. Above, meanwhile, it brings to light its young pure buds, opening shyly as the breasts of virgins. (See: Lyric Poetry: Through the Ages.) Aside from the bloom, out of this tranced absorption with the rot and heat and moisture of the earth, there is distilled the perfume of perfumes from this flower of flowers.

(The nose is surely one of the most impressionable, if not positively erotic, of all our unruly members. I remember a kind old nun, rebuking me for my delight in the spectacle of this world saying, "Beware of the concupiscence of the eye!" I had never heard the word, but I knew what she meant. Then what about the ear? The pores of the skin, the tips of the fingers? We are getting on quicksand. Back, back to the rose, that tempts every mortal sense except the ear, lends itself to every pleasure, and helps by its presence or even its memory, to assuage every mortal grief.)

The rose: its perfume. It is—ten to one—the odor of sanctity that rises from the corpses of holy women, and the oil with which Laïs the Corinthian anoints herself after her bath. Saint Thérèse of Lisieux is shown holding a sheaf of roses, promising her faithful to shower them with roses—that is to say, blessings. The women in Minsky's old Burlesque Theater on the Bowery pinned large red cotton velvet roses over their abused breasts and public thighs, forming a triangle. They then waggled themselves as obscenely as they knew how; they did know how, and it was obscene; and the helpless caricatures of roses would waggle too: the symbol being brought to the final depths of aesthetic and moral imbecility.

"A rose said, 'I am the marvel of the universe. Can it be that a perfume maker shall have the courage to cause me suffering?' " Yes, it is possible. "A nightingale answered, 'One day of joy prepares a year of tears.' " (Note: My translation of a stanza of Omar Khayyam's from the French version.)

This divine perfume from the bone-devouring rose is sometimes got by distilling, a process of purification. The petals are mixed with the proper amount of water, put in the alembic, and the sweetness is sweated out, drop by drop, with death and resurrection for the rose in every drop. Or, and this must be a very old way of doing, one takes the sweet petals, picked tenderly in the morning unbruised, with the dew on them, and lays them gently on a thick bed of fat, beef fat, pork fat, or perhaps oil, just so it is pure, and fat. The perfume seeps from the veins of the rose into the fat, which in turn is mingled with alcohol which takes the fragrance to itself, and there you are. . . . Thinking it over, I am certain there is a great deal more to the art of extracting perfume from petals than this. I got my information from a small French household book, published in 1830, which gives receipts for making all sorts of fascinating messes: liqueurs, bleaching pastes for the complexion, waters of beauty—invariably based on rosewater or rose oil, hair dyes, lip salves, infusions of herbs and flowers, perfumes, heaven knows what. They look plausible on the page, while reading I trust them implicitly, and have never dared to try one of them. One important point the perfume receipt omitted: it did not say you must begin with Damask Roses. In India, in the Balkans, in the south of France, wherever the art of making rosewater and attar of rose is still practiced, as in ancient Cyrenaica whose rose perfume was "the sweetest in the world," there is one only rose used: Rosa Damascena, five-petaled in the Balkans and in India, thirty-petaled in Grasse, and called the Provence Rose. In this Rose of Provence there is perhaps a mixture with Rosa Centifolia, native of the Caucasus—Cabbage Rose to us, to those of us who ever saw it, and smelled it—next to the Damask, the most deeply, warmly perfumed. Once in California, in a nursery, lost in a jungle of strange roses, I asked an old gardener, no doubt a shade too wistfully, "Haven't you a Cabbage Rose, or a Damask, or a Moss Rose?" He straightened up and looked at me wonderingly and said, "Why, my God, I haven't even heard those names for thirty years! Do you actually know those roses?" I told him yes, I did, I had been brought up with them. Slowly, slowly, slowly like moisture being squeezed out of an oak, his eyes filled with tears. "So was I," he said, and the tears dried back to their source without falling. We walked then among the roses, some of them very fine, very beautiful, of honorable breed and proved courage, but the roses which for me are the very heart of the rose were not there, nor had ever been.

They have as many pests as sheep, or bees, two notoriously afflicted races. Aphis, mildew, rust, caterpillars, saw-flies, leaf-cutting bees, thrips, canker worms, beetles, and so on. Spraying has become the bane of rose growers, for the new sorts of roses seem to be more susceptible than the old. I remember my grandmother occasionally out among her roses with a little bowl of soapy water and a small rag. She would wash the backs of a few leaves and dry them tenderly as if they were children's fingers. That was all I ever saw her do in that way, and her roses were celebrated.

Mankind early learned that the rose, except for its thorns, is a benevolent useful flower. It was good to eat, to drink, to smell, to wear, to cure many ailments, to wash and perfume with, to look at, to meditate upon, to offer in homage, piety, or love; in religion it has always been a practical assistant in the working of miracles. It was good to write poetry about, to paint, to draw, to carve in wood, stone, marble; to work in tapestry, plaster, clay, jewels, and precious metals. Besides rose-leaf jam, still made in England, one may enjoy candied rose leaves, rose honey, rose oil—good for the bath or for flavoring cakes and pastries; infusion of roses, a delicious tea once prescribed for many ills; above all, rose-hip syrup, an old valuable remedy in medieval pharmacies, manufactured by monks and housewives. The Spanish Mission fathers brought the Damask Rose—which they called the Rose of Castile—to America and planted it in their dispensary gardens. Rose-hip syrup was one of their great remedies. It was known to cure aches and pains, collywobbles in the midriff, a pallid condition, general distemper, or ill-assortedness. And why not? Modern medical science has in this instance proved once more that ancient herbalists were not just old grannies out pulling weeds and pronouncing charms over them. Rose-hip syrup, say British medical men, contains something like four hundred times more of vitamin C, measure for measure, than oranges or black currants, and whoever drinks freely of it will be largely benefited, if he needs vitamin C, as most of us do, no doubt. They needed it in medieval times, too, and it is pleasant to think that quite large numbers of them got it.

Bear's grease mixed with pounded rose petals made a hopeful hair restorer. The ancient Persians made a rose wine so powerful yet so benign it softened the hardest heart, and put the most miserable wretch to sleep. In Elizabethan England they made a rose liqueur warranted to "wash the mulligrubs out of a moody brain." Mulligrubs is a good word yet in my part of the country, the South, to describe that state of lowered resistance to life now known generally as the "blues." In turn, "blues," in its exact present sense, was a good word in seventeenth-century England, and was brought to America by the early Virginia settlers. Whether they brought roses at first I do not know, nor whether they found any here; but there is a most beautiful rose, single, large-petaled, streaked red and white, called the Cherokee Rose, of a heavenly perfume, which is perfectly at home here. It came from Asia by way of England, however, a long time ago, and has not a drop of Indian blood in it. Maybe the Virginians did bring it—it flourishes best in the Southern states.

The celebrated botanists, rose growers, collectors, hybridizers, perfume makers, as well as the scientific or commercial exploiters of the rose, have all been men; so far as I know, not a woman among them. And naturally in such a large company we find a few who labor restlessly to grow a rose with a six-foot stem; with a thousand petals, and a face broad as a plate;

to color them blue, or black, or violet. The rose being by nature a shrub they could not rest until they made a tree of it. In the same spirit, there are those who embalm them in wax, dip them in dye-stuffs, manufacture them in colored paper, and sprinkle them with synthetic perfume. This is not real wickedness but something worse, sheer poverty of feeling and misdirected energy with effrontery, a combination found in all vulgarizers. The "arrangers" of great music, the "editors" of literary masterpieces, the re-painters of great pictures, the falsifiers of noble ideas—that whole race of the monkey-minded and monkey-fingered "adapters"; the rose too has been their victim. Remy de Gourmont cursed all women in the name of the rose, with the ferocity of perverted love; and aesthetic hypersensibility turned not to hatred but to something even more painful, disgust, nausea, at the weight of false symbol, the hypocritical associations, the sickly sentiment which appeared to have overwhelmed it. With the wild logic of bitterness and disillusion, he cursed the rose, that is, woman, and through it, all those things which had degraded it in his eyes, concluding that the rose itself is vile by nature, and attracts vileness. Only a disappointed lover behaves so unreasonably. He got a brilliant poem out of it, however (*Litanies de la Rose*).

Women have been the treasurers of seedlings and cuttings; they are the ones who will root a single slip in a bottle of water in the corner of a closet; or set out, as the pioneer American women did, on their bitter journeys to the Carolinas, to Kentucky, to Texas, to California, the Middle West, the Indian territories, guarding who knows how their priceless little store of seeds and roots of apples, plums, pears, grapes, and roses—always roses. China Rose, Bengal Rose, Musk Rose, Moss Rose, Briar Rose, Damask Rose—in how many places those very same pioneer rose bushes are blooming yet. But where did all those hedges of wild roses spring from? Were they always there? Gloire de Dijon, Cup of Hebe, Old Blush, Roger Lambelin, Cherokee, Maréchal Niel, Cramoisy —these are some names I remember from Gardens I knew; and Noisette, a small perfect rose, result of the first crossbreeding in this country, a century and a quarter ago. . . . Where did I see that little story about someone advertising a place for sale as an earthly paradise, "the only drawbacks being the litter of rose petals and the noise of nightingales"?

The rose is sacred to religion, to human love, and to the arts. It is associated with the longing for earthly joy, and for eternal life. There is a noticeable absence of them, or flowers of any kind in the textbooks of magic, witchcraft, the Black Arts by any name. The world of evil is mechanistic, furnished with alembics, retorts, ovens, grinding stones; herbs, mainly poisonous; the wheel, but not the rose; hollow circles, zones of safety for the conjuror. The alchemist with his madness for gold—for what did they devote all that hermetic wisdom, that moral grandeur, that spiritual purity they professed but to the dream of making gold? Or of turning pebbles into jewels, as St. John was said to have done? A slander, I do believe, unless taken symbolically. But the evidence is against this: the alchemists meant to make real gold. It is the most grotesquely materialistic of all ends. The witch, with her blood vows and her grave robbing and her animal rites and transformations, how stupid and poor her activities and aims! Where can pictures more coarse and gross and debased be found than in books of magic: they cannot even rouse horror except in the offended eye.

Evil is dull, that is the worst of it, and black magic is the dullest of all evils. . . . Only when the poor metamorphosed Ass can find and eat of good Venus's roses may he be restored again to his right form, and to the reassuring, purely human world of love and music and poetry, reclaimed by the benign sweetness of its petals and leaves from the subhuman mechanistic domain of evil.

And then, the rose of fire: that core of eternal radiance in which Dante beheld the Beatific Vision; this rose still illuminates the heart of Poets:

> ". . . From my little span
> I cry of Christ, Who is the ultimate Fire
> Who will burn away the cold in the heart of Man. . . ."
> Springs come, springs go. . . .
> "I was reddere on Rode than the Rose in the rayne."
> "This smel is Crist, clepid the plantynge of the Rose of Jerico."
> (Edith Sitwell, "The Canticle of the Rose")

And:

> All shall be well and
> All manner of thing shall be well
> When the tongues of flame are in-folded
> Into the crowned knot of fire
> And the fire and the rose are one.
> (T. S. Eliot, "Little Gidding")

1950

A Note on
Pierre-Joseph Redouté
(1750-1840)

For the reproductions of his water colors, he invented a process of printing in colors which he never consented to perfect to the point where it would be completely mechanical. Each one of these prints had further to be retouched by hand. They owe to these light but indispensable retouchings the capricious illusion and movement of life—a life prolonged beyond its term. In effect, the greater part of the roses who posed for Redouté no longer exist today, in nature. Rosarians are not conservators. They have come to create a race of roses, they do not care whether they shall endure, but only that they, the creators, shall give shape to a new race. So the old species disappear little by little; or if they survive, it is not in famous rosaries, which disdain them, but in old gardens, scattered, forgotten, where there is no concern for fashions in flowers.

Jean-Louis Vaudoyer: Les Roses de Bagatelle

Here is an eye-witness description of Pierre-Joseph Redouté: "A short thick body, with the members of an elephant, a face heavy and flat as a Holland cheese, thick lips, a dull voice, crooked fat fingers, a repellent aspect altogether; and under this rind, an extreme fineness of tact, exquisite taste, a profound sense of the arts, great delicacy of feeling, with the elevation of character and constancy in his work necessary to develop his genius: such was Redouté, the painter of flowers, who had as his students all the pretty women in Paris." This is by Joseph-François Grillé, a lively gossip in his time.

A writer of our own time, looking at Redouté's portraits, by Gérard and others, concludes: "In spite of the solid redingote, the ample cravat and the standing collar of the bourgeois, his portraits make one think of some old gardener weathered and wrinkled like a winter apple."

Dear me: I have seen only the engraving after a painting by Gérard, and can find nothing at all strange, much less monstrous, in it. He seems a man of moderate build, in the becoming dress of his age, though plainer than most; with a very good face indeed with rather blunt features, and pleasant, candid, attentive eyes. Perhaps Gérard loved the man who lived inside that unpromising but useful rind, and showed him as he really was.

He was born in Saint-Hubert, Belgium, the son and grandson of artisan-painters, decorators of churches and municipal buildings. His two brothers became also painter-decorators. In the hardy fashion of the times, after a solid apprenticeship to his father, at the age of thirteen he was turned out in the world to make his own way. Dreaming of fame, riches, glory, he roamed all Belgium and Flanders looking for jobs and starving by the way. He took a year of hard work at Liège in the ateliers of famous painters and was sent to Luxembourg to paint portraits of his first royalties, the Princess de Tornaco and others. The Princess was so pleased with his work she gave him letters to present to certain persons of quality residing in Versailles.

In Flanders he studied deeply the painters of the ancient Flemish school. After ten years of this laborious apprenticeship, he joined his elder brother Antoine-Ferdinand in Paris; Antoine-Ferdinand had all that time been unadventurously earning a good living as painter-decorator. Pierre-Joseph helped his brother decorate the Italian Theater, and painted flowers wherever he was allowed. He learned the art of engraving, and he managed to get into the King's Garden, a botanical wonder, in that time, of royal and noble gardens, in order to study, draw and paint plants and flowers. There he met Charles-Louis L'Héritier of Belgium, a man of great wealth, an impassioned botanist and adherent of the classical methods of Linnaeus.

From this time Redouté's history is the straight road to fame, fortune, and the happy life of a man capable of total constancy to his own gifts, who had the great good fortune to be born at the right hour in time, in the right place, and with the pure instinct which led him infallibly to the place where he could flourish and the people who needed and wanted precisely the thing that he could do. The rage for botanical gardening which had been growing for nearly two centuries had reached its climax. Only the royal, the noble, only the newly rich could afford these extravagant collections of rare shrubs, trees, flowers. There were no more simple adorers of flowers, but collectors of rarities and amateur botanists. It was an age of nature lovers, whose true god was science. Redouté was a botanist and a scientist, a decorator with a superior talent for painting. He stepped into the whole company of such combination scientists and decorator-artisans which surrounded and lived by the bounty of rich amateurs. Armed with brush, pencil, microscope, copper plates, stains, colors and acids, they adhered mightily and single-mindedly to their sources of benefits—intellectual bees, they were. Nothing could have been more touching than their indifference to social significance: they hadn't got the faintest notion where the times were driving them, or why; theirs only to pursue their personal passions and pleasures with scientific concentration, theirs to invent new processes of engraving, coloring, more exact representations of the subject in hand. The gardeners were concerned only to invent new roses, the botanists to botanize them, the artist-artisans to anatomize and engrave them. They were good workmen to whom the employment and not the employer was important.

It is astonishing how a world may turn over, and a whole society fall into ruin, and yet there is always a large population which survives, and hardly knows what has happened; indeed, can with all good faith write as a student in Paris did to his anxious father in Bordeaux, at the very height of the troubles of 1792: "All is quiet here," he declared, mentioning casually an execution or so. Later, he gave most painful descriptions of seeing, at every step in the street, the hideous bleeding rags of corpses piled up, uncovered; once he saw seven tumbrils of them being hauled away, the wheels leaving long tracks of blood. Yet there was dancing in the streets (he did not like to dance), bonfires at the slightest pretext (he hated bonfires), and all public places of entertainment were going at full speed. A craze for a new game called Coblentz, later Yo-yo, came to the point that everybody played it no matter where, all the time. When the King was beheaded, in January, 1793, Mercier tells how people rushed to dip handkerchiefs, feathers, bits of paper in his blood, like human hyenas: one man dipped his finger in it, tasted it, and said: "It's beastly salty!" (*Il est bougrement salé!*) Yet no doubt there were whole streets and sections where no terror came. Our student, an ardent Republican and stern moralist, got his four years of tutoring and college, exactly as planned. The Collège de France opened its doors promptly every autumn the whole time he was there.

Redouté, in the center of the royal family, as private painting teacher to the Queen, later appointed as "Designer of the Royal Academy of Sciences," designer in Marie Antoinette's own Cabinet, seemed destined to go almost as untouched by political disasters as the student writing to his father. On the very eve of the revolution, he was called before the royal family in the Temple, to watch the unfolding of a particularly ephemeral cactus bloom, and to paint it at its several stages.

When the Queen was put to death in October, 1793, it was David, patriot-painter, who made the terrible little sketch of her in the cart on her way to the scaffold: a sunken-faced old woman with chopped-off hair, the dress of a fishwife, hands bound behind her, eyes closed: but her head carried as high, her spine as straight, as if she were on her throne. We see for the first time clearly the long curved masculine-looking nose, the brutal Hapsburg jaw. But something else that perhaps David did not mean to show comes through his sparse strokes: as if all the elements of her character in life had been transmuted in the hour of her death—stubbornness to strength, arrogance to dignity, recklessness to courage, frivolity to tragedy. It is wonderful what strange amends David, moved by hatred, made to his victim*

Her friendly, but preoccupied, painter-decorator happened to be in England with L'Héritier, who had done some very fancy work indeed getting away with a treasure of botanical specimens against a capricious government order. The two sat poring over their precious loot in perfect peace while France was being put together again. They returned, and went on with their work under the National Convention, which took great pride in the embellishment of the King's Garden, re-named the Garden of Natural History. (By 1823, after four overturns of the French government, this garden settled down for a good while under the name of the Museum of Natural History of the King's Garden.)

Josephine Bonaparte of course had the most lavish, extravagant collection of rare plants, trees, and flowers at Malmaison, and Redouté be-

---

* In 1790, the Queen's lover, Count Fersen, wrote to his sister: "She is an angel of courage, of conduct, of sensibility: no one ever knew how to love as she does." He had known her since they were both eighteen years old, and had been her lover for more than five years. He had himself all the qualities he found in her, and more.

came her faithful right hand as painter, decorator, straight through her career as Empress, and until her death. In the meantime he was teacher of painting to Empress Marie-Louise; went on to receive a gold medal from the hand of Louis XVIII for his invention of color printing from a single plate; the ribbon of the Legion of Honor was bestowed upon him by Charles X, in 1825; he painted the portrait of the rose named for Queen Marie Amélie; and lived to see his adored pupil Princess Marie-Louise, elder daughter of Louis-Philippe, become Queen of the Belgians.

During one upset or another, his beautiful house and garden at Fleury-sous-Meudon, were almost destroyed; he seems to have invested all the handsome fortune he had made in this place. Yet he simply moved into Paris with his family and went on working. In 1830 again there were the crowds milling savagely in the gardens of the Royal Palace, this time roaring: "Long live the Charter. Down with Charles X! Down with the Bourbons!" Charles went down and Louis-Philippe came in, the last king Redouté was to see. While royal figures came and went in the Tuileries, "that inn for crowned transients," as Béranger remarked, the painters Gérard, Isabey, and Redouté remained a part of the furniture of the Crown, no matter who wore it.

Such a charmed life! Only one of that huge company of men living in the tranced reality of science and art, was for a moment in danger. L'Héritier almost got his head cut off during the first revolution; in 1805 he was killed in the street near his own door—I have seen no account which says why. Did even those who murdered him know why they did it? Did L'Héritier himself know?

The story of Redouté's labors, his teaching, painting, engraving, his valuable discoveries in methods of engraving, coloring plates, and printing, is overwhelming. He worked as he breathed, with such facility, fertility of resources, and abundant energy, he was the wonder of his colleagues, themselves good masters of the long hard day's work. Redouté is said to have painted more than one thousand pictures of roses alone, many of them now vanished; it is on these strange, beautiful portrait-anatomies that his popular fame endures. He loved fame, and was honestly eager for praise, like a good child; but he took no short cuts to gain them, nor any unworthy method. When he invented a certain process of printing in colors, he saw its danger, and stopped short of perfecting it; he did not want any work to become altogether mechanical. All his prints made by this process required to be retouched by hand, for as a good artist he understood, indeed had learned from nature itself, the divine law of uniqueness: that no two leaves on the same tree are ever exactly alike.

His life had classical shape and symmetry. It began with sound gifts in poverty, labor and high human aspirations, rose to honestly won fame and wealth, with much love, too, and admiration without envy from his fellow artists and his students. It went on to very old age in losses and poverty again, with several friends and a royalty or two making ineffectual gestures toward his relief. But then, his friends, both artist and royal, were seeing hard times too. On the day of his death he received a student for a lesson. The student brought him a lily, and he died holding it.

1950

Portrait: Old South

I am the grandchild of a lost War, and I have blood-knowledge of what life can be in a defeated country on the bare bones of privation. The older people in my family used to tell such amusing little stories about it. One time, several years after the War ended, two small brothers (one of them was my father) set out by themselves on foot from their new home in south Texas, and when neighbors picked them up three miles from home, hundreds of miles from their goal, and asked them where they thought they were going, they answered confidently, "To Louisiana, to eat sugar cane," for they hadn't tasted sugar for months and remembered the happy times in my grandmother's cane fields there.

Does anyone remember the excitement when for a few months we had rationed coffee? In my grandmother's day, in Texas, everybody seemed to remember that man who had a way of showing up with a dozen grains of real coffee in his hand, which he exchanged for a month's supply of corn meal. My grandmother parched a mixture of sweet potato and dried corn until it was black, ground it up and boiled it, because her family couldn't get over its yearning for a dark hot drink in the mornings. But she would never allow them to call it coffee. It was known as That Brew. Bread was a question, too. Wheat flour, during the period euphemistically described as Reconstruction, ran about $100 a barrel. Naturally my family ate corn bread, day in, day out, for years. Finally Hard Times eased up a little, and they had hot biscuits, nearly all they could eat, once a week for Sunday breakfast. My father never forgot the taste of those biscuits, the big, crusty tender kind made with buttermilk and soda, with melted butter and honey, every blessed Sunday that came. "They almost made a Christian of me," he said.

My grandfather, a soldier, toward the end of the War was riding along one very cold morning, and he saw, out of all reason, a fine big thick slice of raw bacon rind lying beside the road. He dismounted, picked it up, dusted it off and made a hearty breakfast of it. "The best piece of bacon rind I ever ate in my life," said my grandfather. These little yarns are the first that come to mind out of hundreds; they were the merest surface ripples over limitless deeps of bitter memory. My elders all remained nobly unreconstructed to their last moments, and my feet rest firmly on this rock of their strength to this day.

The woman who made That Brew and the soldier who ate the bacon rind had been bride and groom in a Kentucky wedding somewhere around 1850. Only a few years ago a cousin of mine showed me a letter from a lady then rising ninety-five who remembered that wedding as if it had been only yesterday. She was one of the flower girls, carrying a gilded basket of white roses and ferns, tied with white watered-silk ribbon. She couldn't remember whether the bride's skirt had been twenty-five feet or twenty-five yards around, but she inclined to the latter figure; it was of white satin brocade with slippers to match.

The flower girl was allowed a glimpse of the table set for the bridal banquet. There were silver branched candlesticks everywhere, each holding seven white candles, and a crystal chandelier holding fifty white candles, all lighted. There was a white lace tablecloth reaching to the floor all around, over white satin. The wedding cake was tall as the flower girl and of astonishing circumference, festooned all over with white sugar roses and green leaves, actual live rose leaves. The room, she wrote, was a perfect bower of southern smilax and white dogwood. And there was butter. This is a bizarre note, but there was an enormous silver butter dish, *with feet* (italics mine), containing at least ten pounds of butter. The dish had cupids and some sort of fruit around the rim, and the butter was molded or carved, to resemble a set-piece of roses and lilies, every petal and leaf standing out sharply, natural as life. The flower girl, after the lapse of nearly a century, remembered no more than this, but I think it does well for a glimpse.

That butter. She couldn't get over it, and neither can I. It seems as late-Roman and decadent as anything ever thought up in Hollywood. Her memory came back with a rush when she thought of the food. All the children had their own table in a small parlor, and ate just what the grownups had: Kentucky ham, roast turkey, partridges in wine jelly, fried chicken, dove pie, half a dozen sweet and hot sauces, peach pickle, watermelon pickle and spiced mangoes. A dozen different fruits, four kinds of cake and at last a chilled custard in tall glasses with whipped cream capped by a brandied cherry. She lived to boast of it, and she lived along with other guests of that feast to eat corn pone and bacon fat, and yes, to be proud of that also. Why not? She was in the best of company, and quite a large gathering too.

In my childhood we ate, my father remarked, "as if there were no God." By then my grandmother, her brocaded wedding gown cut up and made over to the last scrap for a dozen later brides in the connection, had become such a famous cook it was mentioned in her funeral eulogies. There was nobody like her for getting up a party, for the idea of food was inseparably connected in her mind with social occasions of a delightful nature, and though she loved to celebrate birthdays and holidays, still any day was quite good enough to her. Several venerable old gentlemen, lifelong friends of my grandmother, sat down, pen in hand, after her death and out of their grateful recollection of her bountiful hospitality—their very words—wrote long accounts of her life and works for the local newspapers of their several communities, and each declared that at one time or another he had eaten the best dinner of his life at her table. The furnishings of her table were just what were left over from times past, good and bad; a mixture of thin old silver and bone-handled knives, delicate porcelain, treasured but not hoarded, and such crockery as she had been able to replace with; fine old linen worn thin and mended, and stout cotton napery with fringed borders; no silver candlesticks at all, and a pound of sweet butter with a bouquet of roses stamped upon it, in a plain dish—plain for the times; it was really a large opal-glass hen seated on a woven nest, rearing aloft her scarlet comb and beady eye.

Grandmother was by nature lavish, she loved leisure and calm, she loved luxury, she loved dress and adornment, she loved to sit and talk with friends or listen to music; she did not in the least like pinching or saving and mending and making things do, and she had no patience with the kind of slackness that tried to say second-best was best, or half good enough. But the evil turn of fortune in her life tapped the bottomless reserves of her character, and her life was truly heroic. She had no such romantic notion of herself. The long difficulties of her life she regarded

as temporary, an unnatural interruption to her normal fate, which required simply firmness, a good deal of will-power and energy and the
proper aims to re-establish finally once more. That no such change took
place during her long life did not in the least disturb her theory. Though
we had no money and no prospects of any, and were land-poor in the
most typical way, we never really faced this fact as long as our grandmother lived because she would not hear of such a thing. We had been a
good old family of solid wealth and property in Kentucky, Louisiana and
Virginia, and we remained that in Texas, even though due to a temporary decline for the most honorable reasons, appearances were entirely to
the contrary. This accounted for our fragmentary, but strangely useless
and ornamental education, appropriate to our history and our station in
life, neither of which could be in the least altered by the accident of
straitened circumstances.

Grandmother had been an unusually attractive young woman, and she
carried herself with the graceful confidence of a natural charmer to her
last day. Her mirror did not deceive her, she saw that she was old. Her
youthful confidence became matriarchal authority, a little way of knowing best about almost everything, of relying upon her own experience for
sole guide, and I think now she had earned her power fairly. Her bountiful hospitality represented only one of her victories of intelligence and
feeling over the stubborn difficulties of life. Her mind and her instinct
ran in flashes of perception, and she sometimes had an airy, sharp, impatient way of speaking to those who didn't keep up with her. She believed
it was her duty to be a stern methodical disciplinarian, and made a point
of training us as she had been trained even to forbidding us to cross our
knees, or to touch the back of our chair when we sat, or to speak until we
were spoken to: love's labors lost utterly, for she had brought up a
houseful of the worst spoiled children in seven counties, and started in
again hopefully with a long series of motherless grandchildren—for the
daughters of that afterwar generation did not survive so well as their
mothers, they died young in great numbers, leaving young husbands and
children—who were to be the worst spoiled of any. She never punished
anyone until she was exasperated beyond all endurance, when she was
apt to let fly with a lightning, long-armed slap at the most unexpected
moments, usually quite unjustly and ineffectually.

Truth was, when she had brought her eleven children into the world,
she had had a natural expectation of at least as many servants to help her

bring them up; her gifts were social, and she should never have had the care of children except in leisure, for then she was delightful, and communicated some of her graces to them, and gave them beautiful memories. We loved the smell of her face powder and the light orange-flower perfume she wore, the crinkled waves of her hair, the knot speared through with a small pointed Spanish comb. We leaned upon her knee, and sniffed in the sweetness of her essential being, we nuzzled her face and the little bit of lace at her collar, enchanted with her sweetness.

Her hands were long since ruined, but she was proud of her narrow feet with their high insteps, and liked to dress them in smooth black kid boots with small spool-shaped heels. When she went "abroad"—that is, shopping, calling, or to church—she wore her original mourning gowns, of stiff, dull, corded silks, made over and refurbished from time to time, and a sweeping crape veil that fell from a peaked cap over her face and to the hem of her skirt in the back. This mourning had begun for her husband, dead only twenty-five years, but it went on for him, and for her daughters and for grandchildren, and cousins, and then brothers and sisters, and, I suspect, for an old friend or so. In this garb, holding up her skirt in front with one black-gloved hand, she would walk with such flying lightness her grandchild would maintain a heated trot to keep pace with her.

She loved to have us say our prayers before bedtime in a cluster around her knees, and in our jealousy to be nearest, and to be first, we often fell fighting like a den of bear cubs, instead of christened children, and she would have to come in among us like an animal trainer, the holy hour having gone quite literally to hell. "Birds in their little nests agree, and 'tis a shameful sight," she would remark on these occasions, but she never finished the rhyme, and for years I wondered why it was a shameful sight for little birds to agree, when Grandmother was rather severe with us about our quarreling. It was "vulgar," she said, and for her, that word connoted a peculiarly detestable form of immorality, that is to say, bad manners. Inappropriate conduct was bad manners, bad manners were bad morals, and bad morals led to bad manners, and there you were, ringed with fire, and no way out.

She was an individual being if ever I knew one, and yet she never did or said anything to make herself conspicuous; there are no strange stories to tell, no fantastic gestures. She rode horseback at a gallop until the year of her death, but it seemed only natural. Her sons had to restrain her from an engineering project, which seemed very simple to her and perhaps was really simple: she had wished to deflect the course of a small river which was encroaching on her land in Louisiana; she knew exactly how it should be done, and it would have made all the difference, she felt. She smoked cubeb cigarettes, for her throat, she would say, and add that she had always imagined she would enjoy the taste of tobacco. She and my father would sit down for a noggin of hot toddy together on cold evenings, or just a drop of good Bourbon before dinner because they enjoyed it. She could not endure to see a horse with its head strung up in a checkrein, and used to walk down a line of conveyances drawn up around the church, saying amiably to the dozing Negro drivers, "Good morning, Jerry; good morning, Uncle Squire," reaching up deftly and loosing the checkrein. The horses hung their heads and so did the drivers, and the reins stayed unfastened for that time, at any rate.

In a family full of willful eccentrics and headstrong characters and unpredictable histories, her presence was singularly free from peaks and edges and the kind of color that leaves a trail of family anecdotes. She left the lingering perfume and the airy shimmer of grace about her memory.

1944

Audubon's Happy Land

The center of St. Francisville is ugly as only small towns trying frantically to provide gasoline and sandwiches to passing motorists can be, but its lanelike streets unfold almost at once into grace and goodness. On the day of our visit, the only sign of special festivity was a splendid old Negro, in top hat, frock coat with nosegay in buttonhole, a black cotton umbrella shading his venerable head, seated before the casually contrived small office where we bought our tickets for the Audubon pilgrimage and were joined by our guide. The old Negro rose, bowed, raised his hat at arm's length to an angle of forty-five degrees more or less, playing his role in the ceremonies not only as a detail of the scene, but as part also of its history. Our guide appeared in a few minutes, tying a flowered kerchief under her chin, *babushka* fashion, as she came. She was dark and thin and soft-voiced, so typically Louisiana French that we thought she must be from New Orleans, or the Bayou Teche country. It turned out that she was from Idaho, lately married to a cousin of the Percys at "Greenwood." No matter; she belonged also, by virtue of love and attachment, as well as appearance, to the scene and its history.

Saint Francis, who preached to the birds, and Audubon, who painted them as no one before or since, are both commemorated in this place. In 1779, the monks of Saint Francis founded the town and christened it. Spain ruled the territory then, though the brothers Le Moyne—Iberville and Bienville—had claimed it three quarters of a century before for France. The Spanish government made a classical error with the classical result. It invited wealthy foreign investors to help settle the country, and the foreign investors ended by taking final possession. These particular foreigners bore such names as Ratliff, Barrow, Wade, Hamilton, Percy; they were all men of substance and of worldly mind, mostly from Virginia and the Carolinas, who obtained by Spanish grant splendid parcels of land of about twelve thousand acres each. These acres formed a subtropical jungle to the very banks of the Mississippi. A man could not, said an old woodsman, sink his hunting knife to the hilt in it anywhere.

The newcomers had on their side the strong arm of slave labor, and definite views on caste, property, morals, and manners. They pushed back the Louisiana jungle mile by mile, uncovered rich lands, and raised splendid crops. They built charming houses and filled them with furniture from France and England. Their silver and porcelain and linen were such as befitted their pride, which was high, and their tastes, which were delicate and expensive. Their daughters sang, danced, and played the harpsichord; their sons played the flute and fought duels; they collected libraries, they hunted and played chess, and spent the winter season in New Orleans. They traveled much in Europe, and brought back always more and more Old World plunder. Everywhere, with ceaseless, intensely personal concern, they thought, talked, and played politics.

In a few short years, these wealthy, nostalgic Americans were, in the phrase of the day, "groaning under the galling yoke of Spain." They forgathered evening after evening in one or another of their mansions and groaned; that is to say, discussed the matter with shrewdness, realism, and a keen eye to the possibilities. They called upon President Madison to lend a hand in taking this territory from Spain, which continued to hold it for some reason long after the Louisiana Purchase. "President Madison," says a local historian of that day, "remained deaf to their cries." The Feliciana planters then stopped crying, organized a small army, and marched on the Spanish capital, Baton Rouge. Harsh as it sounds in such a gentlemanly sort of argument, they caused the Spanish Commandant to be killed as proof of the seriousness of their intentions. They then declared for themselves the Independent Republic of West Florida, with St. Francisville as its capital. A certain Mr. Fulwar Skipwith was elected President. All was done in form, with a Constitution, a Body of Laws, and a flag designed for the occasion. The strategy was a brilliant success. President Madison sent friendly troops to annex the infant republic to the United States of America. This Graustarkian event took place in 1810.

The next year, a Roosevelt (Nicholas), partner in an Eastern steamship company, sent the first steamboat into the Mississippi, straight past St. Francisville and her sister town, Bayou Sara. The days of opulence and glory began in earnest, based solidly on land, money crops, and transportation, to flourish for just half a century.

It is quite finished as to opulence, and the glory is now a gentle aura, radiating not so much from the past as from the present, for St. Francisville lives with graceful competence on stored wealth that is not merely tangible. The legend has, in fact, magnified the opulence into something more than it really was, to the infinite damage of a particular truth: that wealth in the pre-War South was very modest by present standards, and it was not ostentatious, even then. The important thing to know about St. Francisville, as perhaps a typical survivor of that culture, is this: no one there tells you about steamboat wealth, or wears the air of poverty living on its memories, or (and this is the constant, rather tiresome accusation of busy, hasty observers) "yearns for the good old days."

The town's most treasured inhabitant was Audubon, and its happiest memory. This is no afterthought, based on his later reputation. And it is the more interesting when we consider what kind of reputation Audubon's was, almost to the end; nothing at all that a really materialistic society would take seriously. He was an artist, but not a fashionable one, never successful by any worldly standards; but the people of St. Francisville loved him, recognized him, took him to themselves when he was unknown and almost in despair. And now in every house, they will show you some small memento of him, some record that he was once a guest there. The Pirries, of New Orleans and Oakley, near St. Francisville, captured him in New Orleans at the moment when he was heading East, disheartened, and brought him to Oakley for the pleasant employment of teaching their young daughter, Miss Eliza, to dance and draw, of mornings. His afternoons, and some of his evenings, he spent in the Feliciana woods, and we know what he found there.

The Feliciana country is not a jungle now, nor has it been for a great while. The modest, occasional rises of earth, called hills, are covered with civilized little woods, fenced grazing-fields for fine cattle, thatches of sugar cane, of corn, and orchards. Both Felicianas, east and west, are so handsome and amiable you might mistake them for one, instead of twins. For fear they will be confounded in the stranger's eye, the boundaries are marked plainly along the highway. The difference was to me that West Feliciana was holding a spring festival in honor of Audubon, and I, a returned Southerner, in effect a tourist, went straight through East Feliciana, which had not invited visitors, to West Feliciana, which had.

You are to think of this landscape as an April garden, flowering with trees and shrubs of the elegant, difficult kind that live so securely in this climate: camellias, gardenias, crêpe myrtle, fine old-fashioned roses; with simpler things, honeysuckle, dogwood, wisteria, magnolia, bridal-wreath, oleander, redbud, leaving no fence or corner bare. The birds of Saint Francis and of Audubon fill the air with their light singing and their undisturbed flight. The great, dark oaks spread their immense branches fronded with moss; the camphor and cedar trees add their graceful shapes and their dry, spicy odors; and yes, just as you have been told, perhaps too often, there are the white, pillared houses seated in dignity, glimpsed first at a distance through their parklike gardens.

The celebrated oak *allées* are there at "Live Oak," at "Waverly," at "Rosedown," perhaps the finest grove of all at "Highland"—the wide, shaded driveways from the gate to the great door, all so appropriately designed for the ritual events of life, a wedding or a funeral procession, the christening party, the evening walks of betrothed lovers. W. B. Yeats causes one of his characters to reflect, in face of a grove of ancient trees, "that a man who planted trees, knowing that no descendant nearer than his great-grandson could stand under their shade, had a noble and generous confidence." That kind of confidence created this landscape, now as famous, as banal, if you like, as the horse-chestnuts along the Champs Elysées, as the perfume gardens of Grasse, as the canals of Venice, as the lilies-of-the-valley in the forest of Saint-Cloud. It possesses, too, the appeal of those much-visited scenes, and shares their nature, which is to demand nothing by way of arranged tribute; each newcomer may discover it for himself; but this landscape shares its peculiar treasure only with such as know there is something more here than mere hungry human pride in mahogany staircases and silver doorknobs. The real spirit of the place planted those oaks, and keeps them standing.

The first thing that might strike you is the simplicity, the comparative smallness of even the largest houses (in plain figures, "Greenwood" is one hundred feet square; there is a veranda one hundred and ten feet long at "The Myrtles," a long, narrow house), compared not only to the grandeur of their legend, but to anything of corresponding fame you may have seen, such as the princely houses of Florence or the Spanish palaces in Mexico, or, as a last resort, the Fifth Avenue museums of the fantastically rich of two or three generations ago. Their importance is of another kind—that of the oldest New York houses, or the Patrizieren houses in Basel; with a quality nearly akin to the Amalienburg in the forest near Munich, quite the loveliest house I ever saw, or expect to see. These St. Francisville houses are examples of pure domestic architecture, somehow urban in style, graceful, and differing from city houses in this particular, that they sit in landscapes designed to show them off; they are meant to be observed from every point of view. No two of them are alike, but they were all built to be lived in, by people who had a completely aristocratic sense of the house as a dwelling-place.

They are ample and their subtle proportions give them stateliness not accounted for in terms of actual size. They are placed in relation to the south wind and the morning sun. Their ceilings are high, because high ceilings are right for this kind of architecture, and this kind of architecture is right for a hot climate. Their fireplaces are beautiful, well placed, in harmony with the rooms, and meant for fine log fires in the brief winters. Their windows are many, tall and rightly spaced for light and air, as well as for the view outward. All of them, from "Live Oak," built in 1779, to "The Myrtles," built in the 1840's, have in common the beauty and stability of cypress, blue poplar, apparently indestructible brick made especially for the chimneys and foundations, old methods of mortising and pinning, hand-forged nails.

"Live Oak" stands on a green knoll, and, from the front door, one looks straight through the central room to the rolling meadow bordered with iris in profuse bloom. This house is really tired, worn down to the bare grain, the furniture just what might have been left from some remote disaster, but it is beautiful, a place to live in, with its wide, double porches and outside staircase in the early style of the Spanish in Louisiana, its dark paneling, and its air of gentle remoteness.

"Waverly" is another sort of thing altogether, a bright place full of color, where the old furniture is set off with gaily flowered rugs, and the heavy old Louisiana four-poster beds—of a kind to be found nowhere else—are dressed sprucely in fresh curtains. The white pillars of "Waverly" are flat and slender, and the graceful fan-lights of the front door are repeated on the second floor, with an especially airy effect. The vestiges of the old boxwood maze are being coaxed back to life there, and gardenias grow in hedges, as they should.

At "The Myrtles," the flowery iron grille of the long veranda sets the Victorian tone; the long dining-room still wears, between the thin moldings, its French wallpaper from 1840—sepia-colored panels from floor to ceiling of game birds and flowers. The cypress floor is honey-colored, the Italian marble mantelpiece was that day banked with branches of white dogwood. All the rooms are long, full of the softest light lying upon the smooth surfaces of old fruitwood and mahogany. From the back veranda, an old-fashioned back yard, full of country living, lay in the solid shade of grape arbors and trees rounded like baskets of flowers. Chickens roamed and picked there; there was a wood-pile with a great iron wash-pot up-ended against it, near the charred spot where the fire is still built to heat the water.

At "Virginia," we saw George Washington's account-book, made, I believe, at Valley Forge, with all the detailed outlay of that troublesome episode. "Virginia" is by way of being an inn now—that is to say, if travelers happen along they will be put up in tall, canopied beds under fine old quilted coverlets. The large silver spoons in the dining-room came from an ancestor of the Fisher family—Baron de Würmser, who had them as a gift from Frederick the Great. Generous-sized ladles they are, too, paper-thin and flexible. Like so many old coin silver spoons, they appear to have been chewed, and they have been. A thin silver spoon was once considered the ideal object for an infant to cut his teeth upon. But there were dents in a de Würmser soup ladle which testified that some Fisher infant must have been a saber-toothed tiger. "Surely no teething child did that," I remarked. "No," said the hostess, a fleeting shade of severity on her brow. "It was thrown out with the dish-water once, and the pigs got it." Here is the French passport for a Fisher grandfather, dated 1836. It was then he brought back the splendid flowered wallpaper, even now fresh in its discreet colors, the hand-painted mauve linen window-shades on rollers, then so fashionable, replacing the outmoded Venetian blinds; the ornate, almost morbidly feminine drawing-room chairs and sofas.

At "Greenwood," the host was engaged with a group of oil prospectors, for, beneath their charming, fruitful surfaces, the Felicianas are suspected of containing the dark, the sinister new treasure more powerful than gold. If so, what will become of the oaks and the flourishing fields and the gentle cattle? What will become of these lovely houses? "They make syrup and breed cattle here," said our guide; "that keeps 'Greenwood' going very well. Some people [she named them] wanted Mr. Percy to make a dude ranch of this place, but he wouldn't hear of it."

We mentioned our premonitions about St. Francisville if oil should be discovered. Our guide spoke up with the quiet recklessness of faith. "It wouldn't do any harm," she said. "The Feliciana people have had what money can buy, and they have something money can't buy, and they know it. They have nothing to sell. Tourists come here from all over and offer them thousands of dollars for their little things, just little things they don't need and hardly ever look at, but they won't sell them."

"Greenwood" is the typical Southern mansion of too many songs, too many stories—with the extravagant height of massive, round pillar, the too-high ceiling, the gleaming sweep of central hall, all in the 1830 Greek, gilded somewhat, but lightly. There is bareness; space dwarfing the human stature and breathing a faint bleakness. Yet the gentle groves and small hills are framed with overwhelming effect between those columns; effect grandiose beyond what the measuring eye knows is actually there.

It seems now that the builders should have known that this house was the end, never the beginning. It is quite improbable that anyone should again build a house like "Greenwood" to live in. But there it is, with the huge beams of the gallery being replaced, oil prospectors roaming about, and the hostess sitting in her drawing-room with the green-and-gold chairs, the lace curtains fine as bride veils drifting a little; the young girls in jodhpurs are going out to ride. Here, as everywhere else, there were no radios or gramophones going, no telephones visible or ringing; and it seemed to me suddenly that this silence, the silence of a house in order, of people at home, the silence of leisure, is the most desirable of all things we have lost.

At "Highland," descendants in the fourth generation stand in the shade of the oaks planted, as the old House Book records, in January, 1832. The house is older. It has its share of drum tables, fiddle-backed chairs, carved door-frames and wainscoting, but its real beauty lies in the fall of light into the ample, square rooms, the rise of the stair tread, the energy and firmness of its structure. The paneled doors swing on their hand-forged hinges as they did the day they were hung there; the edge of the first doorstep—an immense log of cypress square-hewn—is as sharp as though feet had not stepped back and forth over it for one hundred and forty years.

"Rosedown" is more formal, with its fish pool and eighteenth-century statuary set along the *allée*, and in a semicircle before the conventionally planted garden. The office still stands there, and the "slave bell" in its low wooden frame. The "slave bell" was the dinner-bell for the whole plantation. Above all, at "Rosedown," the Ancestors still rule, still lend their unquenchable life to a little world of fabulous old ladies and a strange overgrowth of knickknacks sprouting like small, harmless fungi on a tree-trunk. Their portraits—Sully seems to have been the preferred painter—smile at you, or turn their attentive heads toward one another; as handsome and as gallant and elegantly dressed a set of young men and women as you would be apt to find blood-kin under one roof. "My great-great-grandfather," said the old, old lady, smiling back again at the high-headed, smooth-cheeked young beau in the frilled shirt-bosom and deep blue, sloping-shouldered coat. His eyes are the same bright hazel as her own. This was the only house in which the past lay like a fine dust in the air.

Steamboats brought wealth and change to St. Francisville once, and oil may do it again. In that case, we are to suppose that new grand pianos would replace the old, square, black Steinways of 1840, as they had in turn replaced the harpsichords. There would be a great deal of shoring up, replacement, planting, pruning, and adding. There would be travel again, and humanistic education. The young people who went away cannot, alas, come back young, but the young there now would not have to go away.

And what else would happen to this place, so occupied, so self-sufficient, so reassuringly solid and breathing? St. Francisville is not a monument, nor a decor, nor a wailing-wall for mourners for the past. It is a living town, moving at its own pace in a familiar world. But it was comforting to take a last glance backward as we turned into the main highway, at Audubon's Happy Land, reflecting that, for the present, in the whole place, if you except the fruits of the earth and the picture postcards at "Rosedown," there was nothing, really nothing, for sale.

1939

A House of My Own

Not long ago, my sister returned to me a bundle of my letters to her, dated from my nineteenth year. My life has been, to say the least, varied: I have lived in five countries and traveled in several more. But at recurring intervals I wrote, in all seriousness: "Next year I shall find a little house in the country and settle there." Meantime I was looking at little houses in the country, all sorts of houses in all sorts of countries.

I shopped with friends in Bucks County long before that place became the fashion. I chose a perfect old stone house and barn sitting on a hill there, renovated it splendidly, and left it forever, all in one fine June morning. In this snapshot style, I have also possessed beautiful old Texas ranch houses; a lovely little Georgian house in Alexandria, Virginia; an eighteenth-century Spanish-French house in Louisiana.

I have stood in a long daydream over an empty, roofless shell of white coral in Bermuda; in several parts of my native South, I admired and would have been glad to live in one of those little, sloping-roofed, chimneyed houses the Negroes live in, houses quite perfectly proportioned and with such dignity in their desolation. In Mexico, I have walked through empty, red-tiled houses, in their patios, and under their narrow, arched cloisters, living a lifetime there in a few hours. In Switzerland, my house was tall, steep-roofed, the very one I chose was built in 1390. It was still occupied, however, with lace curtains at the window and a cat asleep on the window sill. In France, it was a pleasant house, standing flush to the village street, with a garden in back. Indeed, I have lived for a few hours in any number of the most lovely houses in the world.

There was never, of course, much money, never quite enough; there was never time, either; there was never permanency of any sort, except the permanency of hope.

This hope had led me to collect an unreasonable amount of furniture and books, unreasonable for one who had no house to keep them in. I lugged them all with me from Mexico to Paris to New York to Louisiana and back to New York, then stored them, and accepted an invitation to Yaddo, in Saratoga Springs. Yaddo invites artists with jobs to finish to come, and work quietly in peace and great comfort, during summers. My invitation was for two months. That was a year ago, and I am still here, seemingly having taken root at North Farm on the estate. Several times I went away for a few weeks, and when I returned, as the train left Albany, I began to have a sense of homecoming. One day, hardly knowing when it happened, I knew I was going to live here, for good and all, and I was going to have a house in the country. I began to move my personal equivalent of heaven and earth to make it possible. As travelers in Europe make it a point of good taste to drink the wine of the country, so I had always chosen the house of the country. Here, the house of the country is plain, somewhat prim, not large, late Colonial; perhaps modified Georgian would be a useful enough description.

Some friends recommended to me an honest man who knew every farm within miles around. "You can believe every word he says," they assured me. On the first of January, in zero weather and deep snow, I explained to him what I was looking for, and we started touring the countryside. My house must be near Saratoga Springs, my favorite small town of all America that I had seen.* It must be handsomely located in a good, but domestic landscape, with generous acres, well-watered and wooded, and it must not cost above a certain modest sum.

Nodding his head understandingly, he drove me at once sixty miles away into Vermont and showed me a nineteen-room house on a rock-bound spot. He showed me, within the next eighteen days, every sort of house from pink brick mansions on a quarter acre to shingle camp bungalows in wild places far from human habitation. We slogged through snow to our knees to inspect Victorian Gothic edifices big enough to house a boarding school. We crept into desolate little shacks where snow and leaves were piled in the corners of the living-room.

Between each wild goose chase, I repeated, patiently and monoto-

* That was *then!*

nously as a trained crow, my simple wants, my unalterable wishes. At last I reminded him that our friends had told me I could believe every word he said, but until he believed every word I said, too, we could make no progress whatever. And I said good-bye, which seemed to make no impression. Two days later he called again and said perhaps he had a house for me, after all.

That was January 21, 1941. As our car turned into the road, a hen pheasant flew up and struck lightly against the radiator-cap and lost a few breast-feathers. With desperate superstition I got out and picked them up and put them in my handbag, saying they might bring me luck.

We drove for a few miles around Saratoga Lake, turned into an inclined road between a great preserve of spruce and pine, turned again to the right on a small rise, and my honest man pointed into the valley before us. I looked at an old Colonial house, rather small, modified Georgian, with a red roof and several cluttery small porches and sheds clinging to its sides. It sat there in a modest state, surrounded by tall, bare trees, against a small hill of evergreen.

"But that is my house," I told him. "That's mine."

We struggled around it again knee-deep in snowdrifts, peering through windows.

"Let's not bother," I said. "I'll take it."

"But you must see inside first," he insisted.

"I know what's inside," I said. "Let's go to see the owner."

The owner, a woman of perhaps fifty who looked incapable of surprise, had to be told several times, in different phrases, that her house was sold at last, really sold. My honest man had had it on his list for seven long years. Her hopes were about exhausted. I gave him a look meant to be terrible, but he missed it, somehow.

She wanted to tell the history of her house. It was one of the first built in this part of the country, by first settlers, related to Benedict Arnold. It had been lived in since the day it was finished; her own family had been there for eighty-five years. She was the last of her immediate family. With a difficult tear, she said that she had buried all her nearest and dearest from that house; and living there alone as she had been, there were times in the winter evenings when it seemed they were all in the same room with her.

In no time at all, it seems now, the transaction was complete, and I was well seized of my property. I had always thought that was a mere picturesque phrase. It is simply a statement of fact. I am seized of my property, and my property is well seized of me. It is described as having one hundred and five acres of meadow and woodland, with two brooks, a spring, and an inexhaustible well. Besides all this, there are forty acres of molding sand, of which eighteen are under contract to a sand dealer. However, I should not mind this, as the land to be mined for sand lay far away; the operations would be conducted safely out of sight. Of this more later.

I remembered a remark of Mr. E. M. Forster on taking possession of his woods: the first thing he noticed was that his land made him feel heavy. I had become almost overnight a ton weight of moral, social, and financial responsibility, subject to state and county tax, school tax, and an astonishing variety of insurance. Besides the moral, legal, and financial aspects peculiar to myself, the affair had become a community interest. My new-found friends gave me any amount of advice, all seriously good. They were anxious about me. They told me how pleased they were I was going to live there. Other friends drove out to visit, inspect, and approve. My house was solid as a church, in foundation, beams, walls, and roof, and the cellar was an example to all cellars.

Friends came up in the spring from New York, strolled in the meadows, picked flowers, and advised me to practice virtue and circumspection in every act of my new life. There began arriving presents, such as five incredibly elegant very early Victorian chairs and settles, Bohemian mirror glass lamps with crystal-beaded shades, cranberry glass bowls.

My life began to shape itself to fit a neighborhood, and that neighborhood included everybody who came near my house or knew that I had got it. All this is strange new pleasure.

And almost at once I encountered some strange new troubles, oh, a sea of them, some of them surprising, yet once encountered, nothing that does not seem more or less in the natural order of being. For example, the inexhaustible well. It was that for a family who drew water by the pailful, but not enough for two little baths and a new kitchen. I went out the other day to look again at my lovely landscape and my beloved house, indeed I can hardly bear to stay away from them, and there were three strange men pulling up the pump, dropping plumb-lines into the well, and sinking points in the earth here and there. They had also with them a rosy-colored, forked, hazel wand, and they almost blushed their heads off when I knew what it was and asked them if it worked.

"Naw, it's all just a lot of nonsense," said the one who was trying to make it work. They all agreed there was nothing in it, but each of them knew several well-diggers who had seen it work or who could even work it themselves. "There are actually men," said one of them, "who just walk around holding it like this, and when he comes to where there is water, it turns and twists itself right out of his hands." But there wasn't anything to it, just the same, and just the same they never go to look for water without taking one along. They haven't found a well yet, but I do not let my mind dwell on this.

The sand man, thinking that the place was vacated and nobody would know or care, came and leveled over the entire slope of my east meadow within a few steps of the house, before I got into action and persuaded him he was, to say it mildly, not within his rights. There is a great and dreadful scar four feet deep and seventy-five feet long, where I had meant to plant the rose hedge, which must be filled in with tons of soil.

I have a tenant house, which a Southern friend described as something transplanted from *Tobacco Road*. Be that as it may. There are broad plans afoot for it, and I am looking for a tenant farmer. With this in view, I bought, of the best and sturdiest, the following implements: one metal rake, one wooden rake, one hoe, one ax (of the kind used by champion wood-cutters in contests), one handsaw, one spading fork, one mattock, one spade, one brush hook, one snath and blade (medium), one wheelbarrow, one long, dangerous-looking scythe blade, one hammer, one ten-inch file, one grindstone, one four-gallon water-pail, and this is the merest beginning. But I have no tenant farmer.

There is a half-ton of old lumber thrown down on a bed of flowers whose name I do not know, but who were just getting ready to bloom. The sand men hacked a road through my pine woods, taking off great branches of fine trees. Contractors came and went in series. Through the years I have collected a small library of architectural magazines, photographs of old houses before and after, plans for remodeling, and a definite point of view of my own. The first man on the ground looked everything over, listened patiently to my plans and hopes, asked me, "Why take all that trouble for an old house?" and disappeared, never to be seen again. The second was magnificently sympathetic and competent, but he was used to building houses for the Whitneys and Vanderbilts and other racing people in Saratoga, and it was impossible to scale down his ideas.

Others went out, pried up the old random-width floors, tore chunks out of the plaster, knocked bricks out of the chimney, pumped out the well, tested beams, ripped slates off the roof, pulled down sheds and porches, and one by one disappeared. . . . I have a contractor, though. He is Swedish, he has been in this country seventeen years, he is an authority on American Colonial houses, and I decided he should do the work when he went through my house, looked around once, nodded his head, and remarked gently, "Ah, yes, I know just what is here." The house and the furniture are only about ten miles apart now. There remains nothing except to draw them together.

It seems a very long ten miles, perhaps the longest I shall ever travel. I am saving the pheasant feathers to burn, for luck, on the first fire I light in the fine old fireplace with its bake oven and graceful mantelpiece. It will be high time for fires again, no doubt, when I get there.

1941

NOTE. July, 1952: I lived there just thirteen months.

A Letter to the Editor of
The Village Voice

Dear Sir:

It is quite true I enjoy *The Village Voice* very much, and you have very nearly had several unsolicited Letters to the Editor about all sorts of things as they came up: Mailer or No Mailer? Those stories about Gay Street: I lived at 15 Gay Street, 1924. Washington Square: I finished my first short story in Madame Branchard's old rooming house at 61 Washington Square South, in a roaring hot July, 1923. There was a brass plate to Alan (Allan?) Seeger on the wall between my two windows; Madame Branchard is long since dead, and the old house was torn down and part of New York University stands there. Where is the Seeger memorial tablet, I wonder?

My first flat was the second-floor-front at 17 Grove Street, 1920. I was running back and forth between Mexico and New York all the twenties, and took a new flat every time. Jones Street, Charles Street, Bank Street, where didn't I live in the Village during the decade? So you see, I'd just be writing personal reminiscences; have you not had enough of those?

In 1936, when I came back from Europe after many years, I took a flat in Perry Street, Number 64 I seem to remember, and wrote "A Day's Work" afterward right out of the quarrels, pouring down an airshaft, of a family in the next flat. So you see I didn't write because it occurred to me very reasonably: Who cares about all this, but me? But I have live memories—it was a very growing season for me, and though I never did then and do not now think of myself as a Villager in the sense of those to whom it is really home, I have my own affections and attachments, and they are right for me, and I would not have missed being there just when I was there, for anything. Everybody finds his own Village in his own time, and usually gets what he is looking for . . . Tell me some time if there is any little special thing you would like me to write about, how many words and all, and I'll be delighted to try. Meantime, go on sending the V.V. and remind me when my subscription runs out.

1956

The Necessary Enemy

She is a frank, charming, fresh-hearted young woman who married for love. She and her husband are one of those gay, good-looking young pairs who ornament this modern scene rather more in profusion perhaps than ever before in our history. They are handsome, with a talent for finding their way in their world, they work at things that interest them, their tastes agree and their hopes. They intend in all good faith to spend their lives together, to have children and do well by them and each other—to be happy, in fact, which for them is the whole point of their marriage. And all in stride, keeping their wits about them. Nothing romantic, mind you; their feet are on the ground.

Unless they were this sort of person, there would be not much point to what I wish to say; for they would seem to be an example of the high-spirited, right-minded young whom the critics are always invoking to come forth and do their duty and practice all those sterling old-fashioned virtues which in every generation seem to be falling into disrepair. As for virtues, these young people are more or less on their own, like most of their kind; they get very little moral or other aid from their society; but after three years of marriage this very contemporary young woman finds herself facing the oldest and ugliest dilemma of marriage.

She is dismayed, horrified, full of guilt and forebodings because she is finding out little by little that she is capable of hating her husband, whom she loves faithfully. She can hate him at times as fiercely and mysteriously, indeed in terribly much the same way, as often she hated her parents, her brothers and sisters, whom she loves, when she was a child. Even then it had seemed to her a kind of black treacherousness in her, her private wickedness that, just the same, gave her her only private life. That was one thing her parents never knew about her, never seemed to suspect. For it was never given a name. They did and said hateful things to her and to each other as if by right, as if in them it was a kind of virtue. But when they said to her, "Control your feelings," it was never when she was amiable and obedient, only in the black times of her hate. So it was her secret, a shameful one. When they punished her, sometimes for the strangest reasons, it was, they said, only because they loved her—it was for her good. She did not believe this, but she thought herself guilty of something worse than ever they had punished her for. None of this really frightened her: the real fright came when she discovered that at times her father and mother hated each other; this was like standing on the doorsill of a familiar room and seeing in a lightning flash that the floor was gone, you were on the edge of a bottomless pit. Sometimes she felt that both of them hated her, but that passed, it was simply not a thing to be thought of, much less believed. She thought she had outgrown all this, but here it was again, an element in her own nature she could not control, or feared she could not. She would have to hide from her husband, if she could, the same spot in her feelings she had hidden from her parents, and for the same no doubt disreputable, selfish reason: she wants to keep his love.

Above all, she wants him to be absolutely confident that she loves him, for that is the real truth, no matter how unreasonable it sounds, and no matter how her own feelings betray them both at times. She depends recklessly on his love; yet while she is hating him, he might very well be hating her as much or even more, and it would serve her right. But she does not want to be served right, she wants to be loved and forgiven—that is, to be sure he would forgive her anything, if he had any notion of what she had done. But best of all she would like not to have anything in her love that should ask for forgiveness. She doesn't mean about their quarrels—they are not so bad. Her feelings are out of proportion, perhaps. She knows it is perfectly natural for people to disagree, have fits of temper, fight it out; they learn quite a lot about each other that way, and not all of it disappointing either. When it passes, her hatred seems quite unreal. It always did.

Love. We are early taught to say it. I love you. We are trained to the thought of it as if there were nothing else, or nothing else worth having without it, or nothing worth having which it could not bring with it. Love is taught, always by precept, sometimes by example. Then hate, which no one meant to teach us, comes of itself. It is true that if we say I love you, it may be received with doubt, for there are times when it is hard to believe. Say I hate you, and the one spoken to believes it instantly, once for all.

Say I love you a thousand times to that person afterward and mean it every time, and still it does not change the fact that once we said I hate you, and meant that too. It leaves a mark on that surface love had worn so smooth with its eternal caresses. Love must be learned, and learned again and again; there is no end to it. Hate needs no instruction, but waits only to be provoked . . . hate, the unspoken word, the unacknowledged presence in the house, that faint smell of brimstone among the roses, that invisible tongue-tripper, that unkempt finger in every pie, that sudden oh-so-curiously *chilling* look—could it be boredom?—on your dear one's features, making them quite ugly. Be careful: love, perfect love, is in danger.

If it is not perfect, it is not love, and if it is not love, it is bound to be hate sooner or later. This is perhaps a not too exaggerated statement of the extreme position of Romantic Love, more especially in America, where we are all brought up on it, whether we know it or not. Romantic Love is changeless, faithful, passionate, and its sole end is to render the two lovers happy. It has no obstacles save those provided by the hazards of fate (that is to say, society), and such sufferings as the lovers may cause each other are only another word for delight: exciting jealousies, thrilling uncertainties, the ritual dance of courtship within the charmed closed circle of their secret alliance; all *real* troubles come from without, they face them unitedly in perfect confidence. Marriage is not the end but only the beginning of true happiness, cloudless, changeless to the end. That the candidates for this blissful condition have never seen an example of it, nor ever knew anyone who had, makes no difference. That is the ideal and they will achieve it.

How did Romantic Love manage to get into marriage at last, where it was most certainly never intended to be? At its highest it was tragic: the love of Héloïse and Abélard. At its most graceful, it was the homage of the trouvère for his lady. In its most popular form, the adulterous strayings of solidly married couples who meant to stray for their own good reasons, but at the same time do nothing to upset the property settlements or the line of legitimacy; at its most trivial, the pretty trifling of shepherd and shepherdess.

This was generally condemned by church and state and a word of fear to honest wives whose mortal enemy it was. Love within the sober, sacred realities of marriage was a matter of personal luck, but in any case, private feelings were strictly a private affair having, at least in theory, no bearing whatever on the fixed practice of the rules of an institution never intended as a recreation ground for either sex. If the couple discharged their religious and social obligations, furnished forth a copious progeny, kept their troubles to themselves, maintained public civility and died under the same roof, even if not always on speaking terms, it was rightly regarded as a successful marriage. Apparently this testing ground was too severe for all but the stoutest spirits; it too was based on an ideal, as impossible in its way as the ideal Romantic Love. One good thing to be said for it is that society took responsibility for the conditions of marriage, and the sufferers within its bonds could always blame the system, not themselves. But Romantic Love crept into the marriage bed, very stealthily, by centuries, bringing its absurd notions about love as eternal springtime and marriage as a personal adventure meant to provide personal happiness. To a Western romantic such as I, though my views have been much modified by painful experience, it still seems to me a charming work of the human imagination, and it is a pity its central notion has been taken too literally and has hardened into a convention as cramping and enslaving as the older one. The refusal to acknowledge the evils in ourselves which therefore are implicit in any human situation is as extreme and unworkable a proposition as the doctrine of total depravity; but somewhere between them, or maybe beyond them, there does exist a possibility for reconciliation between our desires for impossible satisfactions and the simple unalterable fact that we also desire to be unhappy and that we create our own sufferings; and out of these sufferings we salvage our fragments of happiness.

Our young woman who has been taught that an important part of her human nature is not real because it makes trouble and interferes with her peace of mind and shakes her self-love, has been very badly taught; but she has arrived at a most important stage of her re-education. She is afraid her marriage is going to fail because she has not love enough to face its difficulties; and this because at times she feels a painful hostility toward her husband, and cannot admit its reality because such an admission would damage in her own eyes her view of what love should be, an absurd view, based on her vanity of power. Her hatred is real as her love is real, but her hatred has the advantage at present because it works on a blind instinctual level, it is lawless; and her love is subjected to a code of ideal conditions, impossible by their very nature of fulfillment, which prevents its free growth and deprives it of its right to recognize its human limitations and come to grips with them. Hatred is natural in a sense that love, as she conceives it, a young person brought up in the tradition of Romantic Love, is not natural at all. Yet it did not come by hazard, it is the very imperfect expression of the need of the human imagination to create beauty and harmony out of chaos, no matter how mistaken its notion of these things may be, nor how clumsy its methods. It has conjured love out of the air, and seeks to preserve it by incantations; when she spoke a vow to love and honor her husband until death, she did a very reckless thing, for it is not possible by an act of the will to fulfill such an engagement. But it was the necessary act of faith performed in defense of a mode of feeling, the statement of honorable intention to practice as well as she is able the noble, acquired faculty of love, that very mysterious overtone to sex which is the best thing in it. Her hatred is part of it, the necessary enemy and ally.

1948

"Marriage Is Belonging"

Having never written a word about marriage, so far as I remember,* and being now at the point where I have learned better than to have any theories about it, if I ever had; and believing as I do that most of the stuff written and talked about it is more or less nonsense; and having little hope that I shall add luster to the topic, it is only logical and natural that I should venture to write a few words on the subject.

My theme is marriage as the art of belonging—which should not be confused with possessing—all too often the art, or perhaps only the strategy, and a risky one, of surrendering gracefully with an air of pure disinterestedness as much of your living self as you can spare without incurring total extinction; in return for which you will, at least in theory, receive a more than compensatory share of another life, the life in fact presumably dearest to you, equally whittled down in your favor to the barest margin of survival. This arrangement with variations to suit the circumstances is of course the basis of many contracts besides that of marriage; but nowhere more than in marriage does the real good of the relationship depend on intangibles not named in the bond.

The trouble with me is—always was—that if you say "marriage" to me, instantly the word translates itself into "love," for only in such terms can I grasp the idea at all, or make any sense of it. The two are hopelessly associated, or rather identified, in my mind; that is to say, love is the only excuse for marriage, if any excuse is necessary. I often feel one should be offered. Love without marriage can sometimes be very awkward for all concerned; but marriage without love simply removes that institution

* See preceding. So much for memory.

from the territory of the humanly admissible, to my mind. Love is a state in which one lives who loves, and whoever loves has given himself away; love then, and not marriage, is belonging. Marriage is the public declaration of a man and a woman that they have formed a secret alliance, with the intention to belong to, and share with each other, a mystical estate; mystical exactly in the sense that the real experience cannot be communicated to others, nor explained even to oneself on rational grounds.

By love let me make it clear, I do not refer only to that ecstatic reciprocal cannibalism which goes popularly under the name, and which is indeed commonly one of the earliest biological symptoms (Boy Eats Girl and vice versa), for, like all truly mystical things, love is rooted deeply and rightly in this world and this flesh. This phase is natural, dangerous but not necessarily fatal; so remarkably educational it would be a great pity to miss it; further, of great importance, for the flesh in real love is one of the many bridges to the spirit; still, a phase only, which being passed is too often mistaken for the whole thing, and the end of it. This is an error based on lack of imagination, or the simple incapacity for further and deeper exploration of life, there being always on hand great numbers of people who are unwilling or unable to grow up, no matter what happens to them. It leads to early divorce, or worse. Like that young man whose downward career began with mere murder, this error can lead to infidelity, lying, eavesdropping, gambling, drinking, and finally to procrastination and incivility. These two last can easily have destroyed more marriages than any amount of murder, or even lying.

Let us recall a few generalities about marriage in its practical aspects which are common knowledge, such as: it is one of the most prevalent conditions of the human adult, heading the list of vital statistics, I believe. It has been made very easy to assume, and fairly easy in the legal sense, at least, to abandon; and it is famous for its random assortment of surprises of every kind—leaf-covered booby traps, spiders lurking in cups, pots of gold under rainbows, triplets, poltergeists in the stair closet, and flights of cupids lolling on the breakfast table—anything can happen. Every young married pair believes their marriage is going to be quite different from the others, and they are right—it always is. The task of regulating its unruly impulses is a thorn in the souls of theologians, its social needs and uses the insoluble riddle of law-makers. Through all ages known to man almost everybody, even those who wouldn't be seen dead wearing a wedding ring, having agreed that somehow, in some way, at some time or another, marriage has simply got to be made to work better than it does, or ever has, for that matter. Yet on the whole, my guess is that it works about as well as any other human institution, and rather better than a great many. The drawback is, it is the merciless revealer, the great white searchlight turned on the darkest places of human nature; it demands of all who enter it the two most difficult achievements possible: that each must be honest with himself, and faithful to another. I am speaking here only of the internal reality of marriage, not its legal or even its social aspects.

In its present form it is comparatively modern. As an idea, it must have begun fairly soon after the human male discovered his highly important role in the bringing forth of young. For countless aeons, we are told by those who pretend to know, it was believed that the powers of generation were vested in women alone, people having never been very bright about sex, right from the start. When men at last discovered, who knows how? that they were fathers, their pride in their discovery must have been equaled only by their indignation at having worshiped women as vessels of the Great Mystery when all along they should have been worshiping themselves. Pride and wrath and no doubt the awful new problem of what to do with the children, which had never bothered them before, drove them on to an infinite number of complicated and contradictory steps toward getting human affairs on a sounder basis. And, after all this time (skipping lightly over the first few hundred thousand years of total confusion), in our fine big new busy Western world, we have succeeded in establishing not only as the ideal, but in religious and legal fact (if not altogether in practice), as the very crown and glory of human ties, a one-man-one-woman-until-death sort of marriage, rivaling the swans for purity, with a ritual oath exchanged not only to stick to each other through thick and thin, to practice perfect fidelity, flawless forbearance, a modified bodily servitude, but to love each other dearly and kindly to the end.

All this is to be accomplished in a physical situation of the direst intimacy, in which all claims to the most ordinary privacy may be disregarded by either, or both. I shall not attempt to catalogue the daily accounting for acts, words, states of feeling and even thoughts, the perpetual balance and check between individual wills and points of view, the unbelievable amount of tact, intelligence, flexibility, generosity, and God knows what, it requires for two people to go on growing together and in the same directions instead of cracking up and falling apart.

Take the single point of fidelity: It is very hard to be entirely faithful, even to things, ideas, above all, persons one loves. There is no such thing as perfect faithfulness any more than there is perfect love or perfect beauty. But it is fun trying. And if I say faithfulness consists of a great many things beside the physical, never let it be dreamed that I hold with the shabby nonsense that physical infidelity is a mere peccadillo beneath the notice of enlightened minds. Physical infidelity is the signal, the notice given, that all the fidelities are undermined. It is complete betrayal of the very principle on which love and marriage are based, and besides, a vulgar handing over of one's partner to public shame. It is exactly as stupid as that, to say nothing more.

Yet every day quite by the thousands delightfully honest young couples, promising, capable, sometimes gifted, but in no way superhuman, leap gaily into marriage—a condition which, for even reasonable success and happiness (both words seem rather trivial in this connection), would tax the virtues and resources and staying powers of a regiment of angels. But what else would you suggest that they do?

Then there come the children. Gladly, willingly (if you do not think so, I refer you to the birth records of this country for the past ten years. There haven't been so many young wives having so many babies so fast for at least four generations!) these pairs proceed to populate their houses, or flats—often very small flats, and mother with a job she means to keep, too—with perfect strangers, often hostile, whose habits even to the most adoring gaze are often messy and unattractive. They lie flat on their noses at first in what appears to be a drunken slumber, then flat on their backs kicking and screaming, demanding impossibilities in a foreign language. They are human nature in essence, without conscience, without pity, without love, without a trace of consideration for others, just one seething cauldron of primitive appetites and needs; and what do they really need? We are back where we started. They need love, first; without it everything worth saving is lost or damaged in them; and they have to be taught love, pity, conscience, courage—everything. And what becomes of them? If they are lucky, among all the million possibilities of their fates, along with the innumerable employments, careers, talents, ways of life, they will learn the nature of love, and they will marry and have children.

If this all sounds a little monotonous, and gregarious, well, sometimes it is, and most people like that sort of thing. They always have. It is hardly possible to exaggerate the need of a human being, not a madman, or a saint, or a beast, or a self-alienated genius who is all of these in one, and therefore the scapegoat for all the rest, to live at peace—and by peace I mean in reconciliation, not easy contentment—with another human being, and with that one in a group or society where he feels he belongs. The best, the very best, of all these relationships is that one in marriage between a man and a woman who are good lovers, good friends, and good parents; who belong to each other, and to their children, and whose children belong to them: that is the meaning of the blood tie that binds them, and may bind them sometimes to the bone. Children cut their teeth on their parents and their parents cut their wisdom teeth on each other: that is what they are there for. It is never really dull, and can sometimes be very memorably exciting for everybody. In any case, the blood-bond, however painful, is the condition of human life in this world, the absolute point of all departure and return. The ancient bio-logical laws are still in force, the difference being merely in the way hu-man beings regard them, and though I am not one to say all change is progress, in this one thing, a kind of freedom and ease of mind between men and women in marriage—or at least the possibility of it, change has been all for the better. At least they are able now to fight out their differences on something nearer equal terms.

We have the bad habit, some of us, of looking back to a time—almost any time will do—when society was stable and orderly, family ties stron-ger and deeper, love more lasting and faithful, and so on. Let me be your Cassandra prophesying after the fact, and a long study of the documents in the case: it was never true, that is, no truer than it is now. Above all, it was not true of domestic life in the nineteenth century. Then, as now, it was just as good in individual instances as the married pairs involved were able to make it, privately, between themselves. The less attention they paid to what they were expected to think and feel about marriage, and the more attention to each other as loved and loving, the better they did, for themselves and for everybody. The laws of public decorum were easy to observe, for they had another and better understanding. The Victorian marriage feather bed was in fact set upon the shaky founda-tion of the wavering human heart, the inconsistent human mind, and was the roiling hotbed of every dislocation and disorder not only in mar-riage but all society, which we of the past two generations have lived through. Yet in love—this is what I have been talking about all the time—a certain number of well-endowed spirits, and there are surprisingly quite a lot of them in every generation, have always been able to take their world in stride, to live and die together, and to keep all their strange marriage vows not because they spoke them, but because like centuries of lovers before them, they were prepared to live them in the first place.

Example: A certain woman was apparently a prisoner for life in several ways: already thirty-five or -six years old, supposed to be an incurable invalid, whose father had forbidden any of his children to marry; and above all, a poet at a time when literary women were regarded as monsters, almost. Yet she was able to write, in the first flush of a bride's joy: "He preferred . . . of free and deliberate choice, to be allowed to sit only an hour a day by my side, to the fulfillment of the brightest dream which should exclude me in any possible world."

This could be illusion, but the proof of reality came fifteen years later. Just after her death her husband wrote to a friend: "Then came what my heart will keep till I see her again and longer—the most perfect expression of her love to me within my whole knowledge of her. Always smilingly, and happily, and with a face like a girl's; and in a few minutes she died in my arms, her head on my cheek."

If you exclaim that this is not fair, for, after all, these two were, of course, the Robert Brownings, I can only reply that it is because I sincerely believe they were not so very special that I cite them. Don't be thrown off by that lyrical nineteenth-century speech, nor their fearless confidence not only in their own feelings, but the sympathy of their friends; it is the kind of love that makes real marriage, and there is more of it in the world than you might think, though the ways of expressing it follow the fashions of the times; and we certainly do not find much trace of it in our contemporary literature. It is *very* old-style, and it was, long before the Brownings. It is new, too, it is the very newest thing, every day renewed in an endless series of those fortunate people who may not have one point in common with the Brownings except that they know, or are capable of learning, the nature of love, and of living by it.

1951

Act of Faith:
4 July 1942

Since this war began I have felt sometimes that all our good words had been rather frayed out with constant repetition, as if they were talismans that needed only to be spoken against the evil and the evil would vanish; or they have been debased by the enemy, part of whose business is to disguise fascism in the language of democracy. And I have noticed that the people who are doing the work and the fighting and the dying, and those who are doing the talking, are not at all the same people.*

By natural sympathy I belong with those who are not talking much at present, except in the simplest and straightest of terms, like the young Norwegian boy who escaped from Norway and joined the Canadian forces. When asked how he felt about Norway's fate, he could say only, "It is hard to explain how a man feels who has lost his country." I think he meant it was impossible; but he had a choice, to accept defeat or fight, and he made the choice, and that was his way of talking. There was the American boy going into the navy, who answered the same foolish question: "It's too serious a thing to be emotional about." And the young American wife who was one of the last civilians to escape, by very dangerous and exhausting ways, from a bombarded island where her husband was on active duty. She was expecting her first baby. "Oh yes, I had the baby," she said, matter-of-factly, "a fine healthy boy." And another girl, twenty-one years old, has a six-month-old girl baby and a husband who will be off to the army any day now. She wrote: "I'm glad I have that job. Her Daddy won't have to worry about us."

* Note and read again, December Second, 1969—K. A. P. in Memoriam.

While the talkers have been lecturing us, saying the American people
have been spoiled by too much prosperity and made slack of fiber by too
much peace and freedom, and gloating rather over the painful times we
are about to endure for our own good, I keep my mind firmly on these
four young ones, not because they are exceptional but precisely because
they are not. They come literally in regiments these days, though not all
of them are in uniform, nor should be. They are the typical millions of
young people in this country, and they have not been particularly softened by prosperity; they were brought up on the depression. They have
not been carefully sheltered: most of them have worked for a living
when they could find work, and an astonishing number of them have
helped support their families. They do their jobs and pay their taxes
and buy War Savings Stamps and contribute to the Red Cross and
China Relief and Bundles for Britain and all the rest. They do the work
in factories and offices and on farms. The girls knit and nurse and cook
and are learning to replace the boys in skilled work in war production.
The boys by the thousand are getting off to camp, carrying their little
two-by-four suitcases or bundles. I think of this war in terms of these
people, who are my kind of people; the war they are fighting is my war,
and yes, it is hard to find exactly the right word to say to them. I wait to
hear what they will have to say to the world when this war is won and
over and they must begin their lives again in the country they have
helped to save for democracy.

I wait for that with the most immense and deep longing and hope and
belief in them.

In the meantime let us glance at that theory, always revived in the heat
and excitement of war, that peace makes spirits slothful and bodies
flabby. In this season, when Americans are celebrating the birthday of
our Republic, its most important birthday since that first day of our hard-
won beginnings, we might remember that the men who wrote the Constitution and compiled the Body of Liberties were agreed on the revolutionary theory that peace was a blessing to a country—one of the greatest
blessings—and they were careful to leave recorded their opinions on this
subject. And they were right. Peace is good, and the arts of peace, and its
fruits. The freedom we may have only in peace is good. It was never true
there was too much of either; the truth is, there was never enough, never
rightly exercised, never deeply enough understood. But we have been

making a fairly steady headway this century and a half in face of strong and determined opposition from enemies within as well as from without. We have had poverty in a country able to support in plenty more than twice its present population, yet by long effort we were arriving at an increasing standard of good living for greater and greater numbers of people. One of the prime aims of the democratic form of government was to create an economy in which all the people were to be allowed access to the means and materials of life, and to share fairly in the abundance of the earth. This has been the hardest fight of all, the bitterest, but the battle is by no means lost, and it is not ended, and it will be won in time.

Truth is, the value of peace to us was that it gave us time, and the right to fight for our liberties as a people, against our internal enemies, using those weapons provided for us within our own system of government; and the first result of war with an external enemy is that this right is suspended, and there is the danger that, even if the foreign war is won, the gains at home may be lost, and must be fought for all over again.

It has been the habit and the principle of this people to think in terms of peace, and perhaps to live in rather a too-optimistic faith that peace could be maintained when all the plainest signs pointed in the opposite direction; but they have fought their wars very well, and they will fight this one well, too. And it is no time to be losing our heads and saying, or thinking, that in the disciplines and the restrictions and the heavy taxes and the restraint on action necessary to concerted effort, we have already lost the freedoms we are supposed to be fighting for. If we lose the war, there will be nothing left to talk about; the blessed and sometimes abused American freedom of speech will have vanished with the rest. But we are not going to lose this war, and the people of this country are going to have the enormous privilege of another chance to make of their Republic what those men who won and founded it for us meant for it to be. We aren't going anywhere, that is one great thing. Every single soul of us is involved personally in this war; this is the last stand, and this is our territory. Here is the place and now is the time to put a stop, once and for all, to the stampede of the human race like terrorized cattle over one world frontier after another. We stay here.

And during this period of suspension of the humanities, in the midst of the outrage and the world horror staggering to the imagination, we might find it profitable to examine the true nature of our threatened liberties, and their political, legal, and social origins and meanings, and decide exactly what their value is, and where we should be without them. They were not accidental by any means; they are implicit in our theory of government, which was in turn based on humanistic concepts of the importance of the individual man and his rights in society. They are not mere ornaments on the façade, but are laid in the foundation stone of the structure, and they will last so long as the structure itself but no longer. They are not inalienable: the house was built with great labor and it is made with human hands; human hands can tear it down again, and will, if it is not well loved and defended. The first rule for any effective defense is: Know your enemies. Blind, fanatical patriotism which shouts and weeps is no good for this war. This is another kind of war altogether. I trust the quiet coldness of the experienced fighters, I like their knowing that words are wasted in this business.

1942

The Future Is Now

Not so long ago I was reading in a magazine with an enormous circulation some instructions as to how to behave if and when we see that flash brighter than the sun which means that the atom bomb has arrived. I read of course with the intense interest of one who has everything to learn on this subject; but at the end, the advice dwindled to this: the only real safety seems to lie in simply being somewhere else at the time, the farther away the better; the next best, failing access to deep shelters, bombproof cellars and all, is to get under a stout table—that is, just what you might do if someone were throwing bricks through your window and you were too nervous to throw them back.

This comic anticlimax to what I had been taking as a serious educational piece surprised me into real laughter, hearty and carefree. It is such a relief to be told the truth, or even just the facts, so pleasant not to be coddled with unreasonable hopes. That very evening I was drawn away from my work table to my fifth-story window by one of those shrill terror-screaming sirens which our excitement-loving city government used then to affect for so many occasions: A fire? Police chasing a gangster? Somebody being got to the hospital in a hurry? Some distinguished public guest being transferred from one point to another? Strange aircraft coming over, maybe? Under the lights of the corner crossing of the great avenue, a huge closed vehicle whizzed past, screaming. I never knew what it was, had not in fact expected to know; no one I could possibly ask would know. Now that we have bells clamoring away instead for such events, we all have one doubt less, if perhaps one expectancy more. The single siren's voice means to tell us only one thing.

But at that doubtful moment, framed in a lighted window level with mine in the apartment house across the street, I saw a young man in a white T-shirt and white shorts at work polishing a long, beautiful dark table top. It was obviously his own table in his own flat, and he was enjoying his occupation. He was bent over in perfect concentration, rubbing, sandpapering, running the flat of his palm over the surface, standing back now and then to get the sheen of light on the fine wood. I am sure he had not even raised his head at the noise of the siren, much less had he come to the window. I stood there admiring his workmanlike devotion to a good job worth doing, and there flashed through me one of those pure fallacies of feeling which suddenly overleap reason: surely all that effort and energy so irreproachably employed were not going to be wasted on a table that was to be used merely for crawling under at some unspecified date. Then why take all those pains to make it beautiful? Any sort of old board would do.

I was so shocked at this treachery of the lurking Foul Fiend (despair *is* a foul fiend, and this was despair) I stood a moment longer, looking out and around, trying to collect my feelings, trying to think a little. Two windows away and a floor down in the house across the street, a young woman was lolling in a deep chair, reading and eating fruit from a little basket. On the sidewalk, a boy and a girl dressed alike in checkerboard cotton shirts and skin-tight blue denims, a costume which displayed acutely the structural differences of their shapes, strolled along with their arms around each other. I believe this custom of lovers walking enwreathed in public was imported by our soldiers of the First World War from France, from Paris indeed. "You didn't see that sort of thing here before," certain members of the older generation were heard to remark quite often, in a tone of voice. Well, one sees quite a lot of it now, and it is a very pretty, reassuring sight. Other citizens of all sizes and kinds and ages were crossing back and forth; lights flashed red and green, punctually. Motors zoomed by, and over the great city—but where am I going? I never read other peoples' descriptions of great cities, more particularly if it is a great city I know. It doesn't belong here anyway, except that I had again that quieting sense of the continuity of human experience on this earth, its perpetual aspirations, set-backs, failures and re-beginnings in eternal hope; and that, with some appreciable differences of dress, customs and means of conveyance, so people have lived and moved in the cities they have built for more millennia than we are yet able to account for, and will no doubt build and live for as many more.

Why did this console me? I cannot say; my mind is of the sort that can often be soothed with large generalities of that nature. The silence of the spaces between the stars does not affright me, as it did Pascal, because I am unable to imagine it except poetically; and my awe is not for the silence and space of the endless universe but for the inspired imagination of man, who can think and feel so, and turn a phrase like that to communicate it to us. Then too, I like the kind of honesty and directness of the young soldier who lately answered someone who asked him if he knew what he was fighting for. "I sure do," he said, "I am fighting to live." And as for the future, I was once reading the first writings of a young girl, an apprentice author, who was quite impatient to get on with the business and find her way into print. There is very little one can say of use in such matters, but I advised her against haste—she could so easily regret it. "Give yourself time," I said, "the future will take care of itself." This opinionated young person looked down her little nose at me and said, "The future is now." She may have heard the phrase somewhere and liked it, or she may just have naturally belonged to that school of metaphysics; I am sure she was too young to have investigated the thought deeply. But maybe she was right and the future does arrive every day and it is all we have, from one second to the next.

So I glanced again at the young man at work, a proper-looking candidate for the armed services, and realized the plain, homely fact: he was not preparing a possible shelter, something to cower under trembling; he was restoring a beautiful surface to put his books and papers on, to serve his plates from, to hold his cocktail tray and his lamp. He was full of the deep, right, instinctive, human belief that he and the table were going to be around together for a long time. Even if he is off to the army next week, it will be there when he gets back. At the very least, he is doing something he feels is worth doing now, and that is no small thing.

At once the difficulty, and the hope, of our special time in this world of Western Europe and America is that we have been brought up for many generations in the belief, however tacit, that all humanity was almost unanimously engaged in going forward, naturally to better things and to higher reaches. Since the eighteenth century at least when the Encyclopedists seized upon the Platonic theory that the highest pleasure of mankind was pursuit of the good, the true, and the beautiful, progress, in precisely the sense of perpetual, gradual amelioration of the hard human lot, has been taught popularly not just as theory of possibility but as an article of faith and the groundwork of a whole political doctrine. Mr. Toynbee has even simplified this view for us with picture diagrams of various sections of humanity, each in its own cycle rising to its own height, struggling beautifully on from craggy level to level, but always upward. Whole peoples are arrested at certain points, and perish there, but others go on. There is also the school of thought, Oriental and very ancient, which gives to life the spiral shape, and the spiral moves by nature upward. Even adherents of the circular or recurring-cycle school, also ancient and honorable, somehow do finally allow that the circle is a thread that spins itself out one layer above another, so that even though it is perpetually at every moment passing over a place it has been before, yet by its own width it will have risen just so much higher.

These are admirable attempts to get a little meaning and order into our view of our destiny, in that same spirit which moves the artist to labor with his little handful of chaos, bringing it to coherency within a frame; but on the visible evidence we must admit that in human nature the spirit of contradiction more than holds its own. Mankind has always built a little more than he has hitherto been able or willing to destroy; got more children than he has been able to kill; invented more laws and customs than he had any intention of observing; founded more religions than he was able to practice or even to believe in; made in general many more promises than he could keep; and has been known more than once to commit suicide through mere fear of death. Now in our time, in his pride to explore his universe to its unimaginable limits and to exceed his possible powers, he has at last produced an embarrassing series of engines too powerful for their containers and too tricky for their mechanicians; millions of labor-saving gadgets which can be rendered totally useless by the mere failure of the public power plants, and has reduced himself to such helplessness that a dozen or less of the enemy could disable a whole city by throwing a few switches. This paradoxical creature has committed all these extravagances and created all these dangers and sufferings in a quest—we are told—for peace and security.

How much of this are we to believe, when with the pride of Lucifer, the recklessness of Icarus, the boldness of Prometheus and the intellectual curiosity of Adam and Eve (yes, intellectual; the serpent promised them wisdom if . . .) man has obviously outreached himself, to the point where he cannot understand his own science or control his own inventions. Indeed he has become as the gods, who have over and over again suffered defeat and downfall at the hands of their creatures. Having devised the most exquisite and instantaneous means of communication to all corners of the earth, for years upon years friends were unable even to get a postcard message to each other across national frontiers.* The newspapers assure us that from the kitchen tap there flows a chemical, cheap and available, to make a bomb more disturbing to the imagination even than the one we so appallingly have; yet no machine has been invented to purify that water so that it will not spoil even the best tea or coffee. Or at any rate, it is not in use. We are the proud possessors of rocket bombs that go higher and farther and faster than any ever before, and there is some talk of a rocket ship shortly to take off for the moon. (My plan is to stow away.) We may indeed reach the moon some day, and I dare predict that will happen before we have devised a decent system of city garbage disposal.

This lunatic atom bomb has succeeded in rousing the people of all nations to the highest point of unanimous moral dudgeon; great numbers of persons are frightened who never really had much cause to be frightened before. This world has always been a desperately dangerous place to live for the greater part of the earth's inhabitants; it was, however reluctantly, endured as the natural state of affairs. Yet the invention of every new weapon of war has always been greeted with horror and righteous indignation, especially by those who failed to invent it, or who were threatened with it first . . . bows and arrows, stone cannon balls, gunpowder, flintlocks, pistols, the dumdum bullet, the Maxim silencer, the machine gun, poison gas, armored tanks, and on and on to the grand climax—if it should prove to be—of the experiment on Hiroshima. Nagasaki was bombed too, remember? Or were we already growing accustomed to the idea? And as for Hiroshima, surely it could not have been the notion of sudden death of others that shocked us? How could it be, when in two great wars within one generation we have become familiar with millions of shocking deaths, by sudden violence of most cruel devices, and by agonies prolonged for years in prisons and hospitals and concentration camps. We take with apparent calmness the news of the deaths of millions by flood, famine, plague—no, all the frontiers of danger are down now, no one is safe, no one, and that, alas, really means all of us. It is our own deaths we fear, and so let's out with it and give up our

---

* Fall, 1952. The hydrogen bomb has just been exploded, very successfully, to the satisfaction of the criminals who caused it to be made.

fine debauch of moralistic frenzy over Hiroshima. I fail entirely to see why it is more criminal to kill a few thousand persons in one instant than it is to kill the same number slowly over a given stretch of time. If I have a choice, I'd as lief be killed by an atom bomb as by a hand grenade or a flame thrower. If dropping the atom bomb is an immoral act, then the making of it was too; and writing of the formula was a crime, since those who wrote it must have known what such a contrivance was good for. So, morally speaking, the bomb is only a magnified hand grenade, and the crime, if crime it is, is still murder. It was never anything else. Our protocriminal then was the man who first struck fire from flint, for from that moment we have been coming steadily to this day and this weapon and this use of it. What would you have advised instead? That the human race should have gone on sitting in caves gnawing raw meat and beating each other over the head with the bones?

And yet it may be that what we have is a world not on the verge of flying apart, but an uncreated one—still in shapeless fragments waiting to be put together properly. I imagine that when we want something better, we may have it: at perhaps no greater price than we have already paid for the worse.

1950

A Letter to the Editor
of The Nation

Santa Monica, California
May 11, 1947
Dear Sirs:

It is quite true that strategic positions are occupied methodically by Communists, not only in departments of government here and abroad, but in our schools and universities, the press, the publishing business, industry, the motion pictures. You find them everywhere; they mean business and they are dangerous. But judging by the present drive against the Communists, I should say there are even more fascists in public office, or at least more powerfully placed: the Rankins of this country are as bitter enemies of democratic government as any Communist, and the legislation proposed by them seeks the suppression of all liberty of speech or opinion; if they are not stopped here and now, we shall find ourselves with a "subversive-thoughts" law on our books.

Both fascists and Communists have been strangely successful in persuading the liberals of this country that only a democracy has no right to defend itself from its enemies. Every suggestion that they be curbed in any way has always been met with outcries of wounded democratic feeling from the liberal left, which has defended, on the ground of safeguarding democratic government, the most cynical and base of our so-called civil liberties. I think the liberals had better clear their heads and look the situation in the face before they are driven underground to form a resistance movement to fascism or communism—the end will be the same—in our own country.

Yet in all this maggoty-minded proposed legislation I have seen no suggestion that Communist or fascist conspirators against our government shall be put to death. Let us therefore take a little warning from Mr. del Vayo's interesting article, "Vatican Versus Left in Italy" (*The Nation*, April 5, 1947). Mr. del Vayo says: "Another battle will no doubt be fought over the law on the Defense of the Republic—drafted by Togliatti and approved by the Council of Ministers—which provides sanctions, including the death sentence, against Fascists and Monarchists who conspire against the state."

Italy, we have been told, is to found a democracy. If it is right for a democracy in Italy to execute the death sentence upon Fascists and Monarchists, why not upon Communists too, who are equally its enemies? Granting this, why is it such a crime for a democracy in the United States to put fascist and Communist conspirators in jail, or at least to deprive them of their confidential posts in departments of our government? Does being a democrat morally oblige a man to consent to his own murder? And by what process of reason do the democrats of Italy or of America, to say nothing of Mr. del Vayo, and the editors of *The Nation*, convince themselves that Togliatti, a Communist, means to do anything to help establish a true republic in Italy? Stalin played a sinister game with Hitler when Germany was the center of power for fascism. The Vatican is now that center, and the Communists are playing their old game again. How many jolts of this kind can the liberals of this country take, I wonder, and still preserve their dazzled innocence?

On Communism
in Hollywood

(a report on a
Town Meeting of the Air)

It is a pity John Lardner wasn't there to report the sporting event which took place Tuesday afternoon in Philharmonic Auditorium, but I'll do the best I can.

The name of the hall was the only tranquil thing about the occasion. The word "communism" in the program title brought out a record crowd, and of course a record number of police. Or am I just prejudiced against seeing public assemblies, when political debates take place, being treated as if they were composed of potential criminals? It always reminds me unpleasantly of Berlin in 1932.

As Mr. Denny, the moderator of the Town Meeting of the Air remarked, "This [communism] is a subject on which people feel deeply." He was right. It was a good show. The crowd looked fine, all ages, sizes, colors, and shades of opinion, but all had one common mood.

All were vitally concerned, and at a show of hands it seemed they were divided pretty evenly for one side or the other; they looked fresh as paint on what seemed the hottest day of the year, and they were there to take part. Tempers get more than a little frayed on the platform toward the last, but the audience went right on being opinionated, good humored but decisive and serious.

The celebrated Mr. Denny began with his familiar procedure of laying down rules for the behavior of the audience in order to give the effect he wished over the air. We were reminded that we were all free, respectable

Americans, that millions were listening and we must give an example of good conduct. We were told when to applaud, and what; when to create a subdued hubbub of interaudience discussion, and when to keep our traps shut in a refined manner.

We were instructed that only geese and snakes hiss, but Mr. Denny did not mention the good old universal human custom of saying boo to a goose, which was exactly what happened, often. We were told flatly that when we were pleased, we were free to applaud to our little hearts' content. When we weren't pleased, we were to keep silence.

Just where had I heard that kind of thing before? Where had I seen a little man with a sawed-off moustache standing before a crowd, lifting his hands for the applause to begin, slapping them down on the table for it to cease? I hadn't liked it then, and I still don't. My early-American Jeffersonian-Democrat hackles rose, and though I had not come there planning to hiss or boo, I knew then that I would do both if I felt like it.

It turned out that nearly the whole audience seemed to have been struck with the same notion. The authoritarian Mr. Denny broke into a heavy lather about midway of the broadcast; he looked ready to weep and 10 years older when it finished. I hope that'll learn him, as we say in Texas.

The big trouble with the fight, though—I mean debate—was that the opponents were badly matched as to weight and reach—that is, abilities. The Affirmative, the mother of Miss Ginger Rogers, and State Sen. Jack Tenney, were very, very negative. The Negatives, Mr. Emmet Lavery, president of the Screen Writers Guild, and Mr. Albert Dekker, actor and former state Assemblyman, were extremely affirmative.

Not that the Senator is not a man of many talents. He plays the piano, and writes popular songs, just like the late Mayor Jimmie Walker and Pappy O'Daniel, of Texas. In fact it seems that American politics has had as many musicians as European politics once had painters.

Mr. Dekker took occasion to remind us that the Senator had once called himself a "genial radical," in his piano-playing days. Later he was a Democrat, and now he is a Republican, author of that anthology from his committee reports, *Red Fascism*, as well as the song, "Mexicali Rose," which made him also a good number of non-political enemies. Mr. Lavery is a devout Roman Catholic of Irish descent. Mr. Albert Dekker is a trained actor with a gift for quick indignation backed up by a quick wit.

I am all for fair play, and it is a shame that the so-called Affirmatives had to play their scrub team, the first team and their substitutes having backed down at an embarrassingly late moment. I still think it was pure murder to put Mrs. Lela Rogers, who belongs to the Helen Hokinson-girl school of political thought, and Senator Tenney, who relies strictly on intuition and rumor, in there with Emmet Lavery and Albert Dekker, who stuck to the point and played by the rules.

What good did it do? The ring was a shambles in 15 minutes. You will, I am sure, find ample reports of the official speeches and some of the repartee in other columns of this newspaper. I shall concern myself with the behavior of the debaters before the public as giving a pretty good key to motives and intention and character.

Mr. Lavery and Mr. Dekker certainly got good and mad toward the last, after taking a long course of the most vicious personal baiting from the Affirmatives, who affirmed monotonously with variations that Hollywood was a Hotbed of you-know-what, and Mr. L. and Mr. D. were likewise Reds, Communists, full of high treason.

Mr. Lavery wanted to know why they were up there arguing then, when the Senator's plain duty was to denounce them to the FBI, produce evidence, and see them brought to trial. Mr. Lavery thought that if the Senator was not able to do this, he should let people alone.

The Senator is too seasoned a campaigner not to know that you don't get anywhere in politics letting people alone, and he seized every opportunity to shout, "Red, Communists," into the microphone, whether in turn or out of it. When someone asked Mr. Dekker a question, he only got half a sentence spoken when Senator Tenny shoved in bodily to answer it himself, or at least to prevent it being answered. Mr. Dekker said, "Now you just wait your turn. Everybody here is going to get his chance to talk. This is not one of your hearings."

I thought the roof shook with the applause, and Senator Tenney remarked that the "comrades" seemed to be there in force. I looked carefully, and the whole audience appeared to be applauding, and it occurred to me that there were a great number of people in that house who don't like communism and who will fight it, but not in the Senator's company.

In spite of the large number of hands held up before the program went on the air, when Mr. Denny asked how many believed communism was a threat here, the Senator later got a very modest greeting, and remarked that he was glad to see there were a few Americans in the house, after all. Even his colleague Mrs. Rogers almost got trampled once or twice in the Senator's mad stampede to the microphone, for he knows the value of repetition. Who was it said, Say a thing often enough and people will believe it? Maybe it is an overworked technique by now—it didn't go over so well Tuesday.

At one point Senator Tenney shifted the argument to Catholicism vs. communism, and after calling Mr. Lavery a Red for three quarters of an hour, remarked that if the Communists were able, they'd push him out of the Guild. So why didn't Mr. Lavery push out the Communists? Mr. Lavery explained that he didn't know who they were, in the first place, and in the second, the Guild did not discriminate against members because of religious or political beliefs.

This piece of good American doctrine seemed to exasperate the Senator. "We don't throw out Republicans," said Mr. Lavery going overboard for broadmindedness, and judging by the joyous laughter, there must have been quite a number of Democrats in the house, too.

Well, the point is this, so far as my personal impressions are concerned, and it was those I was asked to give. If I had been on the Affirmative side, I should have been ashamed of my representatives. Just on the score of manners and morals in discussion, on method of argument, on personal dignity and fearlessness, the decision, for my part, went to the Negative. They did succeed in getting some good sense and good thought into the uproar.

And the audience felt this, and expressed itself in a way to refresh one's faith in people, the American people, here and now.

I still don't know how many Communists there are in Hollywood, nor where they are; but I will trust Mr. Dekker and Mr. Lavery and that audience to fight them more effectively than any number of Anti-American Activities Committees, whose activities have seemed to me from the beginning the most un-American thing I know.

1947

A Letter to the Editor of
The Saturday Review
of Literature

Dear Sir:

About the Bollingen-Library of Congress Award for Poetry to Ezra Pound for 1949:

There are a few points in your editorial, (*SRL*, June 11, 1949) and in Mr. Hillyer's articles (*SRL*, June 11 and June 18, 1949) on which I have made the following notes, by way of answering as well as I am able some of his questions, and to ask one or two of my own.

On the origin of the Society of Fellows of the Library of Congress in American Letters, Mr. Hillyer (*SRL*, June 11) has "been unable to discover from the Library how or by whom this impressively titled group of fellows is appointed." Perhaps my own experience will serve as an example. I had my appointment with the title and duties of Fellow of Regional American Literature from Archibald MacLeish, then Librarian of Congress, in January, 1944, to fill out the unexpired term of the late John Peale Bishop, who had resigned because of his illness. Allen Tate, who then occupied the Chair of Poetry as consultant to the Library in that department, was the sponsor who presented my name to Mr. MacLeish when the vacancy was to be filled. I knew nothing of the plan until I received the invitation, which I accepted with delight. The late James Boyd had been Fellow in that chair immediately before Mr. Bishop. I took up where they left off in the work of research into source writings of pioneers and of transient visitors in the early history of this nation—letters, journals, travelers' tales, fiction, poetry (or perhaps rather verse)—with, in my case, special attention to the story of the great migration from Virginia and Pennsylvania to Kentucky. It is an unbelievably rich and vast field, even the small corner I chose for my own, for the whole project would take the working lifetime of one individual. The final aim was to locate all existing documents and rare printings in all the libraries and, so far as possible, private collections, to make lists of them which would be available for reference to the public; also to list the great collection of the Library of Congress in the same way; and, of course, one point was always to look for valuable things which the Library might acquire by gift or purchase. It was deeply interesting, exciting work, and I left it with regret.

Each Fellow was in this way assigned to a particular field, and task, and there was nothing casual or pointless about it; it seems to me particularly appropriate work for writers.

As to the origins of the Society itself: it was founded rather simply by the Fellows, who never pretended or aspired to be more than a group of working artists with a common interest: literature. We talked among ourselves a little about forming some kind of association; the idea grew; one morning we all met and talked over practical details, a few more meetings and the thing was done. I am not much of a joiner, and take very little interest in organizations of any kind, and I have not been active in this one, but I am one of the founders and I feel a real bond with it. I have never attended a meeting but the Consultant in Poetry (Miss Leonie Adams, this year) sends copies of the minutes, full accounts of all proceedings; and I vote by mail, as I wish, without knowing or caring in the least how anyone else is voting.

As to my part in awarding the Bollingen Prize to Ezra Pound, these are the facts: I did not vote on the first list of poets whose names were presented because, due to an error in the address, it did not reach me. The list had been reduced by repeated voting to four candidates before I voted. I accepted this list of four, and voted for Ezra Pound precisely within the limits set by the conditions of the award: of the four final candidates who had volumes of poetry published in this country in 1948, I considered Pound's the best. This is not to say "The Pisan Cantos" are high poetry, and certainly not the best of Pound's poetry, but still my choice among the four, and if I had voted against him, or had abstained, it would have been because I abhor his treason and detest his emotional perversities, for they cannot be called ideas, in politics, and not at all on the grounds provided for my vote. This I think would have been side-stepping the problem, a very serious one, and I was not disposed to side-step. I voted for Ezra Pound in the absence of other and better poets, on the list presented for my choice. Given the same situation, and its consequences, I would do so again. I regret that the award was not withheld until a luckier year, but I do not retract my vote. I should have preferred to vote for John Crowe Ransom or Wallace Stevens; for Louise Bogan, Leonie Adams, Robert Penn Warren, Randall Jarrell, Marianne Moore, Allen Tate, Robert Graves, W. H. Auden, Archibald MacLeish, E. E. Cummings; if they were citizens, T. S. Eliot or Edith Sitwell; and if it were in any way possible, for the late Paul Valéry for "The Cemetery by the Sea," even that one alone. The list could be longer. I love poetry, and especially I love the poetry written by these poets. Their names are good music for these times so celebrated for their literary decline. If this is poetic decline, by all means let us have more of it.

And now a note or two on the tone of the *SRL* articles and editorial: Mr. Hillyer refers to T. S. Eliot as the alien, the expatriate, and calls for his instant downfall on this ground, though it is plain that he would not like Mr. Eliot any better if he had stayed in St. Louis to write his poetry. He is somewhat milder toward W. H. Auden, "A native of Great Britain who is now an American citizen," but still, it is worth mentioning, and it is not intended to add to Mr. Auden's credit. This attitude toward our newly made citizens, of which I must suppose we have quite tens of thousands by now, is indefensible. Mr. Hillyer's personal feelings in the matter are his own, but they should not drive him to using the wrong weapons. I doubt if any serious person changes his citizenship lightly, and it is not a legitimate point to make in any discussion.

Mr. Hillyer is especially indignant because Ezra Pound, having been declared insane, is being comfortably cared for in St. Elizabeth's, and compares his well-being with the wretchedness of our veterans in government mental hospitals. We all know, and have known, that some of our veterans' institutions are not too generously provided for nor too wisely administered; we know, all of us, that even to witness or think about the mere human suffering in those places is enough to crush the soul. There are not only just the maimed and demented from this war, but like an evil shadow lying back of the present, are those living dead grown old in sickness with the most drearily meager provisions for life, from the war before this. . . . Yet I think his argument is altogether wrong. Instead of saying, "Deprive the demented traitor and see that he lives in wretchedness, as a matter of justice," he should begin in another place altogether, using different tactics, different arguments, and for different motives, to do what he can toward the improvement of conditions for the sick soldiers. He must know, we all know, that even if Ezra Pound were put back in the cage they built for him in the Deserters' Camp in Pisa (and a melodramatic piece of nonsense that was, which could not last), it would not by one breath change the situation of one disabled soldier in one bed in any hospital in this country. So why play such a trick on human feelings? To throw them off the point, obscure the question?

I am glad that he is being cared for, I pity his madness;* the evil he has done is hateful to me, I reject it without reservation; but I remember the light that used to shine from his pages when he wrote about something he knew with his heart—poetry—and the beautiful translations, or paraphrases, from the Chinese and the Provençal, and how well he knew that art was not a marginal thing, but lived at the center of being by its own reality; that it was no decoration, but the Stone itself; no matter, he cannot commit treason against that, it is beyond the reach of his mortal part.

In the meantime, I do not believe in the doctrine of the Scapegoat, and I do not like to see one man selected to take the punishment for all those who got away. Even if he recovered, and were convicted of treason, I doubt unless times have changed for the worse, he would suffer the extreme penalty; I hope not. This government, very strong and assured, has always been lenient toward our few traitors, from Benedict Arnold onward. I cannot remember that even one has been put to death.** Perhaps this leniency is explained by the fact that until this war there have been so few of any consequence. Just a year or two ago there was exonerated in an American court another, a woman, who had no talents except for political intrigue of a low kind. She did for Hitler, by radio from Berlin, exactly the same work that Pound did for Mussolini in Italy. She was one of the four (Pound was among them) sentenced to the death penalty subject to capture, by the then Attorney General Francis Biddle. She is living no doubt comfortably in Spain, and the

* I doubted then, and do now, that E.P. was ever mad. K.A.P., February 25, 1969.
** This was pre-Rosenberg.

judge in freeing her in absentia remarked in effect that even if she was working for Nazism, the great point was that she was defending religion and morality. I have heard no complaints about this case, and though she seemed to suffer a debased form of religious mania, I have never heard her called insane. This is no argument for releasing Pound. One injustice does not justify another. But I will admit that this fact has done something to moderate my first indignation against Pound. . . .

Still on this subject, but on a lighter note: In the same number of the *SRL* (June 11) in which Mr. Hillyer and the editors formally declare war to extinction not only on Pound and Eliot, but a whole population of the "new" critics, poets, and, I suppose, prose writers, Mr. Bennett Cerf resurrects an unsavory ghost by telling an amusing—not to me— little story about Mr. Pelham Grenville Wodehouse, whose celebrated character Jeeves was the heart's darling of all those who like that sort of thing. But can it be everyone has forgotten Mr. Wodehouse's career among the Nazis during the war? He did a little talking on the radio, too, and records were made, and played off in England, and there was a pretty how-do-you-do when time came for Mr. Wodehouse to explain. He got off by pleading congenital slackness in the head; his daughter loyally confirmed his defense, and yet can it be that indulgence is shown him because he is a comic writer, to some, and was published at a great price in the *Saturday Evening Post* instead of at five dollars a page or less in one of those beautifully printed subsidized serious literary reviews? I only take this occasion to ask, because at this point I find the whole course of logic of the *SRL* a touch confusing. For Mr. Hillyer claims that the "new" poets are destroying the language at the same time that they sow sedition; they invent words, they quote without giving credit, they use tags from foreign languages, and fall into gibberish with an air of profundity. If this were true, he would be right to protest: and yet, in the pages of this very same number, there appears a review of a new book by Christopher Morley, in which his classical quotations, his foreign language tags, his invented words, his puns, his quips, quirks and quiddities, his prankish, Puckish roysterings among his Bartlett and En- cyclopedia, to say nothing of his Rilke, Donne, Montaigne, and so on, are all commended as the natural carryings-on of a true man of letters. Why? If Morley can do that, why not Eliot? The reviewer says that underneath it all Morley seems to be pretty bitter about something. Well, so is T. S. Eliot. Why all this favoritism?

One thing more: Mr. Hillyer writes about the "new" critics and poets: "Their power in academic circles is beyond appraisal because it is pervasive rather than defined. They have pooled their separate timidities and frustrations gaining strength from each other's weakness, and have succeeded in an age unprepared by education against pretentious cheek."

"An age unprepared by education." At whose door shall we lay this fault? Mr. Hillyer is much scandalized because the Bollingen award is named for Dr. Carl Jung's place in Switzerland, and it was given by Mr. Paul Mellon, who is an admirer of Dr. Jung, who is a professed Fascist (true); and T. S. Eliot is also under the influence of Dr. Jung, and that is why Ezra Pound, a Fascist traitor, got the Mellon money. It is horribly neat, and, if so, reason tells us that the next step is a general campaign against all disciples, friends and admirers of Dr. Jung in this country. This should lead to some interesting scandals. There is no reason why the business should ever end. I did not know the origin of the prize, nor the meaning of its name and did not inquire as I have not inquired into the sources of a great many other prizes and fellowships, because I have a general knowledge that, in many instances, a very small part indeed of some very ill-got fortunes have been returned to society in the form of benefits to the needy. In Western society, the rich have always been made to feel guilty, and no doubt some of them should; all the more reason they should not be hindered in their attempts to make some restitution. Artists sometimes share in this bounty, and I am glad of it. A great many of us are really quite needy. It is just true that if we begin looking gift horses in the mouth, we may find the Night Mare, all teeth and rotten. Mr. Hillyer is on such dangerous ground here I wonder that he is not calling for help.

Yet this is not altogether the point. Mr. Hillyer has first-hand knowledge of Dr. Jung's political beliefs: "I had personal contact with Dr. Jung's Nazism. At luncheon during the Harvard Tercentenary of 1936 (note the date, please) Dr. Jung, who was seated beside me, deftly introduced the subject of Hitler, developed it with alert warmth, and concluded with the statement that from the high vantage point of Alpine Switzerland Hitler's new order in Germany seemed to offer the one hope of Europe."

Hitler, who was a popular idol in Germany at least from 1930 onward, rose to absolute power in 1933. Three years later, the educators at Harvard are so ill-informed about Nazism, so indifferent or so blind to its plain manifestations in the writings of Dr. Jung, they invite him to take part in their Tercentenary, where in his role of honored guest he does spade-work for Hitler. What was a professed Nazi doing as the guest of Harvard so late as 1936? And did Mr. Hillyer rush from that luncheon to speak to some member of the faculty, to the trustees, to the President of Harvard himself, warning them against Dr. Jung? Did he write and publish a piece about it? Did he do anything at all about it? Or did he just forget it until now, when suddenly it pops up as a convenient weapon to use against poets not of his school?

No, I refuse to believe that last line. But ah me, moral indignation is such a powerful weapon, and the American people have such a gift for it, if only they would get together and use all that fury and energy *in time,* and against the sources of our evils; to attack the real powers, the policy-makers, and finally punish the real criminals, the almost-unreachable ones. If this should happen only once, we should then be spared all this dreary aftermath of mean squabbling about a rag here and a tag there. All this hubbub about one wretched man seems not only a little late, but somewhat too easy. During the twenties and thirties, when Ezra Pound was living in Italy, writing his poetry and admiring Mussolini, we must remember that of these three things, at least it was not then disreputable in this country to admire Mussolini. Anyone who cares may run through a file of our most liberal and respectable family magazines (in trade argot, the "quality group"). He may now be dismayed to find how long, and how generously, and how late—almost to the eve of war—Mussolini was praised and supported by influential American newspapers and magazines. And you do remember surely that his policy was supported in more practical ways not only in the United States, but in France and Great Britain. . . . A simple, unpolitical mind like Ezra Pound's might be forgiven for getting a little muddled when asked suddenly to make a right-about-face; he had, in fact, all those years been in quite respectable company, and his real crime seems to have been lack of mental, moral, psychic flexibility, no talent for turning with the political winds. As late as 1939 certain faculty members of a southern University were accepting medals and citations from Mussolini for their services to "cultural relations" (whatever that may mean) between Italy and the United States. Then was the time, dear sirs, for you to have got into this fight.

1949

Opening Speech at Paris Conference, 1952

(International Exposition of the Arts)

Mr. President,
Ladies and Gentlemen,

When I received an invitation to come here to help in this Festival of the Arts as a writer to celebrate our freedom of speech and thought in the arts as well as in government, I thought it was a very beautiful, a very fine thing; I was delighted; for several days, I remained in this euphoric state and then the sinister aspects of the situation occurred to me.

If our freedoms not only as artists, but as citizens, as human beings, were not in great danger, we would not cross seas and far countries to gather here in this citadel of liberty to celebrate them, to boast of what is left of our freedoms.

We would be all of us at home living them and practicing them with that complacency and ease of mind of the truly free. Just the same, this is a great occasion, for perhaps it is the first time we free peoples have gathered together for this purpose and we are here and we are saying just what we like and there will be no penalties and that is not true everywhere.

It was a gift unexpected to me. I have not very much to say in a censorious way; I have not many objections to make, I would just like to say a few things about what goes on in my part of the world.

I have thought lately there has been entirely too much unholy alliance between criticism and the arts, between perhaps the intellectuals and the wars. Do you know, it is not true that the artist is always an intellectual—rather on the contrary—and judging by some of his performances he does not need always to be quite right. He is not an irresponsible, really, but he is a kind of synthesis, a sounding board, a mirror, a sieve, he is an instrument, in fact. He is something being used rather than using and he is not as much the master of his craft and his trade as is a man trained in abstract thought, in criticism, in philosophy, a man who can deal with philosophical and abstract ideas.

The business of the artist is a much stronger and more humane thing: in fact, he really deals with only human matters, with things of this world, and he is so many things because he does mean so many things to so many people.

He has to speak to all of us and interpret for all of us and therefore he is very often a touchstone, or a magnet, he is the sacred madman, he is the prophet and sometimes as a prophet he can prophesy as badly as some of our intellectuals. He can play the fool for the love of God and he does but he shouldn't play the fool for a political party. He then proves himself to be very inept when he goes into politics, and I need not mention any names. We all have our own examples. We all know too many. They don't guess right in their choice of political parties any better than the politicians do and I have often wondered why we require of the artist that he do something he was not born to do and that he do other things that he is not fitted to do instead of letting him go his way to do what he can do and what he must do; because in spite of the fact that probably for the first time in the history of the human race, certainly of the Western World, there has been a great rush, or it looks like this from where I stand, and by quite an overwhelming active majority (but I hope I am wrong) who have decided that art is not necessary, the old morality is not necessary; they think many things are not necessary: ethics are not necessary, love is not necessary, honorable dealings between nations are not necessary.

There are hundreds of good old things that we have decided to do without, and art seems to me one of them.

Well, I think it would be very interesting indeed to see the experiment made, if we, if they have the courage to make it. I was starting to say we but I must say they in this case because I am totally estranged from those who feel and act upon this belief, of living without the human values.

I wonder what would become of us, if we did abandon the arts, if we did just forget them and if we just agreed, in our time, to debase them until they would become irreclaimable, irretrievable. I don't think it will happen but we have gone a little far. This would mean altogether the destruction of the freedom of the artist, and when the artist loses his freedom it only means that everybody else has lost his.

Because the artist is only a human being who belongs to the human race in his place and after all he has his human responsibilities aside from the practice of his art; he is not an outcast, he is a citizen. If he should commit treason against his country, he should expect to be hanged not as an artist but as a citizen, responsible to his society.

So he is not altogether killed always by neglect, by contempt of his best work, but by all these little subtle sorts of things by which we can destroy our possessions; but in my country, I find that they are being killed with kindness, you know; I am afraid they are being strangled with hot butter.

We have a fearful, an unholy alliance between the professors, the universities, the faculties, the critics and the working artist.

And we have, also, an enormous, an immense nursery or cradle system for the fostering of artists. Various funds and grants, foundations, prizes, fellowships and all sorts of ways of helping them to live and I approve of some of them, but alas, the choices of talent are so strange and the committees of selection are so incompetent, it seems to me sometimes, to the case in hand, that it comes to be a very bad thing. It results in a great neglect of a very good and serious young artists and the encouragement of a great deal of perfectly second-rate talent, of the overambitious sort.

So you see, it is not in fact a state-operated thing. No. It really comes of a kind of private philanthropy and from the funds of the universities. But those funds of the great universities are too controlled and increasingly administered by men who are not artists and have very little concept of the meaning of the word. It is too controlled, too limited; it does not really cover the problem.

I think that watching this system grow, and it is growing at a terrific pace in the United States, at first, I thought that anything that anyone could do to help a man survive during the years when he is trying to become an artist, when he is serving his apprenticeship, and trying to prove himself, would be a good thing, and that he should have any help available.

Because I am no believer in this theory that if you have it in you, you will most certainly do your work (we do know now that too much can be destroyed untimely and cannot be replaced and we cannot afford to lose any more by neglect) I am all for any help we can get.

But I should so like to see a little better administration and choice by right people who could discriminate not just between good and bad but between mediocrity and mediocrity which is really more difficult. That is the only thing I think that I have to say in real criticism of this work. But we are not here insisting on the artist being a political person and I think that is a very good thing. They are not chosen for their political beliefs at least.

This is only a little delegation;* this delegation of Americans was not chosen to come here on the basis of our political beliefs and that is a good thing.

We came strictly as artists and we are of quite different political beliefs. We belong to different political parties, we have different religions, we are of different national origins, we have not even the same systems of morals and ethics.

1952

---

* We were six: James Farrell, William Faulkner, Katherine Anne Porter, Allen Tate, Robert Penn Warren, Glenway Wescott.

Remarks on the Agenda

(Conference on the
Arts and Exchange of Persons,
Institute of International Education)

1. *Is foreign experience valuable for the writer, or does it deprive him of
his "roots"? Why not just send his written works?*
A human being carries his "roots" in his blood, his nervous system the
brain cells; no man can get rid of them. Even his attempts to disguise
them will betray his origins and true nature. I think foreign travel and
experience are good for everybody—not just writers, but for writers they
are an invaluable, irreplaceable education in life. Yes, I know; Dante
never left Italy and Shakespeare never left England. We call to mind a
few house-bound women—geniuses too—Jane Austen, Emily Brontë,
Emily Dickinson—but we are not talking now about geniuses, but writers. One thing my fourteen years of travel and living in six foreign countries did for me besides giving me a wonderful time is, I am delighted to
stay at home!

It is an absurd but rather touching little human weakness, but any
number of people would rather see and hear a live author than read his
works.

2. *Are more opportunities for exchange of writers needed?*
Yes, I do think nations should exchange writers and all artists more than
they do; but not officially, not with any political affiliations. Several years
ago when I was in Washington there was some vague talk of sending me
as "cultural attaché" to a Spanish-speaking American country. Our Am-
bassador or Minister to that country turned the entire idea down saying:
"I don't want any culture mixed with my politics." This delighted me,
and I sent him a message through the proper channels: "And I don't

want any politics mixed with my culture!" And I still don't like the mixture.

3. *Should an attempt be made to lift the "iron curtain" through the exchange of writers?*

This is a bear trap of a question. Within my memory, before World War I, we had in effect an open world; no passports needed anywhere in Europe, or in the Americas. Russia, then as now, was closed. It was considered a barbarous government (and it was barbarous in other ways too) because passports were required, and Russian subjects could not leave the country without permission; and the Tsar's secret police and Siberian prison camps were the scandals of the world. (The world itself had quite a few horrors in every country, but Russia was then as now considered the worst.) Writers and artists came and went, even to Russia; they were free as birds at other international frontiers; their books were translated into all languages, and so far as peace, understanding, freedom, between nations is concerned, they might all as well never have left their own back yards. I daresay there is not at this moment a single government in this world which really trusts another government, and we know too well that last year's enemy can be this year's friend, and the other way around; but we can't blame this state of affairs on the writers, and we can't quite expect them to remedy it, either.

4. *What role can or should the U.S. government play in sending writers abroad and bringing writers here?*

The U.S. government might appoint good, well-proved poets and novelists to consular or other foreign posts as the French do, and certain Latin American countries: or appoint first-rate writers for a certain length of time—one, two, three years—as cultural attachés at a salary commensurate with the dignity of the place, to be awarded as an honor. Even the Consular or other foreign service jobs would not be any harder work or take more time than teaching, which is what so many of our best writers do to make a living.

But any political strings attached to any of this would quite simply be fatal, and no honest artist could survive in such a situation.

5. *What are the writer's personal objectives in going abroad? Do these differ from the objectives of most sponsoring organizations?*

I think most writers probably have the same motives as other people—for going abroad. They love to see the world, hear and maybe learn other languages; unfamiliar habits and customs, other peoples' lives and ways of feeling, are so fascinating and exciting and, if one lives there long enough, as I did in Mexico and France, one loves the place and the people; I may never see them again, but I shall never outlive my tenderness and sympathy for those glorious beautiful countries. I suppose the "objective" of a writer is just to live and do his work as well as he can, in his own way and time—his lifetime—and most sponsoring organizations want "production" right now!

6. *What kinds of writers should be selected to go abroad? (Criteria) Who should do the selecting? (Mechanisms)*
a) Good ones. The standard cannot be too high. The Library of Congress has a Chair of Poetry, and I don't know exactly what method they have of choosing but they haven't had a bad poet there yet! The National Institute of Arts and Letters has a pretty good system of choosing their Gold Medalists, and their speakers at the annual wing-ding in May: I have seen an impressive row of talent sitting there waiting to be handed that thousand-dollar grant.
b) For judges, I should look over the committee lists of such organizations. Second-rate judges will not know how to pick first-rate writers.

7. *What should a writer do, if anything, to prepare for a sojourn abroad? Does the writer need assistance or can he do it for himself?*
The only assistance any writer worth his salt needs is enough money to take him where he wants to go and keep him there for as long as he needs to stay. Sometimes he can save up money—if he teaches, for example—and go on a sabbatical year; sometimes he can support himself with free-lance writing, but it is very risky; almost the only hope is a grant or fellowship of some sort, though at this time there are very few that give enough for anyone to live on. Also the grants to what I believe are called "creative" writers, which I suppose means poets, novelists, as distinct from critics, essayists, and journalists, have been cut down to a mere token number in nearly all the foundation; yet I feel that our best poets and novelists are the ones we should send if we are going to send anybody to other countries.

8. *How can the sojourns of visiting writers be made more profitable to themselves and to their sponsors? What obligations does the writer have to a sponsor?*

a) If they are going to a country for the first time, they should have entirely practical advice and information about housing, cost of living, and local conditions. It is better if he knows the language, even slightly. If not he should set himself to speak at once.

b) As to the obligation of the writer to the sponsor, let me again cite my personal experience with the Guggenheim Foundation; their grant took me to Europe for a year, and I managed to stay for five in all. I was worried because the change was a tremendous one for me, full of violent reactions and intense feelings—not unhappy ones, simply unsettling to the last degree. It took me better than a year to settle to work, though I kept enormous notebooks. I wrote to Mr. Henry Allen Moe full of contrition that I hadn't turned out a book in that year. And Mr. Moe wrote that nobody had expected me to! That the grant was not just for the work of that year, but was meant to help me go on for all my life. And this has been true—without that grant, I might have just stayed in Mexico, or here at home; I should certainly not have gone to Europe when I did; and so in the most absolute sense, that Guggenheim Foundation Fellowship has helped to nourish my life as a writer to this day; I am today unable to imagine even faintly what I should have done without my wonderful years in Europe.

The writer owes to his sponsor to write, as well as he is able, in his own time and his own way, exactly what he wishes to write insofar as anyone has ever done that! In fact, he owes to his sponsor exactly what he owes to himself, no more, no less, except thanks!

9. *What can the writer do, if anything, to maintain contact with the country visited after his return home?*

One finds friends anywhere; my way of keeping up is to subscribe to a magazine or newspaper in the languages I can read—French, German, Spanish—and writing and getting letters from friends in those countries I have visited. Isn't this enough, and very pleasant, too? One wouldn't want to make *work* of it!

1956

A Letter to the Editor of
The Yale Review

Dear John:

It is now 6 in the morning of Christmas Eve, though I started this note two days ago. About the statement you sent me, I don't know if either Chiaromonte or Silone ever heard of me, much less would they consider me an intellectual, if they had. And it is of no importance either way.

As for the Declaration signed by the intellectuals of France, I suppose no Western Christian could find any fault with their point of view. Even in the most rigid monastic life with vows of poverty, chastity, and obedience, there is a clause explaining that obedience means only obedience to just and right things: no superior can exact it against conscience or for evil acts. The really shocking thing about the Germans is their insistence that they committed their crimes in the concentration camps (and elsewhere!) merely in obedience to orders. Of course we know what would have happened to them if they had not carried out orders. I have never been tested in this matter, so I cannot judge those who have been. I only say that someway I do not find it a good excuse.

I have been a little surprised that the "intellectuals" in this country have not leaped in a body to protest against prosecution of their French colleagues (among them a few artists, too) and it seems strange to leave the initiative to come from the Italians, some of them old-timers who seem to have kept silence at least at the invasion of (would you believe that I had to look up how to spell Abyssinia, and then realized I should say, Ethiopia). They have not shown any particular interest in human liberty anywhere else, are we sure this is not just a chance for them to attack France safely? Any old thing will do, but this could be a popular cause! I distrust Italy both as enemy and as friend, and never more than when that people champion the cause of the oppressed in some other country.

Well, dear John, I am in favor of the Declaration made and signed by the French intellectuals, and I believe firmly in the right to disobedience and dissent—did you ever read Thoreau on that subject? not because "it is the essence of democracy"—how would I know what is the essence of democracy? I have never seen a democracy in action—but because it is our highest moral duty to protest against the swineries of governments, and that should include our own; so I join with the Italian protest, with as you see rather mixed feelings. . . . I do remember uncomfortably the traditional attitude toward giving aid and comfort to the enemy in wartime: it is called treason, more often than not. I wish I knew more about the personal, political views and affiliations of signers on both Declaration and Protest. I am unenthusiastic about the whole matter: President De Gaulle should be rebuked by some competent party for his irresponsible hasty act in this important question, but I am not sure if the Italians are the ones to take the lead in the matter.

I can't think why your publishing this could be called a "stunt." It seems a legitimate enterprise for a review like yours if ever there was one! There are always afterthoughts as well as forethoughts, but your main true motive is what counts. . . . I discovered a law for myself, and have put it into a little axiom, and I tell it to my writing pupils, and I have never yet found a single exception to it. Here is it: THERE IS NO SUCH THING AS AN EXACT SYNONYM AND NO SUCH THING AS AN UNMIXED MOTIVE. Please give me a by-line on this. And look around a little and tell me if ever you do find an exception. Even God's motives for creating mankind seem to have been unusually mixed!

I look forward to seeing you on January 5th. Meantime, I hope you have a merry time for Christmas, and as good a year as 1961 can possibly be. My own personal future seems very good indeed, but I know there is no separating one's personal concerns from the general fate; the savages and thugs and hoodlums have really broken loose all over the world, we have mob rule and no mistake, so much for our liberal and humane notions!

1961

A Letter to the Editor of
the Washington Post

About that sow's ear into silk purse story in your Oct. 7 issue: Your headlines are charmingly lighthearted: "Silk Purse Is Made of a Sow's Ear Just to Prove That It Can Be Done." By now I suppose that most of us realize that scientists are the most reckless, irresponsible, not to say suicidal, people on earth.

Or do they just lack imagination? For their behavior in regard to all their bomb-inventions to destroy the human race, to end the world before its time, seems to indicate that they do not remember that they will be destroyed too. Or do they just think it is worth it to have all the fun they do have with their murderous experiments?

This is a purely rhetorical question asked by the way. About that sow's ear—I remember very well when this giddy little experiment took place, in 1920 (so long ago as that?), and I said then, and have been saying at intervals ever since, that it was bad enough for scientists to be so frivolous without telling fibs about it.

Our merry little grigs of scientists have not of course in the least made a silk purse or a silk anything else out of a sow's ear. Mr. Stevens now has the foresight to describe what the scientists did make as "a kind of silk" and that is easily the understatement of the year. What they made was an imitation silk purse out of a real sow's ear, and if the directors of the Smithsonian Institution have accepted it on any other terms, I really wouldn't know what to think of them, after all these years of thinking of them as the fountainhead of authority in these matters, the last word in authenticity concerning all that comes to their hands.

I want to make it very clear to these entertaining but misguided men of science: You not only have not made a silk purse out of a sow's ear, but you cannot make a sow, or an ear—or even a silkworm, the only creature that can turn out silk. You may, beginning with a sow's ear, make an imitation silkworm that may turn out a kind of web, or thread. I doubt you can do this, but we'll see—but what that imitation silkworm spins for a cocoon will be imitation silk.

Are you still with me? I am an artist, and I have to keep my feet on the ground and deal with reality, with truth as far as I am able to find it, I have to be practical; and you men of science carrying on your wild games on Cloud Nine, and then telling fibs, make it very hard for me to convince my writing students that indeed, if you consider everything, it is better to acknowledge that only silkworms can make silk, only scientists can make synthetics, and only God can make a silkworm.

1959

Speech of Acceptance

(*to the American Academy of Arts and Letters
on receiving the Gold Medal
for Fiction awarded by the
National Institute of Arts and Letters*)

I was told to write a little speech and I did, but I'm not sure I'm going to read it. Oh, I'll start. It looks all right. I am still amazed at this quite solid emblem of high honor being awarded me: I am told it was won by a very narrow squeak, which gives it rather the look of a good horse-race, and that's always exhilarating. I am charmed to have it, and sincerely glad it did not come earlier. I read lately an observation by Anthony Trollope: "Success is a necessary misfortune of life, but it is only to the very unfortunate that it comes early." I don't know if Mr. Trollope was being sarcastic, but I'm not. I agree entirely with him, quite literally.

I have avoided a career as long as I possibly could, and distrusted Success, in the way that we know it here, all my life. But I worked at my vocation and late in my life, by total hazard, by no design of my own whatever, I wrote a novel that became a modest bestseller.

Up to that time I had been sort of rocking along with my friends and my work and trying to be a good artist and not having much ambition and being quite contented with the nice modest loving little reputation that had been hung around my neck by my friends. But this thing brought me awake quickly.

It was the critics. They had always been very nice to me before, I suppose because they thought I wasn't worth attacking. But I tell you, this time I felt as if I had tripped into a tankful of piranhas, you know, those man-eating fish. They say a small school of them can strip one in thirty seconds, and I think it may be true. But I escaped and am no worse for it, and indeed it taught me something. It's always useful to get your enemies placed. It adds balance to life.

I'm going to leave out something here because this is getting too long. But just the same, I wanted to say that it has been a very difficult life and an exciting and wonderful one. I had at first thought everything was going to come very easy, but it was a long war, and an exhausting one, and I have a feeling now that this medal is a little bit like a laurel leaf put around my brow to show that I nearly won, you know. But just the same, I wouldn't have missed the life that I've had, just as it was, for anything. The years of youth and of being, of becoming, of learning my trade, and making my friends. All those years were wonderful. They are the blessed answer to everything. I have loved my friends who helped me by believing in me, and I thank them now with all my heart and I love them still.

One of my favorite characters in literature is the Wife of Bath. (And I think Chaucer was fond of her too.) Not so much for her history perhaps, but her way of looking at it. And her summing up: "It tickleth me about my heart's root, That I have seen the world as in my time."

I thank you.

1967

BIOGRAPHICAL

The Days Before

> Really, universally, relations stop nowhere, and the exquisite problem
> of the artist is eternally but to draw, by a geometry of his own, the circle
> within which they shall happily *appear* to do so.
>
> H.J.: Preface to *Roderick Hudson.*

We have, it would seem, at last reluctantly decided to claim Henry
James as our own, in spite of his having renounced, two years before his
death, so serious an obligation as his citizenship, but with a disturbing
tendency among his critics and admirers of certain schools to go a step
further and claim him for the New England, or Puritan, tradition.

This is merely the revival and extension of an old error first made by
Carlyle in regard to Henry James the elder: "Mr. James, your New-
England friend," wrote Carlyle in a letter, "I saw him several times and
liked him." This baseless remark set up, years later, a train of reverbera-
tions in the mind of Mr. James's son Henry, who took pains to correct
the "odd legend" that the James family were a New England product,
mentioning that Carlyle's mistake was a common one among the English, who seemed to have no faintest care or notion about our regional
differences. With his intense feeling for place and family relations and
family history, Henry James the younger could not allow this important
error to pass uncorrected. With his very special eyes, whose threads were
tangled in every vital center of his being, he looked long through "a thin
golden haze" into his past, and recreated for our charmed view an almost numberless family connection, all pure Scotch-Irish so far back as
the records run, unaltered to the third generation in his branch of the

233

family; and except for the potent name-grandfather himself—a Presbyterian of rather the blue-nosed caste, who brought up his eleven or was it thirteen children of three happy marriages in the fear of a quite improbable God—almost nothing could be less Puritanic, less New England, than their careers, even if they were all of Protestant descent. The earliest branch came late to this country (1764) according to Virginia or New England standards, and they settled in the comparatively newly opened country of upstate New York—new for the English and Scotch-Irish, that is, for the Dutch and the French had been there a good while before, and they married like with like among the substantial families settled along the Hudson River. Thus the whole connection in its earlier days was spared the touch of the specifically New England spirit, which even then was spreading like a slow blight into every part of the country.

(But the young Henry James feared it from the first, distrusted it in his bones. Even though his introduction to New England was by way of "the proud episcopal heart of Newport," when he was about fifteen years old, and though he knew there at least one artist, and one young boy of European connection and experience, still, Boston was not far away, and he felt a tang of wintry privation in the air, a threat of "assault and death." By way of stores against the hovering famine and siege, he collected a whole closet full of the beloved *Revue des Deux Mondes*, in its reassuring salmon-pink cover.)

Henry James's grandfather, the first William James, arrived in America from Ireland, County Cavan, an emigrant boy of seventeen, and settled in Albany in 1789. He was of good solid middle-class stock, he possessed that active imagination and boundless energy of the practical sort so useful in ancestors; in about forty years of the most blameless, respected use of every opportunity to turn an honest penny, on a very handsome scale of operations, he accumulated a fortune of three million dollars, in a style that was to become the very pattern of American enterprise. The city of Albany was credited to him, it was the work of his hands, it prospered with him. His industries and projects kept hundreds of worthy folk gainfully employed the year round, in the grateful language of contemporary eulogy; in his time only John Jacob Astor gathered a larger fortune in New York state. We may as well note here an obvious irony, and dismiss it: James's grandfather's career was a perfect example of the sort of thing that was to become "typically American," and still is, it happens regularly even now; and Henry James the younger had great good of it, yet it did create the very atmosphere which later on he found so hard to breathe that he deserted it altogether for years, for life.

The three millions were divided at last among the widow and eleven surviving children, the first Henry James, then a young man, being one of them. These twelve heirs none of them inherited the Midas touch, and all had a taste for the higher things of life enjoyed in easy, ample surroundings. Henry the younger lived to wonder, with a touch of charming though acute dismay, just what had become of all that delightful money. Henry the elder, whose youth had been gilded to the ears, considered money a topic beneath civilized discussion, business a grimy affair they all agreed to know nothing about, and neglected completely to mention what he had done with his share. He fostered a legend among his children that he had been "wild" and appeared, according to his fascinating stories, to have been almost the only young man of his generation who had not come to a bad end. His son Henry almost in infancy had got the notion that the words "wild" and "dissipated" were synonymous with "tipsy." Be that as it may, Henry the first in his wild days had a serious if temporary falling out with his father, whom he described as the tenderest and most sympathetic of parents; but he also wrote in his fragment of autobiography, "I should think indeed that our domestic intercourse had been on the whole most innocent as well as happy, were it not for a certain lack of oxygen which is indeed incidental to the family atmosphere and which I may characterize as the lack of any ideal of action except that of self-preservation." Indeed, yes. Seeking fresh air, he fled into the foreign land of Massachusetts: Boston, precisely: until better days should come. "It was an age," wrote his son Henry, "in which a flight from Albany to Boston . . . counted as a far flight." It still does. The point of this episode for our purposes was, that Henry the first mildewed in exile for three long months, left Boston and did not again set foot there until he was past thirty-five. His wife never went there at all until her two elder sons were in Harvard, a seat of learning chosen *faute de mieux*, for Europe, Europe was where they fain all would be; except that a strange, uneasy, even artificially induced nationalism, due to the gathering war between the states, had laid cold doubts on their minds—just where did they belong, where was their native land? The two young brothers, William and Henry, especially then began, after their shuttlings to and from Europe, to make unending efforts to "find America" and to place themselves once for all either in it or out of it. But this was later.

It is true that the elder Jameses settled in Boston, so far as a James of that branch could ever be said to settle, for the good reason that they wished to be near their sons; but they never became, by any stretch of the word, New Englanders, any more than did their son William, after all those years at Harvard; any more than did their son Henry become an Englishman, after all those years in England. He realized this himself, even after he became a British subject in 1914; and the British agree with him to this day. He was to the end an amiable, distinguished stranger living among them. Yet two generations born in this country did not make them Americans, either, and in the whole great branching family connection, with its "habits of ease" founded on the diminishing backlog of the new fortune, the restless blood of the emigrant grandparents ran high. Europe was not so far away as it is now, and though Albany and "the small, warm dusky homogeneous New York world of the mid-century" were dear to them, they could not deny, indeed no one even thought of denying, that all things desirable in the arts, architecture, education, ways of living, history, the future, the very shape of the landscape and the color of the air, lay like an inheritance they had abandoned, in Europe.

"This question of Europe" which never ceased to agitate his parents from his earliest memory was paradoxically the only permanent element in the Jameses' family life. All their movements, plans, interests were based, you might say, on that perpetually unresolved problem. It was kept simmering by letters from friends and relatives traveling or living there; cousins living handsomely at Geneva, enjoying the widest possible range of desirable social amenities; other cousins living agreeably at Tours, or Trouville; the handsomest of the Albany aunts married advantageously and living all over Europe, urging the Henry Jameses to come with their young and do likewise for the greater good of all. There was an older cousin who even lived in China, came back to fill a flat in Gramercy Square with "dim Chinoiseries" and went on to old age in Surrey and her last days in Versailles. There was besides the constant delicious flurry of younger cousins and aunts with strange wonderful clothes and luggage who had always just been there, or who were just going there, "there" meaning always Europe, and oddly enough, specifically Paris, instead of London. The infant Henry, at the age of five, received his "positive initiation into History" when Uncle Gus returned bringing the news of the flight of Louis Philippe to England. To the child, *flight* had been a word with a certain meaning; *king* another. "Flight of kings" was a new, portentous, almost poetic image of strange disasters, it early gave to political questions across the sea a sense of magnificence they altogether lacked at home, where society outside the enthralling family circle and the shimmering corona of friends seemed altogether to consist of "the busy, the tipsy, and Daniel Webster."

Within that circle, however, nothing could exceed the freedom and ease with which artists of all sorts, some of them forgotten now, seemed to make the James fireside, wherever it happened to be, their own. The known and acclaimed were also household guests and dear friends.

Mr. Emerson, "the divinely pompous rose of the philosophical garden," as Henry James the elder described him, or, in other lights and views, the "man without a handle"—one simply couldn't get hold of him at all—had been taken upstairs in the fashionable Astor Hotel to admire the newly born William; and in later times, seated in the firelit dusk of the back parlor in the James house, had dazzled the young Henry, who knew he was great. General Winfield Scott in military splendor had borne down upon him and his father at a street corner for a greeting; and on a boat between Fort Hamilton and New York Mr. Washington Irving had apprised Mr. James of the shipwreck of Margaret Fuller, off Fire Island, only a day or so before. Edgar Allan Poe was one of the "acclaimed," the idolized, most read and recited of poets; his works were on every drawing room or library table that Henry James knew, and he never outgrew his wonder at the legend that Poe was neglected in his own time.

Still it was Dickens who ruled and pervaded the literary world from afar; the books in the house, except for a few French novels, were nearly all English; the favorite bookstore was English, where the James children went to browse, sniffing the pages for the strong smell of paper and printer's ink, which they called "the English smell." The rule of the admired, revered *Revue des Deux Mondes* was to set in shortly; France and French for Henry James, Germany and German for William James, were to have their great day, and stamp their images to such a degree that ever after the English of the one, and of the other, were to be "larded" and tagged and stuffed with French and German. In the days before, however, the general deliciousness and desirability of all things

English was in the domestic air Henry James breathed; his mother and father talked about it so much at the breakfast table that, remembering, he asked himself if he had ever heard anything else talked about over the morning coffee cups. They could not relive enough their happy summer in England with their two babies, and he traveled again and again with them, by way of "Windsor and Sudbrook and Ham Common"; an earthly Paradise, they believed, and he believed with them. A young aunt, his mother's sister, shared these memories and added her own: an incurable homesickness for England possessed her. Henry, asking for stories, listened and "took in" everything: taking in was to be his life's main occupation: as if, he said, his "infant divination proceeded by the light of nature," and he had learned already the importance of knowing in advance of any experience of his own, just what life in England might be like. A small yellow-covered English magazine called *Charm* also "shed on the question the softest lustre" and caused deep pangs of disappointment when it failed to show up regularly at the bookstore.

Henry James refers to all these early impressions as an "infection," as a sip of "poison," as a "twist"—perhaps of some psychological thumbscrew—but the twinges and pangs were all exciting, joyful, mysterious, thrilling, sensations he enjoyed and sought eagerly, half their force at least consisting of his imaginative projection of his own future in the most brilliant possible of great worlds. He saw his parents and his aunt perpetually homesick for something infinitely lovable and splendid they had known, and he longed to know it too. "Homesickness was a luxury I remember craving from the tenderest age," he confessed, because he had at once perhaps too many homes and therefore no home at all. If his parents did not feel at home anywhere, he could not possibly, either. He did not know what to be homesick for, unless it were England, which he had seen but could not remember.

This was, then, vicarious, a mere sharing at second-hand; he needed something of his own. When it came, it was rather dismaying; but it was an important episode and confirmed in him the deep feeling that England had something formidable in its desirability, something to be lived up to: in contrast to France as he discovered later, where one "got life," as he expressed it; or Germany, where the very trees of the great solemn forests murmured in his charmed ear of their mystical "culture." What happened was this: the celebrated Mr. Thackeray, fresh from England, seated as an honored much-at-ease guest in the James library, committed an act which somehow explains everything that is wrong with his novels. "Come here, little boy," he said to Henry, "and show me your extraordinary jacket." With privileged bad manners he placed his hand on the child's shoulder and asked him if his garments were the uniform of his "age and class," adding with brilliant humor that if he should wear it in England he would be addressed as "Buttons." No matter what Mr. Thackeray thought he was saying—very likely he was not thinking at all—he conveyed to the overwhelmed admirer of England that the English, as so authoritatively represented by Mr. Thackeray, thought Americans "queer." It was a disabling blow, recalled in every circumstance fifty years later, with a photograph, of all things, to illustrate and prove its immediate effect.

Henry was wearing that jacket, buttoned to the chin with a small white collar, on the hot dusty summer day when his companionable father, who never went anywhere without one or the other of his two elder sons, brought him up from Staten Island, where the family were summering, to New York, and as a gay surprise for everybody, took him to Mr. Brady's for their photograph together. A heavy surprise indeed for Henry, who forever remembered the weather, the smells and sights of the wharf, the blowzy summer lassitude of the streets, and his own dismay that by his father's merry whim he was to be immortalized by Mr. Brady in his native costume which would appear so absurd in England. Mr. Brady that day made one of the most expressive child pictures I know. The small straight figure has a good deal of grace and dignity in its unworthy (as he feared) clothes; the long hands are holding with what composure they can to things they know; his father's shoulder, his large and, according to the fashion plates of the day, stylish straw hat. All the life of the child is in the eyes, rueful, disturbed, contemplative, with enormous intelligence and perception, much older than the face, much deeper and graver than his father's. His father and mother bore a certain family resemblance to each other, such as closely interbred peoples of any nation are apt to develop; Henry resembled them both, but his father more nearly, and judging by later photographs, the resemblance became almost identical, except for the expression of the eyes—the unmistakable look of one who was to live intuitively and naturally a long life in "the air of the passions of the intelligence."

In Mr. Brady's daguerreotype, he is still a child, a stranger everywhere, and he is unutterably conscious of the bright untimeliness of the whole thing, the lack of proper ceremony, ignored as ever by the father; the slack, unflattering pose. His father is benevolent and cheerful and self-possessed and altogether pleased for them both. He had won his right to gaiety of heart in his love; after many a victorious engagement with the powers of darkness, he had Swedenborg and all his angels round about, bearing him up, which his son was never to have; and he had not been lately ridiculed by Mr. Thackeray, at least not to his face. Really it was not just the jacket that troubled him—that idle remark upon it was only one of the smallest of the innumerable flashes which lighted for him, blindingly, whole territories of mystery in which a long lifetime could not suffice to make him feel at home. "I lose myself in wonder," he wrote in his later years, "at the loose ways, the strange process of waste, through which nature and fortune may deal on occasion with those whose faculty for application is all and only in their imagination and sensibility."

By then he must have known that in his special case, nothing at all had been wasted. He was in fact a most glorious example in proof of his father's favorite theories of the uses and virtues of waste as education, and at the end felt he had "mastered the particular history of just that waste." His father was not considered a good Swedenborgian by those followers of Swedenborg who had, against his expressed principles, organized themselves into a church. Mr. James could not be organized in the faintest degree by anyone or anything. His daughter Alice wrote of him years later: ". . . Father, the delicious infant, couldn't submit even to the thralldom of his own whim." That smothering air of his childhood family life had given him a permanent longing for freedom and fresh air; the atmosphere he generated crackled with oxygen; his children lived in such a state of mental and emotional stimulation that no society ever again could overstimulate them. Life, as he saw it—was nobly resolved to see it, and to teach his beloved young ones to see it—was so much a matter of living happily and freely by spiritual, ethical, and intellectual values, based soundly on sensuous richness, and inexhaustible faith in the goodness of God; a firm belief in the divinity in human nature, God's self in it; a boundlessly energetic aspiration toward the higher life, the purest humanities, the most spontaneous expression of feeling and thought.

Despair was for the elder James a word of contempt. He declared "that never for a moment had he known a skeptical state." Yet, "having learned the nature of evil, and admitted its power, he turned towards the sun of goodness." He believed that "true worship is always spontaneous, the offspring of delight, not duty." Thus his son Henry: "The case was really of his feeling so vast a rightness close at hand or lurking immediately behind actual arrangements that a single turn of the inward wheel, one real response to the pressure of the spiritual spring, would bridge the chasms, straighten the distortions, rectify the relations, and in a word redeem and vivify the whole mass." With all his considerable powers of devotion translated into immediate action, the father demonstrated his faith in the family circle; the children responded to the love, but were mystified and respectful before the theory: they perceived it was something very subtle, as were most of "father's ideas." But they also knew early that their father did not live in a fool's paradise. "It was of course the old story that we had only to *be* with more intelligence and faith—an immense deal more, certainly, in order to work off, in the happiest manner, the many-sided ugliness of life; which was a process that might go on, blessedly, in the quietest of all quiet ways. *That* wouldn't be blood and fire and tears, or would be none of these things stupidly precipitated; it would simply take place by *enjoyed* communication and contact, enjoyed concussion or convulsion even—since pangs and agitations, the very agitations of perception itself, are the highest privilege of the soul, and there is always, thank goodness, a saving sharpness of play or complexity of consequence in the intelligence completely alive."

Blood and fire and tears each in his own time and way each of them suffered, sooner or later. Alice, whose life was a mysterious long willful dying, tragic and ironic, once asked her father's permission to kill herself. He gave it, and she understood his love in it, and refrained: he wrote to Henry that he did not much fear any further thoughts of suicide on her part. William took the search for truth as hard as his father had, but by way of philosophy, not religion; the brave psychologist and philosopher was very sick in his soul for many years. Henry was maimed for life in an accident, as his father had been before him, but he of them all never broke, never gave way, sought for truth not in philosophy nor in religion, but in art, and found his own; showed just what the others had learned and taught, and spoke for them better than they could for themselves, thus very simply and grandly fulfilling his destiny as artist; for it was destiny and he knew it and never resisted a moment, but went with it as unskeptically as his father had gone with religion.

The James family, as we have seen, were materially in quite comfortable circumstances. True the fine fortune had misted away somewhat, but they had enough. If people are superior to begin with, as they were, the freedom of money is an added freedom of grace and the power of choice in many desirable ways. This accounts somewhat then for the extraordinary ability, ease of manners, and artless, innocent unselfconsciousness of the whole family in which Henry James was brought up, which he has analyzed so acutely, though with such hovering tenderness. It was merely a fact that they could afford to be beyond material considerations because in that way they were well provided. Their personal virtues, no matter on what grounds, were real, their kindness and frankness were unfeigned. "The cousinship," he wrote, "all unalarmed and unsuspecting and unembarrassed, lived by pure serenity, sociability, and loquacity." Then with the edge of severity his own sense of truth drew finally upon any subject, he added: "The special shade of its identity was thus that it was not conscious—really not conscious of anything in the world; or was conscious of so few possibilities at least, and these so immediate, and so a matter of course, that it came to the same thing." There he summed up a whole society, limited in number but of acute importance in its place; and having summed up, he cannot help returning to the exceptions, those he loved and remembered best.

There were enough intellectual interests and consciousness of every kind in his father's house to furnish forth the whole connection, and it was the center. Education, all unregulated, to be drawn in with the breath, and absorbed like food, proceeded at top speed day and night. Though William, of all the children, seemed to be the only one who managed to acquire a real, formal university training of the kind recognized by academicians, Henry got his, in spite of the dozen schools in three countries, in his own time and his own way; in the streets, in theaters (how early grew in him that long, unrequited passion for the theater!), at picture galleries, at parties, on boats, in hotels, beaches, at family reunions; by listening, by gazing, dawdling, gaping, wondering, and soaking in impressions and sensations at every pore, through every hair. Though at moments he longed to be an orphan when he saw the exciting life of change and improvisation led by his cheerful orphaned cousins, "so little sunk in the short range," it is clear that his own life, from minute to minute, was as much as he could endure; he had the only family he could have done with at all, and the only education he was capable of receiving. His intuitions were very keen and pure from the beginning, and foreknowledge of his ineducability in any practical sense caused him very rightly to kick and shriek as they hauled him however fondly to his first day of school. There he found, as he was to find in every situation for years and years, elder brother William, the vivid, the hardy, the quick-learning, the outlooking one, seated already: accustomed, master of his environment, lord of his playfellows. For so Henry saw him; William was a tremendous part of his education. William was beyond either envy or imitation: the younger brother could only follow and adore at the right distance.

So was his mother his education. Her children so possessed her they did not like her even to praise them or be proud of them because that seemed to imply that she was separate from them. After her death, the younger Henry wrote of her out of depths hardly to be stirred again in him, "she was our life, she was the house, she was the keystone of the arch"—suddenly his language took on symbols of the oldest poetry. Her husband, who found he could not live without her, wrote in effect to a friend that very early in their marriage she had awakened his torpid heart, and helped him to become a man.

The father desired many things for the childen, but two things first: spiritual decency, as Henry James says it, and "a sensuous education." If Henry remembered his share in the civilizing atmosphere of Mr. Jenks's school as "merely contemplative," totally detached from any fact of learning, at home things were more positive. Their father taught them a horror of piggishness, and of conscious virtue; guarded them, by precept and example, from that vulgarity he described as "flagrant morality"; and quite preached, if his boundless and changing conversation could be called that, against success in its tangible popular meaning. "We were to convert and convert, success—in the sense that was in the general air—or no success; and simply everything that happened to us, every contact, every impression and every experience we should know, were to form our soluble stuff; with only ourselves to thank should we remain unaware, by the time our perceptions were decently developed, of the substance finally projected and most desirable. That substance might be just consummately Virtue, as a social grace and value . . . the moral of all of which was that we need never fear not to be good enough if only we were social enough. . . ."

Again he told them that the truth—the one truth as distinguished from the multiple fact—"was never ugly and dreadful, and (we) might therefore depend upon it for due abundance, even of meat and drink and raiment, even of wisdom and wit and honor."

No child ever "took in" his father's precepts more exactly and more literally than did Henry James, nor worked them more subtly and profoundly to his own needs. He was at last, looking back, "struck . . . with the rare fashion after which, in any small victim of life, the inward perversity may work. It works by converting to its uses things vain and unintended, to the great discomposure of their prepared opposites, which it by the same stroke so often reduces to naught; with the result indeed that one may most of all see it—so at least have I quite exclusively seen it, the little life out for its chance—as proceeding by the inveterate process of conversion."

The little life out for its chance was oh how deeply intent on the chance it *chose* to take; and all this affected and helped to form a most important phase of his interests: money, exactly, and success, both of which he desired most deeply, but with the saving justifying clause that he was able only to imagine working for and earning them honestly— and though money was only just that, once earned, his notion of success was really his father's, and on nothing less than the highest ground did it deserve that name. In the meantime, as children, they were never to be preoccupied with money. But how to live? "The effect of his attitude, so little thought out as shrewd or vulgarly providential, but . . . so socially and affectionately founded, could only be to make life interesting to us at worst, in default of making it extraordinarily paying." His father wanted all sorts of things for them without quite knowing what they needed, but Henry the younger began peering through, and around the corners of, the doctrine. "With subtle indirectness," the children, perhaps most of all Henry, got the idea that the inward and higher life, well rounded, *must* somehow be lived in good company, with good manners and surroundings fitting to virtue and sociability, good, you might say, attracting good on all planes: of course. But one of the goods, a main good, without which the others might wear a little thin, was material ease. Henry James understood and anatomized thoroughly and acutely the sinister role of money in society, the force of its corrosive powers on the individual; the main concern of nearly all his chief characters is that life shall be, one way or another, and by whatever means, a paying affair . . . and the theme is the consequences of their choice of means, and their notion of what shall pay them.

This worldly knowledge, then, was the end-product of that unworldly education which began with the inward life, the early inculcated love of virtue for its own sake, a belief in human affections and natural goodness, a childhood of extraordinary freedom and privilege, passed in a small warm world of fostering love. This world for him was never a landscape with figures, but a succession of rather small groups of persons intensely near to him, for whom the landscape was a setting, the houses they lived in the appropriate background. The whole scene of his childhood existed in his memory in terms of the lives lived in it, with his own growing mind working away at it, storing it, transmuting it, reclaiming it. Through his extreme sense of the appearance of things, manners, dress, social customs, the lightest gesture, he could convey mysterious but deep impressions of individual character. In crises of personal events, he could still note the look of tree-shaded streets, family gardens, the flash of a grandmother's scissors cutting grapes or flowers, fan-shaped lights, pink marble steps; the taste of peaches, baked apples, custards, ice creams, melons, food indeed by the bushel and the barrel; the colors and shapes of garments, the headdresses of ladies, their voices, the way they lifted their hands. If these were all, they would have been next to nothing, but the breathing lives are somewhere in them.

The many schools he attended, if that is the word, the children he knew there, are perfectly shown in terms of their looks and habits. He was terrorized by the superior talents of those boys who could learn arithmetic, apparently without effort, a branch of learning forever closed to him, as by decree of nature. A boy of his own age, who lived in Geneva, "opened vistas" to him by pronouncing Ohio and Iowa in the French manner: an act of courage as well as correctness which was impressive, surrounded as he was by tough little glaring New Yorkers with stout boots and fists, who were not prepared to be patronized in any such way. Was there anybody he ever thought stupid, he asked himself, if only they displayed some trick of information, some worldly sleight of hand of which he had hitherto been ignorant? On a sightseeing tour at Sing Sing he envied a famous ciminal his self-possession, inhabiting as he did a world so perilous and so removed from daily experience. His sense of social distinctions was early in the bud: he recognized a Dowager on sight, at a very tender age. An elegant image of a "great Greek Temple shining over blue waters"—which seems to have been a hotel at New Brighton called the Pavilion—filled him with joy when he was still in his nurse's arms. He had thought it a finer thing than he discovered it to be, and this habit of thought was to lead him far afield for a good number of years.

For his freedoms were so many, his instructions so splendid, and yet his father's admirable, even blessed teachings failed to cover so many daily crises of the visible world. The visible world was the one he would have, all his being strained and struggled outward to meet it, to absorb it, to understand it, to be a part of it. The other children asked him to what church he belonged, and he had no answer; for the even more important question, "What does your father *do?*" or "What business is he in?" no reply had been furnished him for the terrible occasion. His father was no help there, though he tried to be. How could a son explain to his father that it did no good to reply that one had the freedom of all religion, being God's child; or that one's father was an author of books and a truth-seeker?

So his education went forward in all directions and on all surfaces and depths. He longed "to be somewhere—almost anywhere would do—and somehow to receive an impression or an accession, feel a relation or a vibration"; while all the time a performance of *Uncle Tom's Cabin,* which gave him his first lesson in ironic appreciation of the dowdy, the overwrought and underdone; or Mrs. Cannon's mystifyingly polite establishment full of scarfs, handkerchiefs, and colognes for gentlemen, with an impalpable something in the air which hinted at mysteries, and which turned out to be only that gentlemen, some of them cousins, from out of town took rooms there; or the gloomy show of Italian Primitives, all frauds, which was to give him a bad start with painting—such events were sinking into him as pure sensation to emerge from a thousand points in his memory as knowledge.

Knowledge—knowledge at the price of finally, utterly "seeing through" everything—even the fortunate, happy childhood; yet there remained to him, to the very end, a belief in that good which had been shown to him as good in his infancy, embodied in his father and mother. There was a great deal of physical beauty in his family, and it remained the kind that meant beauty to him: the memory of his cousin Minnie Temple, the face of his sister Alice in her last photograph, these were the living images of his best-loved heroines; the love he early understood as love never betrayed him and was love at the latest day; the extraordinarily sensitive, imaginative excitements of first admirations and friendships turned out to be not perhaps so much irreplaceable as incomparable.

What I am trying to say is that so far as we are able to learn, nothing came to supplant or dislocate in any way those early affections and attachments and admirations.

This is not to say he never grew up with them, for they expanded with his growth, and as he grew his understanding gave fresh life to them; nor that he did not live to question them acutely, to inquire as to their nature and their meaning, for he did; but surely no one ever projected more lovingly and exactly the climate of youth, of budding imagination, the growth of the tender, perceptive mind, the particular freshness and keenness of feeling, the unconscious generosity and warmth of heart of the young brought up in the innocence which is their due, and the sweet illusion of safety, dangerous because it must be broken at great risk. He survived all, and made it his own, and used it with that fullness and boldness and tenderness and intent reverence which is the sum of his human qualities, indivisible from his sum as artist. For though no writer ever "grew up" more completely than Henry James, and "saw through" his own illusions with more sobriety and pure intelligence, still there lay in the depths of his being the memory of a lost paradise; it was in the long run the standard by which he measured the world he learned so thoroughly, accepted in certain ways—the ways of a civilized man with his own work to do—after such infinite pains: or pangs, as he would have called them, that delight in deep experience which at a certain point is excruciating, and by the uninstructed might be taken for pain itself. But the origin is different, it is not inflicted, not even invited, it comes under its own power and the end is different; and the pang is *not* suffering, it is delight.

Henry James knew about this, almost from the beginning. Here is his testimony: "I foresee moreover how little I shall be able to resist, throughout these notes, the force of persuasion expressed in the individual *vivid* image of the past wherever encountered, these images having always such terms of their own, such subtle secrets and insidious arts for keeping us in relation with them, for bribing us by the beauty, the authority, the wonder of their saved intensity. They have saved it, they seem to say to us, from such a welter of death and darkness and ruin that this alone makes a value and a light and a dignity for them. . . . Not to be denied also, over and above this, is the downright pleasure of the illusion yet again created, the *apparent* transfer from the past to the present of the particular combination of things that did at its hour ever so directly operate and that isn't after all then drained of virtue, wholly wasted and lost, for sensation, for participation in the act of life, in the attesting sights, sounds, smells, the illusion, as I say, of the recording senses."

Brother William remained Big Brother to the end, though Henry learned to stand up to him manfully when the philosopher invaded the artist's territory. But William could not help being impatient with all this reminiscence, and tried to discourage Henry when he began rummaging through his precious scrapbags of bright fragments, patching them into the patterns before his mind's eye. William James was fond of a phrase of his philosopher friend Benjamin Paul Blood: "There is no conclusion. What has concluded, that we might conclude in regard to it?"

That is all very well for philosophy, and it has within finite limits the sound of truth as well as simple fact—no man has ever seen any relations concluded. Maybe that is why art is so endlessly satisfactory: the artist can choose his relations, and "draw, by a geometry of his own, the circle within which they shall happily *appear* to do so." While accomplishing this, one has the illusion that destiny is not absolute, it can be arranged, temporized with, persuaded, a little here and there. And once the circle is truly drawn around its contents, it too becomes truth.

First version: July, 1943
Revised: 27 February 1952

Homage to
Ford Madox Ford

Several years ago Ford Madox Ford remarked to me, at Olivet—and to how many others? I don't know—with a real pride and satisfaction, that he had a book to show for every year of his life. Now he knew as well as anyone that no man can write sixty *good* books, he said himself there were books on that list he was willing to have out of print forever. But at the time of writing them, he had believed firmly each book was going to be good; in any case, each book was as good as he was capable of making it at that moment, that given circumstance; and in any case he could not have stopped himself from the enterprise, because he was a man of letters, born and bred. His life work and his vocation happened to be one and the same thing. A lucky man, in spite of what seems, sometimes, to the onlooker, as unlucky a life as was ever lived.

His labors were constant, his complicated seeking mind was never for one moment diverted from its speculations on the enduring topic of literature, the problems of creation, the fascinating pitfalls of technique, the moral, psychic, aesthetic aspects of art, all art, any one of the arts. He loved to live the life of the artist, he loved to discover, foster, encourage young beginners in what another admirer of his, Glenway Wescott, has described as "this severe and fantastic way of life." Toward the end, when he was at Olivet, Ford described himself as "an old man mad about writing." He was not really an old man—think of Hardy, think of Tolstoy, think of Yeats—and his madness was an illuminated sanity; but he had, when he wrote this, intimations of mortality in him, and he had always practiced, tongue in cheek, that "pride which apes humility." It pleased him to think of himself in that way; and indeed, when you consider his history, the tragic mischances of his life, his times of glory and success alternating with painful bouts with poverty and neglect, you might think, unless you were an artist, that he was a little mad to have run all the risks and to have taken all the punishment he did take at the hands of fortune—and for what? I don't think he ever asked himself that question. I doubt greatly he ever seriously considered for one moment any other mode of life than the life he lived. I knew him for twelve years, in a great many places and situations, and I can testify that he led an existence of marvelous discomfort, of insecurity, of deep and pressing anxiety as to his daily bread; but no matter where he was, what his sufferings were, he sat down daily and wrote, in his crabbed fine hand, with pen, the book he was working on at the moment; and I never knew him when he was not working on a book. It is not the moment to estimate those books, time may reverse his own severe judgment on some of them, but any of you who have read the Tietjens cycle, or *The Good Soldier*, must have taken a long step forward in your knowledge of craftsmanship, or just what it takes to write a fine novel. His influence is deeper than we are able to measure, for he has influenced writers who never read his books, which is the fate of all masters.

There was in all something so typical, so classical in his way of life, his history, some phases of his career, so grand in the old manner of English men of letters, I think a reading of his books and a little meditation on his life and death might serve at once as guiding sign and a finger of warning to all eager people who thoughtlessly, perhaps, "want to write." You will learn from him what the effort really is; what the pains, and what the rewards, of a real writer; and if that is not enough to frighten you off, you may proceed with new confidence in yourself.

1942

Gertrude Stein:
Three Views

"EVERYBODY IS A REAL ONE"

All I know about Gertrude Stein is what I find in her first two books, *Three Lives* and *The Making of Americans*. Many persons know her, they tell amusing stories about her and festoon her with legends. Next to James Joyce she is the great influence on the younger literary generation, who see in her the combination of tribal wise woman and arch-priestess of aesthetic.

This is all very well; but I can go only by what I find in these pages. They form not so much a history of Americans as a full description and analysis of many human beings, including Gertrude Stein and the reader and all the reader's friends; they make a psychological source book and the diary of an aesthetic problem worked out momently under your eyes.

One of the many interesting things about *The Making of Americans* is its date. It was written twenty years ago (1906–1908), when Gertrude Stein was young. It precedes the war and cubism; it precedes *Ulysses* and *Remembrance of Things Past*. I doubt if all the people who should read it will read it for a great while yet, for it is in such a limited edition, and reading it is anyhow a sort of permanent occupation. Yet to shorten it would be to mutilate its vitals, and it is a very necessary book. In spite of all there is in it Gertrude Stein promises all the way through it to write another even longer and put in it all the things she left unfinished in this. She has not done it yet; at least it has not been published.

Twenty years ago, when she had been living in Paris only a few years, Gertrude Stein's memory of her American life was fresh, and I think both painful and happy in her. "The old people in a new world, the new people made out of the old, that is the story that I mean to tell, for that is what really is and what I really know." This is a deeply American book, and without "movies" or automobiles or radio or prohibition or any of the mechanical properties for making local color, it is a very up-to-date book. We feel in it the vitality and hope of the first generation, the hearty materialism of the second, the vagueness of the third. It is all realized and projected in these hundreds of portraits, the deathlike monotony in action, the blind diffusion of effort, "the spare American emotion," "the feeling of rich American living"—rich meaning money, of course—the billion times repeated effort of being born and breathing and eating and sleeping and working and feeling and dying to no particular end that makes American middle-class life. We have almost no other class as yet. "I say vital singularity is as yet an unknown product with us." So she observes the lack of it and concerns herself with the endless repetition of pattern in us only a little changed each time, but changed enough to make an endless mystery of each individual man and woman.

In beginning this book you walk into what seems to be a great spiral, a slow, ever-widening, unmeasured spiral unrolling itself horizontally. The people in this world appear to be motionless at every stage of their progress, each one is simultaneously being born, arriving at all ages and dying. You perceive that it is a world without mobility, everything takes place, has taken place, will take place; therefore nothing takes place, all at once. Yet the illusion of movement persists, the spiral unrolls, you follow; a closed spinning circle is even more hopeless than a universe that will not move. Then you discover it is not a circle, not machinelike repetition, the spiral does open and widen, it is repetition only in the sense that one wave follows upon another. The emotion progresses with the effort of a giant parturition. Gertrude Stein describes her function in terms of digestion, of childbirth: all these people, these fragments of digested knowledge, are in her, they must come out.

The progress of her family, then, this making of Americans, she has labored to record in a catalogue of human attributes, acts and emotions. Episodes are nothing, narrative is by the way, her interest lies in what she calls the bottom natures of men and women, all men, all women. "It is important to me, very important indeed to me, that I sometimes understand every one. . . . I am hoping some time to be right about every one, about everything."

In this intensity of preoccupation there is the microscopic observation of the near-sighted who must get so close to their object they depend not alone on vision but on touch and smell and the very warmth of bodies to give them the knowledge they seek. This nearness, this immediacy, she communicates also, there is no escaping into the future nor into the past. All time is in the present, these people are "being living," she makes you no gift of comfortable ripened events past and gone. "I am writing everything as I am learning everything," and so we have lists of qualities and defects, portraits of persons in scraps, with bits and pieces added again and again in every round of the spiral: they repeat and repeat themselves to you endlessly as living persons do, and always you feel you know them, and always they present a new bit of themselves.

Gertrude Stein reminds me of Jacob Boehme in the way she sees essentials in human beings. He knew them as salt, as mercury; as moist, as dry, as burning; as bitter, sweet or sour. She perceives them as attacking, as resisting, as dependent independent, as having a core of wood, of mud, as murky, engulfing; Boehme's chemical formulas are too abstract, she knows the substances of man are mixed with clay. Materials interest her, the moral content of man can often be nicely compared to homely workable stuff. Sometimes her examination is almost housewifely, she rolls a fabric under her fingers, tests it. It is thus and so. I find this very good, very interesting. "It will repay good using."

"In writing a word must be for me really an existing thing." Her efforts to get at the roots of existing life, to create fresh life from them, give her words a dark liquid flowingness, like the murmur of the blood. She does not strain words or invent them. Many words have retained their original meaning for her, she uses them simply. Good means good and bad means bad—next to the Jews the Americans are the most moralistic people, and Gertrude Stein is American Jew, a combination which by no means lessens the like quality in both. Good and bad are attributes to her, strength and weakness are real things that live inside people, she looks for these things, notes them in their likenesses and differences. She loves the difficult virtues, she is tender toward good people, she has faith in them.

An odd thing happens somewhere in the middle of this book. You will come upon it suddenly and it will surprise you. All along you have had a feeling of submergence in the hidden lives of a great many people, and unaccountably you will find yourself rolling up to the surface, on the outer edge of the curve. A disconcerting break into narrative full of phrases that might have come out of any careless sentimental novel, alternates with scraps of the natural style. It is astounding, you read on out of chagrin. Again without warning you submerge, and later Miss Stein explains she was copying an old piece of writing of which she is now ashamed, the words mean nothing: "I commence again with words that have meaning," she says, and we leave this limp, dead spot in the middle of the book.

Gertrude Stein wrote once of Juan Gris that he was, somehow, saved. She is saved, too; she is free of pride and humility, she confesses to superhuman aspirations simply, she was badly frightened once and has recovered, she is honest in her uncertainties. There are only a few bits of absolute knowledge in the world, people can learn only one or two fundamental facts about each other, the rest is decoration and prejudice. She is very free from decoration and prejudice.

1927

SECOND WIND

Spirals and corkscrews are whirlwinds if we spin a big top and not stop. Not stop nor drag a herring. She confused them all, yet called every day offering new feather pillows. If you wish to amuse yourself you may have your palm read, or do you drink gin? There is also the flea circus, and there is a Congressman. Romance is useful knowledge; America is romance, but you must first live in Paris. Theaters and ticker tape and the states to escape. Ticker tape and ticker tacker, tick tack toe.

> Now you know.
> This is so.
> This sounds silly.
> As you please.
> Now I will explain.

She mentioned a little of everything reasonable in order not to tell the secret. When the photographs came she said there had been a mistake. Dead things when they go dead go dead and do not come alive. They go dead. They said yes it is pretty but we miss the color. This was ended then.

This was not all. This was another one a younger one a sadder one a wiser one a smaller one a darker one with gray skin being reading the Making of Americans three times all summer. It was ended then. But you say she is wiser then why is she sadder then it is not sadder to be wiser then. Oh, yes, but when things go dead it is different.

You don't understand. Let me tell you then.

We were saying it is different now it was different then it is finished now it was finished then you may go up close and look if you like. This is an American habit with romance.

In *Useful Knowledge* you will look for sex to vex. There is no sex to vex. Look visibly. Stimulation is one and irritation is another. Another to smother Americans, who wear glasses and read if a hat is dropped suddenly. They send white wedding cake too in painted boxes. We are told this is being American, but it is not pleasant. She says it is pleasant. I doubt doubt it. If this is being American I doubt it. If this is being making romance I doubt it. If this is owning the earth I doubt it. If I doubt it it is sometimes necessary to let this be all. Iowa is not Maine Maine is not Iowa Louisiana is not either there are many states.

> In Spain there is no rain.
> Mr. Lewis.
> Mr. Lewis.

Page Mr. Wyndham Lewis on this page. Page on page. Why does he rage and when. Not American being human Mr. Lewis calls her Gerty and says she stammers. Who will be enemies because his name is not Gerty and he stammers. Being stammering is being Mr. Lewis in one way and being stammering is being Gerty in another way and it's all in the day. This way today. Being stammering together is a chorus and a chorus being stammering together is thinking. Thinking being stammering. Many rivers but only two rivers. There will be only a few two rivers with furry edges. The cost is nothing. The cost is nothing much. Much. Much is what you pay for. Only a few. Two by two and one by one. Two is too few.

> Now all together.
> Repetition makes subways.
> I know what I am saying and if you flatter me I am insulted.

1928

THE WOODEN UMBRELLA

. . . I want to say that just today I met Miss Hennessy and she was carrying, she did not have it with her, but she usually carried a wooden umbrella. This wooden umbrella is carved out of wood and looks like a real one even to the little button and the rubber string that holds it together. It is all right except when it rains. When it rains it does not open and Miss Hennessy looks a little foolish but she does not mind because it is after all the only wooden umbrella in Paris. And even if there were lots of others it would not make any difference.

Gertrude Stein: *Everybody's Autobiography*

When Kahnweiler the picture dealer told Miss Stein that Picasso had stopped painting and had taken to writing poetry, she confessed that she had "a funny feeling" because "things belonged to you and writing belonged to me. I know writing belongs to me, I am quite certain," but still it was a blow. ". . . No matter how certain you are about anything belonging to you if you hear that somebody says it belongs to them it gives you a funny feeling."

Later she buttonholed Picasso at Kahnweiler's gallery, shook him, kissed him, lectured him, told him that his poetry was worse than bad, it was offensive as a Cocteau drawing and in much the same way, it was unbecoming. He defended himself by reminding her that she had said he was an extraordinary person, and he believed an extraordinary person should be able to do anything. She said that to her it was a repellent sight when a person who could do one thing well dropped it for something else he could not do at all. Convinced, or defeated, he promised to give back writing to its natural owner.

Writing was no doubt the dearest of Miss Stein's possessions, but it was not the only one. The pavilion atelier in rue de Fleurus was a catch-all of beings and created objects, and everything she looked upon was hers in more than the usual sense. Her weighty numerous divans and armchairs covered with dark, new-looking horsehair; her dogs, Basket and Pépé, conspicuous, special, afflicted as neurotic children; her clutter of small tables each with its own clutter of perhaps valuable but certainly treasured objects; her Alice B. Toklas; her visitors; and finally, ranging the walls from floor to ceiling, giving the impression that they were hung three deep, elbowing each other, canceling each other's best effects in the jealous way of pictures, was her celebrated collection of paintings by her collection of celebrated painters. These were everybody of her time whom Miss Stein elected for her own, from her idol Picasso (kidnapped bodily from brother Leo, who saw him first) to miniscule Sir Francis Rose, who seems to have appealed to the pixy in her.

Yet the vaguely lighted room where things accumulated, where they appeared to have moved in under a compulsion to be possessed once for all by someone who knew how to take hold firmly, gave no impression of disorder. On the contrary, an air of solid comfort, of inordinate sobriety and permanence, of unadventurous middle-class domesticity—respectability is the word, at last—settled around the shoulders of the guest like a Paisley shawl, a borrowed shawl of course, something to be worn and admired for a moment and handed back to the owner. Miss Stein herself sat there in full possession of herself, the scene, the spectators, wearing thick no-colored shapeless woolen clothes and honest woolen stockings knitted for her by Miss Toklas, looking extremely like a handsome old Jewish patriarch who had backslid and shaved off his beard.

Surrounded by her listeners, she talked in a slow circle in her fine deep voice, the word "perception" occurring again and again and yet again like the brass ring the children snatch for as their hobby horses whirl by. She was in fact at one period surrounded by snatching children, the literary young, a good many of them American, between two wars in a falling world. Roughly they were divided into two parties: those who were full of an active, pragmatic unbelief, and those who searched their own vitals and fished up strange horrors in the style of *transition*. The first had discovered that honor is only a word, and an embarrassing one, because it was supposed to mean something wonderful and was now exposed as meaning nothing at all. For them, nothing worked except sex and alcohol and pulling apart their lamentable Midwestern upbringings and scattering the pieces. Some of these announced that they wished their writings to be as free from literature as if they had never read a book, as indeed too many of them had not up to the time. The *transition* tone was even more sinister, for though it was supposed to be the vanguard of international experimental thought, its real voice was hoarse, anxious, corrupted mysticism speaking in a thick German accent. The editor, Eugene Jolas, had been born in the eternally disputed land of Alsace, bilingual in irreconcilable tongues, French and German, and he spoke both and English besides with a foreign accent. He had no mother tongue, nor even a country, and so he fought the idea of both, but his deepest self was German: he issued frantic manifestoes demanding that language be reduced to something he could master, crying aloud in "defense of the hallucinative forces," the exploding of the verb, the "occult hypnosis of language," "chthonian grammar"; reason he hated, and defended the voice of the blood, the disintegration of syntax—with a special grudge against English—preaching like an American Methodist envangelist in the wilderness for "the use of a language which is a mantic instrument, and which does not hesitate to adopt a revolutionary attitude toward word syntax, going even so far as to invent a hermetic language, if necessary." The final aim was "the illumination of a collective reality and a totalistic universe." Meanwhile Joyce, a man with a mother tongue if ever there was one, and a master of languages, was mixing them in strange new forms to the delight and enrichment of language for good and all.

Miss Stein had no problems: she simply exploded a verb as if it were a soap bubble, used chthonian grammar long before she heard it named (and she would have scorned to name it), was a born adept in occult hypnosis of language without even trying. Serious young men who were having a hard time learning to write realized with relief that there was nothing at all to it if you just relaxed and put down the first thing that came into your head. She gave them a romantic name, the Lost Generation, and a remarkable number of them tried earnestly if unsuccessfully to live up to it. A few of them were really lost, and disappeared, but others had just painted themselves into a very crowded corner. She laid a cooling hand upon their agitated brows and asked with variations, What did it matter? There were only a few geniuses, after all, among which she was one, only the things a genius said made any difference, the rest was "just there," and so she disposed of all the dark questions of life, art, human relations, and death, even eternity, even God, with perfect Stein logic, bringing the scene again into its proper focus, upon herself.

Some of the young men went away, read a book, began thinking things over, and became the best writers of their time. Humanly, shamefacedly, they then jeered at their former admiration, and a few even made the tactical error of quarreling with her. She enjoyed their discipleship while it lasted, and dismissed them from existence when it ended. It is easy to see what tremendous vitality and direction there was in the arts all over the world; for not everything was happening only in France; life was generated in many a noisy seething confusion in many countries. Little by little the legitimate line of succession appeared, the survivors emerged each with his own shape and meaning, the young vanguard became the Old Masters and even old hat.

In the meantime our heroine went on talking, vocally or on paper, and in that slow swarm of words, out of the long drone and mutter and stammer of her lifetime monologue, often there emerged a phrase of ancient native independent wisdom, for she had a shrewd deep knowledge of the commoner human motives. Her judgments were neither moral nor intellectual, and least of all aesthetic, indeed they were not even judgments, but simply her description from observation of acts, words, appearances giving her view; limited, personal in the extreme, prejudiced without qualification, based on assumptions founded in the void of pure unreason. For example, French notaries' sons have always something strange about them—look at Jean Cocteau. The Spaniard has a natural center of ignorance, all except Juan Gris. On the other hand, Dali had not only the natural Spanish center of ignorance, but still another variety, quite malignant, of his own. Preachers' sons do not turn out like other people—E. E. Cummings, just for one. Painters are always little short round men—Picasso and a crowd of them. And then she puts her finger lightly on an American peculiarity of our time: ". . . so perhaps they are right the Americans in being more interested in you than in the work you have done, although they would not be interested in you if you had not done the work you had done." And she remarked once to her publisher that she was famous in America not for her work that people understood but for that which they did not understand. That was the kind of thing she could see through at a glance.

It was not that she was opposed to ideas, but that she was not interested in anybody's ideas but her own, except as material to put down on her endless flood of pages. Like writing, opinion also belonged to Miss Stein, and nothing annoyed her more—she was easily angered about all sorts of things—than for anyone not a genius or who had no reputation that she respected, to appear to be thinking in her presence. Of all those GI's who swarmed about her in her last days, if anyone showed any fight at all, any tendency to question her pronouncements, she smacked him down like a careful grandmother, for his own good. Her GI heroes Brewsie and Willie are surely as near to talking zombies as anything ever seen in a book, and she loved, not them, but their essential zombiness.

Like all talkers, she thought other people talked too much, and there is recorded only one instance of someone getting the drop on her—who else but Alfred Stieglitz? She sat through a whole session at their first meeting without uttering one word, a feat which he mentioned with surprised approval. If we knew nothing more of Stieglitz than this we would know he was a great talker. She thought that the most distressing sound was that of the human voice, other people's voices, "as the hoot owl is almost the best sound," but in spite of this she listened quite a lot. When she was out walking the dogs, if workmen were tearing up the streets she would ask them what they were doing and what they would be doing next. She only stopped to break the monotony of walking, but she remembered their answers. When a man passed making up a bitter little song against her dog and his conduct vis-à-vis lamp posts and house walls, she put it all down, and it is wonderfully good reporting. Wise or silly or nothing at all, down everything goes on the page with the air of everything being equal, unimportant in itself, important because it happened to her and she was writing about it.

She had not always been exactly there, exactly that. There had been many phases, all in consistent character, each giving way in turn for the next, of her portentous being. Ford Madox Ford described her, in earlier Paris days, as trundling through the streets in her high-wheeled American car, being a spectacle and being herself at the same time. And this may have been near the time of Man Ray's photograph of her, wearing a kind of monk's robe, her poll clipped, her granite front and fine eyes displayed at their best period.

Before that, she was a youngish stout woman, not ever really young, with a heavy shrewd face between a hard round pompadour and a round lace collar, looking more or less like Picasso's earliest portrait of her. What saved her then from a good honest husband, probably a stockbroker, and a houseful of children? The answer must be that her envelope was a tricky disguise of Nature, that she was of the company of Amazons which nineteenth-century America produced among its many prodigies: not-men, not-women, answerable to no function in either sex, whose careers were carried on, and how successfully, in whatever field they chose: they were educators, writers, editors, politicians, artists, world travelers, and international hostesses, who lived in public and by the public and played out their self-assumed, self-created roles in such masterly freedom as only a few early medieval queens had equaled. Freedom to them meant precisely freedom from men and their stuffy rules for women. They usurped with a high hand the traditional masculine privileges of movement, choice, and the use of direct, personal power. They were few in number and they were not only to be found in America, and Miss Stein belonged with them, no doubt of it, in spite of a certain temperamental passivity which was Oriental, not feminine. With the top of her brain she was a modern girl, a New Woman, interested in scientific experiment, historical research, the rational view; for a time she was even a medical student, but she could not deceive herself for long. Even during her four years at Radcliffe, where the crisp theories of higher education battle with the womb-shaped female mind (and "they always afterward seemed foolish" to her at Radcliffe, she said, meaning perhaps the promoters of these theories) she worried and worried, for worrying and thinking were synonyms to her, about the meaning of the universe, the riddle of human life, about time and its terrible habit of passing, God, death, eternity, and she felt very lonely in the awful singularity of her confusions. Added to this, history taught her that whole civilizations die and disappear utterly, "and now it happens again," and it gave her a great fright. She was sometimes frightened afterward, "but now well being frightened is something less frightening than it was," but her ambiguous mind faced away from speculation. Having discovered with relief that all knowledge was not her province, she accepted rightly, she said, every superstition. To be in the hands of fate, of magic, of the daemonic forces, what freedom it gave her not to decide, not to act, not to accept any responsibility for anything—one held the pen and let the mind wander. One sat down and somebody did everything for one.

Still earlier she was a plump solemn little girl abundantly upholstered in good clothes, who spent her allowance on the work of Shelley, Thackeray, and George Eliot in fancy bindings, for she loved reading and *Clarissa Harlowe* was once her favorite novel. These early passions exhausted her; in later life she swam in the relaxing bath of detective and murder mysteries, because she liked somebody being dead in a story, and of them all Dashiell Hammett killed them off most to her taste. Her first experience of the real death of somebody had taught her that it could be pleasant for her too. "One morning we could not wake our father." This was in East Oakland, California. "Leo climbed in by the window and called out that he was dead in his bed and he was." It seems to have been the first thing he ever did of which his children, all five of them, approved. Miss Stein declared plainly they none of them liked him at all: "As I say, fathers are depressing but our family had one," she confessed, and conveys the notion that he was a bore of the nagging, petty sort, the kind that worries himself and others into the grave.

Considering her tepid, sluggish nature, really sluggish like something eating its way through a leaf, Miss Stein could grow quite animated on the subject of her early family life, and some of her stories are as pretty and innocent as lizards running over tombstones on a hot day in Maryland. It was a solid, getting-on sort of middle-class Jewish family of Austrian origin, Keyser on one side, Stein on the other: and the Keysers came to Baltimore about 1820. All branches of the family produced their individual eccentrics—there was even an uncle who believed in the Single Tax—but they were united in their solid understanding of the value of money as the basis of a firm stance in this world. There were incomes, governesses, spending money, guardians appointed when parents died, and Miss Stein was fascinated from childhood with stories about how people earned their first dollar. When, rather late, she actually earned some dollars herself by writing, it changed her entire viewpoint about the value of her work and of her own personality. It came to her as revelation that the only difference between men and four-footed animals is that men can count, and when they count, they like best to count money. In her first satisfaction at finding she had a commercial value, she went on a brief binge of spending money just for the fun of it. But she really knew better. Among the five or six of the seven deadly sins which she practiced with increasing facility and advocated as virtues, avarice became her favorite. Americans in general she found to be rather childish about money: they spent it or gave it away and enjoyed it wastefully with no sense of its fierce latent power. "It is hard to be a miser, a real miser, they are as rare as geniuses it takes the same kind of thing to make one, that is time must not exist for them. . . . There must be a reality that has nothing to do with the passing of time. I have it and so had Hetty Green . . ." and she found only one of the younger generation in America, a young man named Jay Laughlin, who had, she wrote, praising him, avarice to that point of genius which makes the true miser. She made a very true distinction between avarice, the love of getting and keeping, and love of money, the love of making and spending. There is a third love, the love of turning a penny by ruse, and this was illustrated by brother Michael, who once grew a beard to make himself look old enough to pass for a G.A.R. veteran, and so disguised he got a cut-rate railway fare for a visit home during a G.A.R. rally, though all the men of his family fought on the Confederate side.

The question of money and of genius rose simultaneously with the cheerful state of complete orphanhood. Her mother disappeared early after a long illness, leaving her little nest of vipers probably without regret, for vipers Miss Stein shows them to have been in the most Biblical sense. They missed their mother chiefly because she had acted as a buffer between them and their father, and also served to keep them out of each other's hair. Sister Bertha and Brother Simon were simpleminded by family standards, whatever they were, Brother Leo had already started being a genius without any regard for the true situation, and after the death of their father, Brother Michael was quite simply elected to be the Goat. He had inherited the family hatred of responsibility—from their mother, Miss Stein believed, but not quite enough to save him. He became guardian, caretaker, business manager, handy-man, who finally wangled incomes for all of them, and set them free from money and from each other. It is pleasant to know he was a very thorny martyr who did a great deal of resentful lecturing about economy, stamping and shouting about the house with threats to throw the whole business over and let them fend for themselves if they could not treat him with more consideration. With flattery and persuasion they would cluster around and get him back on the rails, for his destiny was to be useful to genius, that is, to Miss Stein.

She had been much attached to her brother Leo, in childhood they were twin souls. He was two years older and a boy, and she had learned from Clarissa Harlowe's uncle's letter that older brothers are superior to younger sisters, or any boy to any girl in fact. Though she bowed to this doctrine as long as it was convenient, she never allowed it to get in her way. She followed her brother's advice more or less, and in turn he waited on her and humored and defended her when she was a selfish lazy little girl. Later he made a charming traveling companion who naturally, being older and a man, looked after all the boring details of life and smoothed his sister's path everywhere. Still, she could not remember his face when he was absent, and once was very nervous when she went to meet him on a journey, for fear she might not recognize him. The one thing wrong all this time was their recurring quarrel about who was the genius of the two, for each had assumed the title and neither believed for a moment there was room for more than one in the family. By way of proving himself, brother Leo took the pavilion and atelier in the rue de Fleurus, installed himself well, and began trying hard to paint. Miss Stein, seeing all so cozy, moved in on him and sat down and began to write—no question of trying. "To try is to die" became one of her several hundred rhyming aphorisms designed to settle all conceivable arguments; after a time, no doubt overwhelmed by the solid negative force of that massive will and presence, her brother moved out and took the atelier next door, and went on being useful to his sister, and trying to paint.

But he also went on insisting tactlessly that he, and not she, was the born genius; and this was one of the real differences between them, that he attacked on the subject and was uneasy, and could not rest, while his sister reasoned with him, patiently at first, defending her title, regretting she could not share it. Insist, argue, upset himself and her as much as he liked, she simply, quietly knew with a Messianic revelation that she was not only a genius, but *the* genius, and sometimes, she was certain, one of not more than half a dozen real ones in the world. During all her life, whenever Miss Stein got low in her mind about anything, she could always find consolation in this beautiful knowledge of being a born genius, and her brother's contentiousness finally began to look like treason to her. She could not forgive him for disputing her indivisible right to her natural property, genius, on which all her other rights of possession were founded. It shook her—she worried about her work. She had begun her long career of describing "how every one who ever lived eats and drinks and loves and sleeps and talks and walks and wakes and forgets and quarrels and likes and dislikes and works and sits"—everybody's autobiography, in fact, for she had taken upon herself the immense task of explaining everybody to himself, of telling him all he needed to know about life, and she simply could not have brother Leo hanging around the edges of this grandiose scheme pinching off bits and holding them up to the light. By and by, too, she had Alice B. Toklas to do everything for her. So she and her brother drifted apart, but gradually, like one of Miss Stein's paragraphs. The separation became so complete that once, on meeting her brother unexpectedly, she was so taken by surprise she bowed to him, and afterward wrote a long poem about it in which her total confusion of mind and feeling were expressed with total incoherence: for once, form, matter and style stuttering and stammering and wallowing along together with the agitated harmony of roiling entrails.

There are the tones of sloth, of that boredom which is a low-pressure despair, of monotony, of obsession, in this portrait; she went walking out of boredom, she could drive a car, talk, write, but anything else made her nervous. People who were doing anything annoyed her: to be doing nothing, she thought, was more interesting than to be doing something. The air of deathly solitude surrounded her; yet the parade of names in her book would easily fill several printed pages, all with faces attached which she could see were quite different from each other, all talking, each taking his own name and person for granted—a thing she could never understand. Yet she could see what they were doing and could remember what they said. She only listened attentively to Picasso—for whose sake she would crack almost any head in sight—so she half-agreed when he said Picabia was the worst painter of all; but still, found herself drawn to Picabia because his name was Francis. She had discovered that men named Francis were always elegant, and though they might not know anything else, they always knew about themselves. This would remind her that she had never found out who she was. Again and again she would doubt her own identity, and that of everyone else. When she worried about this aloud to Alice B. Toklas, saying she believed it impossible for anyone ever to be certain who he was, Alice B. Toklas made, in context, the most inspired remark in the whole book. "It depends on who you are," she said, and you might think that would have ended the business. Not at all.

These deep-set, chronic fears led her to a good deal of quarreling, for when she quarreled she seems to have felt more real. She mentions quarrels with Max Jacob, Francis Rose, with Dali, with Picabia, with Picasso, with Virgil Thomson, with Braque, with Breton, and how many others, though she rarely says just why they quarrelled or how they made it up. Almost nobody went away and stayed, and the awful inertia of habit in friendships oppressed her. She was sometimes discouraged at the prospect of having to go on seeing certain persons to the end, merely because she had once seen them. The world seemed smaller every day, swarming with people perpetually in movement, full of restless notions which, once examined by her, were inevitably proved to be fallacious, or at least entirely useless. She found that she could best get rid of them by putting them in a book. "That is very funny if you write about any one they do not exist any more, for you, so why see them again. Anyway, that is the way I am."

But as she wrote a book and disposed of one horde, another came on, and worried her afresh, discussing their ludicrous solemn topics, trying to understand things, and being unhappy about it. When Picasso was fretful because she argued with Dali and not with him, she explained that "one discusses things with stupid people but not with sensible ones." Her true grudge against intelligent people was that they talked "as if they were getting ready to change something." Change belonged to Miss Stein, and the duty of the world was to stand still so that she could move about in it comfortably. Her top flight of reasoning on the subject of intelligence ran as follows: "The most actively war-like nations could always convince the pacifists to become pro-German. That is because pacifists were such intelligent beings they could follow what any one is saying. If you follow what any one is saying then you are a pacifist you are a pro-German . . . therefore understanding is a very dull occupation."

Intellectuals, she said, always wanted to change things because they had an unhappy childhood. "Well, I never had an unhappy childhood, what is the use of having an unhappy anything?" Léon Blum, then Premier of France, had had an unhappy childhood, and she inclined to the theory that the political uneasiness of France could be traced to this fact.

There was not, of course, going to be another war (this was in 1937!), but if there was, there *would* be, naturally; and she never tired of repeating that dancing and war are the same thing "because both are foward and back," while revolution, on the contrary, is up and down, which is why it gets nowhere. Sovietism was even then going rapidly out of fashion in her circles, because they had discovered that it is very conservative, even if the Communists do not think so. Anarchists, being rarities, did not go out of fashion so easily. The most interesting thing that ever happened to America was the Civil War; but General Lee was severely to be blamed for leading his country into that war, just the same, because he must have known they could not win; and to her, it was absurd that anyone should join battle in defense of a principle in face of certain defeat. For practical purposes, honor was not even a word. Still it was an exciting war and gave an interest to America which that country would never have had without it. "If you win you do not lose and if you lose you do not win." Even as she was writing these winged words, the Spanish Civil War, the Republicans against the Franco-Fascists, kept obtruding itself. And why? "Not because it is a revolution, but because I know so well the places they are mentioning and the things there they are destroying." When she was little in Oakland, California, she loved the big, nice American fires that had "so many horses and firemen to attend them," and when she was older, she found that floods, for one thing, always read worse in the papers than they really are; besides how can you care much about what is going on if you don't see it or know the people? For this reason she had Santa Teresa being indifferent to faraway Chinese while she was founding convents in Spain. William Seabrook came to see her to find out if she was as interesting as her books. She told him she was, and he discovered black magic in the paintings of Sir Francis Rose. And when she asked Dashiell Hammett why so many young men authors were writing novels about tender young male heroines instead of the traditional female ones, he explained that it was because as women grew more and more self-confident, men lost confidence in themselves, and turned to each other, or became their own subjects for fiction. This, or something else, reminded her several times that she could not write a novel, therefore no one could any more, and no one should waste time trying.

Somehow by such roundabouts we arrive at the important, the critical event in all this eventful history. Success. Success in this world, here and now, was what Miss Stein wanted. She knew just what it was, how it should look and feel, how much it should weigh and what it was worth over the counter. It was not enough to be a genius if you had to go on supporting your art on a private income. To be the center of a recondite literary cult, to be surrounded by listeners and imitators and seekers, to be mentioned in the same breath with James Joyce, and to have turned out bales of titles by merely writing a half-hour each day: she had all that, and what did it amount to? There was a great deal more and she must have it. As to her history of the human race, she confessed: "I have always been bothered . . . but mostly . . . because after all I do as simply as it can, as commonplacely as it can say, what everybody can and does do; I never know what they can do, I really do not know what they are, I do not think that any one can think because if they do, then who is who?"

It was high time for a change, and yet it occurred at hazard. If there had not been a beautiful season in October and part of November, 1932, permitting Miss Stein to spend that season quietly in her country house, the *Autobiography of Alice B. Toklas* might never have been written. But it was written, and Miss Stein became a best-seller in America; she made real money. With Miss Toklas, she had a thrilling tour of the United States and found crowds of people eager to see her and listen to her. And at last she got what she had really wanted all along: to be published in the *Atlantic Monthly* and the *Saturday Evening Post*.

Now she had everything, or nearly. For a while she was afraid to write any more, for fear her latest efforts would not please her public. She had never learned who she was, and yet suddenly she had become somebody else. "You are you because your little dog knows you, but when your public knows you and does not want to pay you, and when your public knows you and does want to pay you, you are not the same you."

This would be of course the proper moment to take leave, as our heroine adds at last a golden flick of light to her self-portrait. "Anyway, I was a celebrity." The practical result was that she could no longer live on her income. But she and Alice B. Toklas moved into an apartment once occupied by Queen Christina of Sweden, and they began going out more, and seeing even more people, and talking, and Miss Stein settled every question as it came up, more and more. But who wants to read about success? It is the early struggle which makes a good story.

She and Alice B. Toklas enjoyed both the wars. The first one especially being a lark with almost no one getting killed where you could see, and it ended so nicely too, without changing anything. The second was rather more serious. She lived safely enough in Bilignin throughout the German occupation, and there is a pretty story that the whole village conspired to keep her presence secret. She had been a citizen of the world in the best European tradition; for though America was her native land, she had to live in Europe because she felt at home there. In the old days people paid little attention to wars, fought as they were out of sight by professional soldiers. She had always liked the notion, too, of the gradual Orientalization of the West, the peaceful penetration of the East into European culture. It had been going on a great while, and all Western geniuses worth mentioning were Orientals: look at Picasso, look at Einstein. Russians are Tartars, Spaniards are Saracens—had not all great twentieth-century painting been Spanish? And her cheerful conclusion was, that "Einstein was the creative philosophic mind of the century, and I have been the creative literary mind of the century also, with the Oriental mixing with the European." She added, as a casual afterthought, "Perhaps Europe is finished."

That was in 1938, and she could not be expected to know that war was near. They had only been sounding practice *alertes* in Paris against expected German bombers since 1935. She spoke out of her natural frivolity and did not mean it. She liked to prophesy, but warned her hearers that her prophecies never came out right, usually the very opposite, and no matter what happened, she was always surprised. She was surprised again: as the nations of Europe fell, and the Germans came again over the frontiers of France for the third time in three generations, the earth shook under her own feet, and not somebody else's. It made an astonishing difference. Something mysterious touched her in her old age. She got a fright, and this time not for ancient vanished civilizations, but for this civilization, this moment; and she was quite thrilled with relief and gay when the American army finally came in, and the Germans were gone. She did not in the least know why the Germans had come, but they were gone, and so far as she could see, the American army had chased them out. She remembered with positive spread-eagle patriotism that America was her native land. At last America itself belonged to Miss Stein, and she claimed it, in a formal published address to other Americans. Anxiously she urged them to stay rich, to be powerful and learn how to use power, not to waste themselves; for the first time she used the word "spiritual." Ours was a spiritual as well as a material fight; Lincoln's great lucid words about government of the people by the people for the people suddenly sounded like a trumpet through her stammering confession of faith, she wanted nothing now to stand between her and her newly discovered country. By great good luck she was born on the winning side and she was going to stay there. And we were not to forget about money as the source of power; "Remember the depression, don't be afraid to look it in the face and find out the reason why, if you don't find out the reason why you'll go poor and my God, how I would hate to have my native land go poor."

The mind so long shapeless and undisciplined could not now express any knowledge out of its long willful ignorance. But the heart spoke its crude urgent language. She had liked the doughboys in the other war well enough, but this time she fell in love with the whole American army below the rank of lieutenant. She "breathed, ate, drank, lived GI's," she told them, and inscribed numberless photographs for them, and asked them all to come back again. After her flight over Germany in an American bomber, she wrote about how, so often, she would stand staring into the sky watching American war planes going over, longing to be up there again with her new loves, in the safe, solid air. She murmured, "bless them, bless them." She had been impatient with many of them who had still been naïve enough to believe they were fighting against an evil idea that threatened everybody; some of them actually were simple enough to say they had been—or believed they had been—fighting for democratic government. "What difference does it make what kind of government you have?" she would ask. "All governments are alike. Just remember you won the war." But still, at the end, she warned them to have courage and not be just yes or no men. And she said, "Bless them, bless them."

It was the strangest thing, as if the wooden umbrella feeling the rain had tried to forsake its substance and take on the nature of its form; and was struggling slowly, slowly, much too late, to unfold.

1947

Ole Woman River:
A Correspondence with
Katherine Anne Porter

I was accused of many ignoble motives when I wrote "The Wooden Umbrella." The most painful being an accusation that I had waited until a writer was dead to launch my attack. This was not true, for I have the letter dated November 17, 1939, from Margaret Marshall, then one of the editors of *The Nation*, saying that she was glad I was enjoying the prospect of writing about Gertrude Stein. She was referring to *Everybody's Autobiography*, and later I also read the *Autobiography of Alice B. Toklas*.

University of Colorado
Boulder, Colorado

Dear Katherine Anne:

I am in the throes of second sight again and about to go to Europe, with a feeling I shall not get back. No doubt I shall, but there is the feeling and a short closed vista to the inward eye, so I am getting my loose ends in order and the enclosed is one of them. I am sending it, with the original letter, to the Stein Collection at Yale, since I can think of nothing else to do with it. I cannot destroy it because of my feeling for Gertrude and I can't publish it because of my feeling for you, so this seems to me to be the solution, sprung as it is.

Good luck and everything.

Donald Sutherland

Note to Dr. Donald Gallup of the Yale University Library, on sending those papers to the Stein Collection there.
re: Katherine Anne Porter.

I first met KAP in 1942. I liked her very much, as I liked her writing. I had the impression, from our conversations, that she liked Gertrude

Stein and her writing as I did, since she said that all anyone had to know about character was already contained in *The Making of Americans.* Or something very like that, and more than I would have said of the book myself. I also understood that she knew Gertrude Stein and had had the traditional difficulty with the small tables and chairs in Gertude Stein's studio at 27 rue de Fleurus, but I may easily have been mistaken about that. In any case, KAP and I get along very well and she was kind enough to try to get an early book of mine published.

In 1945 I was in Paris, a G.I. about to return to America, and Gertrude Stein asked me to send her from America when I got back there *The Feather Merchants*, since it was beneath the intellectual dignity of her other friends. So on my return I sent her the book, and two others, one of them *Pale Horse, Pale Rider* by KAP, with the hope that Gertrude Stein could get it to a French publisher. I thought it would go very well into French and improve relations, since at that time the French seemed to consider *Gone With the Wind* our utmost.

Gertrude Stein wrote to my wife and me in November, 1945, as follows:

> My dear friends:
> The package of books came, thanks so much, do you want them back after we are through, you know there was a funny story, one day a young gentleman called and he sent in a note saying that he was the nephew of Katherine Anne Porter. Then he came in and I said gently and politely, do I know your aunt, I am afraid said he you have never met, and said I politely who is she, and he went quite white and said you know and I said no, and then he decided to take it as a joke, but it was a blow, he had evidently traveled far on his nephewship. As a matter of fact no I have (not) been able to do much with either of the ladies, just plain not, but Alice is more hopeful, I suppose I have gotten kind of fed both in painting and in writing with school work, I like honest chromos but school no . . .

The rest of the letter has nothing to do with KAP. After Gertrude Stein's death in 1946 KAP published her long essay on Gertrude Stein, attacking her and her work. There may or may not be a connection between the essay and the episode of the nephew; I rather think not, and that the malice of the essay is a natural result of having once liked the subject of it before an intellectual conversion against the subject. At any rate I have not published this letter, since I am obliged to KAP and fond of her and of her work when it is not criticism. I have shown the letter to a few friends, and unfortunately a garbled reference to the contents did appear in print. Otherwise, the letter is not known. I want it kept so until after my death, unless KAP decides otherwise and wishes to reply to it.

Donald Sutherland

P.S. The other "lady" in question was of course Eudora [Welty].

117 East 17th Street
New York 3, N.Y.
2 June 1953

Dear Donald:

It would have been better for you to have written to me before sending my book to Gertrude Stein. For it happens I had and have, a superb translator, Marcelle Sibon, and my first book, *Flowering Judas*, was brought out exactly in that year 1945 in Paris, and I must say we were all surprised at how well it was received. *Pale Horse, Pale Rider* was brought out later, and *The Leaning Tower* is on its slow way. So it was a pity, I think, that by the kind intentions of my friends, I was twice exposed to the attentions of Miss Stein; the fact that I did not hear of either incident for a good while afterward doesn't help much.

Now then to the mean little gossip which is the subject of your note to the Yale Library Collection. It is good of you not to believe the ignoble motives so eagerly attributed to me by others in my article about Gertrude Stein. Yet I think well of you, and think therefore there is no call to insult you by congratulating you on having a decent mind. . . . If you published such a slander against me, even with your disclaimer, it would be a great wrong committed for a very small cause. By putting it in the Yale Collection, you make it available to anyone who wishes to use it: but I am all for keeping the record as straight as we can; and you are certainly right not to destroy it. Time takes care of everything. If this is the worst that is said of me in letters and gossip, I am very lucky indeed.

I went with Allen and Caroline Tate to see Miss Stein, it must have been in the winter of 1933: I can only fix the date by remembering other events of the time: it was after I came back from Basel, which was December, 1932: and before I was married in Paris, which was March, 1933 . . . doesn't matter, except I should never have thought of going if the Tates had not asked me, and it certainly seemed a matter of no importance. I had never had any intention of going there, for in spite of my liking for certain things in Miss Stein's work, I had long since lost my early notions that there was any vitality in her work. Miss Stein and Miss Toklas both were perfectly friendly and courteous, no incident of any kind marked the visit: and my deep feeling of boredom and futility and sense of suffocation simply came from the atmosphere itself; I have never been able to describe it, but I have suffered it more than once, in many situations; it is simply a message to me from my deepest instincts that I am in the wrong place with the wrong people. These "instincts," believe me, no matter what their origin, are deeply right, and when I try to override them, ignore them, they bide their time, but they punish me for my inattention or willfulness. So it was. I got away as soon as I could, and, of course, never went back. It never occurred to me then or later to ask whether Miss Stein ever even heard my name, and if she had, there was no reason for her to remember it. I had published one little unknown book. If she got clippings of reviews, she might have noticed my parody review of *Useful Knowledge*, the book which caused me to reconsider her work, five years before I saw her and to decide that Miss Stein was on the whole a bore, and a little of a fraud.

But this was my own private critical opinion, I felt no urge to make a crusade of it. Then I simply did not read anything further—I had read *Tender Buttons, Three Lives, The Making of Americans,* and *Useful Knowledge,* and surely that was enough on which to base my judgment. It seemed plain to me that Miss Stein was not for me. Then in 1937 some publisher (just looked it up—Random House) sent me a copy of *Everybody's Autobiography.* I was asked to review it by someone else: I do not remember who (*Note), it can't matter. So I read it and read it, and made notes, and finally wrote the review almost to the end, and called it "The Wooden Umbrella." This was the piece published by *Harper's* in, I think, 1947. I had tired of the whole thing, had no interest, did not finish it but put it away among my papers and forgot it. Then I read the *Autobiography of Alice B. Toklas,* and made a few notes from that; in the meantime, you remember, we had the rise of Hitler, the long dictatorship of Mussolini, the war in Spain, and finally our war, and by that time I was in Santa Monica, California; and all the notes about Miss Stein's G.I.'s, her ride in the war plane, her quoted words were all taken from the published stories about her; and by this time I was getting her *placed,* her relation to the times and what her attitude really meant in political, human, all sorts of terms; I thought her a blight on everything she touched, and I think so more than ever. So I finished up the article I was writing about her, meaning it to be the first of two; in the second I meant to deal with her work and the underlying idea, if it can be called that.

Now then, you were the first to expose me to Miss Stein, really; but I did not know this until this morning. My good friend Sylvia Beach was the agent of the second exposure. My nephew, then a very young, eager, inexperienced man, in active service in the Army, had been sent to Dijon to the University during his service in the occupying army in Germany. He went up to Paris when he could, and I sent him to Sylvia Beach, who was very kind to him and sent him on to certain persons he wanted to meet. (This weakness for "meeting" people I have never been able to understand or sympathize with much, but it exists, it is I suppose harmless.) So Sylvia, a great partisan of mine, no doubt confirmed in my nephew's mind the notion that his aunt K. A. was not only a great writer, but a very famous one. I must not be held accountable for their charming illusion, based as it was on pride and love. So Miss Beach sends our Innocent Abroad off to Miss Stein, and he full of doubts as to whether he would be received, whether he could justify intruding on the great artist (he respected artists in those days, at least), and Sylvia—I can just *hear* her!—said: "All you have to do is tell her you are K.A.P.'s nephew!" Sylvia is the soul of honor and honesty. Why she thought this I shall never know, but I do know she would never purposely have misled anyone; she undoubtedly believed what she was saying. So did my nephew, more's the pity. For out of that completely paltry little episode, there has come a nastiness like this we are talking about. Paul told me the story thus: that when he spoke to her, feeling the need to explain his presence, he said that Sylvia Beach had sent him, and that he was K.A.P.'s nephew. And that Miss Stein said, very clearly and carryingly, so that everybody in the room heard it, "K.A.P.? Who is she?" He says nothing of turning pale, I don't suppose he knew he did, but he did say he was very confused and embarrassed, as well he might have been, and as no doubt she meant him to be. But what surprises me is that Miss Stein would remember and tell this incident. It varies from her victim's in two particulars: he says nothing of a note, and she does not seem to have been very gentle or polite; but standards do vary in these things. And you call my criticism of her malicious, but you do not mention her malice in accusing him of traveling on his nephewhood. He did not, except on the bad advice of someone he trusted, and he has not in any particular to this day. In fact he has felt it as a liability, and is even somewhat overscrupulous. He will not let me help him.

Now then, the point of all this is exactly: I invited my nephew to come and visit with me awhile on the West Coast to rest up from his four years or more in the Army. He did, and at one time or another, telling stories of his adventures, he told me this story about Gertrude Stein. But not before my article was written, and not before I had decided to publish it. . . . She had died meanwhile, and I brought it up to date a little—the original piece, as you see, had been begun nearly ten years before; and I was troubled that I had not finished it and published it before her death because I realized that I could also be accused of base motives in withholding it. I had not withheld it. I had simply finished it in its own time, an editor of *Harper's*, a friend of mine, who knew it was in existence, thought it very timely, and asked me for it. . . . But I did not know this story of my nephew's until *afterward*. Meantime he *had* told it to several young men he knew in Paris, it evidently had troubled him, and a great many people seem to have known it long before I did. This gave someone his big chance to write to *Harper's* magazine and tell the story (my nephew's version, so we know where he got it), and accuse me of taking my base revenge in the form of this article. I did not answer it because I did not know yet. It is a thing too cheap and mean even to talk about, and yet the circumstances certainly do give such minds all they need to work on. It is a matter exactly of my word against theirs—a very loaded kind of dice, for they are not interested in facts. Nice fresh dirty gossip is good enough for them.

I am glad that you "rather think" that I did not do such a thing. And again I am amazed at the way men tear the vitals out of each other's work, and even personal lives, in the name of literary criticism, and everybody accepts this. But when a woman writes criticism, it is always female malice if she says a harsh word . . . I studied both *Autobiographies* carefully a number of years, and I hesitated long because I did not want to be unjust, and if you knew the depths of my feeling and intellectual opposition to that entire school and epoch, that whole view, in the round, you would understand better that "The Wooden Umbrella" was an exercise in self-restraint and understatement. I am sorry you do not like my criticism, but that is anybody's right; it does not affect my right to say what I think. But I do resent the questioning of my motives and my good faith; they are wrong to attribute their own baseness to me.

Now then, I think this probably clears up the matter. I am sorry you thought it worth troubling about, but I answer you because as you say, in effect, we have always been friendly and got on well, in spite of the differences in our tastes and ideas of literature. Reading your letter again, I note that you do not want your note to the Yale Collection available until after your death. . . . I am keeping of course a copy of this letter and naturally it is not to be seen by anyone but yourself, now or ever. I shall keep it in my papers and have not yet decided what disposition I shall make of them, but my will provides that no letters of mine to anyone at all shall ever be published or shown in any collection. I have advised as many friends as I can reach that they may as well return my letters to me, for there is nothing else to be done with them.

However, the publication of certain letters, such as those of Hart Crane, make me feel that maybe I should not leave my name and reputation at their mercy. . . . I have in mind to tell that really ugly story, but have been so revolted by it I have never had the courage to endure the revival in my memory. But the deathly odors of old lies and evil acts keeps seeping up as from a plague pit. I am sickened by it, but I suppose one day or another I must tell, as the saying is, "my side of it." It is a dreary prospect.

Now I hope you get to Europe and return when you like. Unless you have some definite plans for controlling the tenure of your life, you must know by now as I do that premonitions of fatality sometimes mean only that we are so set on changing something we are quite willing to die in the attempt. Of course, I should like to think this is true of you. But in any case at all let me know as you wish to tell of what happens to you in your change.

I woke very merry and well this morning, meaning to do a day's work; this letter of yours has quite disheartened me: I have never been anxious about my reputation either as a person or as artist; am not now. It always seemed very simple and natural to be an artist, I can't quite understand the hubbub about such a normal state. But it really does hurt me to be slandered; that no doubt is a weakness, but I confess it.

With all good wishes,

Yours,
Katherine Anne

(*Note) Dear Donald, what I remembered to have said about *The Making of Americans* was, that it was a source book of characters for novelists; that almost every sort of nature and temperament was there mentioned and partially described, though there was no attempt to fill them out or carry their histories through . . . this seemed then to me what was wrong and still does. Art does not imitate the shapelessness of life, that is, the shapeless, fragmentary life which most individuals see. . . .

The artist must work some order into what I have called somewhere else "his little handful of chaos." This is what Miss Stein could not do, or would not. I feel that she discovered that she could not, and so made for herself a kind of theory to justify her incapacity. I know you have explained her very well in your book. But you did not convince me, for your book is wonderfully thought out, ordered, the most formal plea for disorder and general chaos I ever read. I enjoyed it thoroughly but I can't take it as an argument for what you are trying to prove. That is paradox without any reservations, isn't it? Life is one bloody, horrible confusion, and the one business of the artist is to know it, admit it, and manifest his vision of order in the human imagination: he simply mustn't be sloppy and he must know what he is doing and he mustn't elevate his weaknesses into dogma. I am writing in a fearful hurry and this is as near as I can come at this moment to my meaning. So far as it goes, you may take it for an incomplete expression of a principle of my being.

Yours,
Katherine Anne

Donald Sutherland
1607 Bluebell
Boulder, Colorado
June 4, 1953

Dear Katherine Anne:

I am sorry my letter sent a promising day of yours off its course, but I hope this is the end of that particular headache, for both of us. I am only distressed now that I wrote in such haste that I went by ear and seem to have said "I rather think" (meaning I think, rather, that, etc.) with a heavy accent on the *rather*, whereas it reads to the eye like a terribly patronizing and impertinent phrasing. Well, God damn. As to "malice":

first, what men say against each other and their writing has motivations for which the exact words could not go through the mail, by and large (or have you any idea?), and malice is by comparison venial if not a positive virtue. BUT I do think the feminine mind lives and breathes in the personal and the sensory and when you go on the attack, even with fasting and prayer and purity of heart, you come out with the substance and texture of gossip and cannot really get beyond moral ideas, so that there has never been a woman critic and I think there never will be, except where the specific gifts are at their best, as when Edith Sitwell is on the subject of the texture of Pope or the misdeeds of Wyndham Lewis. So I think you are wasting your time on criticism—as I am, for that matter, though for other reasons, naturally. And of course, we shall both go on doing it, God damn again, and I think the reason we do it is that there hasn't been a decent critic since Coleridge (in English) and we feel that *some* criticism should be done, so we rush away from our real business to do it. But anything less than Coleridge is really not, at this time of day, worth doing. *I* got into criticism only because there was none, of Gertrude Stein's work (in 1946), worth measuring.

I think you are in for it with the Hart Crane business; it will be decades before we get back to his poetry from his life. I don't know what the new disturbance is, not having seen his letters, but I suppose in NYC there is a nuisance; out here it is very easy to ignore anything whatever, and I can go by the old maxim: Never Reply to Anything. I could, even with more to reply to.

You are quite right about a radical change. I have just been made a full professor, and that doesn't sound bad, but when it happens to you it is terrible; it brings you smack up against the question of who you are and what have you done with the last couple of decades. The trouble is that one has, morally, to go on for a while yet until the attack on the position—by McCarthy and the like—is driven back, and this could be turned into an excuse for just holding on interminably. So it is not so much a fatality as a serious impasse and a matter of seeing and pushing through it.

As to writing and "criticism" I so see my way ahead very well, from ontology to punctuation, and it is a matter now of starting off irrevocably, and whole hog. I think what I am moving into is a variety of romanticism, with its wits about it so to say; at any rate I think you may like what comes of it if anything does, and that would be a relief from this awkward situation of holding such perfectly opposite opinions of Stein. Naturally the difference goes deep but it doesn't seem to work as an opposition except at that point.

Thank you for having enjoyed my book even so, and forgive me for having ruined your day with the business of the letter.

Gilberte* and I both send our very best.

Donald

117 East 17th Street
New York 3, N.Y.
10 June 1953

Dear Donald:

All human beings of no matter what sex or gradation of sex, live partly in the personal and sensory, and partly in the abstract and supersensory or—in too many cases—the sub-sensory, and you don't get out of this that easily with me!

All art comes out of human nature, not just one part, but every cell of it; and so does criticism. You seem to speak as if criticism was some sort of purely scientific apparatus, like a surgeon's kit or a chemistry laboratory, where art, the human organism or tissue is subjected to a purely impersonal or abstract analysis. There is no such thing as the purely abstract or the purely intellectual, anyway. Even criticism such as yours of Gertrude Stein's work carries such a charge of the sensory and personal it fairly pulsates through and between the lines. Judging merely by what I read of criticism, whether by men or women, men are quite as motivated by these forces as women; if you are not a good critic, it is for precisely the same reason that I am not—our minds and feelings work better in other ways, and why this is so, nobody knows at all. It occurs to me sometimes that the real difference between the sexes, emotionally and intellectually considered, is that women feel less need for asserting themselves by analyzing and judging everything; they do not, in a word, feel a need to be God. This could have some relation perhaps to their biological function, it has been advanced as theory, but no one really knows. . . . My criticism has been well received by other critics, male and female, generally. One or two, and not the best ones, have attempted to drag the old red herring of Sex over the trail; Robert Penn Warren said to me, "You've invaded what men like to feel is their peculiar territory, so you must expect to catch a few bricks!" I told him I had noticed a

* His wife.

long time ago that nothing infuriated people like hearing someone say, "I think . . ." and this goes double for women thinking in the presence of a certain kind of man who wishes to feel—it is purely an emotional matter—that women have no right to exercise their intellectual powers. And again, actually men are the most virulent and persistent gossips I know, and at a level which shames me for the human race. . . . Yes, I do have an idea, an awfully good one, of men's motives and even those unmailable words in which they express them. (But I know so many different kinds of people, men and women, that any generality I make about any of them just rises up and slaps back at me within two lines, so I have about given that up.)

I can't agree about the absence of good criticism since Coleridge. He is maybe impossible to beat on his own grounds, which were extensive; but even here and now we have some fine gifts in that line. No one critic is good for everything, any more than any one artist can do every sort of thing. And if, as you say, women can't get beyond moral ideas, well that is better than never arriving at them at all, much less transcending them. (Simone de Beauvoir's theory is that women, by some chargeable mischance of human affairs, live in immanence, men in transcendence. I can only say, some do and some don't, either way.)

One little human truth is that opinionated people don't hold much with other people's opinions, and it is a great pleasure to some of them to be able to ascribe incurable defects, such as belonging to a certain sex; or base motives, or lack of understanding, to anyone whose views they disagee with.

Let's not play that silly little game. "For it is neither just nor fit/That poets should each other eat." * You are welcome to disagree with me as much as you choose, criticize my work as severely as you like; but please don't expose yourself by putting it on the grounds that I am a woman, or criticize other work out of personal feelings. I can really dislike the work of someone really deeply; disagree with them about everything, and yet like the person very well. So I confess I have refused to write even reviews about certain writers because I know it might endanger friendship. You may say this proves what you were saying about the personal. Well, I value my human associations in this one little short painful life. I do not think so well of my critical faculty as to risk such a loss on it. Wanda Landowska once said, about an argument with some English friends over the ascription of some old music—who wrote it exactly and when?—

* A jingle often repeated by Ford Madox Ford.

which she let drop, saying, "Friendship is more important than truth." I would not go so far: but I know friendship when I see it, and none of us, not one man or woman in the whole world, since we got up on our hind legs and started looking for the Truth, has ever been sure he has found it. No matter what they say, and no matter how much blood they are willing to shed in defense of their belief. I intend to go on looking for my little fragment, though, with my entire sensory and intellectual being, coming up once in a while with some finding or other . . . what else did anyone ever do? And I mean to use every part of my entire nature for what it is worth—why work with fragments when you need all you have?

And going back to the prime cause of this little encounter, you forget that the piece about Miss Stein was meant to be a personal portrait—a self-portrait in fact, gathered feature by feature from her own two books of autobiographical writings, and it *was* an attempt to explain by implication why I thought her no artist: she was never able to get out of her own narcissistic preoccupation with herself, that terrible blinding, crippling love of the self-lover for his own reflection in the mirror. There have been some wonderful illuminations of this state by those in it: valuable exactly as illuminations: but not for me to accept their findings as doctrine or a way of being for me. Chaos *is*—we are in it. My business is to give a little shape and meaning to my share of it. . . .

Never mind. Go your way as you must, I go as I must. This is not a question to be settled. I *am* happy you are going "whole hog"—that is, finally, the only way to go. Never ask the end—it was in your beginning anyway. I wish you well. Good remembrance and affection to your wife, whom I remember so clearly as admirable and lovable.

Yours,
Katherine Anne

117 East 17th Street
New York 3, N.Y.
4 July 1953

Dear Donald:

You are right, I am not interested in reputations at all. Not interested in careers, "celebrities": and I sympathize with your feeling about certain things being more becoming to men than to women—I hadn't thought of criticism, or anything that particularly had to do with the mind or imagination: for example, there aren't and never have been any first-rate women composers, I can't think why, but it seems to be a fact. I don't think that composing would be unbecoming to women, if they were any good at it. If a first-rate one ever comes along, I shan't feel that she should be discouraged on the grounds of sex. But yes, I do think a woman admiral could easily be ridiculous, and certain forms of athletics are very unbecoming to women, and I know for certain that Nature or Something meant for Aristotle to be a man and Joan of Arc a woman. (No matter if she did straddle a horse and wave a sword, hers was a most womanly career and purpose. Her feelings were completely feminine.) St. Thomas was rightly a man, and St. Theresa of Avila a woman: they were both tremendous geniuses and there is no question of rivalry or inequality. They don't get in each other's way at all. If a woman bullfighter turned out, however, to be as good as Joselito or Sánchez Mejías, I should still think she was absurd and badly out of place.

Your very interesting male view that a woman speaking her mind critically makes herself less interesting—believe me, it works both ways. I have more than once been quite charmed with a man until I read his book. After that, I didn't care to know anything more about him! Both sexes do love a certain amount of mystery and foggy foggy dew in the other.

Now, you say, you are getting deep in Romanticism. At odds no doubt with the "neoclassical, neocatholic school." Once, many years ago, Yvor Winters called me "outrageously romantic" and I took it for the smack-down it was supposed to be. John Crowe Ransom led a whole school of critics and poets in one direction for years, and then right-about-faced and began leading another set practically in the opposite direction. Writers are continually announcing these changes of heart and mind, and they always have a name for each one. . . . Well, I never knew what I was. I have been called so many things it would confuse me if I let my mind dwell on it. I'm Ole Woman River, I just keep rollin' along! And this, I think, is a really feminine habit—we don't seem to need to classify ourselves or join a trend, or name our school. What I always hoped for myself was that I might keep a warm heart and cultivate a cool head; and it is astonishing how many kinds of literature I have been able to love and admire and accept, having just such a delight in the working of the human faculties in such a variety and complexity.

Yours,
Katherine Anne

Eudora Welty and
A Curtain of Green

Friends of us both first brought Eudora Welty to visit me two and a half years ago in Louisiana. It was hot midsummer, they had driven over from Mississippi, her home state, and we spent a pleasant evening together talking in the cool old house with all the windows open. Miss Welty sat listening, as she must have done a great deal of listening on many such occasions. She was and is a quiet, tranquil-looking, modest girl, and unlike the young Englishman of the story, she has something to be modest about, as *A Curtain of Green* proves.

She considers her personal history as hardly worth mentioning, a fact in itself surprising enough, since a vivid personal career of fabulous ups and downs, hardships and strokes of luck, travels in far countries, spiritual and intellectual exile, defensive flight, homesick return with a determined groping for native roots, and a confusion of contradictory jobs have long been the mere conventions of an American author's life. Miss Welty was born and brought up in Jackson, Mississippi, where her father, now dead, was president of a Southern insurance company. Family life was cheerful and thriving; she seems to have got on excellently with both her parents and her two brothers. Education, in the Southern manner with daughters, was continuous, indulgent, and precisely as serious as she chose to make it. She went from school in Mississippi to the University of Wisconsin, thence to Columbia, New York, and so home again where she lives with her mother, among her lifelong friends and acquaintances, quite simply and amiably. She tried a job or two because that seemed the next thing, and did some publicity and newspaper work; but as she had no real need of a job, she gave up the notion and settled down to writing.

She loves music, listens to a great deal of it, all kinds; grows flowers very successfully, and remarks that she is "underfoot locally," meaning that she has a normal amount of social life. Normal social life in a medium-sized Southern town can become a pretty absorbing occupation, and the only comment her friends make when a new story appears is, "Why, Eudora, when did you write that?" Not how, or even why, just when. They see her about so much, what time has she for writing? Yet she spends an immense amount of time at it. "I haven't a literary life at all," she wrote once, "not much of a confession, maybe. But I do feel that the people and things I love are of a true and human world, and there is no clutter about them. . . . I would not understand a literary life."

We can do no less than dismiss that topic as casually as she does. Being the child of her place and time, profiting perhaps without being aware of it by the cluttered experiences, foreign travels, and disorders of the generation immediately preceding her, she will never have to go away and live among the Eskimos, or Mexican Indians; she need not follow a war and smell death to feel herself alive: she knows about death already. She shall not need even to live in New York in order to feel that she is having the kind of experience, the sense of "life" proper to a serious author. She gets her right nourishment from the source natural to her—her experience so far has been quite enough for her and of precisely the right kind. She began writing spontaneously when she was a child, being a born writer; she continued without any plan for a profession, without any particular encouragement, and, as it proved, not needing any. For a good number of years she believed she was going to be a painter, and painted quite earnestly while she wrote without much effort.

Nearly all the Southern writers I know were early, omnivorous, insatiable readers, and Miss Welty runs reassuringly true to this pattern. She had at arm's reach the typical collection of books which existed as a matter of course in a certain kind of Southern family, so that she had read the ancient Greek and Roman poetry, history and fable, Shakespeare, Milton, Dante, the eighteenth-century English and the nineteenth-century French novelists, with a dash of Tolstoy and Dostoievsky, before she realized what she was reading. When she first discovered contemporary literature, she was just the right age to find first W. B. Yeats and Virginia Woolf in the air around her; but always, from the beginning until now, she loved folk tales, fairy tales, old legends, and she likes to listen to the songs and stories of people who live in old communities whose culture is recollected and bequeathed orally.

She has never studied the writing craft in any college. She has never belonged to a literary group, and until after her first collection was ready to be published she had never discussed with any colleague or older artist any problem of her craft. Nothing else that I know about her could be more satisfactory to me than this; it seems to me immensely right, the very way a young artist should grow, with pride and independence and the courage really to face out the individual struggle; to make and correct mistakes and take the consequences of them, to stand firmly on his own feet in the end. I believe in the rightness of Miss Welty's instinctive knowledge that writing cannot be taught, but only learned, and learned by the individual in his own way, at his own pace and in his own time, for the process of mastering the medium is part of a cellular growth in a most complex organism; it is a way of life and a mode of being which cannot be divided from the kind of human creature you were the day you were born, and only in obeying the law of this singular being can the artist know his true directions and the right ends for him.

Miss Welty escaped, by miracle, the whole corrupting and destructive influence of the contemporary, organized tampering with young and promising talents by professional teachers who are rather monotonously divided into two major sorts: those theorists who are incapable of producing one passable specimen of the art they profess to teach; or good, sometimes first-rate, artists who are humanly unable to resist forming disciples and imitators among their students. It is all well enough to say that, of this second class, the able talent will throw off the master's influence and strike out for himself. Such influence has merely added new obstacles to an already difficult road. Miss Welty escaped also a militant social consciousness, in the current radical-intellectual sense, she never professed communism, and she has not expressed, except implicitly, any attitude at all on the state of politics or the condition of society. But there is an ancient system of ethics, an unanswerable, indispensable moral law, on which she is grounded firmly, and this, it would seem to me, is ample domain enough; these laws have never been the peculiar property of any party or creed or nation, they relate to that true and human world of which the artist is a living part; and when he dissociates himself from it in favor of a set of political, which is to say, inhuman, rules, he cuts himself away from his proper society—living men.

There exist documents of political and social theory which belong, if not to poetry, certainly to the department of humane letters. They are reassuring statements of the great hopes and dearest faiths of mankind and they are acts of high imagination. But all working, practical political systems, even those professing to originate in moral grandeur, are based upon and operate by contempt of human life and the individual fate; in accepting any one of them and shaping his mind and work to that mold, the artist dehumanizes himself, unfits himself for the practice of any art.

Not being in a hurry, Miss Welty was past twenty-six years when she offered her first story, "The Death of a Traveling Salesman," to the editor of a little magazine unable to pay, for she could not believe that anyone would buy a story from her; the magazine was *Manuscript,* the editor John Rood, and he accepted it gladly. Rather surprised, Miss Welty next tried the *Southern Review,* where she met with a great welcome and the enduring partisanship of Albert Erskine, who regarded her as his personal discovery. The story was "A Piece of News" and it was followed by others published in the *Southern Review,* the *Atlantic Monthly,* and *Harper's Bazaar.*

She has, then, never been neglected, never unappreciated, and she feels simply lucky about it. She wrote to a friend: "When I think of Ford Madox Ford! You remember how you gave him my name and how he tried his best to find a publisher for my book of stories all that last year of his life; and he wrote me so many charming notes, all of his time going to his little brood of promising writers, the kind of thing that could have gone on forever. Once I read in the *Saturday Review* an article of his on the species and the way they were neglected by publishers, and he used me as the example chosen at random. He ended his cry with 'What is to become of both branches of Anglo-Saxondom if this state of things continues?' Wasn't that wonderful, really, and typical? I may have been more impressed by that than would other readers who knew him. I did not know him, but I knew it was typical. And here I myself have turned out to be not at all the martyred promising writer, but have had all the good luck and all the good things Ford chided the world for withholding from me and my kind."

But there is a trap lying just ahead, and all short-story writers know what it is—The Novel. That novel which every publisher hopes to obtain from every short-story writer of any gifts at all, and who finally does obtain it, nine times out of ten. Already publishers have told her, "Give us first a novel, and then we will publish your short stories." It is a special sort of trap for poets, too, though quite often a good poet can and does write a good novel. Miss Welty has tried her hand at novels, laboriously, dutifully, youthfully thinking herself perhaps in the wrong to refuse, since so many authoritarians have told her that was the next step. It is by no means the next step. She can very well become a master of the short story, there are almost perfect stories in A *Curtain of Green*. The short story is a special and difficult medium, and contrary to a widely spread popular superstition it has no formula that can be taught by correspondence school. There is nothing to hinder her from writing novels if she wishes or believes she can. I only say that her good gift, just as it is now, alive and flourishing, should not be retarded by a perfectly artificial demand upon her to do the conventional thing. It is a fact that the public for short stories is smaller than the public for novels; this seems to me no good reason for depriving that minority. I remember a reader writing to an editor, complaining that he did not like collections of short stories because, just as he had got himself worked into one mood or frame of mind, he was called upon to change to another. If that is an important objection, we might also apply it to music. We might compare the novel to a symphony, and a collection of short stories to a good concert recital. In any case, this complainant is not our reader, yet our reader does exist, and there would be more of him if more and better short stories were offered.

The stories in A *Curtain of Green* offer an extraordinary range of mood, pace, tone, and variety of material. The scene is limited to a town the author knows well; the farthest reaches of that scene never go beyond the boundaries of her own state, and many of the characters are of the sort that caused a Bostonian to remark that he would not care to meet them socially. Lily Daw is a half-witted girl in the grip of social forces represented by a group of earnest ladies bent on doing the best thing for her, no matter what the consequences. Keela, the Outcast Indian Maid, is a crippled little Negro who represents a type of man considered most unfortunate by W. B. Yeats: one whose experience was more important than he, and completely beyond his powers of absorption. But the really unfortunate man in this story is the ignorant young white boy, who had innocently assisted at a wrong done the little Negro, and for a most complex reason, finds that no reparation is possible, or even desirable to the victim. . . . The heroine of "Why I live at the P.O." is a terrifying family poltergeist, when one reconsiders it. While reading, it is gorgeously funny. In this first group—for the stories may be loosely classified on three separate levels—the spirit is satire and the key grim comedy. Of these, "The Petrified Man" offers a fine clinical study of vulgarity—vulgarity absolute, chemically pure, exposed mercilessly to its final subhuman depths. Dullness, bitterness, rancor, self-pity, baseness of all kinds, can be most interesting material for a story provided these are not also the main elements in the mind of the author. There is nothing in the least vulgar or frustrated in Miss Welty's mind. She has simply an eye and an ear sharp, shrewd, and true as a tuning fork. She has given to this little story all her wit and observation, her blistering humor and her just cruelty; for she has none of that slack tolerance or sentimental tenderness toward symptomatic evils that amounts to criminal collusion between author and character. Her use of this material raises the quite awfully sordid little tale to a level above its natural habitat, and its realism seems almost to have the quality of caricature, as complete realism so often does. Yet, as painters of the grotesque make only detailed reports of actual living types observed more keenly than the average eye is capable of observing, so Miss Welty's little human monsters are not really caricatures at all, but individuals exactly and clearly presented: which is perhaps a case against realism, if we cared to go into it.

She does better on another level—for the important reason that the themes are richer—in such beautiful stories as "Death of a Traveling Salesman," "A Memory," "A Worn Path." Let me admit a deeply personal preference for this particular kind of story, where external act and the internal voiceless life of the human imagination almost meet and mingle on the mysterious threshold between dream and waking, one reality refusing to admit or confirm the existence of the other, yet both conspiring toward the same end. This is not easy to accomplish, but it is always worth trying, and Miss Welty is so successful at it, it would seem her most familiar territory. There is no blurring at the edges, but evidences of an active and disciplined imagination working firmly in a strong line of continuity, the waking faculty of daylight reason recollecting and recording the crazy logic of the dream. There is in none of these stories any trace of autobiography in the prime sense, except as the author is omnipresent, and knows each character she writes about as only the artist knows the thing he has made, by first experiencing it in imagination. But perhaps in "A Memory," one of the best stories, there might be something of early personal history in the story of the child on the beach, estranged from the world of adult knowledge by her state of childhood, who hoped to learn the secrets of life by looking at everything, squaring her hands before her eyes to bring the observed thing into a frame—the gesture of one born to select, to arrange, to bring apparently disparate elements into harmony within deliberately fixed boundaries. But the author is freed already in her youth from self-love, self-pity, self-preoccupation, that triple damnation of too many of the young and gifted, and has reached an admirable objectivity. In such stories as "Old Mr. Marblehall," "Powerhouse," "The Hitch-Hikers," she combines an objective reporting with great perception of mental or emotional states, and in "Clytie" the very shape of madness takes place before your eyes in a straight account of actions and speech, the personal appearance and habits of dress of the main character and her family.

In all of these stories, varying as they do in excellence, I find nothing false or labored, no diffusion of interest, no wavering of mood—the approach is direct and simple in method, though the themes and moods are anything but simple, and there is even in the smallest story a sense of power in reserve which makes me believe firmly that, splendid beginning that this is, it is only the beginning.

> But now that so much is being changed,
> is it not time that we should change? Could
> we not try to develop ourselves a little,
> slowly and gradually take upon ourselves
> our share in the labor of love? We have been
> spared all its hardship . . . we have been
> spoiled by easy enjoyment. . . . But what if
> we despised our successes, what if we
> began from the beginning to learn the
> work of love which has always been done
> for us? What if we were to go and become
> neophytes, now that so much is changing?
>
> Rainer Marie Rilke

A Sprig of Mint
for Allen

A sixtieth birthday is impressive, what the Mexicans call *una bola de años*, a ball of years; it represents a triumph of durability and vitality, and at least a partial victory of the spirit in what turned out, after all, to be a pretty long war. I am particularly impressed when it occurs to someone I have known since he was twenty-seven years old, already a poet of great gifts and a critic of severe and obstinate character—I mean by that, with his caliber of mind, a good critic. Ah well, here he is, and how did he get here? I am reminded again that, though a year is added to my life every twelve months, and every year in the sweet month of May I celebrate with love and praise the recklessness of my father and mother, I cannot budge the friends of my youth out of *their* youth in my mind and heart: there they remain in a frame of light with a backdrop of blue sky and green field—it does not occur to me that anybody is getting older except myself. I am not taking it very hard, either, not speeding it up unnecessarily—there is all the time in the world.

So, as for my friend Allen Tate, I know well he is a grandfather and has been one for a great while, but it happened to him so early he was the youngest grandfather I ever knew personally. It did nothing to age him in my eyes. When some of John Crowe Ransom's friends, Allen among them, invited me to Mr. Ransom's sixtieth birthday party, I thought it quite all right, very natural for him, because I had never seen him when he was younger; yet even then I felt that sixty is a little young

to begin giving testimonials and memorials and getting our special numbers of magazines. It might put notions in a man's head about getting
old. So I delight in the spectacle of our dear John Crowe Ransom, how
successfully he has resisted all the well-meaning, admiring attempts of
his misguided loving friends to embalm him while he is still walking
around thinking live thoughts.

I am, as you see, against this whole project of making a production of
Allen's sixtieth birthday; he is simply not old enough yet, he still has
much to do. I nearly made it, not quite as usual, to Robert Frost's eight-
ieth birthday party. That is more like it. A great poet who survives in his
powers to that age should be given a public vote of thanks and all the
honors lying around loose at the time. But Allen cannot be called venerable by any stretch of the word and he shouldn't be summed up at this
point. If you plan to give a gay birthday party with plenty of champagne
and music and dancing and flowers, do invite me. I may not get there,
but I'd like being invited. Let's not be solemn about the passing of time
and the reputations of our literary men. Allen's is safe, I think—let's let
him live and grow. It is splendid to think another good poet has lived to
be sixty years old, for the real ones do grow in grace as they go on—I am
remembering Hardy, Yeats, Frost, Eliot—so I wish my old friend joy of
his years in health and just the right degree of disturbance, upset, uproar,
and controversy that he can best thrive on to write his poetry. Many
happy returns of the day, with my love.

> Beauty, who creates
> All sweet delights for men,
> Brings honor at will, and makes the false seem true
> Time and again.
>
> (Pindar)

1959

On First Meeting
T. S. Eliot*

Cousin, if one lives long enough, everything will come, even death, even a promised photograph. I was so long in getting hold of this myself, I almost forgot why I had it at all; then, in moving, papers get packed away and forgotten. Quite often I find mss. of stories half finished that I can hardly believe I ever started.

I saw T. S. Eliot for the first time when he was here last (New York, opening of his play, *The Cocktail Party*), and this is an astonishingly fine likeness of him as of right now, so far as any photography may be trusted at all. He is a charming, sweet-mannered man, with beautiful conversation. I have seen only a very few real geniuses, great persons in their gifts and achievements, and it occurred to me again on meeting this one that those I have seen shared in common the simplicity and dignity of manner that does come with long experience of living, thinking and feeling about art, about human beings, about religion or ideas or emotions as *realities; working* as artists, blessed be, they seem naturally to outgrow, to shed, all kinds of fears and the horrid affectations and other nonsense that come of fears. They lose self-importance, and the vanity of impressing their personalities on others; I feel that this poet was never much afflicted with either.

It had been a very long ordeal: I didn't get to the last party until

* This was originally included in a letter from Miss Porter to a distant relative. The letter was accompanied by a photograph of the poet.

nearly ten in the evening, but he had been honored almost to exhaustion: a huge long luncheon, a crowded cocktail party, a vast dinner, and a roaring late party with all three floors of a good-sized house densely populated by a frenetic glass-in-hand crowd. There were at least a dozen well-known literary drunks, besides non-literary ones, swarming around him at once, whirling and changing places, being elbowed away and striving back, grabbing him, patting him, *owning* him, trying to claw each other away from him.

He didn't resist, but he didn't give way, either; it was quite something to see and remember in the way of self-possession without self-assertion, gentleness without weakness, a St. John of the Cross sort of thing, and at what a party, too!

I shook hands with him and he smiled and drew me into the ring and asked me to sit by him, and I did; but only for a few seconds and a few words, then I escaped before I should be torn in pieces. Miss Marianne Moore, at a good distance, holding her glass of fruit juice, observed the behavior of a certain gentleman not carrying his liquor too well, and remarked in her beautiful velvet voice, "That man is simply speckled all over like a trout with impropriety . . ." which I must write down for you before it gets away from me. I wandered away from group to group and managed to find somebody to bring me a few drinks, and finally not able to bear the scrimmage, I went home. I looked back for a glimpse of the poet as I went. He was as serene and collected as if he sat easily in the void of the hurricane, where no doubt he *does* sit. One doesn't arrive there without a struggle, and the marks are on him as you see, but they are no disfigurement.

This is never to hint that he was a teakwood Buddha without nerves or a queasy midriff. He drank quite what he wanted and seemed to enjoy it and carried it perfectly, only toward the end of this preposterous day he looked paler and thinner and taller, and there was a light dew on his brow and the back of his neck, and he smiled a little more perseveringly, and was more inclined to confine his remarks to simple assent: "Yes indeed!" or "Quite!" I am happy to have seen him and I was charmed with him.

1961

Flannery O'Connor at Home

I saw our lovely and gifted Flannery O'Connor only three times over a period, I think, of three years or more, but each meeting was spontaneously an occasion and I want to write about her just as she impressed me.

I want to tell what she looked like and how she carried herself and how she sounded standing balanced lightly on her aluminum crutches, whistling to her peacocks who came floating and rustling to her, calling in their rusty voices.

I do not want to speak of her work because we all know what it was and we don't need to say what we think about it but to read and understand what she was trying to tell us.

Now and again there hovers on the margin of the future a presence that one feels as imminent—if I may use stylish vocabulary. She came up among us like a presence, a carrier of a gift not to be disputed but welcomed. She lived among us like a presence and went away early, leaving her harvest perhaps not yet all together gathered, though, like so many geniuses who have small time in this world, I think she had her warning and accepted it and did her work even if we all would like to have had her stay on forever and do more.

It is all very well for those who are left to console themselves. She said what she had to say. I'm pretty certain that her work was finished. We shouldn't mourn for her but for ourselves and our loves.

After all, I saw her just twice—memory has counted it three—for the second time was a day-long affair at a Conference and a party given by Flannery's mother in the evening. And I want to tell you something I

think is amusing because Flannery lived in such an old-fashioned Southern village very celebrated in Southern history on account of what took
place during the War. But in the lovely, old, aerie, tall country house
and the life of a young girl living with her mother in a country town so
that there was almost no way for her knowing the difficulties of human
beings and her general knowledge of this was really very impressive because she was so very young and you wondered where—how—she had
learned all that. But this is a question that everybody always asks himself
about genius. I want to just tell something to illustrate the Southern
custom.

Ladies in Society there—in that particular society, I mean—were
nearly always known, no matter if they were married once or twice, they
were known to their dying day by their maiden names. They were called
"Miss Mary" or whoever it was. And so, Flannery's mother, too; her
maiden name was Regina Cline and so she was still known as "Miss
Regina Cline" and one evening at a party when I was there after the
Conference, someone mentioned Flannery's name and another—a
neighbor, mind you, who had probaby been around there all her life—
said, "Who is Flannery O'Connor? I keep hearing about her." The
other one said, "Oh, you know! Why, that's Regina Cline's daughter:
that little girl who writes." And that was the atmosphere in which her
genius developed and her life was lived and her work was done. I myself
think it was a very healthy, good atmosphere because nobody got in her
way, nobody tried to interfere with her or direct her and she lived easily
and simply and in her own atmosphere and her own way of thinking. I
believe this is the best possible way for a genius to live. I think that
they're too often tortured by this world and when people discover that
someone has a gift, they all come with their claws out, trying to snatch
something of it, trying to share something they have no right even to
touch. And she was safe from that: she had a mother who really took
care of her. And I just think that's something we ought to mention,
ought to speak of.

She managed to mix, somehow, two very different kinds of chickens
and produced a bird hitherto unseen in this world. I asked her if she
were going to send it to the County Fair. "I might, but first I must find a
name for it. You name it!" she said. I thought of it many times but no
fitting name for that creature ever occurred to me. And no fitting word
now occurs to me to describe her stories, her particular style, her view of

life, but I know its greatness and I see it—and see that it was one of the great gifts of our times.

I want to speak a little of her religious life though it was very sacred and quiet. She was as reserved about it as any saint. When I first met her, she and her mother were about to go for a seventeen-day trip to Lourdes. I said, "Oh, I wish I could go with you!" She said, "I wish you could. But I'll write you a letter." She never wrote that letter. She just sent a post card and she wrote: "The sight of Faith and affliction joined in prayer—very impressive." That was all.*

In some newspaper notice of her death, mention of her self-portrait with her favorite peacock was made. It spoke of her plain features. She had unusual features but they were anything but plain. I saw that portrait in her home and she had not flattered herself. The portrait does have her features, in a way, but here's something else. She had a young softness and gentleness of face and expression. The look—something in the depth of the eyes and the fixed mouth; the whole pose fiercely intent gives an uncompromising glimpse of her character. Something you might not see on first or even second glance in that tenderly fresh-colored, young, smiling face; something she saw in herself, knew about herself, that she was trying to tell us in a way less personal, yet more vivid than words.

That portrait, I'm trying to say, looked like the girl who wrote those blood-curdling stories about human evil—NOT the living Flannery, whistling to her peacocks, showing off her delightfully freakish breed of chickens.

I want to thank you for giving me the opportunity to tell you about the Flannery O'Connor I know. I loved and valued her dearly, her work and her strange unworldly radiance of spirit in a human being so intelligent and undeceived by the appearance of things. I would feel too badly if I did not honor myself by saying a word in her honor: it is a great loss.

1964

---

* She *did* write that letter, which was misplaced for a number of years—a very good letter, which I found when going over my papers for the University of Maryland. The line I remembered was this marvel of composure in the face of Death itself and her own death.

From the Notebooks:
Yeats, Joyce, Eliot, Pound

Boulder, Colorado. July, 1942. The death of James Joyce distressed me more than any other since the death of Yeats. How the tall old towers are falling: these were the men I most admired in my youth: I discovered Yeats for myself; he was the first contemporary poet I read, and the first poem was in a magazine in 1915:

> There is a Queen in China, or maybe 'tis in Spain
> And birthdays and holidays such praises can be heard
> Of her unblemished loveliness, a whiteness without stain
> You might think her that sprightly girl
> Was trodden by a bird.*

If this is not quite exact, it is the way I remembered it for years and years before I saw it again in a collection. But beginning there, and with his *Celtic Twilight*, a book which seems to have disappeared, I followed Yeats with the most faithful adoring love, and discovered a new shining world. Joyce came a little later, but not much. I read *Dubliners* in 1917, and that was another revelation, this time of what a short story might be,

---

* "His Phoenix." It was later collected in the volume *The Wild Swans at Coole* (1919) and appears as follows:

> There is a Queen in China, or maybe it's in Spain,
> And birthdays and holidays such praises can be heard
> Of her unblemished lineaments, a whiteness with no stain,
> That she might be that sprightly girl trodden by a bird.

even though I had believed that *Chekov* had written the last one worth reading, until then.

As between these two great artists, I should say that Yeats was the greater imagination; Joyce did not have greatness in the grand manner, as Yeats did: Joyce had a dryness of heart, and very limited perceptions of human nature. Yeats *grew* great, the only kind of greatness, really: as if all his life he was fulfilling some promise to himself to use every cell of his genius to its fullest power. Yesterday's newspaper was just sent over to me with an account of Joyce which reminded me of the day I first heard of his death. He died in his second war exile, two variations of his perpetual exile. He was a homeless man, the most life-alienated artist of our time. Yet more than anybody, he gave fresh breath and meaning to language, and new heart, new courage, new hope to all serious writers who came after him. Rest his soul in peace.

I saw him only once. When I first went to Paris, in February, 1932, he was already world-famous, half-blind, surrounded by friends all faithful to him, apparently, but jealous of each other, watching him for signs of favor, each claiming to be first, trying to prevent anyone new from coming near him: and on the outer rim of this group was a massed ring of eager followers trying to get into the sacred circle: it was pretty grim to witness even from a safe distance: but he had reached that point of near defenselessness against the peculiar race of people who live in reflected glory: I did not wish to see him, or speak to him—what was there to say? And it was no doubt true that no new acquaintance could do more than disturb or bore him. But I never went near him, and this idea of him was presented to me as the true state of affairs by Sylvia Beach, Eugene and Maria Jolas, by Ford Madox Ford, by all of the many persons I knew there who had known Joyce, and befriended him for years. I think, too, that most of them had quarreled more or less among themselves about Joyce, and in a way, with Joyce himself. Sylvia most certainly had good cause for her belated resentment of his callous use of her life; but no one I knew was really easy in regard to him: he seems to have been a preposterously difficult man to get along with. His blindness was like the physical sign of his mind turning inward to its own darkness: after all, if the accounts now given are true, it seems not to have been the optic nerves but his teeth: and at last his intestines killed him.

One evening a crowd gathered in Sylvia's bookshop to hear T. S. Eliot read some of his own poems. Joyce sat near Eliot, his eyes concealed under his dark glasses, silent, motionless, head bowed a little, eyes closed most of the time, as I could plainly see from my chair a few feet away in the same row, as far removed from human reach as if he were already dead. Eliot, in a dry but strong voice, read some of his early poems, turning the pages now and again with a look very near to distaste, as if he did not like the sound of what he was reading. I had been misled by that too-often published photograph showing him as the young Harvard undergraduate, hair sleekly parted in the middle over a juvenile, harmless face. The poet before us had a face as severe as Dante's, the eyes fiercely defensive, the mouth bitter, the nose grander and much higher bridged than his photographs then showed; the whole profile looked like a bird of prey of some sort. He might have been alone, reading to himself aloud, not once did he glance at his listeners.

Joyce sat as still as if he were asleep, except for his attentive expression. His head was fine and handsome, the beard and hair very becoming to the bony thrust of his skull and face, the face of "a too pained whitelwit," as he said it, in the bodily affliction and prolonged cureless suffering of the mind. . . .

To those of my own generation and after, I can only say, what would we have done without him? He had courage for all of us, and patience beyond belief, and the total intensity of absorption in his gift, and the will to live in it and for it in spite of hell: and more often than not, it was hell: but as bad and worse things have happened to many quite good men who suffered quite as much, who had no gift, no toy, no special mystery of their own, to console them.

Washington, D.C. May 9, 1965. Note: Quite years later, in Washington, D.C., I went to visit Ezra Pound at St. Elizabeth's, where he held limited but lively open house for a parade of friends. I looked about the place as I left—a huge sort of plant, with thousands upon thousands of persons of all ages and kinds, in every degree of insanity. I inquired and it was as I suspected: Ezra Pound was the only poet in the place! Naturally I said nothing at the time, but went away with my delicious impression that either poets are more level-headed than other men—or are they just harder to catch? In any case, I doubted then and do doubt that Ezra Pound was ever for a moment insane. He was just a complete, natural phenomenon of Unreason.

1965

Romany Marie, Joe Gould
—Two Legends Come to Life

(*a letter to* The Village Voice)

Romany Marie's charming rosy-edged reminiscences which you published lately, and your notice of Joe Gould's death in a mental hospital,
remind me of two strange episodes that have stayed in my memory thirty
years or a little less.

In the early twenties and on I spent a great deal of time in Mexico,
and when I was in Greenwich Village I took very little part in the goings-
on there. Everybody I knew, however, knew Romany Marie, her series of
wonderful places where you saw simply everybody from all over the
world, the warmth of her heart and the goodness of her coffee. Friends
of mine who knew her—and it seemed that all of them did—offered to
take me to visit her; I don't remember why I never went.

I met her in the country at a kind of boarding farm where writers and
artists went in the summer, when I was trying to do some work. But it
wasn't much more quiet there than in town, for a writer named Leonard
Cline, who wrote glib high-voltage novels, quite mad, drunken and impossible to quell or shake off when he went on the rampage, which was
every night and often every day as well, made life so devilish for most of
us—there were about a dozen of us scattered around in the barns and
icehouses and chicken coops as well as the main house—that I was on
the point of giving up and leaving when Romany Marie came up to
spend a weekend with Cline and his wife.

She was a swarthy, weathered, beautiful woman in early middle life,

301

calm and smiling and wearing her gypsy clothes as if she were born to the patteran, though everybody knew she was no gypsy, she said so herself. She just liked the idea of gypsies and decided to look like one.

She lent color and a kind of reality to the vaguely formless existence of the farm, and in the evening we all built a fire and sat around it singing, believe it or not, until Leonard Cline got off on his mad high horse, when we scattered and Romany Marie came to my place, the icehouse, to spend the night. I barred the doors and put out the lights, and Leonard Cline careered and howled around the place, and beat on the doors demanding that we let him in, for a wearisome while. Romany Marie listened to the din in perfect calmness, but I was quite exhausted after a great while of it; and she suggested that while Cline was beating on the front door, we should take our cot mattresses—thin little rags they were—out the back door, and take refuge in the woods up the hill. We did this, running and hauling our mattresses after us. We sat there, in the moony woods, hearing the poor madman shouting and raging below, until at last his wife persuaded him to go in their house. We smoked and talked awhile about all sorts of things, and of Cline Romany Marie said: "Oh, we must pity him. He is so much more unhappy than he can possibly make anybody else!"

We finally slept, and the next thing I knew, it was daylight, I smelled cigarette smoke, heard the rustle of Romany Marie's four or five long ruffled gay-colored skirts, and saw her stamping out her live cigarette with her bare foot. She rubbed her hands over her face, smoothed her hair, shook out her skirts, and was ready to go. I felt terribly disheveled, which I was, and could hardly wait to make our breakfast coffee.

Odd thing is, I don't remember anything more about this episode, or how it ended, but Romany Marie and I were friends after that; whenever I went to see her, this wild night was our point of reference and our cheerful common memory. This must have been in 1926 or '27: I went later to Bermuda, back to Mexico, and on to Europe, and didn't see her for nearly ten years. But when I went back, with another old friend of hers, she remembered instantly, and we talked again about our flight to the woods, and Romany Marie said, with the transfiguring power of her memory: "Oh, weren't we like two nymphs pursued by a satyr?" It is now years again since I have seen her, and I hope to see her soon, for I know she will be sitting there with that marvelous air of repose and gentle confidence, not changed at all, and I will say: "Marie, Marie,

Marie, do you remember that night in the woods?" and she will say—but of course I don't know exactly the words she will speak, but she will smile her same smile, and remember.

(Note: Some time afterward, Leonard Cline murdered his best friend with a shotgun in a country house after a night of furious drunken brawling. And a good while later, he was found dead in his bed. There was always the feel of death in the air where he was, and our flight was not just altogether humorous, one way of getting rid of an intolerable nuisance. He was always dangerously violent.)

And then, Joe Gould! I did not know him, only by sight, and the sight was always a sad one. He was regarded with a kind of indulgence and pity by his friends, but everyone seemed to realize there was nothing anyone could do to help him, and I have heard some of them tell comic stories about him by the hour; he was in his way as living a legend as Romany Marie.

But one evening I was at a party with my friends Slater and Sue Brown, and I remember Robert Coates and his wife, Elsa, Malcolm and Peggy Cowley, Hart Crane, and I think others, but I don't remember who. The front door to the flat had a wide, old-fashioned keyhole, and was approached by a longish narrow hall. Slow wavering steps were heard in this hall, and Slater Brown said warningly "Shsh—wait a minute—be quiet!" And we all were silent and looked toward the door. The footsteps paused outside. Slater tiptoed and peered through the keyhole, and looked into an eye peering right back at him. It was, as Slater had feared, Joe Gould. He moved silently away, we all kept quiet, and after a very few seconds I'm sure, though it seemed longer, the slow steps dragged away.

This was only a little while before I went back to Mexico in 1930, very early spring. I never saw him again, or knew where he was, or what had become of him until the other day when I saw your story about his death.

1957

Jacqueline Kennedy

I saw Mrs. Kennedy only twice—first, at the Inaugural Ball in the Armory in Washington; second, at the dinner in honor of the Nobel Prize winners, in the White House. In each of these glimpses she looked like all her photographs, those endless hundreds of images of her cast on screens and printed pages everywhere through the short, brilliant years of her public career beside her husband; only, in breathing life she was younger, more tender and beautiful. She had the most generous and innocent smile in the world, and her wide-set eyes really lighted up when she spoke to her guests. Old-fashioned character readers of faces believed that this breadth between the eyes was the infallible sign of a confiding, believing nature, one not given to suspicions or distrust of the motives of others. It might very well be true. On account of this feature, a girl reporter described her as resembling a lioness. I do not think she resembles a lioness in the least, but I am ready to say she is lionhearted. A merrier, sweeter face than hers never dawned upon the official Washington scene—so poxed with hardbitten visages, male and female, that bring joy to nobody—but even the swiftest of first glances could not mistake it for a weak face. It was and is full of strong character and tragic seriousness lying not quite dormant just under the surface, waiting for the Furies to announce themselves.

Certain members of her family, and long-term friends surmised these latencies, but could not name them—someone of them called her a "worrier." This is obviously not the word to name her special kind of hand-to-hand immediate concentration on the varied demands and emergencies of her days all through her life as we have known it—which may be called the ordeal by camera—but it is easy to see how a by-stander, no matter how near the relationship, might misread her, never having seen in action the austerity, the reserve force and the spiritual discipline which no one expects in so young a creature. There had not been any occasion sufficient to call them out. She had been such a fashionable sort of young girl, brought up in the most conventional way: the good schools, the travel, the accomplishments and sports, the prepared social life. The whole surface was smooth as satin; she even wore clothes almost too well, a little too near the professional model. But she outgrew this quickly and was becoming truly elegant at an unusually early age. She had the mistaken daydream that many very nice girls do have, that to be a newspaper reporter and go about pointing cameras at perfect strangers was a romantic adventure. She got over this speedily too, and became herself the target of every passing camera and every eager beaver of a reporter who could get near her. And what a record they gave us of a life lived hourly in love with joy, yet with every duty done and every demand fulfilled: nothing overlooked or neglected.

Remember that veiled head going in and out of how many churches, to and from how many hospitals and institutions and official functions without number: that endless procession of newly sprung potentates to entertain royally! And always her splended outdoor life—water-skiing with Caroline, both their faces serenely happy, fearless; driving a pony cartfull of Kennedy children, the infant John John on her lap; going headfirst off that hunter at the rail fence, and in perfect form too, her face perhaps not exactly merry, but calm, undismayed. An expert, trained fall that was; one would have to ride a horse to know how good it was, and what a superb rider Mrs. Kennedy is.

There is another snapshot of her going at a fine stride on her beautiful horse; and always that lovely look of quiet rapture in her high-spirited, high-stepping play. She never seemed happier than when swimming or skating or water-skiing, or sailing, or riding, or playing with her children. Who will forget the pictures of her in sopping wet slacks, bare feet, tangled hair, blissful smile, on the beach; with her husband nearby, rolling in the sand, holding Caroline, still in her baby-fat stage, at arm's length above him?

All of us heard, I'm sure, some lively stories of the pitched battles of early marriage, and there were dire predictions that little good would come of it. Nonsense! What would you expect of two high-strung, keen-witted, intensely conscious and gifted people deeply in love and both of them with notions of their own about almost everything? It was not in the stars for that pair to sink gently into each other's arms in a soft corner, murmuring a note of music in perfect key. It seems to have been a good, fair, running argument in the open—heaven knows there was no place for them to hide; eyes, ears and cameras were everywhere by then —and we know that things were coming out well. We could see it in their expressions as time ran on, and the cameras intercepted their glances at each other, saw them off guard at moments of greeting, of parting, their clasped hands as they came out of the hospital after Patrick was born—anybody could see that the marriage was growing into something grand and final, fateful and tragic, with birth and death and love in it at every step. Their lives were uniting, meshing firmly in the incessant uproar and confusions of the most incredibly complicated situation imaginable. But they were young, they were where they wanted to be, they loved what they were doing and felt up to it; and they dealt every day, together in their quite different ways, supporting and balancing each other, with a world in such disorder and in the presence of such danger, international and domestic, as we have not seen since Hitler's time. And the entertainments, the music, the dancing, the feasting— there hasn't been such a born giver of feasts in the White House, a First Lady who recognized that a good part of her duties were social, since Dolley Madison. Mrs. Kennedy had the womanly knack of making even dull parties appear to be pleasures. But the manner of the President and his wife to each other was always simple, courteous and pleasant, without gestures, without trying. It was a pleasant thing to see, and I began to be grateful for those swarming pestiferous cameras that could show me such reassuring steadfastness with such grace and goodness.

The only moment of uneasiness I ever saw in Mrs. Kennedy's pictured face was at the first showing of the *Mona Lisa* in Washington, when somebody concerned in the arrangements did something awkward, I forget what; she looked distressed. We know now she was expecting her fifth child, five within a period of little more than seven years: she had already lost two, and was to lose Patrick. Every child had cost her a major operation or a serious illness. This is real suffering, and yet she ceded nothing to the natural pains of women, but bore her afflictions as part of her human lot, rose and went about her life again.

I remember so vividly how she looked at the Inaugural Ball. In that vast place more fit for horse shows than balls, the stalls where we sat were railed in with raw pine, champagne was chilled in large zinc buckets such as they water horses in at country race tracks; there were miles and miles of droopy draperies and a lot of flags, and a quite impressive display of jewels and furs and seriously expensive-looking clothes. Also we listened to a peculiarly pointless program of popular songs: first, the Sidewalks of New York kind of stuff, then Negro jazz, not the best of its kind either; besides two or three bloodcurdling little ditties dedicated to Mrs. Kennedy; and I believe, I am not certain, that they were sung and played by the composers, young women who should have been warned off. It was acutely embarrassing; and altogether it was the oddest mixture of international grandeur and the tackiest little county fair you ever saw. I love county fairs, and I love grand occasions; but I don't like them mixed. So I remarked on the spot—still having the Coronation of Queen Elizabeth II in mind's eye—that we would never, it was clear, as a nation, learn how properly to conduct our ceremonial events.

The taking of the oath, outdoors in January, if you please, had been a series of gaffes. But that was over, and the young First Lady came to the big Ball at the Armory, one of five or six, I believe, going on all over town, and sat there in her white gown, motionless as a rose on its stem, watching her husband adoringly. She went away early, for John John had been born seven weeks before.

Later, by a year or more maybe, at the dinner given in the White House for the various Nobel Prize winners, and runners-up, we were having cocktails in the East Room, and I saw and greeted all sorts of delightful old acquaintances I hadn't seen for twenty years and may never see again—I seem nearly always to be somewhere else!—when the strains of "Hail to the Chief" gave us the cue to set down our glasses and turn toward the great door. There was no roll of drums, no silver-trumpet fanfare, no; just a wistful, rather wiggly little tune, very appealing and sweet, and there stood the President and Mrs. Kennedy before us, amiable and so good-looking and so confident, with all the life and all the world before them, and why should it ever end? Very happily and easily we formed a long line and went past them shaking their hands lightly—think of all the hands they had to shake every day!—and then we went on to dinner and a merry party afterward, and it was all so gentle, and reassuring, in that lovely house, so well done and so easy.

Atmosphere, tone, are very elusive things in a house, and they depend entirely on the persons who live there. . . . The White House that evening was a most happy place to be, and I shall never see it again, for I wish to remember it as it was then. What style they had, those young people! And what looks. . . .

Then I went to Europe and came back a year later, on All Souls' Eve, to Washington. And now I am writing this, on the 22nd of December, 1963, on the day of the Month's Mind Mass, and the memorial lighting of candles at the Lincoln Memorial. The perpetual light that Mrs. Kennedy set at the President's grave can be seen from almost any point in this city. This light is only one of the many things Mrs. Kennedy asked for and received during that night of November 22.

I have a dear friend whose beloved wife died not long ago, and he wrote me an account of her going away, and he said: "I never heard of, or imagined, such an admirable performance!" I knew exactly what he meant, and within a few days I witnessed Mrs. Kennedy's performance, at the great crisis of her life, and it was flawless, and entirely admirable; I have no words good enough to praise it. The firmness with which she refused to leave the body of her husband, keeping her long vigil beside him, but not idly, not in tears, planning and arranging for his burial to the last detail. What relentless will she showed, fending off the officious sympathy of all those necessary persons who swarm about tragic occasions, each anxious to be of service, true, but all too ready to manage and meddle. She refused to be cheated of her right to this most terrible moment of her life, this long torment of farewell and relinquishment, of her wish to be conscious of every moment of her suffering: and this endurance did not fail her to the very end, and beyond, and will not fail her.

What I think of now is the gradual change in that lovely face through the fiercely shattering years when she and her husband raced like twin rockets to their blinding personal disaster which involved a whole world. Among the last pictures I remember is Mrs. Kennedy as she stood with her two children in the cold light of a late-fall day—and you don't have such perfectly well-behaved children at their age unless you have known how to love them and discipline them!—watching the President's coffin being carried from the White House on its way to the Rotunda. She stood there staring a little sidelong, as if she could not dare to look directly. The first shock was over, that head-on collision with death in one of its most wasteful and senseless forms had taken place without warning, as it always does, but the dazed blind look was gone from her eyes, replaced by a look of the full knowledge of the nature of Evil, its power and its bestial imbecility. She stared with dawning anger in her eyes, in the set of her mouth, yet with the deepest expression of grief I have ever seen, a total anguish of desolation, but proud, severe, implacable.

No one who witnessed that three-day funeral service, in presence or by screen, can ever say again that we, as a nation cannot properly conduct the ceremonies of our state. We have been well taught.

1964

COTTON
MATHER

(work in progress)

Author's Note: *These three chapters are part of my history of the Salem Witch-craft, chosen from eleven chapters written in Bermuda in 1929.*

Affectation of
Praehiminincies
(A.D. 1663-1675)

Maria Mather bore many children, some of them afflicted, and she accepted all her griefs and theirs with formal resignation. Not so much with this first child, Cotton. She spent on him the freshness of her maternal passion as if there would never be another. Stray glimpses of her, caught through a web of small-chronicle, show her praying and fasting for his sake, careful that his first words should be a prayer. Cotton seemed sound enough after the first precarious months of his life: in his second year he was undeniably frail, and when he formed his first pious words, his parents were horrified to discover that he stammered. There was no defect in the organ of speech, it was a nervous condition, and he could not utter a word without a painful struggle.

Dedicated as he was to the church, family pride, family reputation, family vocation were all at stake and in a fair way to be lost. It was obvious to the young parents that the devil had made an immediate assault upon an enemy he had reason to fear even in the cradle. They communicated their dismay to the child. The fate of his soul and the success of his career in the world were identified in earliest impressions with the necessity for loosening the catch in his speech. With precocious understanding he sat in his oak high chair, brought from England by grandfather Mather, and prayed to be cured of his stammer.

When he was three years old, he could read and spell, and his serious education began in the free school of Mr. Benjamin Thompson. Family legend contends that he was an apostle from the first, and stammer or no, he began at once to lead his schoolmates in prayer. At playtime he preached little sermons to them. The feebler wits of the school listened and were impressed, but sturdier spirits made fun of him, poked him and pinched him when the master was not by, and gave him the joy of suffering for his principles. Increase Mather liked to believe that his child was a saint at three years, and resented the treatment he received. He encouraged him in his unutterable priggishness, and soothed his vanity by explaining that persecution was the fate of good souls in a wicked world. He also cautioned the schoolmaster to be gentle with his child. The Mathers were all tender parents in an epoch of systematic brutality toward the young. Richard Mather had been so dreadfully flogged and kicked by his schoolmaster that his childhood was embittered. Much as he longed for an education, he had begged his father to take him from school. His father sympathized and persuaded him to endure for the sake of learning. Richard overlived the experience, but not the effects of it, nor the memory, and all his life he spoke against the popular cruelties to children, and was tender with his own. Increase was even more indulgent: he was almost unique in his age because he did not beat his young, but rather erred to the opposite extreme.

The special consideration he received in school gave Cotton a certain advantage over his playmates. He found himself supported in his apostolic attitude not only at home, but by public opinion, and this early became confused in his mind with the voice of God. The primer lessons were composed of moral maxims, and he learned that "The Butterfly, in gaudy Dress, the worthless Coxcomb doth express." He was offered such fallacies of natural history as "The Crocodile, with watery eyes, O'er man and every creature cries." Infant religiosity was praised in such bold rhyme-schemes as "Young Obadias, David, Josias, All were pious."

These infantile studies could not detain him long. He swallowed the primer and the horn-book, moved into the next grade, added Greek, Latin and arithmetic to his list, and proceeded upward without pause. "Zerxes the Great did die, and so must you and I . . ." was the primer lesson that stuck fast in his mind and urged him to a feverish speed. Death was at his shoulder, he might be stricken at any moment, he had no time to lose, he must hurry!

In his fifth year he resolved to be great. "He expected it, and therefore he bore and did many things, and disregarded all difficulties." This is

Cotton's son Samuel, writing a long generation later, in the Mather fashion presenting with minute filial care a selected phase of his parent's career.

This inflated self-importance of the infant Cotton was a reflection of the family feeling. He was surrounded by every possible attitude of moral grandeur, a tallness and solemnity of manner utterly unrelieved by any sense of proportion. He "played saint" in imitation of his elders. And saintliness carried a certain social prestige. He went to services in a meeting house where the pews were carefully allotted according to social position, and he could not help seeing that he sat with his mother in the very front pew while his father occupied the pulpit. In his dangerous precocity, he absorbed everything without discrimination, and began to imitate the methods of his elders. He soon mastered the technique of exacerbating his sensibilities in prayer, and could burst into a flood of nervous tears at the crisis of a petition, precisely as his father and mother did, and as sometimes the whole congregation did, bowing in shaken rows while their anguished groans ascended to heaven.

He believed that New England was the most important country in the world, and Boston the greatest city, and his family the most distinguished of all families, and this belief remained almost unmodified into his middle age. To a natural personal arrogance the Mathers added theological pride, and a jealous vanity that showed an alarming tendency to resent slights real or apparent. People were continually uncomfortable in the presence of Increase Mather for fear they might do or say something damaging to his feelings. Respect for the clergy had been an article of faith in the early colony. The outward observances of this respect survived, but the spirit was weakening, and Increase was sensitive to the slightest breeze of change in this regard.

Cotton adored his father, and his grandfather Mather he revered as a solemn presence stalking through his infant days giving reproof and admonition in his overpowering voice. But to his grandfather John Cotton went his secret hero worship. He was dead, but mother and grandmother conspired to keep his memory alive in a romantic aura of all that was courtly, superb, learned and charming in this world. The city of Boston itself was his breathing monument, and Sarah Mather could not praise him enough.* It was natural that the admired husband who had called

---

* In Boston, England, John Cotton married, as his second wife, a young widow, Sarah Story. He used to call her his "dear sweetheart and comfortable yokefellow."

her tender names should somewhat overshadow the living one with whom she shared the chilly pieties of old age. It was true that a miracle had saved Richard Mather for New England. The ship that brought him almost sank in the harbor, everyone agreed there was no natural cause why it should have remained afloat, but God spared all for the sake of bringing Richard Mather safely to shore. This was a miracle clearly, but insignificant compared to the blazing comet that hovered above Boston during Grandfather Cotton's last sickness, disappearing on the day of his death.

A godless innkeeper had been made uncomfortable by John Cotton's presence as a guest, professing himself unable to curse and damn with that saint under his roof. Once John Cotton had prayed for the dying child of his bitter enemy, Pastor Wilson, and the child had recovered at once. The man who had sworn to John Cotton's nonconformity before the High Commission had fulfilled prophecy by dying of the plague under a hedge; Mr. Leverett, who swore to a lie in defense of John Cotton and Christ's kingdom, was even now in New England, safe with honor. His reward had been certain, visible and negotiable, the just end of virtue.

Little Cotton imbibed these stories, and the system of ethics they were designed to illustrate, as revealed truth. The more marvelous the tale, the more farfetched the moral, the easier for him to believe. Daily proofs of the family greatness were shown to him. He saw his father, when involved in a doctrinal dispute, turn to Richard Mather for consultation. When Richard wished to clench an argument, he turned to the writings of John Cotton, and the disputants were silenced.

Before his milk-teeth were loosened, the child assumed the task of outpraying and outdoing these spiritual giants. His stammer grew worse, and his parents kept days of humiliation for his relief. The house was filled with lamentations of suffering souls engaged in begging off from the cruelties of an implacable, invisible Presence that hourly threatened them with fresh calamities. Cotton had thought at first it was the Devil who had tied his tongue. Now it appeared that the visitation might be from God, enraged at some mysterious failure of holiness in Cotton's soul. Appalled, much confused, he wept and implored with the others,

---

Years later, Richard Mather married, as his second wife, John Cotton's widow, Sarah. In the meantime, John and Sarah Cotton's daughter, Maria, had married Increase, eldest son of Richard Mather. They were the parents of Cotton Mather.

not without some pardonable pride in his elevated situation at the very center of a divine mystery.

Cotton had been absorbing knowledge from Mr. Thompson, from his father, and from the thousand-odd books on his father's shelves. It was already the finest collection in the colony, where every family of any pretension prided itself on the possession and at least a quoting knowledge of good literature. It was socially correct to be known as a great reader: respect for the learning implicit in books increased, as times passed, into a nostalgia for the world of urbane European culture, and every ship brought fresh consignments of the latest works, not all of them theological or moralistic, to adorn the homes and minds of New Englanders who leaned with undiscriminating confidence on the printed word. Increase Mather had the foundations of true learning, and he read for love, even for amusement at times; the young Cotton had the desire to be learned and above all to be called learned, and he read voraciously everything he could lay hands upon. His memory was photographic, and at six years his little head was a mere rubbish heap of printed matter. He was then turned over to the famous pedagogue, Mr. Ezekiel Cheever, to be prepared for Harvard. Cheever was pious and a master of languages, and his unpleasant fondness for beating small boys caused him to enjoy a notable reputation as a disciplinarian. But he did not apply the ferule to Increase Mather's prodigious child. Even he was not so bold as that. All Boston was familiar with the father's sensitiveness about his son who was born a genius and a saint besides. Cotton pursued his apostolic labors among his classmates and devoured knowledge with an inhuman persistency that would be quite incredible if all the records of his later life did not bear witness to his unwearying pursuit of a single idea. This idea took on monstrous shapes and sizes, it sprouted in a thousand variations, but it remained essentially unaltered: the single aspiration of Cotton Mather to identify publicly and unmistakably his personal interests and ambitions with the will of God.

Harvard had lived up to the expectations of its founders and was the pride of New England, considered a cultural center equal to anything England could show. It was now an affront to local self-esteem to send promising young men to Europe for their degrees. Harvard was more than a university: it was a political hostage. Its rights, its very existence, were bound up with the first charter, and anything that menaced the charter menaced Harvard. It was the stamping ground of the clerical party: the whole death struggle of the theocratic state was to be enacted here, and the times were ripening for it. The destructive third generation was rising, critical of its grandfathers, cheerfully casual about the rather musty notions of its fathers. Harvard held firmly to its original aim of fitting the sons of ministers for the ministry, but many of them thus prepared fell away from their vocation and entered other professions, or even went into trade. Merchants' sons who had no intention of entering the church were now admitted, a little grudgingly. It was necessary to admit them, for otherwise they would go to England for their education and return with minds expanded beyond the permissible limits of provincial life: or worse, they might not come back at all. This had happened often enough.

A thirteenth-century schoolman would have approved the curriculum, with its heavy emphasis on logic, rhetoric and syntax, its geometry and arithmetic and astronomy, but alas, no music. A smattering of physics, a long list of dead languages, Greek, Syriac, Chaldee, Hebrew: and Latin, now on the point of dying out as the peculiar language of scholars. The students read the Bible exhaustively in all languages. In addition, and this was most important, the "scholar must understand that the end of his life was to know good, and Jesus Christ which is eternal good," and to attain this they read the scriptures and prayed publicly twice a day. Blasphemy was first among the seven major offenses, and its variations were minutely classified. The sinner was punished by a flogging, attended by prayer.

Into this ample lap of learning the great Ezekiel Cheever literally kicked his pupils, having first prepared them thoroughly in Greek, Latin, and the fear of God. At twelve years Cotton Mather had absorbed all that Cheever could teach. On June 22, 1675, Increase Mather wrote in his diary that Cotton had gone to live at the College. "The God of all Grace be with him, and never leave nor forsake him, but bless him and make him a blessing wherever he shall be, amen!"

The president and the instructors were prepared to treat the young genius very handsomely, granting him the same privileges and exemptions he had enjoyed under Cheever. The students were not so complacent. An unpleasant episode occurred almost at once. On the following 11th of July, Increase received dark news from his son. His cousin, John Cotton III, son of John Cotton II of Plymouth, brother of Maria, had joined with some older lads and hazed the newcomer severely. Also they made him run errands for them, and there were hints of harsher things. No doubt they were a set of young savages, but no doubt either that young Cotton Mather was supremely irritating in his assumptions of superiority, not only to the students but to the instructors. He complained with tears to his father.

Increase visited his brother-in-law at Plymouth, and commanded him to discipline his son, who was even now getting a reputation for wildness. He then called the overseers together, and laid his grievances before them. Many differences had been smoldering for a great while between Mr. Mather and the other fellows of the Corporation, and from this entirely legitimate pretext began a quarrel that brought numberless hidden grudges to light. His colleagues promised the enraged father to abolish the student custom of forcing the freshmen to act as fags for the older youths. In the matter of hazing, carried on secretly and with remarkable solidarity, they confessed themselves helpless. They would do what they could. This was merely a surface abuse, said Increase Mather. The trouble lay deeper. He was not interested in the custom itself. He merely demanded that his own son be protected from the brutalities of his classmates. This they could not promise.

Ten days afterward, the father was still seething. He rode again to Cambridge and held a long conference with acting President Orian Oakes and Mr. Thomas Danforth, a Corporation member. He threatened to take Cotton from Harvard if they could not insure him respectful treatment from the students, regardless of seniority. Mr. Oakes pleaded that this would be a great mistake, very harmful to Cotton's future, and asked that he be left where he was. He assured the injured father it was nothing like so serious as Cotton seemed to think, but could give no acceptable reason why the students were mistreating him. Increase felt sure—and he was right—that the persecution was no mere boyish prank, but the material result of a true jealous animosity. The boy was at a painful age, and was mentally overgrown and bodily small and fragile. He had a beautiful face and very careful manners, and was absolutely skinless in his contact with strangers. The effort to overcome his stammer kept him in a continual nervous tension: his desire to make a perfect impression caused him to assume a fantastic preciosity of address. All his life he had been shielded, flattered and adored by his family and friends, and, except for his very first school days, he had suffered not one rumor of a world of physical shocks and psychic cruelties. His school-mates had in them merely the very human desire to hurt and wound a creature who had rather too easy a time of it: the perfectly savage and natural impulse to destroy what they could not understand or sympa-thize with. Cotton's state was pitiable, all the more so because he had nothing within himself to combat the disaster. He suffered blindly and appealed to his father: and his father, dismayed to the soul at the pre-dicament of his adored child, could only storm and rage and provoke fresh disturbances. He left Cotton at the College and went away angry.

At the August commencement Cotton had new woes to confide. Among other things, the Fellows of the Corporation had called the stu-dents into a special meeting and had remonstrated with them severely for tattling of College affairs to the outside world. Cotton felt this was aimed at him for the crime of confiding in his parent. Increase wondered what they meant by the outside world. Was he not a member of the Corporation? Cotton said the students were whispering among them-selves that Increase Mather wanted to be president of Harvard, and this was the reason for his highly critical attitude toward everything that was done there.

This was a real blow. He did wish to be president, it was the dearest ambition of his life, and it galled him that a set of upstart boys had divined and spoken lightly of his closely guarded secret. At the next Cor-poration meeting, Mather took the aggressive in earnest and provoked an open quarrel. He threatened to resign his fellowship. The Fellows and the President, he charged, had abused him in allowing his son to be abused, and they had wronged him in allowing the students to slander him by saying he wished to be president.

Mr. President Oakes was astounded and embarrassed at this frankness. He protested he had never heard of such a thing. With a great show of diplomacy he attempted to reassure Mr. Mather, and probably wished the mischief-making Cotton far away. He thought it would be a great pity if Mr. Mather resigned from his place; as Mr. Mather thought so too, and was merely waiting for an invitation to relent, that part of the business passed over swiftly. The scandal about his ambitions was more difficult. Mr. Oakes said something about this, too, but with less effect. He declared that nobody believed, or had even hinted, that Mr. Mather desired to be president. That Mr. Mather *should* someday be made pres-ident, no one had much doubt: and if there was any uneasiness in connection with this, it was simply the fear that Mr. Mather might in such an event remove the College to Boston. His prejudice against Cambridge was a matter of common knowledge.

After being driven to the wall by further arguments from the still unpacified Mr. Mather, Mr. President Oakes owned with some desperation that there were persons who thought that Mr. Mather was not always so plain and outright about things as he might be, but begged him not to let this trouble him. No doubt jealousy was at the bottom of it, for the interests of Harvard touched everyone keenly, and as for himself, he wished nothing better than to see Mr. Mather settled in the president's chair at Cambridge.

Further than this magnanimity no man could be asked to go. But Mr. Mather retorted that if he should ever be persuaded to accept the presidency of Harvard, it would be at the cost of great self-denial, and sacrifice of his personal welfare. The Mathers father and son were never to lose an occasion to repeat that every step of their lives for the public good had been accomplished at the expense of their private interests.

Mr. Oakes was tremendously impressed by this, assented to everything, and promised Mr. Mather that he should be treated with more respect in the future. The discussion had shifted so subtly from its prime base that Cotton was for the moment no longer the center of attention. Mr. Thatcher and Mr. Danforth, two Fellows of somewhat progressive, or anti-Mather, tendencies, were not so agreeable, and refused pointblank to humor the whims of one that they persisted in regarding as a mere Corporation member like themselves. As nothing less than complete victory would satisfy Increase Mather, he again took horse and rode to see the governor.

Leverett must have shuddered to see him coming. Mather was a gadfly to the governor and the magistrates as well as to Oakes and the Fellows. He harried their flanks in the matter of political and social reforms, as he pursued the faculty of the College with warnings about heresies and apostasies. Mather visited the magistrates in turn, admonishing them of their duties, criticizing their conduct of public affairs and laying fresh programs before them. When his advice was disregarded, as it was all too often, he fell into a fever of resentment and prayed against the enemies of God and New England and Increase Mather.

On his visit, the governor was tactful and sympathetic. He promised to intervene in the College trouble, and everything should be righted at once. Mr. Mather was to rest easy about his son. The situation simmered down a little, but nothing had been resolved. Mather kept a day of humiliation because all his labors seemed so fruitless. "I do but cumber the ground," he groaned. In this episode he perceived that the whole country was in a perilous state. The College seemed doomed to go down under its present woeful management. Moreover the Indians were again rising in force, and the English were not receiving the customary aid from God. The abomination of witchcraft seemed about to devour a people lost in atheisms. The powers of darkness appeared to be getting a firm grip on New England. He wrote to country ministers and asked them to send him particularized and authenticated instances of diabolic possessions and enchantments such as might have come to their attention. The country ministers were delighted with the idea, and highly curious documents began to come in to the North Street parsonage. Mather was much heartened by the unexpected results of his request. He decided to make a book of them, a book that should be a solemn warning and a horrid example.

Cotton had committed an indiscretion in the belief that his father was all-powerful. His father's failure to revenge Cotton's personal wrongs gave a severe check to his faith, and threw him into a new phase of doubts and inner searchings. He saw himself for the first time in direct relation to a world existing outside of himself, grossly self-sufficient, powerful, intractable, immersed in affairs utterly strange to him, entrenched in a point of view not his, and, above all, personally hostile to him. Hitherto he had cultivated a self-doubt, spiritual humiliation, as a rite. In his conflicts with God, with Evil, with his own soul, he emerged finally triumphant, always. In his first encounter with the world, the monster he was born to control and to win for God, he was defeated, bruised, and left prostrate.

Moreover, in his anxiety to uphold his own prestige at college, he had brought on a premature crisis in his father's affairs, embarrassed his cause, and thrown the whole orderly procession off the track. It was a symptomatic episode: he had begun his dual career of assistant and obstructionist to his father. The long struggle between filial piety and ambitious self-interest was on. He had meant to be a spiritual lord of life in college, and he had simply precipitated a rather nasty row involving his father in a series of undignified gestures. He fell into gloom, for if he dimmed the radiance of his father, he darkened all his own prospects.

No Mather was ever lacking in self esteem, and all of them believed, in their more exalted moments, that the world was in substantial agreement with their estimate of themselves. For Cotton, this encounter with a group of lads carefully selected from his own caste, but never quite his equals, for that was impossible, dedicated like himself to a life of holiness in the sacred vocation, gave him a problem in realism very hard to reconcile with his stubborn fantasy of personal grandeur.

He bore it badly. He fell into a deep self-pity and wept in a chagrin that he tried vainly to metamorphose into a state of penitence and purification. It was quite hopeless: he was lost, rejected of God and man, there was no refuge from his inner demon. He suddenly began to stammer again, and all the careful work of his childhood was swept away. The fear of death took hold of him: no literary invention this time, no planned invitation to pleasant horror, no fixed contemplation of the King of Terrors until the imagination was lashed into a foam. Perfect cold inexorable fear crept into his flesh and along his nerves: death became a reality to him. This brought on a long course of afflictions; he feared he had sinned away his day of grace, as the hopeless Calvinistic phrase would have it. He was driving himself unmercifully at his studies, because now above all times he must stand at the head of his classes. He quarreled quietly and bitterly with his cousin John Cotton: and afterwards spent long hours examining his conscience, appalled at what he found there. Night after night he lay sweating and sleepless, clenched upon himself, waiting for the stroke of death, with his soul in disorder and unable to prepare itself for eternity. The foulness of his thoughts and the abominable behavior of his body disconcerted utterly that portion of his mind dedicated to the intellectual pursuit of sainthood. Until now his sins had been mostly rhetorical, he accused himself in general of all the enormities, not knowing what they might be, but in his blithe vanity assuming that he was the chief of sinners. Now in his adolescent upheavals, his pains and monstrous dreams and nervous shudderings, his uncontrollable mental and physical states, he recognized the precise, full nature of sin, and his moral collapse threatened to become complete. He believed his shocking experiences to be unique in the world, and shameful beyond words, and he went with a sense of guilt within, and, what was always terrifying to him, a fear of losing his reputation if anyone should suspect his infamous state.

At home, his brothers Samuel and Nathaniel were violently ill. They had worms, the plague of children in that day. Nathaniel and then Samuel almost yielded up the ghost in prolonged vomiting attacks. Cotton went home and Maria clasped again this most beloved of her children, and they spent a long dark day of tears together, praying for the sick. Increase was almost afraid to pray, for the cause seemed lost: "Now I thought it might be some discouragement to Cotton in case he should see his poor sinful father's prayers were not heard; yet I humbly pleaded it with God."

Salad oil and a clyster were also invoked, and ipecac, and the poor little wretches were dragged through to life. In this moment of relief, Cotton confided the state of his soul, more burdened than any flesh could be, to his father.

He found comfort. His father was not horrified. On the contrary, he was much encouraged at these signs of the death struggle of the Old Adversary in his son. He explained it all so clearly: that these agonies were the first signs of true conversion: and they spent the evenings praying and reading and talking together in the quiet study, among the friendly books, far from the bitter distractions of the world. These hours were very calming to them both, for Cotton was tranquilized to learn that his bodily rebellions were not new in the history of the soul's adventures, and Increase felt growing up by his side a confidant and disciple. Their companionship grew toward equality, and Increase began to confide somewhat of his interests and his problems with his ungrateful and sinful congregation, and those obdurate, hard-hearted fellows of the Corporation who were undoubtedly ruining Harvard.

Increase Mather was very quietly doing a dangerous and subversive thing in a political way. Two of the regicides, Whalley and his son-in-law, Goffe, were moldering in perpetual exile in Connecticut. Increase was one of their agents, and he protected them well, sending and receiving their letters for them, and managing their affairs so adroitly that they were never apprehended. Cotton learned with awe that his admirable father could defy the King of England for reasons of conscience: that New England was a separate country owing no loyalty to any power but the Congregationalist church: and of all the factions within this sacred edifice, the faction headed and controlled by his father was in the right. His spirits revived, their joint defeat at the college seemed less important.

Though one single Synod had refuted eighty-two heresies, thus outstripping Arius by two, yet new ones cropped up like wild grass, and Increase was kept busy quoting his father and his father-in-law at the heretics, with added doctrine of his own. By now they had almost forgotten Calvin, only his tremendous idea, borrowed from Zwingli, remained: and the struggle set up in the ordinary mind by the doctrine of predestination had resolved itself into a mere Manichean warfare between the almost equally matched, separate and authoritative powers of good and evil. Increase Mather was a scourge to the provincial theologians, rising at them in this fashion:

"As for your errors respecting discipline, sacraments, their covenants, etc., I can bear with them yea, and these Arminian heterodoxia respecting Christ's dying for these reprobates doth not much trouble me. But your denying the meritorious obedience of Christ is such desperate heresy as no man that liveth with Jesus Christ in the Christian religion can in sincerity . . . bear with. Nevertheless, I still desire to respect you, and earnestly beseech Christ to let you see your error."

After receiving a letter or two of this kind, the startled rural prophet would ordinarily sink into a permanent silence.

On such examples Cotton formed his style and his point of view. He improved on them both with stouter language and even denser stubbornness. His character was now definitely formed, his mind at fourteen had reached the limit of its growth: all else afterward was mere expansion in the sense of things observed and memorized, a collected mass of information, but the actual capacity of his mind was measured finally at adolescence. He was a typical wonder-child.

Now his personality exhibited strange contradictions. He laughed and wept easily, and though tears were comprehensible to those about him, his tendency to merriment was very disconcerting. He lacked the sober caustic humor and hard cruel wit which appertained to the character of the English Puritan: possibly to all Puritans of all races and epochs. His gayety was spontaneous if somewhat nervous, and because he believed it sprang from an unworthy levity in his nature he tried to suppress it. This in turn led him to attempt an impressive dignity and profundity of manner, which degenerated into sheer youthful pomposity, and caused him to suffer some ridicule in other places than Harvard. This was the beginning of his hysteria and habit of making frightful puns. At first he made them as jests, hoping to amuse his hearers. Later the habit became automatic, and he played on words in contexts that shocked his hearers: that do, indeed, startle the reader even today. (John Cotton, for suavity and gentleness, he described outright as a "soft bag of Cotton," and he lamented that the stone from which Richard Mather suffered proved to be his tombstone.) He was bemused by the mysteries of his physical being and hoped to conquer himself by systematic discipline. He prayed intensively by rule, and began to increase his days of fasting in secret, and to read erudite treatises on the mechanics of meditation. Thus early he was an expert technician, and was forever inventing exercises calculated to advance his cause in Heaven, and on earth. After a fast he always felt more authoritatively spiritual, and this would call to mind the lost state of his little brothers and sisters. They had their own schemes for personal piety, and they could seldom be persuaded to follow his lead in devotion. It was the Mather pride. They would do their own praying. Nathaniel was especially individualistic. He ended by influencing Cotton.

For some years it was nip and tuck between Cotton and his brother Nathaniel for the family laurels of sainthood. "It may be truly written on his grave that study killed him," Cotton wrote long afterward. "His candle would burn until after midnight, until, as his own phrase has it, he thought his very bones would fall asunder." Nathaniel's bones were troublesome at best. He was so frail he could not walk until far past the time for walking. Horrible pains in his joints crippled him recurrently for long periods: he suffered an epileptic stroke that affected his tongue, and for several years he stammered worse than his brother. Even in this state, and handicapped by six years juniority, he threatened to outpace Cotton not only in piety but in learning.

The Mather pride afflicted him to a degree, and he awakened the conscience of Cotton, who, being proud with a difference, might have gone all his life mistaking this dark voice for a virtue, except for Nathaniel who overlooked nothing. When Nathaniel abased himself for whittling a stick on Sunday, and, for fear of being seen, hid himself behind a door while he whittled, Cotton could do no less than search himself for misdeeds even more subtle: they called themselves atheists, and admitted with mutual tears that they deserved hell. They supplemented each other admirably: while Cotton assisted Nathaniel in languages and mathematics, Nathaniel assisted Cotton in the finer points of moral self-torture. All of the children ate, drank, and breathed despair of God's mercy, and their sufferings began even in babyhood. Later, when he was editing his private papers, Cotton destroyed his own records until his eighteenth year, but preserved Nathaniel's long monotonous plaints of mental and bodily disease. He perceived that Nathaniel had a literary style worth his study. In keeping his own diary afterwards, he selected from his brother's papers many passages that he felt were equally pertinent to his state, and copied them in as his own entries. "O make my tongue a Tree of Life," sang poor Nathaniel, and the phrase seemed such a happy one it reappears regularly through all the years of Cotton's own petitions.

Nathaniel wrote: "What shall I do? *What shall I do to be saved?* Without a Christ, I am *undone, undone* forevermore! O for a Christ! O for a Christ! Lord give me a Christ or I die!" These are the unpleasant rhythms of a misplaced emphasis: and to increase the confusion, both brothers were confused about their sexual status. Both of them sought their God in the role of vestal virgins. Nathaniel at this time, and Cotton much later, employed a curious symbolism. "Oh, Lord Jesus, I come to thee! Who am I that I should be married to the King of Glory? I do accept Thee for my head and husband."

The family interests and interior distractions did not prevent Cotton from achieving the highest record for scholarship at Harvard. He mastered Hebrew beyond the requirements, and began to compile his own systems of physics and logic. His vacations were spent in his father's library, where he read himself into headaches, and cudgeled his brains to think up new religious exercises.

Daily he rose from the family table, an abundant board where he enjoyed himself sinfully, and repaired to his study, there to invite an attack of indigestion by instructing himself in doctrine and meditation on the state of his soul. The house was not large, and Maria Mather had almost completed her work of bringing ten children into the world. Slaves, bonded servants, and visiting relations were stowed away somehow, and by excellent management father and eldest son were comfortably secluded in separate studies. Cotton, pacing measuredly back and forth, would select a theme. Doctrinally he posed himself a question. He then considered the causes, the effects, the adjuncts, as well as the opposites and resemblances of his theme. As his theme was invariably himself, his sinfulness, the question how best he might repent and stand well in the sight of God, he arrived logically at a general examination of his conscience, which resolved inevitably into a minute consideration of concrete sins; in the course of events there followed a severe expostulation with himself, and at last a resolution, increasing in imaginative momentum, to repent on the strength of the grace offered with the new Covenant.

The results were monotonously the same. Terror would strike through his carefully contrived defenses, the true and awful meaning of these words and ceremonies would suddenly become clear, shattered he would fall to the floor weeping and imploring to be saved from eternal damnation. All his uncertainties and disappointments would rush upon him, and he would sob dolefully with his forehead on the floor. Later he would rise, make himself tidy, for he was fastidious in his dress, and, seated at his desk, he would record his crisis in detail, with pride and self-congratulation in his achievement.

At home everything was quite perfect. No one disturbed or criticized him, friends and parents admired him fondly, and even in far-away England Uncle Nathaniel was aware of his nephew's importance. He thought Cotton a remarkable child and sent him a "Brachygraphic fitted to the Latin tongue," and insisted that he learn it at once and teach it to his brothers and sisters. Himself, he had not time nor patience for it, it looked very difficult, but shorthand was a branch of learning he desired to see in the family. It had the prestige of novelty and exclusiveness: "Brachygraphic is not known nor practised anywhere in Europe but in England." The gift and the advice went unregarded, and he wrote anxiously about his character-book, saying he had been unable to find another. Cotton Mather depended on longhand to the end of his days.

In this same year there are other glimpses of Cotton seen outside the official biographical records of his youth. Uncle John Cotton, minister at Plymouth, was head of a household reasonably afflicted, reasonably pious and somehow cheerful. As a small-town pastor he was aware that his family lacked the advantages of the metropolis. Also he seemed to have forgotten the little incident of his son helping to terrorize Cotton at Harvard two years before. He was continually writing to his sister Maria, enclosing a few shillings and wanting in return a piece of sealing wax, or several yards of good black cotton ribbon or a modest length of green galloon. At times he wished his sister to buy these things on credit at the same shop where she had bought his wife's cloak and he would pay for all in the spring. He sent an occasional barrel of good salt beef for their winter use, and in turn he hoped they would take his son John under their roof for counsel and prayer. No denying, the contrast between young John and his cousin Cotton was so marked that even John's father must admit and deplore it. He would make up all expense by sending tubs of butter and other necessities.

Increase was in no particular haste to grant this request, for later still another inducement was offered: John Cotton was training a little Negro slave for his dear brother in Christ Increase. The child was only seven but would be very useful for cutting wood and drawing water. He was being properly prepared for these duties, for even now he could answer the question, Who made him?

Then he wrote suggesting an alternative: "Concerning your son Cotton, that he may live here with me this winter: God hath given him grace, and his learning is above what those of his standing have usually attained to, whence he is able to do good to others: and you know it is recorded as the honour of your blessed father that at fifteen years he was called to be a schoolmaster; and why may not his grandson have it put into the records of his life, that before that age he was accounted worthy to be so employed?"

The third John Cotton was hopelessly in arrears with his studies, and his lately persecuted cousin was being haled to the rescue. Cotton was to have comfortable board free of charge. He would return to Boston in the spring with five pounds of silver in his pocket, besides what money other Plymouth families would be happy to pay him for private tutoring. He should have the tenderest treatment, and, as a final argument, it was suggested that the change of air might save Cotton from the smallpox, for Boston was in the midst of one of its frequent plagues.

Cotton could not be tempted by anything. The trouble with his uncles on both sides of the family was that they could not comprehend the altitude of his destiny. Shorthand! What had he to do with that? Tutoring! He did not in the least desire to compete with his grandfather Mather on these grounds, and the money was no inducement. He was perfectly comfortable at home. He remained at Harvard and near his father. Into the records of his life went a very grand letter to his Uncle John:

"I know your candour will not charge me with idleness. Your courtesy will not implead me for forgetfulness, and most of all, you will not without reason accuse me of unwillingness to serve you in what I may, even *usque ad aras*, and if possible, there." He then pleaded delicate health, and "uncertainty of conveyance, and that again seconded by other evocations." He was in fact a busy and important young man, and his Plymouth relations quite evidently needed to be reminded of it. Yet he was not without his generous will to helpfulness. He called upon his muddied shoes to testify how unweariedly he sought the Plymouth boat, "who" (the shoes) "in this time when Boston is become another Lutetia (q. *luto sata*) do proclaim they wanted a pair of goloshooes when travelling near the dock-head." He declared he would fling salt upon the tail of time, or persuade the wind and tide to be favorable to his design if he had the power: but he had not. In short he labored to prove his scholarship and let his uncle know he had no intention of burying himself in Plymouth during the winter season of study.

Then he turned to a subject made for his pen. "Never was it such a time in Boston. Boston burying places never filled so fast. It is easy to tell the time when we did not use to have the bells tolling for burials on a Sabbath day by sunrise: to have seven buried on a Sabbath night after meeting. To have coffins crossing each other as they have been carried in the street—to have, I know not how many corpses following each other close at their heels—to have thirty-eight die in one week." * Still, smallpox or no, he would not come to Plymouth. Providence had been tender in his own family. He had been touched slightly. Brother Nathaniel and sister Sarah also, but sister Maria went out of her head for several days and they feared to lose her. His father's prayers had been responsible undoubtedly for the mildness of this affliction, yet he assured his uncle he was even now preparing himself for the worst, in case Providence should suffer a change of mood.

This air of royal condescension toward his Plymouth relations was a faithful reflection of his father's attitude. The family correspondence was a little one-sided. John Cotton was always affectionately respectful, a little apologetic. He was the poorer of the two, but was always offering small tributes. He was always pressed for money and trying to explain it: he was after all unable to send the little Negro because there were no clothes in the house fit to send him in. The Mathers replied seldom, in the tone of those who held the deciding vote. The near relations were often mystified by the inexplicable remoteness of their distinguished kinsmen. Time and again they forgot themselves and treated the Mathers quite simply. They were soon recalled to a sense of their impropriety.

---

* Borrowed in spots from Dekker's account of the Plague in London.

A Goat for Azazel
(A.D. 1688)

Martha Goodwin, fourteen-year-old, elder daughter of a pious brick mason named John Goodwin, was behaving very strangely. She had been behaving with conspicuous strangeness since she was eleven years old and it had long been suspected that she was in the grip of a diabolical possession. Cotton Mather early noted her symptoms and marked their progress. The Goodwins lived in Charlestown, and during a Sabbath visit to his father-in-law, John Phillips, Mather heard an encouraging bit of gossip.

Not only Martha, but all four of Goodwin's children had fallen, almost overnight, into a state of mind very puzzling and sinister. Little Mercy, seven years old, was in a continual tantrum. She yelled and her body grew rigid while she was being dressed; she refused to do the useful household task suitable to her age; and she would not, without a fearful struggle, allow herself to be put to bed at the customary hour. Naturally the Devil found an easy abiding-place in the bodies of children, conceived as they were, poisoned to the bone with original sin, but a sound beating would usually dislodge him. He sat firmly in this child against all such persuasions. The slightest rebuke from her parents affected her like a lightning shock. She fell prone, turned blue in the face, her eyes rolled upward and her teeth clenched in a paroxysm of lockjaw. The elder son, sixteen years old, shouted that he was a wolf, retired into corners and howled bestially. The third child, John, suffered with shooting pains, and showed signs of epilepsy. He would sprawl on the floor and scream that he could not get up again because his head was nailed to the floor.

Martha was a pretty, inventive, restless girl. She suffered all the afflictions of the others, with a few added symptoms acutely her own.

One afflicted child had been troublesome enough, but four of them succeeded in terrorizing their parents completely. They called on their pastor and several other ministers to come and help them rout the invisible hosts that had chosen their humble household as a battlefield.

The last minister to be invited was Cotton Mather. With his genius for instant action, Cotton Mather was the first man there. The prayer-meeting was called for an afternoon. He arrived alone, early in the morning, held his prayer service by himself, recognized at a glance all the signs of true demoniacal possession in the children, and advised their father to look about for the witch.

At this the children howled in dead earnest, and their sufferings were redoubled. By the time the other ministers arrived, among them Mr. John Hale of Beverly and Mr. Samuel Noyes of Salem, the children had been struck stone-deaf and could not hear the prayers. When the reverend gentlemen produced their Bibles, the devil-possessed were provoked to roll on the floor and kick at them.

The uproar continued for days, amid daily festivals of prayer and the fascinated attentions of the neighbors. The sufferings of the children rivaled those of the children of Sweden, Mather's favorite witch ground. Pins were discovered sticking lightly under their skins. They vomited pins and nails and other unnatural substances. They wore themselves out with acrobatic feats, bending backwards until their heads touched their heels, while their arms and legs appeared to be wrenched from the sockets by invisible hands.

At nightfall, recovered somewhat, they would eat hearty suppers and settle down for a good sleep. Cotton Mather suggested a three-day fast, and they weakened noticeably under it. Being fed again, their torments were renewed with sinister complications.

Martha named the witch. Some time before, she had quarreled with the laundress, a girl of her own age, accusing her of stealing some linens. The girl was the daughter of Bridget Glover, an Irish woman who supported her family, with the help of her older children, by washing clothes for the neighbors. She was considered a little crazy, because she was excitable, and when she was excited she spoke Gaelic. But she had a free command of vituperation in English and her loose way of talking offended a great many people. She was a Catholic, really worse than a Quaker, and she had been called a witch more than once.

Bridget Glover joined in the quarrel and defended her child. She went over to the Goodwin house and shouted angrily and made incoherent threats. It was a foolish row over the back fence, but through skillful handling by Cotton Mather it became the most sensational episode in Boston for the next six months. The exact words spoken by Bridget Glover will never be known. Indeed, the facts of the case cannot now be learned, for it was recorded by Cotton Mather, who was interpreting by a formula, and the event followed the perfect classical pattern. Each member of the Goodwin family gave a different version of her speeches, but all agreed that she had spoken repeatedly of the Devil and had cursed them in the manner of a witch. Cotton Mather conferred with his friend Mr. Hale, who agreed with him that this was matter for the authorities. Bridget Glover was formally accused of witchcraft, and brought before the magistrates for examination.

When they began to question her, so the story runs, she stammered a moment, lapsed into Gaelic, and never again spoke a word of English. It was necessary to conduct her trial through an interpreter. There is little doubt that she was full of fairy lore, a firm believer in ancient signs and wonders. This was not strange, nor even criminal. Good Congregationalists had to be reminded from the pulpit, now and again, that they must not turn the sieve and shears, wear amulets, and recite charms when they dug for healing herbs. The records are so confused in Bridget's case that there is no way of knowing what arts she practiced. The Irish bravado overcame her when confronted by her enemies, and she boasted that indeed she was a witch, and a good one. She had done all they charged her with, and more; she hinted she could tell great things if she pleased.

The interpreters said so, at least. They also interrupted, on their own responsibility, to add that she appeared to be dominated in turn by a black magic superior to her own and was restrained from telling tales by being forced to talk in a language which the demons believed no one else in Boston could understand. The crack-brained logic of the demons left their servant defenseless, and the trial went on smoothly.

Point by point the evidence corresponded with the best traditions. Rag figures stuffed with goat's wool were found in her house and produced in court. She admitted she had made them, and said her way of tormenting her victims was to wet her finger in her mouth and stroke these dolls. The Goodwin children were brought in, fell to roaring at the sight of her, and when she touched one of the dolls they flew obligingly into fits.

Cotton Mather sat at the examination and took his endless notes. It was better than he had hoped for.

The witch was invited to name her counsel. "Have you no one to stand by you?" asked a magistrate.

"I have," she said, and looked pertly into the air. "No, he's gone!"

She explained, the faithful interpreters said, that she meant her Prince. This seemed so curious they doubted if she was sane. Half a dozen physicians came to talk with her. They inquired first about the state of her soul. "You ask me a very solemn question, I cannot tell what to say to it." They desired her to repeat the Pater Noster. She stumbled in some of the passages and excused her bad Latin by saying she could not pronounce those words if they gave her all the world. The doctors, too, had read the best authorities on witchcraft. They decided that she was sane, and a witch.

Cotton Mather, in his own account of this episode, told how he posted himself with the interpreters outside her cell, where they heard her quarreling with her spectral demon, saying she had confessed to revenge herself for his falseness to her. Mather harried the fantastical creature, visiting her almost every day as she sat chained in her cell. In rambling wild talk she let her fancy go, according to the interpreters: and told of meetings with her Prince in company with other worshipers of his, though she would not name them; and confessed that she knew her Prince to be the Devil. Mather told her that her Prince had cheated her badly. "If that be so, I am sorry," said Bridget. She refused to answer some of his questions, explaining that her spirits forbade her to speak. As a Catholic she so feared and hated his heretic prayers that she implored him not to pray for her until her spirits gave her leave to listen.

She was found guilty and sentenced to be hanged. Mather could not rest on this. He went around and collected all the neighborhood gossip about her. Festering grievances and old hatreds were reopened; a Mrs. Hughes remembered that her small son had waked one night crying that a woman was in the room, she had reached under the bedclothes and tried to tear out his bowels. She said that Bridget, when accused of this, had confessed it was herself in specter. This Mrs. Hughes, under Mather's questioning, enjoyed great refreshment of memory. A friend of hers had died six years before, declaring with her last breath that Bridget Glover had murdered her in specter. Further—and this is the perfect Mather touch—the dying woman had warned Mrs. Hughes to remember this, for in six years there would be great occasion to mention it.

The six years were now finished. After sitting in prison for some months, Bridget Glover was taken out and hanged. On the scaffold she spoke out clearly and strongly in Irish. The interpreter came down off the ladder and translated the speech to Mather, waiting below. She said that the children would not be relieved by her death, for there were others besides herself had a hand in their sufferings.

This was truth with unconscious irony. The ones who had a hand in it published this statement at once, and the Goodwin children fell into fresh complexities of torment.

Cotton Mather sat in the Goodwin house and urged the wretched little animals onward. They had begun with a fine holiday of rebellion, and now found themselves caught in a horrible device that really frightened them. They were no longer allowed to invent their own tortures, but suffered assault from without. Invisible hands smacked them rudely, and large bruises appeared on their bodies to prove it. On being assured that the specters had done it, they said they could see the shadows moving about the room. Demoralized with terror, they would point them out, and Cotton Mather would aim a blow at this place. Strangely enough, the child who pointed, though his back was turned, would receive a stout thwack also. Howling, he would speak the names that occurred, or had been suggested, to him, and Cotton Mather wrote them down, with the comment that all the persons named had been since suspected of witchcraft. Invariably, he would observe within a few days that a suspected woman would be wearing an unaccountable bruise on the very part of her body where he had struck at her specter a few days previously. He does not explain how he went about making these discoveries. He failed in gathering enough evidence to justify the arrest of any one of them.

The solemn farce went on. The children were now quite bewildered, but they still had presence of mind enough to remember the main issue. During all the months that Bridget Glover sat chained waiting for her death, they concerned themselves with putting off the bedtime hour, getting out of their chores, and escaping family prayer. The neighbors crowded in as to a deathbed. This was better than a deathbed or a hanging, for it had the tang of novelty and supernatural danger. The children barked, purred, growled, leaped like wild animals, and attempted to fly like birds, or like witches. The watchers restrained them from harming themselves. When they pulled their neck-cloths so tightly they almost choked, someone was always on hand to relieve them. They almost fell in the fire, and they almost drowned themselves, but someone nearby hauled them out in the nick of time. If anyone dared to touch a Bible, those religion-surfeited infants almost died. They tore their clothes and broke glasses and spilled their cups, and mewed with delight; and to save their lives they could not do the simplest task without making a frightful mess of it. No one dared to punish them—were they not innocent victims of the Devil?

Mather continued to tell them the specters had done everything, and did not fail verbally to point the way to grace. "Child, pray to the Lord Jesus Christ," he admonished them in turn. Immediately their teeth clenched over their tongues and they stared at him. "Child, look to Him," he advised, and their eyes were pulled instantly so far into their heads he professed a fear that they would never emerge again.

This grew monotonous, and Mather chose the interesting member of the family for closer observation. He took Martha to live in his house. She was gifted, pretty, and full of wit, and the others were merely noisy and stubborn and tiresome.

Away from the stuffy disordered cottage, Martha behaved herself very nicely at first. The big fine Mather house, with its handsome furniture, silver, books, servants, impressed her. Good food, a soft bed, and the gentleness of Abigail, Mather's young wife, were very disarming. Everything was pleasant except the persistent praying and the constant watching of all her movements.

She grew restless in a few days. In a voice of distress she announced to Cotton Mather that They had found her out, and at once she had a fit of choking and her throat swelled until she was threatened with strangulation. Mather held her and stroked her throat until the fit passed. Whenever the fits returned, he could always cure her with this stroking, a remedy in common use by the lower order of witches.

For several months the Mather household lived in tumult. Martha was the center of attraction, and she repaid the attentions given her. A dozen times a day Mather forced her to her knees to pray with her. She clapped her hands over her ears and declared They were raising such a clamor she could not hear a word. At times she walked with a heavy limp, and she explained that They had clamped Bridget Glover's chain on her leg. Mather would strike at the invisible chain and it would fall away. In his headlong battle with the Devil, he used with precision the methods of witchcraft described by those professional witchfinders Perkins, Gaule, Bernard; and Martha responded properly. She surmised hidden silver in the well, and it was found there. She spoke in strange languages, and "her belly would on a sudden be puft up strangely," one of the marks of diabolical possession as quoted by Increase Mather in his useful table; now, I believe, noted as one of the common symptoms of intestinal worms; and she did all these things with high dramatic effect.

She was forever getting into states where Cotton Mather must hurry to her rescue, and at times his powers of exorcism were tried severely. After a while, her mood would change into a charming gayety. For days she would talk, "never wickedly," wrote Mather with affectionate admiration, "but always wittily and beyond herself." He loved wit and gayety, and he dared not confess this taste to the society he lived in; but he could not deny himself the perverse joy he took in Martha's youth and spirits. She was so entertaining in these moods he could not reprove her. His role of religious guardian and exorcist forbade him to play a foil to her, and her spirits flashed themselves away in empty air, unsatisfied. Relapsing into her dark mood, she would say, "I want to steal, or be drunk—then I would get well."

Martha was the first, and the most imaginative, of all the girls who were to follow her in a blind destructive rebellion against the perversion of life through religion, in the theocratic state. Revolt was working in all directions; it was fermenting in politics, in the church, in labor, in the economic system; after two generations the whole body of society was heaving with premonitions of change. The children merely followed their sure instincts, but they were not understood, and Cotton Mather at twenty-eight years was in a position of power he was in no way fitted to assume. He used any weapon that came his way, but his personal desires blinded his judgment, and so he chose badly. He was bound to make of this absurd episode an issue of first importance in the history of his career, and he succeeded. He had proved his power as a witchfinder in the case of Bridget Glover, and he believed that a cure of Martha would establish finally the supernatural authority he craved: to be marked and set apart as the intimate of God, the most potent enemy of the Devil in New England, and in the world. First he must convince the governor and the magistrates and the ministers of Boston that he could truly cast out devils. The rest would follow.

Martha's personality was a disturbing element, not to his greater plan but in his secret self. Neither of them realized fully the nature of the tension between them, and they played a gruesome game of Blind-Man's Buff. She tormented and tantalized him endlessly, and he held her and prayed with her while she struggled in her recurrent frenzies. At times these scenes were mere romps between them; at other moments they touched the edge of horror: he stared fascinated as she flung herself down before him writhing, crying for him to save her from her demons. He listened to her blasphemies as long as he dared, then stroked and soothed her into calm. She would work herself into a dangerous state and kick and strike at him; but always the blow that began in violence ended in a light pat of the fingertips or a soft nudge of the toe.

Day and night were the same to Martha. She would rise out of her sleep crying that her devil-horse was waiting for her. Mounting a chair, she would gallop about the room. Once, seated on air in the posture of a woman on horseback, she galloped up a flight of stairs, and Mather admired this feat so much he almost forgot its devilish inspiration. In this mood her boisterous humor grew very broad in the best seventeenth-century manner. If her stomach made sounds of disturbed digestion, she would exclaim, "Something is going away from me!," clasp her head in her palm and complain of faintness. Mather, listening solemnly for some statement from the demon inhabiting her, would declare indeed he had heard the squeaking of a mouse. If he tried to persuade her to speak the Holy Name, she would answer flippantly, "Oh, you know what it is! It is G and O and D!"

All profitable and edifying literature threw her into confusion. Books in favor of the Quakers calmed her, but she could not endure a word against them. She enjoyed Popish books, and went blind at the sight of the Assembly catechism. She hugged the accursed book of common prayer to her bosom, calling it her Bible. Mather noted with mystification and some chagrin that his own books worked like a poison in her. He gave her his story of bewitched Ann Cole, of Hartford, who was unutterably pious, even in her fits. Ann Cole's pieties gave Martha the worst convulsions of all.

It began to look as if the battle were lost, for Mather was so enchanted with her vitality and imagination he was losing control over her. Her tenderness then took an odd turn. She decided to flatter him outrageously. Flying as if pursued by an army of devils she burst in at his study door, paused with a sigh of relief, and told him she had come there for sanctuary. The devils could not enter there, the place was holy and God forbade it to them. She sat the whole afternoon by his side, demurely reading the Bible. At dark she went to the door and set her foot experimentally over the threshold. Her ghostly steed was waiting for her, her devils seized her, and she was off on her wild career seated on air.

Mather had waited long for some demonstration that his study was in fact a holy of holies. He wished for definitive proof. He pursued her, and dragged her again over the magic doorsill. She resisted furiously, fell, scuffled with her feet, and threw her weight upon him so that he was almost forced to carry her outright. After incredible toil the goal was gained and the delightful miracle repeated itself. They were both out of breath, but she recovered first, stood up beaming, and said, "Now I am well!"

This was plainly a marvel very creditable to them both. Mather called in several ministers and repeated the scene successfully half a dozen times before witnesses who infallibly would spread the story in its proper light. It then occurred to him, or was suggested, that further demonstrations of this kind were dangerous, as savoring slightly of witchcraft in themselves. Besides, it was no longer necessary. Martha for no apparent reason became perfectly subdued.

It was now early fall. Abigail was expecting her third child, and the constant excitement had wearied her. She lived in deep retirement, and no comment of hers is recorded concerning this episode. Martha was to stay on for a while to insure her recovery. She spent her afternoons reading pious books in Mather's study, and the household quieted down.

During this inexplicable period of calm, Mather began preparing his pamphlet on Martha's case, together with a sermon entitled "The Nature and Reality of Witchcraft." Martha grew very annoyed at this, and her manner toward him underwent a mysterious change. Previously she had treated him with some respect, even in her rages; she had made love to him in her primitive way. Now she was bold and impudent; with her cutting young-girl wit she slashed at her patron and protector. He was startled and displeased at the new kind of demon that had got into Martha. Possibly she had not believed he was taking it all so seriously.

When she discovered how completely she had befooled him, she was a changed girl.

In all his life no one had dared to interrupt Cotton Mather at his holy labors. Martha knocked loudly at his door whenever she pleased, and invented scandalous pretexts to annoy him. "There is someone below would be glad to see you!" she shouted one day. Mather went down, found no one, and scolded her for telling falsehoods. She retorted, "Mrs. Mather is always glad to see you!"

He understood nothing about women, and he never learned anything about them; this outburst of jealousy confounded him. A dozen times a day she was at his door, and would have him out on one excuse or another. The attention that had been given her was not going to be diverted to a sermon about her if she could help it. She threw heavy books and other objects at him, being careful not to hit him. She would follow him upstairs and down, heckling and ridiculing him about his foolish sermon, vowing she would revenge herself on him for writing it.

She rummaged through his papers, a desperate impertinence, and got hold of his precious document on witchcraft. She had read it while he was writing it, at least a hundred times, says Mather. Now she could not get one word of it straight, but made a parody of it as she went, with such aptness and humor Mather laughed in spite of himself. At once she grew very earnest, and in a bitter voice she prophesied that he "should quickly come to disgrace by that history."

She told him every day as clearly as she could in symbolic acts and words that she was making him ridiculous, but his obsessional self-concentration kept him blinded. He went on exhibiting her, and she rose to her audiences like the gifted actress she was.

A number of young ministers came to witness her performances. Mather talked to them in Latin; if he told her to look to God, he said, her eyes would be fairly put out. The clever girl clenched her eyelids. This was impressive, and they began trying her demon with languages. He knew Greek and Hebrew also. The Indian dialects floored the demon, and the gentlemen conversed in these. Then they all knelt and prayed affectionately for Martha, while she sprawled gracelessly on the floor, with her belly swelled strangely, and made croaking noises. She whistled, sang, shouted, and covered her ears to shut out the painful sound of prayer. Rising to her knees, she tried to strike Mather, could not, and begged the others to strike him for her: "He has wounded me in the *head!"* she wept. "Lord, have mercy on a daughter vexed with a Devil," prayed Mather. Martha sank her voice into her throat, as if a demon of grisly humor spoke within her: "There's two or three of us."

This was almost the end. Martha's energies were about exhausted, her inventiveness would go no further. In the evening of this day, she grew merry for a while, and later went quietly to bed. In the night she began weeping terribly, and when Mather went to quiet her she told him she repented of all she had said and done. She was beginning to realize her situation and to be ashamed.

At Christmas, she relapsed and gave a lively imitation of a drunken person, babbling and reeling and spewing. Mather was pained, insisted that she had had nothing to drink, and ended by admiring her talent for impersonation. She recovered shortly, wept again, and made one of her enigmatic remarks: "They will disgrace me when they can do nothing more." Mather thought she spoke of her demons.

Martha was growing up. She knew well that her day was over. A sudden sickness came upon her. She pulled and tossed and moaned and sweated in some profound disturbance, crying out that she was afraid to die alone, someone must die with her. Even in this state, she paraphrased a psalm so brilliantly that Mather was amazed again, for the last time. She resigned herself to death, prophesied Indian wars and a great tragedy upon the country, and recovered.

Her brothers and small sister, without Martha to inflame them, had been reduced to their usual behavior. Mather sent her home.

Here Martha's personal history ceases, but not the consequences of this fateful period of her life. She became, Mather recorded merely, very docile, very silent; and remained a submissive Christian girl. He made a legend of her, and the drama of Martha Goodwin and Bridget Glover took hold of the popular imagination and was recalled again and again during the Salem Witchcraft, four years later.

Mather preached his sermon on the nature and reality of witchcraft, and afterward published it, an initiate statement of the inner organization of the witch cult in New England, and elsewhere, its rules, ceremonies, feasts, and dark purposes. He was gradually persuading himself that the putting to death of witches was a blood-sacrifice tending to placate the Devil. His mind was a little confused between the role played by the ancient Hebrew scape-goat and an obscure doctrine of the early Christians that Christ shed his blood not as an offering to God the Father for the remission of sins but as an act of propitiation to the Devil on behalf of mankind. A passage from the witchcraft section of his *Magnalia Christi Americana* is poetically applicable to Bridget Glover's part in the Goodwin episode: "When two goats were offered unto the Lord (and only unto the Lord) we read that one of them was to fall by lot to Azazel . . . it is no other than the name of the Devil himself."

1940

A Bright Particular Faith
(A.D. 1700)

In her sixteenth year of marriage, Abigail, wife of Cotton Mather, the brilliant and celebrated Boston minister, miscarried of her eleventh child. Her physicians pronounced it a false conception. Mather at once observed a day of humiliation in his study, inquiring of his soul if he had ever troubled the Church with any false conceptions of doctrine, that this calamity should be visited upon him.

Abigail was dangerously ill, and her husband set aside a day of fasting and prayer for her. But he was cold in his devotions and it occurred to him sadly that a man cannot believe what he will, when he will. He reassured himself by saying that he feared her death so terribly he could not pray for her life. He brooded at length on the inconveniences of a motherless family—five of their children had survived—the coming perils of his own wifeless state, and in his brooding he was buffeted with impure thoughts, his mind dwelling with persistent carnality on Abigail. He was disconcerted and ashamed, gave it up, and set another day for fasting, by way of cleansing his imagination of Abigail the woman before he should pray for Abigail the soul.

He knelt by her bedside with his children present, and there, he records in his diary, he felt the rays of a particular faith, a definite belief that she would recover. Later he returned to his study, and this particular faith was intensified by intimate assurances from Heaven that she would not die at present. He resolved, in writing, that if the Lord would spare

343

his Good Thing he would be wise and chaste and holy in his conversation with her ever afterward. He hastened to tell Abigail the happy news that she was to be spared to him.

She grew worse immediately. On the next Sunday she appeared to be dying, and the physician was sent for out of the public assembly. Mather's faith suffered a shock, but the fit passed over.

That evening he went to bed and slept soundly, but they called him up at midnight, saying her hour was near. He sat praying the rest of the night. Next morning he felt confident his prayers were being heard, for Abigail still breathed. He set himself now to wrestle in earnest, and his wife's deathbed was transformed into a battlefield where Mather fought another of his distinguished engagements with God.

Terrible complications set in: fever, shivering fits, salivation; and Abigail lay silent, neither living nor dying. Mather saw that one fast would not do, and he devoted three days to her cause. On a Tuesday he prayed for her again, but his mind wandered off to other affairs, and having established the precious necessary mood of intimacy with God he took advantage of it to pray for the political situation in England. His old enemy, Joseph Dudley, head of a powerful party entirely opposed to Mather, had recently been made Governor, and Mather rightly feared the outcome. It proved, he admitted, a day of no great enjoyments.

As if to rebuke his straying thoughts, Abigail grew worse the following day, and fell into a heavy coma. This was a severe trial, but Mather reflected that he held out under it stoutly, which would in time make the certain blessing the more blessed. He prepared several petitions to be presented to Queen Anne, and devoted another day to Abigail, praying meanwhile for strength to preach before the new Governor the next morning. He was writing and sending complaints against Dudley secretly to England, but he planned to gain Dudley's friendship to all appearances; and God, Who inspired him in his campaign, would not, he hoped, allow his plan to fail.

On this day of prayer his familiar shining angel appeared: that baroque being who brought, on several occasions, the most consoling messages of encouragement: and assured him that Abigail would not die; further, that the Mather family should enjoy some particular glory because of this sad experience. He opened his psalm book and sang, and the pages fell open themselves infallibly renewing the promises he had wrested from God. This heartened him so much, he preached with amazing vigor and success before Dudley. He described a good man to the Governor and the congregation, with a wealth of adroit touches which formed a flattering but fairly recognizable portrait of Dudley himself. . . .

Abigail sank lower into darkness; no prayer and no human hand could raise her. Mather wrote in his diary that her death was evil enough, but he in it dreaded most of all the blow to his particular faith, a defeat too personal for him to endure. A note of arrogance crept into his prayers: he demanded the life of Abigail as proof of his own ambassadorship between heaven and earth. His wife would not flatter his hopes. She contented herself with thanking him for his courtesy and attention, and told him she was grateful for his goodness to her when she was no longer of any service to him.

In the sixth week Mather observed another fast for Abigail, and against the small-pox, and in behalf of New England now going to war against the French. Abigail took a turn for the worse, an extreme suffering came upon her; he knelt by her to watch her die. She rallied and her husband kept his seventh fast for her. He was almost wearied out and half defeated. For the first time, he verbally offered her to the Lord and submitted to all the sorrowful consequences of her death. When he rose from his knees he felt certain that she would live.

His mind at rest for the moment, he prepared the sermon he had preached for Dudley, and gave it to be printed and distributed. He also tossed off a little sermon on Sins of Omission, and certain members of his congregation had it published.

Abigail lay quietly. She could not die and she would not try to live. The physicians pronounced her illness mortal. Mather kept a vigil for her. He lay on the floor and wept, so thinly clothed that the hard floor hurt his tender bones and he complained of this as he cried to God to spare him Abigail. This time, as if his suffering bones had touched devine compassion, Abigail rallied a little. He renewed his supplications. She failed again. Once more he was called out of his sleep: "I am kept up all night that I may see her die, and therewith the terrible death of my prayer and faith." Yet, when again he attempted to resign her, some spark of hope refused to be quenched and he comforted himself with the thought that God had sent this affliction upon Abigail for the express purpose of trying his own faith.

On a Sunday toward the end of August, after preaching and praying in the morning, he was sitting alone in his house when he received a ghostly intimation that Heaven would speak to him in a very familiar manner, if he would wait in a suitable posture. A voice said to him: "Go into your great Chamber and I will speak with you."

He went in and cast himself upon the floor, far away from the noisy children, away from the speechless Abigail. He wept exorbitantly and confessed his own loathsomeness: he was worthy only to be thunder-struck into dust and ashes. After a short period of self-torture, the ritual-istic frenzy came, his tears poured in a flood upon the floor, and he talked aloud in a broken voice:

"And now my Father is going to tell, what he will do for me; my Father loves me, and will fill me with his love, and will bring me to everlasting life. My Father will make me a Chosen Vessel, to do good in the world. My Father will yet use me to glorify his Christ, and my Op-portunities, my precious Opportunities to do so, shall be after a most astonishing manner continued and multiplied. Particularly, my treatise of, THE TRIUMPHS OF CHRISTIANITY, my Father will send his holy angels to look after it, and it shall not be lost." (This manuscript had been mysteriously misplaced and it was causing him great distress.) "The condition of my dear Consort, my Father will give me to see his wonderful favor in it. My Father will be a Father to my children, too: He will provide for them, and they shall every one of them serve Him throughout the ages."

He rose calm and refreshed, with a heavenly impression upon his soul.

A public day of prayer relieved him momentarily from the duty of keeping a private one; he kept a day of thanksgiving instead, because Abigail still lingered, after fourteen weeks. The day before this thanks-giving, Abigail had sunk into apathy and seemed again to be dying. Still, he kept his day, and resolutely thanked God for all; and his faith that she would live revived once more.

August and September passed, and Abigail kept to her bed, with alter-nations of energy and collapse. Mather began to be troubled by a recur-rent thought. Maybe he had been inattentive to the precise meaning of that particular faith he had cherished in the matter. He now persuaded himself that her many crises had passed immediately after each day of prayer he offered for her; and it came to him that the Lord was keeping her with them to test their prayer and faith with patience and to teach them resignation. "It may be, after the Lord has given me demonstrations, of His being loth to deny me anything that I importunately ask of Him, and therefore doth one month after another delay the thing I fear: yet I must at last encounter the Death which I have deprecated, when both my wife and I shall be better prepared for it."

He doubted that he had rightly interpreted the messages he had received. He had believed that God meant in the end to do him the enormous favor of restoring Abigail. It now occurred to him that this may have been a hasty, a shortsighted conclusion. Maybe, in a word, it was better that Abigail should die: "The Lord may have blessings in store for me, and my poor Family, beyond anything I can at present imagine, or indeed, would be willing to imagine."

Abigail's sickness prevented him from accepting an important invitation to preach out of town. He accepted this rebuke from Heaven with a number of useful reflections. He was not altogether forsaken, he assured himself: several towns invited him later, and he was able to fill his engagements with great success. In the first part of October he conducted a public fast at South Church, and wrestled with the Lord in prayer for near two hours together. He noted that by some particular dispensation of Providence he was much in demand for such occasions.

Abigail had lain for twenty weeks. She was now an uncomplaining shadow but still she could not die. Symptoms of tuberculosis set in. Mather kept another vigil for her. He was so tired he could not keep awake. Disheartened, he left the case with God, and opened his grandfather Richard Mather's Bay Psalmbook to sing a verse or two. The pages fell open at the lines:

> And there was not among their tribes
> A feeble person told.

"Lord," he thought, "this won't be fulfilled until the resurrection of the dead. The tribes of the raised will not have one feeble person among them!" It was an omen that Abigail must die. He said, "Lord, Thy will be done," and slept.

The next night, Abigail had a strange dream. A solemn man appeared in her chamber, accompanied by a woman so pitiably wretched and meager that Abigail praised God she was not yet so badly off as this. The man proposed a remedy for her relief. For the terrible pain in her breast, he said, "Let them cut the warm wool from a living sheep, and apply it warm to the grieved pain. Next, for her salivation, take a tankard of spring water, and over the fire dissolve an agreeable quantity of mastics and of gum isinglass: drink this liquor now and then to strengthen the glands, which ought to have been done a great while ago."

Her principal physician saw no harm in trying this remedy. To the surprise of everyone, she rose in a few days from her bed, and came into her husband's study, where they knelt and prayed together. For a time she improved and Mather turned with relief to his interrupted literary activities. The first copies of his masterpiece, the *Magnalia Christi Americana*, had lately come over from England, and the sight of it consoled and repaid him for all his long privations.

In November, Abigail took once more to her bed. A serious epidemic of small-pox had broken out in Boston. Mather wrote a pamphlet for the comfort of plague sufferers, and distributed it himself. Immune as he was, from a mild attack of small-pox in his youth, he visited constantly in the foul-smelling sealed chambers of the sick, and carried the contagion home to his children.

Little Nibby came down, and then young Increase, then Nancy, and their nurse. The house was in dreadful disorder, and Mather in desperation essayed a day of fasting as a cure for all. Closing himself in, he tried to escape the confusion of drugs and disease. It was not to be. His study was the warmest and most comfortable room in the house, and the winter cold could not be kept out of the drafty nursery. With a groan he surrendered his refuge to the children.

"God sanctifies this to me, to humble me," he wrote in his diary, "for not serving Him as I should have done in my study: which provokes Him to chase me out of it."

Warm and sheltered by three thousand books, the children lay blinded and sore and wretched. They cried for their mother, who did not answer, being now shielded in indifference to this world. They cried for relief and comfort from their father, and the harassed man came a dozen times a day to pray with them. Freely and fervently and anxiously on each occasion he implored God to take them all if it pleased His will. They began to recover.

Abigail's sudden decline had been a shock, and Mather was stricken with tenderness for her. He spent most of his time in her room, praying for her "as agreeably" as he could. He no longer measured his strength against the determined assault of death, but prepared her for the end. He would entertain her for hours at a time with descriptions of heaven, assuring her that she would most certainly go there. She made no further resistance, and on Tuesday, the first of December, 1701, the agony set in, there could be no doubt of it this time.

Mather wrote: "The desire of my eyes is this day to be taken from me." She remained conscious, prayed a little, said she was happy to die. Her husband at this late moment was touched with a painful doubt: he implored her to tell him faithfully what fault she had seen in him that she might have wished away. He could not let her go without asking what she really thought of him. He had never inquired before. Abigail did not fail him. She answered that she had not seen any fault in him: "and that God had made his conversation exceedingly serviceable to her, to bring her nearer to Himself."

This perfectly reserved answer satisfied him for the present, but he wondered at it afterward, he said. Two hours before her death he knelt by her and took her hands, and made a ceremony of relinquishment: "With her then in my hands, I solemnly and sincerely gave her up to the Lord: and in token of my real resignation, I gently put her out of my hands, and laid away a most lovely hand, resolving that I would never touch it any more."

Abigail submitted, and though she had called for him often before she did not ask for him again. Years after he evoked and rewrote this scene many times, with a great appreciation of its dramatic rightness, and a pleased sense of his own handsome part in it. Abigail had been a good habit with him, the harmless solvent of his carnal needs, a shield against sin, the Good Thing given from the Lord. It was fitting that he should be prostrated by her loss, and he was prostrated several hours. She spoke her last words to her father, "Heaven, heaven will make amends for all."

Mather wrote in his diary: "She lived with me, just as many years as she had lived in the world before she came to me, with an addition of the seven months wherein her dying languishments were taking her from me": thus did the clock in his brain tick away time: "When I had been married to her just sixteen years . . . God began to take her from me. I said then to my father, 'I seem to feel in my mind, the bodings of a dark cloud hanging over my family.' The cloud came on, and now, see what was in it!"

On the Friday following Abigail was given a very honorable funeral. It was socially as distinguished as the wedding had been: which Mather described as the most famous wedding ever seen in that part of the world. Mather set himself the task of glorifying Christ in his affliction, and distributed certain of his religious pamphlets among the hundred friends who had taken turns in watching at the bedside. To each copy he attached a poem he had written for the occasion.

He fasted and prayed the day after the funeral. Five days later he preached a sermon about the prophet Ezekiel's wife. He was touched with a wonderful demonstration from the Lord of the love his congregation bore him. The people were planning to build a costly tomb for Abigail and her five children. . . .

Now he had time to pause and reflect. He perceived that the astonishing sting in his wife's death was the miscarriage of his particular faith. That was the intolerable affront that wiped out his personal grief. He tried to arrange his memories of her. There is very little of Abigail in his diary. She sits perpetually in shadow, hands folded over her enlarging womb. There is very little record of her in the social life of the times, though she was beautiful, rich, and of good family. She went very seldom with him to the many dinners given in the houses of their friends. Other women attended; even Hannah Sewall, who bore fourteen children, and yet had time and energy to visit about with her husband, to take trips to the country to eat cherries and raspberries, to assist at births, or special meetings and fasts. Rarely Abigail.

Mather made no comment during her lifetime on her temperament, nor hint of her personal appearance beyond a generalized reference to her beauty, and coy hints as to the carnal charms of her person. After her death, he gradually realized her as a separate being, and, released from the necessity for restraint, he freed his long-bound thoughts from this marriage as death had freed his body. Almost overnight, he became a relieved and thankful widower.

He saw clearly that his deepest prayers had been truly answered. If Abigail had lived, she must have continued an invalid, in continual languor and weakness and sorrow. He could not help commending himself for having endured so cheerfully all the fatigues of her long suffering; indeed she had praised him herself, in an oblique way: "I shall make you all weary," she said, during her last days, and added at once, knowing her husband must instantly take everything to himself, "I don't mean you, Mr. Mather!" He remembered this now with self-congratulations. He reflected that his own health must have suffered if he had run the venture of sleeping with her: undoubtedly he would have gone into a consumption, and the children, thus deprived of their main parent, would have received bad educations. His imagination ran footloose: then, too, she was of a melancholy temper. She had wept for months when her father married a second time, though the marriage was a desirable one. Her youngest brother, carrying several hundred pounds of Mather's money, had fallen into the hands of the French; she had been inconsolable, not for the money but for her brother. Her second and favorite brother had gone to London, sick, hoping to work a cure by the sea-voyage; he came to say good-bye to her, and she bade him farewell quietly enough, but after he was gone "she broke out in a more than ordinary passion and agony and said, that she desired God would never let her live to hear of the death of that young man!" The brother had died, and everyone had been at great pains to conceal the event from her. Mather recalled too that her elder brother was "a profane and sottish fellow," a disgrace to his family. She died without knowing this. If she had lived to learn these things, manifestly his own position would have been insupportable.

He sat day after day with gathering thankfulness reviewing all the probabilities of his misfortune if Abigail had not died. The assured permanence of her absence was a blessing, even though tendered in such a disconcerting form. Little by little the idea grew within him that death and Abigail had been secretly, firmly allied against him. He perceived with astonishment that he had not fought the will of God, but her will, in her death. She had defeated him, had overruled his prayers with her own. Chagrin changed to definite resentment. He repented of his prayers for her life, his resentment included her very family to whom he felt himself still bound by the tenuous threads of this dissolved marriage. He had always hated them, and they hated him; and this hatred was never softened in that generation. He decided almost at once to marry again. He had, in fact, several months before Abigail's death, noticed with intense wishfulness a witty and light-hearted young gentlewoman whom he now hoped to make the second Mrs. Mather. . . .

Children are the most embarrassingly observant of all animals. Nancy, having fallen about this time into convulsions and a malignant fever, lay speechless all one day. Her father fasted, and made a prayer resigning the child, and prayed for an easy and speedy death for her. In the evening she suddenly revived and remarked with some spirit: "I heard my father give me away today, but I shall not die this time, for all that!"

1934

she was of a melancholy temper. She had wept for months, when her father married a second time, though the marriage was a desirable one. Her youngest brother, although several hundred pounds of Mathos' money, had followed the bankers that told it, she had been inconsolable, not for the principal but her brother. Her second and favorite brother had gone to London and, hoping to work a cure, he she said voyage, gave me to say good bye to her, and she bade him take it all patiently. "I wish there he was gone." She bade one that he is than ordinary be kind and happy and prayed and that she disturbed God would never let her live in hope of the hearts of that young man." The brothers had each and every one had by that great pains to conceal the worst from her. Mother recollected that her elder brother was to return, the hitherto fellow. While her in his family, she died without knowing this. If she had used to learn these things, manifestly his own, perhaps would have been disappointable.

He sat day after day with gathering thankfulness reviewing all the propensities of his misconduct, as Abigail had once said. The sins of her, absence of her absence, were blessings of an though rendered to her a disconcerting form, little by little the idea grew within him that death and vengeance had been extorted, numbly giving pause, and of singular charged with astonishment that he had not thought the will of God, half her will in her death. She had deleted to him indeed remedied by prayers with the scorn of her prayer to definite resentment. He released of his prayers as of her life, his resentment indeed between himself to them, she felt himself still bound to those anxious fringes of this, disturbed universe. He had always hated them, and they hated him, and they hated was never reduced to that gratitude. He decided throughout at once to take revenge, as he had in fact, some months before Abigail's death, thought of with a rather thankfulness a way, and it thickened a young gentleman, whom she now hoped to make the second Mrs. Mathos.

Children are the most confirming observant of all animals. Some having fallen short this one into a convulsion, and, as if against her, in a speechless all one day. Her father raised and made a noise roughly of the child, and prayed for an vain, and spoke again for her, in the evening she suddenly revived and remarked with some spirit, "I heard my father give me a new order, but I shall see death in time, for all that."

MEXICAN

Why I Write About Mexico

(*a Letter to the Editor
of* The Century)

I write about Mexico because that is my familiar country. I was born near San Antonio, Texas. My father lived part of his youth in Mexico, and told me enchanting stories of his life there; therefore the land did not seem strange to me even at my first sight of it. During the Madero revolution I watched a street battle between Maderistas and Federal troops from the window of a cathedral; a grape-vine heavy with tiny black grapes formed a screen, and a very old Indian woman stood near me, perfectly silent, holding my sleeve. Later she said to me, when the dead were being piled for burning in the public square, "It is all a great trouble now, but it is for the sake of happiness to come." She crossed herself, and I mistook her meaning.

"In heaven?" I asked. Her scorn was splendid.

"No, on earth. Happiness for men, not for angels!"

She seemed to me then to have caught the whole meaning of revolution, and to have said it in a phrase. From that day I watched Mexico, and all the apparently unrelated events that grew out of that first struggle never seemed false or alien or aimless to me. A straight, undeviating purpose guided the working of the plan. And it permitted many fine things to grow out of the national soil, only faintly surmised during the last two or three centuries even by the Mexicans themselves. It was as if an old field had been watered, and all the long-buried seeds flourished.

About three years ago I returned to Mexico, after a long absence, to study the renascence of Mexican art—a veritable rebirth, very conscious, very powerful, of a deeply racial and personal art. I was not won to it by any artificial influence; I recognized it at once as something very natural and acceptable, a feeling for art consanguine with my own, unfolding in a revolution which returned to find its freedoms in profound and honorable sources. It would be difficult to explain in a very few words how the Mexicans have enriched their national life through the medium of their native arts. It is in everything they do and are. I cannot say, "I gathered material" for it; there was nothing so mechanical as that, but the process of absorption went on almost unconsciously, and my impressions remain not merely as of places visited and people known, but as of a moving experience in my own life that is now a part of me.

My stories are fragments, each one touching some phase of a versatile national temperament, which is a complication of simplicities: but I like best the quality of aesthetic magnificence, and, above all, the passion for individual expression without hypocrisy, which is the true genius of the race.

I have been accused by Americans of a taste for the exotic, for foreign flavors. Maybe so, for New York is the most foreign place I know, and I like it very much. But in my childhood I knew the French-Spanish people in New Orleans and the strange "Cajans" in small Louisiana towns, with their curious songs and customs and blurred patois; the German colonists in Texas and the Mexicans of the San Antonio country, until it seemed to me that all my life I had lived among people who spoke broken, laboring tongues, who put on with terrible difficulty, yet with such good faith, the ways of the dominant race about them. This is true here in New York also, I know: but I have never thought of these people as any other than American. Literally speaking, I have never been out of America; but my America has been a borderland of strange tongues and commingled races, and if they are not American, I am fearfully mistaken. The artist can do no more than deal with familiar and beloved things, from which he could not, and, above all, would not escape. So I claim that I write of things native to me, that part of America to which I belong by birth and association and temperament, which is as much the province of our native literature as Chicago or New York or San Francisco. All the things I write of I have first known, and they are real to me.

1923

Notes on the Life and Death of a Hero[*]

The author of *The Itching Parrot* was born November 15, 1776, in Mexico City, baptized the same day, in the parish church of Santa Cruz y Soledad, and christened José Joaquín Fernández de Lizardi.

His parents were Creoles (Mexican-born Spaniards), vaguely of the upper middle class, claiming relationship with several great families. They were poor, she the daughter of a bookseller in Puebla, he a rather unsuccessful physician, a profession but lately separated from the trade of barber. They made an attempt to give their son the education proper to his birth, hoping to prepare him for the practice of law.

The child, who seems to have been precocious, willful, and somewhat unteachable, spent his childhood and early youth in an immensely Catholic, reactionary, socially timid, tight-minded atmosphere of genteel poverty and desperately contriving middle-class ambitions. Though his parents' heads were among the aristocracy, their feet threatened daily to slip into the dark wallow of the lower classes, and their son witnessed and recorded their gloomy struggle to gain enough wealth to make the worldly show that would prove their claim to good breeding. There was no other way of doing it. In Spain, as in Europe, scholarship might be made to serve as a second choice, but in Mexico there was no place for

* Preface to *The Itching Parrot* (*El Periquillo Sarmiento*), by J. J. Fernández de Lizardi. Translated from the Spanish by K.A.P. Copyright 1942 by Doubleday & Company, Inc.

scholarship. The higher churchly honors were reserved for the rich and nobly born; as for the army, it offered for a young Mexican only the most ignoble end: a father could wield as the last resort of authority the threat to send his son to be a soldier.

The outlook was pretty thin for such as our hero. But he was to prove extraordinarily a child of his time, and his subsequent career was not the result of any personal or family plan, but was quite literally created by a movement of history, a true world movement, in which he was caught up and spun about and flung down again. His life story cannot be separated in any particular from the history of the Mexican Revolutionary period. He was born at the peak of the Age of Reason, in the year that the thirteen states of North America declared themselves independent of England. When he was a year old, the United States government decreed religious freedom. In Mexico the Inquisition was still in power, and the Spanish clergy in that country had fallen into a state of corruption perhaps beyond anything known before or since. The viceregal court was composed entirely of Spanish nobles who lived in perpetual luxurious exile; the Indian people were their natural serfs, the mixed Indian and Spanish were slowly forming a new intractable, unpredictable race, and all were ruled extravagantly and unscrupulously by a long succession of viceroys so similar and so unremarkable it is not worth while to recall their names.

The French Revolution occurred when Lizardi was about fourteen years old. At twenty, he was a student in the University of Mexico, College of San Ildefonso. It is not likely that any newfangledness in social or political theory had yet managed to creep in there. There was very little thinking of any kind going on in Mexico at that time, but there were small, scattered, rapidly increasing groups of restless, inquiring minds, and whoever thought at all followed eagerly the path of new doctrines that ran straight from France. The air was full of mottoes, phrases, name-words for abstractions: Democracy, the Ideal Republic, the Rights of Man, Human Perfectibility, Liberty, Equality, Fraternity, Progress, Justice, and Humanity; and the new beliefs were based firmly on the premise that the first duty of man was to exercise freedom of conscience and his faculty of reason.

In Mexico as in many other parts of the world, it was dangerous to mention these ideas openly. All over the country there sprang up secret political societies, disguised as clubs for literary discussion; these throve for a good many years before discussion became planning, and planning led to action and so to revolution.

In 1798, his twenty-second year, Lizardi left the university without taking his bachelor's degree, perhaps because of poverty, for his father died about this time, and there seems to have been nothing much by way of inheritance. Or maybe he was such a wild and careless student as he describes in *El Periquillo*. It is also possible that he was beginning to pick up an education from forbidden sources, such as Diderot, d'Alembert, Voltaire, Rousseau. At any rate, he never ceased to deplore the time he had spent at acquiring ornamental learning, a thing as useless to him, he said, as a gilded coach he could not afford to keep up. The fact seems to be, his failure was a hard blow to his pride and his hopes, and he never ceased either to bewail his ignorance. "To spout Latin is for a Spaniard the surest way to show off his learning," he commented bitterly, and himself spouted Latin all his life by way of example. In later days he professed to regret that his parents had not apprenticed him in an honest trade. However, there was no help for it, he must live by his wits or not at all.

After he left the university without the indispensable academic laurel that would have admitted him to the society of the respectably learned, he disappeared, probably penniless, for seven long years. These years of the locust afterwards were filled in suitably with legends of his personal exploits as a revolutionary. He was supposed to have known Morelos, and to have been in active service with the early insurgents. He says nothing of this in his own account of his life, written a great while afterwards: it is probable that he was a public scrivener in Acapulco. In 1805 he returned to Mexico City and married Doña Dolores Orendain, who brought him a small dowry. As late as 1811 he appears to have been a Justice of the Peace in Taxco, when Morelos took that town from the Viceroy's troops, and was said to have delivered secretly a store of royalist arms and ammunition to Morelos. For this act he was supposed to have been arrested, taken to Mexico, tried and freed, on the plea that he had acted not of his own will but under threat of death from Morelos' insurgents.

The particularly unlikely part of this story is that the royalist officers would never have taken the trouble to escort Lizardi, an obscure young traitor to the Spanish throne, all the way from Taxco to Mexico City for trial. It is still a long road, and was then a terrible journey of several days.

They would have shot him then and there, without further ceremony. A more unlikely candidate than Lizardi for gun-toting was never born. He shared with all other humanist reformers from Erasmus onward a hatred of war, above all, civil war, and his words on this subject read like paraphrases from Erasmus' own writings, as indeed many of them were. Lizardi's services to his country were of quite another kind, and his recompense was meager to the last degree.

Just when those agile wits of his, which he meant to live by, first revealed themselves to him as intransigent and not for sale, it is difficult to discover. As late as 1811 he wrote a poem in praise of the Virgin of Guadalupe, who had protected the capital city and defeated by miracle the insurgent army led by Hidalgo. He wrote another entirely loyal and conventional poem to celebrate the accession of Philip VII to the Spanish throne. He belonged with the Liberal faction, that is, he opposed alike the excesses of the extreme insurgents and the depravities of the viceroys, he began by believing himself to be a citizen of the world, wrote against narrow patriotism, and refused to put himself at the service of any lesser cause than that of absolute morality, in every department of state and church. His literary career began so obscurely that it is difficult to trace its beginnings, but by 1811 he was writing and publishing, on various presses in Mexico City, a copious series of pamphlets, poems, fables, dialogues, all in the nature of moral lectures with rather abstract political overtones, designed to teach broadly social sanity, political purity, and Christian ethics. These were sold in the streets, along with a swarm of broadside, loose-leaf literature by every kind of pamphleteer from the most incendiary Mexican nationalist to the most draggletailed anonymous purveyors of slander and pornography.

A series of rapid events occurred which brought Lizardi out into the open, decided the course of his beliefs and therefore of his acts, and started him once for all on his uncomfortable career as perpetual dissenter. In 1810 the Council of Cádiz decreed the freedom of the press, for Spain and her colonials. The Viceroy of Mexico, Xavier Vanegas, believed, with his overworked board of censors, that the Mexican press had already taken entirely too much freedom for itself. He suppressed the decree, by the simple means of refraining from publishing it.

By July, 1811, the insurgent army under Hidalgo had been defeated, and late in that month the heads of Hidalgo and his fellow heroes, Aldama, Jiménez, and Allende, were hanging as public examples in iron cages at Guanajuato. The Empire was re-established, with Vanegas still Viceroy, and during that year and into the next, the censorship of the press became extremely severe. Every printer in Mexico was required to show a copy of every title he published, and among the items that showed up regularly were quite hundreds of flimsy little folders with such names as "The Truthful Parrot," in which a loquacious bird uttered the most subversive remarks in the popular argot of the lower classes, mixed freely with snatches of rhyme, puns in Mexican slang, and extremely daring double meanings. There were such titles as "The Dead Make No Complaints"; "The Cat's Testimony," a fable imitating La Fontaine; "It Is All Right to Cut the Hair But Don't Take the Hide Too," which in Spanish contains a sly play on words impossible to translate; "There Are Many Shepherds Who Shall Dance in Bethlehem," another punning title, meaning that many priests shall go to Belén (Bethlehem), the great prison which exists still in Mexico City; "Make Things So Clear That Even the Blind May See Them"; "Even Though Robed in Silk, a Monkey Is Still a Monkey"; "All Wool Is Hair," which has a most salty double meaning; "The Nun's Bolero," concerning scandals in convents; "The Dog in a Strange Neighborhood"; "The Devil's Penitents"—these were only a few of the provocations Lizardi showered upon the censors, the royalist party, the church, venal politicians of all parties, social and political abuses of every kind. The censors could hardly find a line that did not contain willful but oblique offense, yet nothing concrete enough to pin the author down on a criminal charge, so the Council of Safety contented itself with harrying him about somewhat, suppressing his pamphlets from time to time, forbidding various presses to publish for him, and threatening him occasionally with worse things.

But it is plain that Lizardi had discovered that he was, in particular, a Mexican, and a patriotic one, though still in general a citizen of the world. It would seem that those truly heroic heads of Father Hidalgo and the others in Guanajuato had brought him down from the airy heights of abstract morality to a solid and immediate field of battle. For, in June, 1812, three months before the new constitution took effect, Viceroy Vanegas, who seems to have been a rather weak, shortsighted man, alarmed by the continued rebelliousness of a people he had believed he had conquered, took a fateful step. He issued an edict condemning to death all churchmen of regular or secular state who might take part in the revolution. This clause dealt with those many priests who rose to take the place of Father Hidalgo. All officers from the rank of sublieutenant upwards were condemned to death. There were all over the country an immense number of captainless men who went independently into battle. These were to be decimated on the spot wherever captured. This last clause might seem to have covered the business; but the Viceroy added a final generous provision for wholesale slaughter. After such decimation, those who by chance had escaped death were, if convenient, to be sent to the Viceroy for suitable punishment. If this was not convenient, it was left to the discretion of each commandant to do with them as he saw fit.

So far, the edict was in its nature a fairly routine measure in times of emergency. But there was a further clause condemning to death all authors of incendiary gazettes, pamphlets or other printed matter. This was sensational, considering that unpublished decree granting freedom of the press. The liberal wing of the Constitutionalist (or royalist) party, together with all the forces that aimed for a peaceable settlement and some sort of compromise with the revolutionists, protested against this edict and advised the Viceroy seriously against such drastic means. The Viceroy did not cancel the edict, but as a sop to public opinion, he did publish the Cádiz decree on October 5, 1812, and the Mexican press, theoretically at least, was free.

Lizardi was ready to take advantage of this freedom. He leaped into print just four days later with the first number of his first periodical, which had for title his own pen name, *The Mexican Thinker*. For two numbers he praised the glories of a free press and the wonders of liberty, but in the third he broke out in high style against the whole Spanish nation, its pride, its despotism; against the corruptions of the viceregal court, the infamies of officials in every station. Seeing that no revenge overtook him, he dared further in a later number: "There is no civilized nation which has a worse government than ours, and the worst in America, nor any other vassal country that has suffered more harshly in its arbitrary enslavement." He turned upon the Spanish governors the very words they had used against Hidalgo. "Cursed monsters," he wrote, and printed, and sold in the streets to be read by all, "you despots and the old evil government are responsible for the present insurrection, not as you say the Cura Hidalgo. It is you together who have stripped our fields, burned our villages, sacrificed our children and made a shambles of this continent."

It is worth noticing here that among his fellow pamphleteers, Lizardi was famous for his moderate language and his courtesy in debate.

No consequences followed this wrathful page. Lizardi went on safely enough until the ninth number, published on December 2, 1812. He devoted this number to an appeal to the Viceroy Vanegas to revoke at least that clause of the edict against revolutionaries which called for the trial of insurgent priests before a military court. He also wrote a personal letter to the Viceroy, timed the publication date to coincide with the Viceroy's Saint's Day, and appeared at court with a specially printed copy. With his own hands he delivered this little bombshell into the very hands of Vanegas, and received the viceregal thanks.

It is hardly probable that Vanegas troubled to examine the papers given him, but the Council of Safety, alarmed, informed him of its contents. The following day the Viceroy and his council suspended the freedom of the press, "for reason of the unsettled conditions of the country." They sent for Lizardi's printer, manager of the Jáurigui press, who admitted that Lizardi had written the offending article.

On the fifth of December they ordered Lizardi to appear before the Court. He disappeared into ineffectual hiding in the house of a friend, Gabriel Gil, where, at three o'clock in the morning, December 7, he was seized and taken to prison. He wrote the story ten years later at great length, and he was still as indignant as he was the day it occurred, but he was proud, also, of the number of men who came to help with the arrest. There were more than seventy of the "dirty birds."

It must be remembered that, under the edict, Lizardi was in danger of death. It would appear his jailers set out methodically to terrorize him, and they succeeded. It does not appear that his judges had any intention of sentencing him to death, but the whole proceedings had the air of making a stern example of troublesome scribblers. They put him in the death cell, where he passed a hideous night, expecting a priest to come to administer the last rites, expecting to be tortured, mistaking the rattle of the jailor's keys for chains. In the morning they took him before a judge he knew, and suspected of having headed the plot to imprison him, where he had to listen patiently to a great deal of foul insult and injury.

Lizardi, in the speeches of his celebrated hero, El Periquillo, declared repeatedly that he feared physical violence more than anything else. The Periquillo is merry and shameless about it, for cowardice is possibly the most disgraceful trait known to man in Mexico, but his author did not find it amusing in himself. Later in his defense to the Viceroy he admitted quite simply that he had refused to obey the first summons to appear because he feared violence and not because he had a sense of guilt. His fears were reasonable. Worse had happened to other men for less cause, or at any rate for no more.

Still, when he gathered that harsh language was probably going to be the worst of it, and he was not going to be tortured and hanged, or at any rate, not that day, he recovered his spirits somewhat and took a rather bantering tone with his infuriated questioners. He was a tall, slender man of a naturally elegant manner, of the longheaded, well-featured Hidalgo kind; his portrait shows a mouth sensitive almost to weakness, and a fine alert picaresque eye. His judges, being also Spanish, and prone to judge a man's importance by his dress—a reflection of his financial state, which was in turn proof of his caste—were inclined to doubt he was so dangerous as they had thought, since Lizardi at that moment was "emaciated, pallid, of shabby appearance," with his "black cloak smeared and crumpled from using it as a bed" in his cell; ten years after he remembered with regret that he had no time to clean it properly before having to show himself. Lizardi told them that indeed they were right, not he but two ladies, one respectable, the other plebeian, had written the articles. They insisted humorlessly that he explain himself. He sobered down and confessed himself as the author. "The respectable lady was the constitution of Cádiz, which allowed him to write on political questions; the plebeian was his own ignorance which had misled him into believing the Viceroy would not be angered by a request to revoke an edict distasteful to the people."

Their ferocity rose at this, they demanded an account of his whole life, and pursued him with questions meant to trap him until, seeing the affair still threatened to be serious, he grew frightened again and implicated his friend Gabriel Gil as well as Carlos María Bustamante, an active insurgent, and writer, who had "warned him his life was in danger and advised him to leave the city."

Probably because of these interesting bits of evidence and not, as Lizardi boasted years afterwards, on account of his own astuteness, for he certainly does not seem to have shown any, the sentence of solitary confinement was lifted, he was remanded to the common jail among a number of his comrade insurgent prisoners and Gil was arrested.

Feeling himself betrayed by the man whom he had befriended at so much danger to himself, Gil said that Lizardi had come to him in distress, and that he, Gil, had done his best to persuade him to obey the summons. Gil then went on to make a bad matter worse by saying that Lizardi had confided that a certain friend had told him he could escape safely with five hundred insurgents who were about to leave the city.

In panic, Lizardi denied this and involved another friend, Juan Olaeta, who had, Lizardi said, offered to allow him to escape with the insurgents. Olaeta, brought before the judges, passed on the responsibility to an unnamed priest from Toluca, who had overheard a conversation between two persons unknown to him, concerning the plans of five hundred insurgents who were about to leave the city. Olaeta's part had been merely an offer to Lizardi to take him to the priest. Lizardi insisted to Olaeta's face that Olaeta had "told him the Tolucan priest would arrange for his escape with the insurgents. Olaeta insisted that Lizardi had misunderstood him, and the two, together with Gabriel Gil, were sent back to jail." If they were in the same cell, it must have been a frightfully embarrassing situation for Lizardi. And he was not done yet.

After nine days in prison, exhausted by repeated questioning and anxieties, he wrote a personal appeal to the Viceroy saying in effect and in short that he had acted innocently in handing him the protest against the edict and that before giving it he had shown it to a priest who approved of it, and by way of justifying himself further, he added with appalling lack of ethical sense that Carlos María Bustamante, and a Doctor Peredo had "written with more hostility than he against the same edict." He continued to drag names into the business, adding that of a Señor Torres, and even blaming his error on them.

The first Judge advised the Viceroy to turn Lizardi's case over to the Captain General and the Military Court. Lizardi asked for bail which was his constitutional right, but it was refused. He was handed about from court to court, military and civil, for months, gradually modifying his statements, or retracting, or insisting that he had been misunderstood. Gil and Olaeta were freed, Bustamante, Torres and Peredo were never arrested at all, and Bustamante, an admirable and heroic spirit, never held any grudge against him, but wrote well of him afterwards. But Lizardi lingered on in jail, writing to the Viceroy, asking for an attorney, asking that his case be turned over to the war department, being mysteriously blocked here and there by hostile agencies, and there he might have stayed on to the end if Vanegas had not been succeeded as Viceroy on March 4, 1813, by Calleja.

Lizardi began a fresh barrage of importunities and explanations to this new, possibly more benign power. He praised him for the good he hoped for from him, and published this praise as a proclamation of the Thinker to the People of Mexico. This got him no new friends anywhere and did not get him his liberty either. He was allowed now and then to visit his family, which consisted of his wife, a newly born daughter, and four unnamed members which, dependent upon him, were almost starving. He had supported them somewhat while in prison by getting out number 10 and number 11 of *The Mexican Thinker*, in December, and number 12 and number 13 in January, but in a considerably chastened and cautious style.

One of its periodic plagues came upon Mexico City and raged as usual, and the churches were crowded with people kissing the statues and handing on the disease to each other. In one number of *The Thinker*, Lizardi advised them to clean up the streets, to burn all refuse, to wash the clothes of the sick not in the public fountains but in a separate place, not to bury the dead in the churches, and as a final absurdity, considering the time and place, he counseled them to use the large country houses of the rich as hospitals for the poor. None of these things was done, the plague raged on and raged itself out.

Lizardi also wrote a statement of his quarrel with the existing state of politics, but a very discreet one, and he could think of no better remedy, his own situation being still perilous as it was, than that both sides in the struggle should obey the counsels of Christ and love one another.

Naturally this sloppy thinking brought upon him the contempt of all sides. The royalists thought no better of him than before, and the liberals, who favored the new constitution, now distrusted him, as they had no intention of loving either an out-and-out royalist or any insurgent, and as for the insurgents themselves, they damned Lizardi freely.

All this was going on, remember, while our hero was still in prison.

In Mexico there was the celebrated "Society of Guadalupe," the most effective of such societies which, under cover of more polite interests, were at the service of Morelos and kept him well informed of events in the capital. The new Viceroy, Calleja, proved to be an even more bitter enemy of the insurgents than Vanegas had been, and Lizardi's unfortunate eulogy of Calleja had been sent to Morelos with a note by a member of the Society of Guadalupe. "This person," said the note, "is not worth your attention, because when they imprisoned him, he showed his weakness, and has written several pamphlets praising this damnable government, and has most basely harmed several men."

At last the Viceroy, finding no new things against Lizardi, wearied of the case; the last judge who took it over recommended that Lizardi be set free, and so he was, on July 1, 1813, after nearly seven months in prison. "Enough to ruin me, as I was ruined, with my family," he wrote.

This is the least handsome episode of Lizardi's life, and he behaved like a green recruit stampeded under his first fire, who may yet become as good a soldier as any man. Lizardi became a better soldier than most, and if he had been once afraid to die, he was not afraid to suffer a long, miserable existence for the sake of his beliefs. He was by no means ruined. He had scarcely been scotched. He returned to his dependents, his six-month-old daughter and the wife who had almost died at her birth, to a brazier without coals and a cupboard without food; and sat down at once to write indignantly against all the causes of misery and the effects of injustice in this maddening world.

The Holy Office of the Inquisition had recently been abolished by decree. Lizardi, with that unbelievable speed of his, wrote a history of that institution, a very bitter history, and he rejoiced over its downfall. He published it on September 30, 1813, as a number of *The Thinker,* and went on with his many projects for local reforms, not attacking the government except by indirection. He wrote against ignorant doctors; against the speculators in food who hoarded for higher prices; he wrote rebuking the Creoles, telling them they had the vices of both the Indians and the Spaniards. If he had poured boiling oil upon them he could not have offended them more bitterly. He wrote against the depravity of the lower classes, and the plague of thieves, beggars, and drunkards in the streets. In November he enjoyed a small popular triumph. A crowd gathered at sight of him and cheered him in the street, shouting that he told them the naked truth. ("La Verdad Pelada" was one of his most lively efforts.) But no royalist or liberal or insurgent or priest or anyone that mattered then was in this cheering rabble; these were the shirtless ones, the born losers no matter which side might win. They shouted his name, and worsened his reputation, but they did not follow his advice and could not if they would. They liked him because he was sharp and angry, full of their own kind of humor, and talked to them in their own language. It was the first time they had ever seen their own kind of talk in print. The flattery was great and they responded to it; for a few centavos they could buy this highly flavored reading matter which expressed all their secret wrongs and grudges and avenged them vicariously; and his words worked afterwards in their thoughts; they trusted him and believed him.

In December, 1813, three months after Lizardi's attack, the Inquisition was reestablished. The absolutist monarch Ferdinand VII after his eclipse was back on the throne of Spain, and all grudgingly granted liberties were at an end again for Spain and her colonies.

Lizardi was by then a man without a party indeed. For in that month someone of the Society of Guadalupe sent Morelos a marked copy of Lizardi's attack on the native-born Mexicans, commenting: "Merely to show you how this author abuses us. We know his weakness since the time of his imprisonment, and we wish that in the press of Oaxaca you shall give him a good shaking up [literal translation] as a mere sycophant."

And one month later, January 14, 1814, a priest called the attention of the head Inquisitor, Flores, to *The Mexican Thinker*'s denunciation of the Inquisition. More than a year later Flores sent the article to two priests for examination, and in June, 1815, they denounced it as "a mass of lies, impostures, iniquitous comparisons, scandals, seductions, offensive to pious ears, injurious to the sanctity of the sovereign Popes, and the piety of our monarch."

Once more the harassed manager of the Jáuregui press was tracked down, this time by an officer of the Inquisition. The printer said that Lizardi lived in Arco Street, number 3, tenement A, then reconsidered and said Lizardi had lived there when he wrote the article but was now living in Prieto Nuevo Street. Lizardi was always moving about from one poverty-stricken tenement in a shabby back street to another. Nothing more came of this affair just then.

The only sign Lizardi gave that he knew he had been denounced to the Inquisition was a softening in the tone of his indignation, a generally lowered quality of resistance, a methodical search for themes on which he might express himself freely without touching too dangerous topics. That year he wrote some rather sensible plans for relieving the sufferings of lepers; against gambling and gambling houses; and criticisms of the prevailing system of public education. He began a campaign for modern education, based on the ideas of Blanchard, a Jesuit priest who had modified Rousseau's theories as expressed in *Emile* "to suit the needs of Christian education."

Sometime during 1815 Lizardi tried a new series of pamphlets under a single title, "Alacena de Frioleras," meaning a cupboard of cold food, scraps, leftovers. He fell into disgrace with the censors at the second number, and was refused license to print it. He was bitterly discouraged but not without some resources still. He decided to try his hand at a novel; what censor would look for political ideas in a paltry fiction?

Lizardi's friend Dr. Beristain, a man of letters, who was writing and compiling a Library of Northern Spanish Americana, did not agree with the censors, but declared Lizardi to be "an original genius, native of New Spain." Dr. Beristain also believed that Lizardi, for his knowledge of the world and of men, and for his taste in literature, merited to be called "if not the American Quevedo, at least the Mexican Torres Villaroel . . . he has now in hand a life of Periquito Sarmiento, which judging by what I have seen of it, much resembles Guzman de Alfarache."

The censor's report for February, 1816, mentions the appearance of *El Periquillo* from the prologue to chapter 6; in July, another series of chapters; the third series was suppressed on November 29, 1816, because it contained an attack on the system of human slavery.

This is the first mention of that book, undertaken as Lizardi's last hope of outwitting the censorship, as well as of making a living by its sales as it was being written. He finished it, but it was not published in full until after his death.

There followed a long dreary period of pamphlet writing, against bullfighting, against dandyism—his Don Catrín remains a stock character in that line until today—calendars, almanacs, stainless essays on morals and manners, hymns and little songs for children. In the meantime the insurgents, who had been growing in strength, were weakened and the Liberal-Constitutionalist party got into power. At once they suppressed both the Inquisition and the Board of Press Censorship, and at once Lizardi was ready for them. He founded a small periodical called *The Lightning Conductor* and began to tell again the naked truth.

There were to be several changes of government yet during Lizardi's lifetime, but there was never to be one he could get along with, or accept altogether. After twenty-four numbers of *The Lightning Conductor*, he could not find a printer who would risk printing his periodical for him.

Lizardi by no means defended the entire Constitutionalist idea, he only defended those tendencies which led to such reforms as he had just witnessed in regard to the Inquisition and the censorship. But in doing this he offended again the rockbound royalist clergy, who used the whip of spiritual authority to force their parishioners to oppose the constitution, as it curtailed the Spanish power and automatically their own. These and all other die-hard royalists hated Lizardi; the insurgents distrusted him. He was a gadfly to the Viceroy, always addressing complaints directly to him: he was opposed to war still, civil war above all, and considered the insurgents to be almost as obnoxious to the good of the country as the royalists themselves. He considered himself "as Catholic as the Pope," but the clergy hated and attacked him bitterly. A priest named Soto wrote such a vicious pamphlet against him that the censors suppressed it.

During that period, almost frantic in his hornets' nest of personal and public enemies, Lizardi found time and a little money to open a reading room, where for a small fee the public might read the current books, newspapers, pamphlets. Almost nobody came to read, he lost his money and closed the place after a few months.

The struggle between Mexico and Spain was approaching the grand climax, and with peculiar timeliness Lizardi did precisely the thing calculated to get him into trouble. In February, 1821, Augustín Iturbide and Canon Monteagudo, at the head of the Anti-constitutionalist party, boldly declared themselves ready to separate Mexico from Spain, without any further compromises. The Liberal party had held out for an independence to be granted by Spain, peacefully. The new constitution granted when Vanegas was Viceroy had been a makeshift affair, with no real concessions in it. Iturbide's party appeared to be only the acting head of the insurgents, for this seizing of independence for Mexico was exactly what the insurgents had been fighting for all along. Iturbide, with an ambition of his own, decided to use the strength of the insurgents and the growing nationalist spirit to his own ends. He and Monteagudo published their program as the Plan of Iguala.

In the meantime, Lizardi had been writing on this topic, too. Just four days after the Plan of Iguala was published, Lizardi printed a pamphlet which was described as a serio-comic dialogue between two popular and sharp-tongued characters called Chamorro and Dominiquín. They discussed the possibilities of independence for Mexico, and looked forward to the day of freedom, believed it would be a good thing for both countries, but still hoped it might be granted legally by the Spanish government.

The liberal constitutionalist but still very royalist government, with its free press, saw nothing to laugh at in this work, suppressed it at once, arrested Lizardi and kept him in jail for several days. On this occasion he flattered no one, implicated no one, and retracted nothing. He was released, and wrote a halfhearted pamphlet on the beauties of reconciliation between factions. And in his next pamphlet he stated boldly a change of mind. "It is true that if we do not take our independence by force of arms, they will never concede us our liberty by force of reason and justice."

When he had been imprisoned, he was accused of being a follower of Iturbide, and a supporter of the Plan of Iguala. Lizardi replied merely that he had not known about the plan when he wrote his own suggestions; in effect no answer at all, and perhaps true in itself. But immediately after this last pamphlet boldly counseling the violent way to freedom, the next thing we know, Lizardi is showing a letter from Iturbide to a certain Spaniard, and this Spaniard is supplying him with money and equipment and a horse, and Lizardi, by urgent request of Iturbide, is riding toward Tepotzotlan to take charge of the insurgent press there. This press was devoted entirely to the doctrine of Mexican independence and the necessity of gaining it by force.

Iturbide's troops fought their way steadily through the country toward Mexico City, and Lizardi was close on their heels with his press turning out patriotic broadsides. Iturbide entered the capital in triumph on September 21, 1821. The great deed was accomplished, the eleven years of revolutionary war came to a close, and Mexico was declared an independent government. Lizardi naturally entered the city in triumph also, with his press still going at top speed. Let the censors fume. He had a whole victorious army with him.

There was still no thought in anyone's mind of establishing a Republic. Lizardi expressed the hopes of the victors clearly: that Iturbide should be made Emperor by acclamation, at the first session of Congress. "Oh," cried our misguided hero, who had waited so long to espouse any faction, and now had taken to heart so utterly the wrong one, "may I have the joy of kissing once the hand of the Emperor of America, and then close my eyes forever in death."

How little becoming to Lizardi was this new garment of acquiescence.

It was never made for him and he could not carry it off. Two month
later his eyes, closed in enthusiasm, were opened violently, he gazed
clearly upon the object of his infatuation, and rejected it. He saw tha
Iturbide had done as other ambitious men do. He had used the force o
a great popular movement to seize power for himself, and meant to se
himself up as head of a government more oppressive if possible than the
old.

Lizardi wrote a pamphlet called "Fifty Questions to Whoever Care
to Answer Them," and the questions were very embarrassing to the new
Emperor, to the church authorities leagued with him, and to all who had
promised reforms in government. Iturbide had at least gone through the
formality of having himself elected Emperor, and Lizardi accused the
priests of controlling the election. They called Lizardi unpatriotic, hos
tile to religion, accused him of political ambitions. Iturbide was discon
certed by the sudden defection of a man to whom he had given money
and a press and a horse to boot, and finding that Lizardi was abusing the
freedom of the press, urged that a new censorship be established.

Finding himself the chief obstacle to that freedom of the press which
had now become his main object in life, Lizardi proceeded to multipl
his offenses. Freemasonry had been creeping in quietly from France b
way of Spain. It was the nightmare of the Church everywhere and two
Popes had issued bulls against it: Clement XII in 1738, Benedict XIV i
1751. The alarmed clergy in Mexico republished these bulls in 1821, and
by way of response Lizardi wrote a pamphlet called painly "A Defens
of the Freemasons." He used arguments that were in the main those of a
good Christian, an informed Catholic and a fairly good student of the
Bible. It was also a heated, tactless and illogical performance, and the
Church simply came down on him like a hammer. Nine days after the
pamphlet was published, Lizardi was publicly and formally excommuni
cated by the board of ecclesiastical censorship, and the notice wa
posted in all the churches.

So it was done at last, and The Thinker passed a little season in hel
which made all his former difficulties seem, as he would say, "like frui
and frosted cake." He was kept more or less a prisoner in his own house
where by the rules no member of his own household was supposed to
speak to him, or touch him, or help or serve him in any way.

It is improbable that this state of affairs ever existed in that family
but the neighbors would not speak to his wife or daughter, they had

great hardships procuring food, and no servant would stay in the house. When he ventured out certain persons drew aside from him; at least once a small mob gathered and threatened to stone him; a group of friars also threatened to come and beat him in his own house, and he advised them defiantly to come well prepared. They did not come, however. He had no defenders for no one would defend an excommunicated man. His wife went to appeal to the Vicar-General, who would not allow her to approach or speak, but waved her away, shouting, "In writing, in writing," since it was forbidden to speak to any member of his family.

Lizardi, announcing that he was "as Catholic as the Pope," which in fact he does not seem to have been, began to defend himself. It was a sign of the times that he could still find presses to print his pamphlets. He appealed to Congress to have the censure of the Church lifted within the prescribed legal period, and asked that body to appoint a lawyer to defend him in the secular courts, but nothing was done in either case. He continued to harry the government, giving sarcastic advice to Iturbide, and recorded with pride that after he had been cut off from human kind by his excommunication his friends were more faithful than ever. It is true he did enjoy some rather furtive moral support from radical sources, but he was bold as if he had all society on his side. He wrote a second defense of the Freemasons, wrote a bitter defense of his entire career and beliefs in the famous "Letter to a Papist," and dragged on his miserable life somehow until 1823, when Iturbide was overthrown by General Antonio López de Santa Ana, head of a "Federalist" party which pretended to found a Republic based on the best elements of the American and French models. It turned out to be another dictatorship which lasted for about thirty years, with Santa Ana at its head. The Catholic Church was still the only recognized religion, a blow to Lizardi, but he took hope again. The appearance of the written Constitution deceived him momentarily, and as unofficial uninvited member of the Federalist party he began again agitating for all those reforms so dear to his heart: Freedom of the press, first, last and forever, compulsory free education, religious liberty, liberty of speech and universal franchise, and naturally, almost as a result of these things, justice, sweet justice, for everybody, regardless of race, class, creed or color.

Almost at once he found himself in jail again.

He gives his account of it as follows, tongue in cheek: "In the month of June (1823), I was imprisoned for writing an innocent little paper

called 'If Congress Sits Much Longer We Shall Lose Our Shirts.' I d
scribed a dream I had in which a set of petty thieves were debating th
best way of robbing us . . . they denounced me . . . on the strengt
of the title alone, arrested me and I was forced to labor again in my ow
defense." ("Letter to a Papist.")

This must have blown over, for on the 20th of that same June he wa
again prisoner in St. Andrés' hospital, but this was probably one of tho
dreary mischances which befall poor people unable to keep up with th
rent: at any rate he insulted the landlady and she threw him out of th
house, lock, stock, and barrel, accusing him of defamation of her chara
ter. He got out of this, too, and in revenge wrote a poem called "Epith
lamium" in which he seems to have married off the judge and the lan
lady with appropriate ribaldry; but they could do nothing as he men
tioned no names.

By then no printer would publish for him: he appears to have got hol
of a press of his own, but the authorities forbade newsboys to sell h
papers in the streets. At last he left the city for a while, but there was n
fate for him in such a case except death in exile. He returned and late i
December, 1823, he wrote a letter to the ecclesiastical board of censo
ship, saying he would no longer attempt to defend himself by civil lav
and asked for absolution. This was granted and the documents we
published in a periodical in January, 1824.

"Time will mend all things," he wrote at about this time, "in effec
today this abuse will be remedied, tomorrow, another . . . in eight o
ten years everything will go as it should." He lived by, and for, th
illusion, but these are the words of a mortally weary man. He had neve
been strong and he was already suffering from the tuberculosis of whic
he was to die. He had at this time an intimation of approaching death.

He began a small bi-weekly sheet called *The Yokel and the Sacristan*
and in June, 1825, a number of this was pronounced heretical. He wa
given eight days in which to make a reply, and asked for three month
which was not granted. He allowed himself even a little more time tha
he had asked for, then made an evasive and unsatisfactory reply. He wa
not pursued any further about this.

The reason may have been that Lizardi had quarreled successfull
even triumphantly, just five months before, with the Bishop of Sonor
This Bishop had issued a manifesto pronouncing the new Federali
Constitution of Mexico Anti-Catholic (in spite of that clause legalizin
the Church alone which had so nearly broken Lizardi's spirit). Th

Bishop argued for the divine right of Kings, and said that God had been deprived of his rights. Lizardi replied with a defense of the republican form of government, in his usual animated style. The public response to him was so great a governmental commission waited upon the Bishop, escorted him to Acapulco and put him on board a ship which returned him to Spain for good. And Santa Ana's government suddenly gave Lizardi a pension of sixty-five pesos a month "to reward him for his services to the revolution, until something better could be found." The something better was the editorship of the official organ of the new government, called *The Gazette*, at a salary of 100 pesos a month. For the times, this was not a bad income for a man who had never had one and this short period was the only one of his life in which Lizardi was free from financial misery. He was at once pestered by his enemies who coveted no doubt the fortune he had fallen into, and though he went on with the job for a year or two, in the end he quarreled with everybody and was out of favor again. . . .

So it went, to the end. The rest of the history has to do with suits for defamation, plays about to be produced and failing, troubles with the censors, suppressions rather monotonously more of the same. "Let the judges answer whether they are fools or bought men," he wrote, when they found for his enemy in a slander trial. He maintained this spirit until the end. He wrote publicly denying that he had ever yielded to the ecclesiastical censors, or asked for absolution. The fact is clear that if he had not done so, the sentence of excommunication would never have been lifted. He boasted of his prudence in the business, and hinted at secret, important diplomatic strategy. Let it go. In the end, it was a matter of yielding, or of starving his family and himself to death.

In 1825, General Guadalupe Victoria, then President, proclaimed the end of slavery. One might have thought this would please Lizardi, and perhaps it did in a measure. But at once he discovered that the proclamation referred only to Negro slaves, and to the outright buying and selling of human flesh. It did not refer to the slavery of the Indian, which he found as bitter and hopeless under the Creole Republic as it had been under the Spanish Viceroys. . . . He pointed out this discrepancy, and insisted that it should be remedied. By that time, he had such a reputation for this kind of unreasonableness, the new government decided to ignore him as far as they were able. He was dismissed from consideration as a crackbrained enthusiast.

By the end of April, 1827, Lizardi knew that death was near. Someone reported on his state of health: he was "a mere skeleton." Lying in bed, he wrote and had printed his "Testament and Farewell of The Mexican Thinker." At some length, and with immense bitterness, he repeated for the last time his stubborn faiths, his unalterable beliefs, his endless opposition to every form of social, political, and human wrong, to every abuse of power and to every shade of dishonesty, particularly the dishonesty of those in power. He still considered himself as Catholic as the Pope, but he could not admit the infallibility of His Holiness. He still did not believe in the apparitions of saints, calling them "mere goblins." He was as good a patriot as ever, but he was still no party man, and he could not condone in the republican government those same abuses he had fought in the days of the Empire. With sad irony he willed to his country "A Republic whose constitution denies religious freedom; a Cathedral on which the canons would at the first opportunity replace the Spanish coat of arms; an ecclesiastical chapter which ignores the civil law altogether; streets full of stray dogs, beggars, idle police; thieves and assassins who flourish in criminal collusion with corrupt civil employees," and so on as ever, in minute detail, no evil too petty or too great for attack, as if they were all of one size and one importance. I think this does not argue at all a lack of the sense of proportion, but is proof of his extraordinary perception of the implicit relationship between all manifestations of evil, the greater breeding and nourishing the lesser, the lesser swarming to support and confirm the greater.

He advised the President of the Republic to get acquainted with the common people and the workers, to study his army and observe the actions of his ministers; and he desired that his wife and friends should not make any loud mourning over him; they were not to light candles around him, and they were to bury him not in the customary friar's robe, but in the uniform of a soldier. Further, he wished that his wife would pay only the regular burial fees of seven pesos, and not haggle with the priest, who would try to charge her more for a select spot in the cemetery. He wished that his epitaph might be: "Here lies the ashes of The Mexican Thinker, who did what he could for his country."

For long days and nights he strangled to death slowly in the wretched little house, number 27, Fuente Quebrado (The Broken Fountain), with his wife and young daughter watching him die, unable to relieve his sufferings with even the most rudimentary comforts, without medical attendance, without money, almost without food. He called two priests to hear his final confession, wishing them to be witnesses for each other that he had not died without the last rites; but he put off receiving Extreme Unction because he hoped the ritual might be attended by a number of former friends who believed him to be a heretic. The friends for some reason failed to arrive for this occasion. Lizardi lingered on, hoping, but no one came; and on June 27, still hoping, but refusing the ceremony until his witnesses should arrive, he died. Almost at once it was rumored abroad that he died possessed of the devil. The friends came then, to see for themselves, and his pitiable corpse was exposed to public view in the hovel where he died, as proof that the devil had not carried him off.

The next day a few former acquaintances, his family and a small mob of curious busybodies followed the body of Fernández de Lizardi to the cemetery of San Lázaro, and buried him with the honors of a retired Captain. Neither the epitaph that he composed for himself, nor any other, was inscribed on his gravestone, for no stone was ever raised. His wife died within four months and was buried beside him. His fifteen-year-old daughter was given in charge of a certain Doña Juliana Guevara de Ceballos, probably her godmother, or a female relation, who seems to have handed her over to the care of another family whose name is not known. This family removed to Vera Cruz shortly, and there Lizardi's daughter died of yellow fever.

So the grave closed over them all, and Mexico almost forgot its stubborn and devoted Thinker. The San Lázaro cemetery disappeared, and with it his unmarked grave. His numberless pamphlets disappeared, a few into private collections and storerooms of bookshops; a great many more into moldering heaps of wastepaper. In effect, Lizardi was forgotten.

His novel, his one novel that he had never meant to write, which had got itself suppressed in its eleventh chapter, is without dispute The Novel of the past century, not only for Mexico but for all Spanish-speaking countries. It was published in full in 1830, three years after Lizardi's death, and there were eight editions by 1884. In spite of this, in 1885 there appeared an edition, "corrected, explained with notes, and adorned with thirty fine illustrations," and announced as the second edition, though it was really the ninth.

After that, no one troubled any more to number editions correctly or not. Until the recent disaster in Spain, a big popular press in Barcelona reprinted it endlessly at the rate of more than a million copies a year, on pulp paper, in rotten type, with a gaudy paper cover illustrating some wild scene, usually that of the corpse-robbing in the crypt. In Mexico I used to see it at every smallest sidewalk book stall; in the larger shops there were always a good number of copies on hand, selling steadily. It was given to the young to read as an aid to manners and morals, and for a great while it must have been the one source of a liberal education for the great mass of people, the only ethical and moral instruction they could have, for Lizardi's ideas of modern education got no foothold in Mexico for nearly a century after him.

It is not to be supposed that anybody ever read a picaresque tale for the sake of the sugar plums of polite instruction concealed in it, but Lizardi had the knack of scattering little jokes and curious phrases all through his sermons, and he managed to smuggle all his pamphlets into the final version of *El Periquillo*. They were all there, at great length; the dog in the strange neighborhood, the dead who make no noise, the monkey dressed in silk; with all his attacks on slavery, on bullfighting, on dishonest apothecaries and incompetent doctors; his program for enlightened education, his proposals for cleaning the city in time of plague; against the vicious and mercenary clergy, the unscrupulous politicians; against gambling, against—ah well, they are all there, and the trouble for the translator is getting them out again without leaving too many gaps. For try as he might, by no art could the good Thinker make his dreary fanatic world of organized virtue anything but terrifying to the reader, it was so deadly dull. But once these wrappings are stripped from the story, there is exposed a fine, traditional Rogue's Progress, the history of a true pícaro, a younger brother of Guzman de Alfarache, as Dr. Beristain said, or of Gil Blas. He has English relations too—Peregrine Pickle, Roderick Random, Tom Jones, all of that family of lucky sinners who end well. In the best style, more things happen to El Periquillo than might reasonably happen to one man, events move at top speed, disasters pile up; but he comes through one way or another, shedding his last misadventure with a shake of his shoulders, plunging straightway into the next. Like all his kind, he is hard and casual and thickskinned and sentimental, and he shares their expedient, opportunist morality, which always serves to recall to his mind the good maxims of his early upbringing when his luck is bad, but never once when it is good.

The typical pícaro also is always the incomplete hero of his own story, for he is also a buffoon. Periquillo is afflicted with the itch, he loses his trousers during a bullfight in the presence of ladies, he is trapped into the wrong bed by the malice of his best friend, he is led again and again into humiliating situations by wits quicker than his own.

Living by his wits, such as they are, he is a true parasite, attaching himself first to one then another organism to feed upon. He is hardly ever without a "master" or "mentor" or "patron" and this person is always doing something for him, which El Periquillo accepts as his right and gives nothing, or as little as possible, in return.

Only once does he feel real gratitude. After leaving the house of the Chinese Mandarin, improbable visitor from the Island Utopia, whom Periquillo has succeeded in gulling for a while, he has been beaten and called a pimp by three girls. None of his other disgraces could equal this, so he gets drunk and goes to hang himself. He fails of course, goes to sleep instead, and wakes to find himself robbed and stripped to the shirt by wayside thieves. He is rescued by a poor old Indian woman who clothes and feeds him. In an untypical rush of tenderness, he embraces and kisses the unsightly creature. This is almost the only truly and honestly tender episode in the book, uncorrupted by any attempts to point a moral, for Lizardi's disillusionment with human nature was real, and based on experience, and most of his attempts to play upon the reader's sentiments ring false.

As El Periquillo's adventures follow the old picaresque pattern, so do those of the other characters, for they are all pretty much fairly familiar wares from the old storehouse. But the real heroes of this novel, by picaresque standards, are some of El Periquillo's comrades, such as Juan Largo, and the Eaglet. One is hanged and one dies leading a bandit raid, neither of them repents or ponders for a moment, but goes to his destined end in good form and style. Juan Largo says, "A good bullfighter dies on the horns of the bull," and El Periquillo answers that he has no wish to die a bullfighter's death. Indeed, he wants no heroics, either in living or dying. He wants to eat his cake and have it too and to die at last respectably in a comfortable bed surrounded by loving mourners. He does it, too. A thoroughly bad lot.

As in all picaresque literature, the reader has uneasy moments of wondering whether it is the hero or the author who is deficient in moral sensibility; or whether the proposed satire has not staggered and collapsed under its weight of moral connotation. When Januario is about to become a common thief, there is a long and solemn dialogue between him and Periquillo, Januario holding out firmly against Periquillo's rather cut-and-dried exhorations to honesty, or at any rate, as a last resort, plain prudence. Januario there repeats word for word the whole Catechism. Having done this, he goes out on his first escapade, and is half successful—that is he escapes from the police, but leaves his swag. On this occasion, Lizardi, by the demands of the plot, is hard beset to have Periquillo present, a witness, yet innocent. The best he can manage is to have him act as lookout, by distracting the watchman's attention and engaging him in conversation. Periquillo then believes that this act does not involve him in the least, and is most virtuously outraged when he is arrested and accused as confederate.

Again, Periquillo, in prison, and watching for a chance to cheat at cards, reflects at length and piously on the illicit, crafty methods of the trusty for turning a dishonest penny by cheating the prisoners. Thinking these thoughts, Periquillo refrains from cheating only because he realizes that he is in very fast company and will undoubtedly be caught at it. Don Antonio, a jail mate, formerly a dealer in contraband, in telling his story of how he lost his ill-gained fortune, innocently assumes and receives the complete sympathy of his hearers, not all of them mere thugs either. This Don Antonio, by the way, who is meant to shine as an example of all that is honorable, upright and unfortunate in human nature, is certainly one of the most abject and nitwitted characters in all fiction. He is smug, pious, dishonest, he feels dreadfully sorry for himself, and his ineptitude and bad management of his affairs cause much suffering to innocent persons. In fact, Lizardi was singularly uninspired in his attempts to portray virtue in action. In his hands it becomes a horrid device of boredom, a pall falls over his mind, he retreats to the dryest kind of moral saws and proverbs. He seemed to realize this, seemed to know that this kind of goodness, the only kind he dared recommend or advertise, was deadly dull. He tried to make it interesting but could not, and turned again with relief to his tough thieves and merry catchalls and horners and unrepentant bandits. Their talk is loose and lively, their behavior natural; he cheers up at once and so does his reader.

A contemporary critic complained that the book was "an uneven and extravagant work in very bad taste . . . written in an ugly style, with a badly invented plot . . . made worse by the author's treatment." He then confessed that what really annoyed him was the author's choice of characters, who were all from the lowest walks of life. They talked and behaved exactly like the vulgar people one saw in the streets, and their language was the sort heard in taverns. This left-handed praise must have pleased Lizardi, who had aimed at precisely this effect. The critic went on to say that the vices of polite society were perhaps no less shocking, but they seemed less gross because it was possible to gloss them over, decorate them, polish them up a bit, and make them less ridiculous. "When a rich man and a poor man drink together," answered Lizardi, in a little jingle, "the poor man gets drunk, but the rich man only gets merry."

Lizardi's infrequent flights into a more rarefied social atmosphere are malicious, comic, and a conventional caricature, designed to confirm in his lower-class readers all their worst suspicions regarding the rich and titled. Now and again he drags in by the ears a set speech on the obligations of nobility to be truly noble and of the poor to be truly virtuous, in the most Lizardian sense of those words, but he makes it clear that he has no real hopes that this will come to pass.

For him, the very rich and the very poor are the delinquent classes, to use a current sociological phrase. He called aloud for the pure mediocrity of morals and manners, the exact center of the road in all things. The middling well off, he insisted, were always good, because they practiced moderation, they were without exorbitant desires, ambitions, or vices. (That this was what made them middling was what Lizardi could never see, and that only those born to the middling temperament, rather than middling fortune, could practice the tepid virtues.) Every time El Periquillo falls into poverty, he falls also into the vices of the poor. When by his standards he is rich, he practices at once the classical vices of the rich. His feelings, thoughts, and conduct contract and expand automatically to the measure of his finances. He was always astounded to meet with morality in the poor, though he did meet it now and then, but never once did he find any good among the rich. His favorite virtue was generosity, and particularly that generosity practiced toward himself, though he almost never practiced it toward others. Even during a period of relative respectability, financially speaking, when El Periquillo is planning to marry, he discusses with Roque, one of his fly-by-night friends, the possibility of Periquillo's Uncle Maceta standing as security for the bridegroom's finery at the tailor's and the silversmith's, along with a plot to rid himself of his mistress, a girl whom he had seduced from a former employer. All goes smoothly for a time: the Uncle is complacent, the mistress is thrown out of the house in good time, the marriage takes place, with bad faith on both sides, El Periquillo's transitory small fortune is thrown away on fast living, and the Uncle is rooked out of his money. El Periquillo comments that it served him right for being such a stingy, unnatural relative.

So much for the Parrot as the faulty medium of Lizardi's social and moral ideas: some of his other characters were hardly less successful in this role . . . for example, his army officer, a colonel, in Manila.

This man is a brilliant example of what a military man is not, never was, could not in the nature of things be, yet Lizardi introduces him quite naturally as if he believed him to be entirely probable. The Colonel is full of the most broadly socialistic ideas, democratic manners, with agrarian notions on nationalism. He believes that rich deposits of gold and silver are a curse to a country instead of the blessings they are supposed to be, and that the lucky country was one which must depend upon its fruits, wool, meats, grain, in plenty but not enough to tempt invaders. He notes that Mexico and the Americas in general are deplorable examples of that false wealth which caused them to neglect agriculture and industry and fall prey to rapacious foreigners. . . . The Colonel, in his fantasy, is no more strange than the entire Manila episode. El Periquillo is deported there as a convict. It is hardly probable that Lizardi ever saw Manila, though there was a legend that he had visited there during the vague "lost years." It is more probable that while he lived in Acapulco he listened to stories of storm and shipwreck and life in strange ports. That he loved the sea is quite plain, with a real love, not romantic or sentimental; he expresses in simple phrases a profound feeling for the deep waters and the sweet majesty of ships. But otherwise, the Manila episode has the vague and far-fetched air of second-hand reporting.

It is not his moral disquisitions, then, nor his portrayal of character, nor his manner of telling his story, that keeps El Periquillo alive after more than a hundred years: it is simply and broadly the good show he managed to get up out of the sights and sounds and smells of his native town. His wakes, funerals, weddings, roaring drunken parties, beggars in their flophouses, the village inns where families rumbled up in coaches, bringing servants, beds, food, exactly as they did in medieval Europe: they all exist with extraordinary vividness, and yet there is very little actual description. There are dozens of scenes which stick in the memory: Luisa standing in the door, greeting with cool scorn her former lover; the wake with the watchers playing cards through the night, and as their own candles give out, borrowing one by one the blessed candles from the dead; the robbing of the corpse, with its exaggerated piling of horror upon horror; the hospital scenes, the life in prisons; all this is eyewitness, first-hand narrative, and a worm's-eye view beside. It is a true picture of the sprawling, teeming, swarming people of Mexico, ragged, eternally cheated, crowding about the food stalls which smoke along the market side, sniffing the good smells through the dirt and confusion, insatiably and hopelessly hungry, but indestructible. Lizardi himself was hungry nearly all his life, and his Periquillo has also an enormous, unfailing preoccupation with food. He remembers every meal, good or bad, he ever ate, he refers punctually three times a day to the fact that he was hungry, or it was now time to eat: "And my anxious stomach," says Periquillo, in one of the more painful moments of his perpetual famine, "was cheeping like a bird to gobble up a couple of plates of chile sauce and a platter of toasted tortillas." Even in exile, in Manila, when he had almost forgotten persons he had known, could hardly remember the lovely face of his native city, he still remembered with longing the savory Mexican food. . . .

Lizardi was once insulted by a picayune critic, who wrote that his work was worthless and he himself a worthless character who wrote only in order to eat. This was not altogether true, for if it had been, Lizardi might easily have been much better fed than he was: but he did, having written, do what he could to sell his work to gain his bread, and though he did not choose the easy way, still he was bitterly stung by this taunt, poor man, and to save his pride, mentioned that at least he had lived by what he made, and not squandered his wife's dowry.

The Thinker's style has been admired as a model of clarity in Mexican literature by some of his later friends, but I think that must be the bias of loyalty. By the loosest standard, that style was almost intolerably wordy, cloudy, vague, the sentences of an intricate slovenliness, the paragraphs of inordinate length; indeed it was no style at all, but merely the visible shape of his harassed mind which came of his harassed life. He nearly always began his pamphlets, as he began his novel, with great dignity, deliberation and clearness, with a consciously affected pedantry, with echoes of the grand manner, a pastiche of Cervantes or Góngora, but he knew it could not last; he knew also his readers' tastes; he could do no more than promise a patchwork, and patchwork it was. There are times too when it is apparent he wrote at top speed in order to get the number finished and handed to the printer, needing desperately the few pesos the sale would bring him, padding and repeating, partly because his mind was too tired to remember what he had written, and partly because he must give his readers good weight for the money, or they would not buy.

The censors complained constantly of his obscenity and use of double meanings, and indeed he was a master in this mode. All of his writings I have seen are full of sly hints and some not so sly, curious associations of ideas one would need to be very innocent indeed to miss. The Mexican love them with a special affection, the language is a honeycomb of them no doubt Lizardi enjoyed writing them, and it was a certain device for catching his readers' undivided attention. He did not need to invent anything, he had only to listen to the popular talk, which was and is ripe and odorous. Some of it is very comic and witty, some of it simply nasty humorless, and out of place in a translation where the meaning could be conveyed only by substituting a similar phrase in English, since they are often untranslatable in the technical sense. And was he—to imitate one of his own rhetorical questions—so simple as to believe that his reader would take the trouble to wade through his moral dissertations if he did not spice them with the little obscenities they loved? He was not, and he did his best by them in the matter of seasoning. At least a hundred million readers have found his novel savory, and perhaps a few of them repaid his hopes by absorbing here and there in it a little taste of manners and morals, with some liberal political theory besides. Certainly the causes for which he fought have been never altogether defeated, but they have won no victory, either: a lukewarm, halfway sort of process the kind of thing that exasperated him most, that might well end by disheartening the best and bravest of men. Lizardi was not the best of men, nor the bravest, he was only a very good man and a very faithful one. If he did not have perfect courage or judgment, let him who has require these things of him.

Miss Porter
Adds a Comment

(*a Letter to the Editor of*
The Nation)

Dear Sirs:

A number of persons, some of them good friends, all of them well
disposed to my work, have confessed that they simply (simply!) could
not be interested in *The Itching Parrot*. Some of them don't like the
picaresque novels in any language. Others thought it not a good example
of the kind. And others thought it was cut too much. (I agree.) This
dismayed me as translator, for I found the book interesting in Spanish
and naturally have an indulgent eye for the curtailed version in English.
This is not altogether self-love, for I had a regiment (or anyway a squad)
of collaborators and advisers, some of them extremely well informed on
the subject and all of them marvelously opinionated. Also I was guided
in the first working over by a *borrador* made by Mr. Pressly, a good
knowledgeable, if sketchy, translation. Toward the end I took flight in
the most cowardly manner, leaving the manuscript to its fate, pretending
not to know what was being done to it; and I am not half so sorry as I
should be, perhaps, when I consider the great number of serious, good
criticisms I have had by letter from real authorities in the Spanish language, Spanish and South American literature, and intelligent admirers
of Lizardi. And I feel that Mr. Elder certainly made the very best of his
part of a bad bargain, for the final cutting is pretty adroit, I think.

My share in the book has been well rewarded in Mr. Duff's scholarly and courteous defense of my motives and methods in publishing the book in its present—and first—English version. He is most reassuring. All my gratitude to Mr. Duff for supporting me in the matter of untranslatable idiom, slang and double meanings. The only way to translate them would be to hold up the progress of the story with a paragraph of explanation for every such word or phrase. For example: "*Toda lana es pelo,*" or "All wool is hair," is that all? Why, how pointless. Indeed? Look it up in the dictionary. As for my tidying up the Parrot, and turning him into a Macaw, that may have happened. But I did not assume "the manner of the eighteenth-century masters of realism." That manner is Lizardi's, and I found it comfortable because of the special influence upon me of eighteenth-century English prose: notably that of Lawrence Sterne; and Lizardi's style comes into English in just that manner. Even his slang, his racy phrases, have a mixture of formality in them, and as for the straightaway course, I open the book at random and translate at sight the first paragraph under my eye: "That which they call Fortune appeared quickly to have wearied of favoring me. I formed a close friendship with two rich merchants of Vera Cruz, who proposed to me that I should share with them in the negotiation of certain interesting contraband on board the frigate *Amphytrite.* . . ." Call that what you please, firm and simple, or eighteenth-century, or just plain prose, it is as near an exact translation as my mortal powers will allow. . . .

I have always been in favor of publishing the full and complete document, whatever it may be. I detest edited historical papers, novels cut in half when brought from one language to another. Yet, in the end, I consented and for a good reason. There was absolutely no prospect of getting it published in the original form. I should know, after ten years' trying, and fourteen publishers' rejections. I have the first version, in four big fat typewritten volumes, with a map of Mexico City for 1770 or thereabouts, a portrait of Lizardi, and the illustrations which appeared in the 1884 edition. They will probably never see daylight. The present version, I decided, was certainly better than none, for Mr. Duff is right in his belief that the book is important, and for precisely the reasons he gives.

As an inadequate expression of my thanks to Mr. Duff, I shall send him a copy of the translation, to judge for himself (God willing that there is room for it on a ship and the ship shall arrive). I stand by the translation, what there is of it. I wish it were all to do over again, perhaps it would be better next time. I shall be glad to see a full translation published by someone else. I can't do it again, there is not time, I must go on to the next thing. . . .

1943

Leaving the Petate

The petate is a woven straw mat, in shape an oblong square, full of variations in color and texture, and very sweet smelling when it is new. In its ordinary form, natural colored, thick and loosely contrived, it is the Mexican Indian bed, an ancient sort of sleeping mat such as all Oriental peoples use. There is a proverb full of vulgar contempt which used to be much quoted here in Mexico: "Whoever was born on a *petate* will always smell of the straw." Since 1910, I shall say simply to fix a date on changes which have been so gradual it is impossible to say when the transition actually was made, this attitude has disappeared officially. The *petate*, an object full of charm for the eye, and immensely useful around any house, is no longer a symbol of racial and economic degradation from which there is no probable hope of rising. On the contrary, many of the best 1920 revolutionists insisted on smelling of the straw whether they were born on the *petate* or not. It was a mark of the true revolutionary to acknowledge Indian blood, the more the better, to profess Indian points of view, to make, in short, an Indian revolution. All the interlocking advances of the *mestizo* (mixed Spanish and Indian) revolution since Benito Juárez have been made for the Indian, and only secondarily by him—much as the recent famous renascence of Indian sculpture and painting was the work of European-trained *mestizos*. No matter: this article is not going to deal with grand generalities. I am interested in a few individual human beings I have met here lately, whose lives make me believe that the Indian, when he gets a chance, is leaving the *petate*.

And no wonder. He wraps himself in his *serape*, a pure-wool blanket woven on a hand loom and colored sometimes with vegetable dyes, and lies down to rest on his *petate*. The blankets are very beautiful, but they are always a little short, and in this table-land of Mexico at least, where the nights are always cold, one blanket is not enough. The *petate*, beautiful as it is, is also a little short, so the man curls down on his side, draws his knees up and tucks his head down in a prenatal posture, and sleeps like that. He can sleep like that anywhere: on street corners, by the roadside, in caves, in doorways, in his own hut, if he has one. Sometimes he sleeps sitting with his knees drawn up to his chin and his hat over his eyes, forming a kind of pyramid with his blanket wound about him. He makes such an attractive design as he sits thus: no wonder people go around painting pictures of him. But I think he sleeps there because he is numbed with tiredness and has no other place to go, and not in the least because he is a public decoration. Toughened as he may be to hardship, you can never convince me he is really comfortable, or likes this way of sleeping. So the first moment he gets a chance, a job, a little piece of land, he leaves his *petate* and takes as naturally as any other human or brute being to the delights of kinder living. At first he makes two wooden stands, and puts boards across them, and lays his *petate* on a platform that lifts him from the chill of the earth. From this there is only a step to thin cotton mattresses, and pillows made of lumps of rags tied up in a square of muslin, and thence. . . .

There were presently three women near me who had lately left the *petate*: Consuelo, Eufemia and Hilaria. Consuelo is the maid of a young American woman here, Eufemia was my maid, and Hilaria is her aunt. Eufemia is young, almost pure Aztec, combative, acquisitive, secretive, very bold and handsome and full of tricks. Hilaria is a born intriguer, a carrier of gossip and maker of mischief. Until recently she worked for a hot-headed Mexican man who managed his servants in the classical middle-class way: by bullying and heckling. This gentleman would come in for his dinner, and if it was not ready on the instant, he would grab his hat and stamp shouting into the street again. "My señor has an incredibly violent nature," said Hilaria, melting with pride. But she grew into the habit of sitting in my kitchen most of the time, whispering advice to Eufemia about how best to get around me; until one day the señor stamped around his house shouting he would rather live in the streets than put up with such a cook, so Hilaria has gone back to her native village near Toluca—back, for a time at least, to her *petate*. She has never really left it in spirit. She wears her *reboso*, the traditional dark-colored cotton-fringed scarf, in the old style, and her wavy black hair is braided in two short tails tied together in the back. Her niece Eufemia came to me dressed in the same way, but within a week she returned from her first day off with a fashionable haircut, parted on the side, waved and peaked extravagantly at the nape—"In the shape of a heart," she explained—and a pair of high-heeled patent-leather pumps which she confessed hurt her feet shockingly.

Hilaria came over for a look, went away, and brought back Eufemia's godmother, her cousins and a family friend, all old-fashioned women like herself, to exclaim over Eufemia's haircut. They turned her about and uttered little yips of admiration tempered with rebuke. What a girl! but look at that peak in the back! What do you think your mother will say? But see, the curls on top, my God! Look here over the ears—like a boy, Eufemia, aren't you ashamed of yourself! and so on. And then the shoes, and then Eufemia's dark-red crochet scarf which she wore in place of a *reboso*—well, well. . . .

They were really very pleased and proud of her. A few days later a very slick pale young man showed up at the house and with all formality explained that he was engaged to marry Eufemia, and would I object if now and then he stopped by to salute her? Naturally I should never object to such a thing. He explained that for years upon years he had been looking for a truly virtuous, honorable girl to make his wife, and now he had found her. Would I be so good as to watch her carefully, never allow her to go on the street after dark, nor receive other visitors? I assured him I would have done this anyhow. He offered me a limp hand, bowed, shook hands with Eufemia, who blushed alarmingly, and disappeared gently as a cat. Eufemia dashed after me to explain that her young man was not an Indian—I could see that—that he was a barber who made good money, and it was he who had given her the haircut. He had also given her a black lace veil to wear in church—lace veils were once the prerogative of the rich—and had told her to put aside her *reboso*. It was he who had advised her to buy the high-heeled shoes.

After this announcement of the engagement, Eufemia began saving her money and mine with miserly concentration. She was going to buy a sewing machine. In every department of the household I began to feel the dead weight of Eufemia's sewing machine. Food doubled in price, and there was less of it. Everything, from soap to a packet of needles, soared appallingly until I began to look about for a national economic crisis. She would not spend one penny of her wages, and whenever I left town for a few days, leaving her the ordinary allowance for food, I always returned to find the kitten gaunt and yelling with famine and Eufemia pallid and inert from a diet of tortillas and coffee. If all of us perished in the effort, she was going to have a sewing machine, and if we held out long enough, a brass bed and a victrola.

In the meantime, Consuelo came down with a mysterious and stubborn malady. Her young American woman briskly advised her to go to one of the very up-to-date public clinics for treatment. Consuelo at once "went Indian," as her employer defines that peculiar state of remoteness which is not sullenness nor melancholy, nor even hostility—simply a condition of not-thereness to all approach. So long as it lasts, a mere foreigner might as well save his breath. Consuelo is Totonac, speaks her own tongue with her friends, is puritanically severe, honest and caretaking. Her village is so far away you must travel by train for a day or so, and then by horseback for two days more, and in her sick state she turned with longing to this far-off place where she could get the kind of help she really trusted.

Somehow she was prevented from going, so she called in a *curandera* who came from this same village. A *curandera* is a cross between a witch wife and an herb doctor. She steeped Consuelo in home-made brews and incantations, and what we had feared was a tumor the *curandera* identified as a rib which had been jarred from its moorings. Whatever it was, Consuelo recovered, more or less. Consuelo has two cousins who left the *petate* and are now nurses in a famous American homeopathic sanitarium. They send her long lists of dietary rules and hygienic counsels, which her American employer follows with great effect. Consuelo prefers to stick to her own witch doctors, and lets the foreign ones alone.

Hilaria is a *curandera,* and so is Eufemia in a limited way, and both of them remind me very much of the early American housewife who kept her family medicine chest supplied with her own remedies from tried recipes. They have extensive herb knowledge, and Eufemia was always bringing me a steaming glassful of brew for every smallest discomfort imaginable. I swallowed them down, and so ran a gamut of flavors and aromas, from the staggering bitterness of something she called the "prodigious cup" to the apple-flavored freshness of manzanilla flowers. Hilaria pierces ears when the moon is waning, to prevent swelling, and ritually dabs the ear with boiling fat, which should be an excellent antiseptic. To cure headache, a bottle of hot water at the feet draws the pain from the head. This works better if the sign of the cross is made over the head and the bottle. Every benefit is doubled if given with a blessing, and Eufemia, who knows the virtues of rubbing alcohol, always began my alcohol bath with "In the name of the Father, and of the Son, and of the Holy Ghost, may this make you well," which was so gracious an approach I could hardly refuse to feel better.

She agrees with Hilaria that a small green *chile* rubbed on the outer eyelid will cure inflammation of the eye, but you must toss it over your shoulder from you, and walk hastily away without glancing back. During my illness she moistened a cloth with orange-leaf water and put it on my head as a cure for fever. In the morning I found between the folds a little picture of the Holy Face. Eufemia takes up readily with every new thing, and uses iodoform, lysol, patent toothpaste, epsom salts, bicarbonate of soda, rubbing alcohol and mustard plasters very conveniently. Hilaria sticks firmly to her native herbs, and to cure colds puts a plaster of *zapote*—a soft black fruit—heated red hot, on the chest of her patients. Both remedies are remarkably helpful. But Eufemia is leaving the *petate*, and Hilaria is going back to it.

I sympathized with Eufemia's ambitions, even to her fondness for toilet articles of imported German celluloid, her adoration for Japanese cups and saucers in preference to the Mexican pottery which I so love. But I had not reckoned on providing a dowry for a young woman, and the time came for us to part. I set the day two weeks off, and she agreed amiably. Then I gave her her month's wages and two hours later she had packed up her bed and sent it away. Her young man came in and professed astonishment at the state of affairs. "She is not supposed to go for two weeks," I told him, "and at least she must stay until tomorrow." "I will see to that," said the oily Enrique, "this is very surprising." "Tomorrow she may go and welcome, in peace," I assured him.

"Ah, yes, peace, peace," said Enrique. "Peace," I echoed, and we stood there waving our hands at each other in a peculiar horizontal gesture, palms downward, crossing back and forth at our several wrists, about eye level. Between us we wore Eufemia down, and there was peace of a sort.

But in the meantime, she had no bed, so she slept that night on a large *petate* with two red blankets, and seemed very cheerful about it. After all, it was her last night on a *petate*. I discovered later that it was Enrique who had suggested to her that she leave at once, so they might be married and go to Vera Cruz. Eufemia will never go back to her village. She is going to have a brass bed, and a sewing machine and a victrola, and there is no reason why a good barber should not buy a Ford. Her children will be added to the next generation of good little conservative right-minded dull people, like Enrique, or, with Eufemia's fighting spirit, they may become *mestizo* revolutionaries, and keep up the work of saving the Indian.

My new cook is Teodora. "Think of Eufemia going away with just a barber," she says. "My cousin Nicolasa captured a chauffeur. A chauffeur is somebody. But a barber!"

"Just the same, I am glad she is married," I say.

Teodora says, "Oh, not really married, just behind the church, as we say. We marry with everybody, one here, one there, a little while with each one."

"I hope Eufemia stays married, because I have plans for her family," I tell her.

"Oh, she will have a family, never fear," says Teodora.

1931

The Fiesta of Guadalupe

I followed the crowd of tired burdened pilgrims, bowed under their loads of potteries and food and babies and baskets, their clothes dusty and their faces a little streaked with long-borne fatigue. Indians all over Mexico had gathered at the feet of Mary Guadalupe for this greatest *fiesta* of the year, which celebrates the initiation of Mexico into the mystic company of the Church, with a saint and a miracle all her own, not transplanted from Spain. Juan Diego's long-ago vision of Mary on the bare hillside made her Queen of Mexico where before she had been Empress.

Members of all tribes were there in their distinctive costumes. Women wearing skirts of one piece of cloth wrapped around their sturdy bodies and women wearing gaily embroidered blouses with very short puffed sleeves. Women wearing their gathered skirts of green and red, with blue *rebosos* wrapped tightly around their shoulders. And men in great hats with peaked crowns, wide flat hats with almost no crown. Blankets, and *serapes*, and thonged sandals. And a strange-appearing group whose men all wore a large square of fiber cloth as a cloak, brought under one arm and knotted on the opposite shoulder exactly in the style depicted in the old drawings of Montezuma.

A clutter of babies and dolls and jars and strange-looking people lined the sidewalks, intermingled with booths, red curtained and hung with paper streamers, where sweets and food and drinks were sold and where we found their astonishing crafts—manlike potteries and jars and wooden pails bound with hard wrought clasps of iron, and gentle lacework immaculately white and unbelievably cheap of price.

I picked my way through the crowd looking for the dancers, that curious survival of the ancient Dionysian rites, which in turn were brought over from an unknown time. The dance and blood sacrifice were inextricably tangled in the worship of men, and the sight of men dancing in a religious ecstasy links one's imagination, for the moment, with all the lives that have been.

A woven, moving arch of brilliant-colored paper flowers gleaming over the heads of the crowd drew me near the gate of the cathedral as the great bells high up began to ring—sharply, with shocking clamor, they began to sway and ring, their ancient tongues shouting notes of joy a little out of tune. The arches began to leap and flutter. I managed to draw near enough to see, over the fuzzy poll of sleeping baby on his mother's back. A group of Indians, fantastically dressed, each carrying an arch of flowers, were stepping it briskly to the smart jangle of the bells. They wore tinsel crowns over red bandanas which hung down their necks in Arab fashion. Their costumes were of varicolored bits of cloth, roughly fashioned into short skirts and blouses. Their muscular brown legs were disfigured with cerise and blue cotton stockings. They danced a short, monotonous step, facing each other, advancing, retreating, holding the arches over their crowns, turning and bowing, in a stolid sarabande. The utter solemnity of their faces made it a moving sight. Under their bandanas, their foreheads were knitted in the effort to keep time and watch the figures of the dance. Not a smile and not a sound save the mad hysteria of the old bells awakened from their sleep, shrieking praise to the queen of Heaven and the Lord of Life.

Then the bells stopped, and a man with a mandolin stood near by, and began a quiet rhythmic tune. The master of ceremonies, wearing around his neck a stuffed rabbit clothed in a pink satin jacket, waved the flagging dancers in to line, helped the less agile to catch step, and the dancing went on. A jammed and breathless crowd and pilgrims inside the churchyard peered through the iron fence, while the youths and boys scrambled up, over the heads of the others, and watched from a precarious vantage. They reminded one irresistibly of a menagerie cage lined with young monkeys. They spraddled and sprawled, caught toeholds and fell, gathered themselves up and shinned up the railings again. They were almost as busy as the dancers themselves.

Past stalls of fruits and babies crawling underfoot away from their engrossed mothers, and the vendors of images, scapulars and rosaries, I walked to the church of the well, where is guarded the holy spring of water that gushed from beneath Mary's feet at her last appearance to Juan Diego, December twelve, in the year of grace fifteen and thirty-one.

It is a small darkened place, the well covered over with a handsomely wrought iron grating, through which the magic waters are brought up in a copper pail with a heavy handle. The people gather here and drink reverently, passing the pail from mouth to mouth, praying the while to be delivered of their infirmities and sins.

A girl weeps as she drinks, her chin quivering. A man, sweating and dusty drinks and drinks and drinks again, with a great sigh of satisfaction, wipes his mouth and crosses himself devoutly.

My pilgrimage leads me back to the great cathedral, intent on seeing the miraculous Tilma of Juan Diego, whereon the queen of Heaven deigned to stamp her lovely image. Great is the power of that faded virgin curving like a new moon in her bright blue cloak, dim and remote and immobile in her frame above the soaring altar columns.

From above, the drone of priests' voices in endless prayers, answered by the shrill treble of boy singers. Under the overwhelming arches and the cold magnificence of the white altar, their faces lighted palely by the glimmer of candles, kneel the Indians. Some of them have walked for days for the privilege of kneeling on these flagged floors and raising their eyes to the Holy Tilma.

There is a rapt stillness, a terrible reasonless faith in their dark faces. They sigh, turn toward the picture of their beloved Lady, printed on the garment of Juan Diego only ten years after Cortes had brought the new God, with fire and sword, into Mexico. Only ten years ago, but it is probable that Juan Diego knew nothing about the fire and sword which have been so often the weapons of the faithful servants of our Lady. Maybe he had learned religion happily, from some old gentle priest, and his thoughts of the Virgin, ineffably mysterious and radiant and kind must have haunted him by day and by night for a long time; until one day, oh, miracle of miracles, his kindled eyes beheld her, standing, softly robed in blue, her pale hands clasped, a message of devotion on her lips, on a little hill in his own country, the very spot where his childhood had been passed.

Ah well—why not? And I passed on to the steep winding ascent to the chapel of the little hill, once a Teocalli, called the Hill of Tepeyac, and a scene of other faiths and other pilgrimages. I think, as I follow the path, of those early victims of Faith who went up (mighty slowly and mighty heavily, let the old Gods themselves tell you) to give up their beating hearts in order that the sun might rise again on their people. Now there is a great crucifix set up with the transfixed and bleeding heart of one Man nailed upon it—one magnificent Egoist who dreamed that his great heart could redeem from death all the other hearts of earth destined to be born. He has taken the old hill by storm with his mother, Mary Guadalupe, and their shrine brings the Indians climbing up, in silent groups, pursued by the prayers of the blind and the halt and the lame who have gathered to reap a little share of the blessings being rained upon the children of faith. Theirs is a doleful litany: "In the name of our Lady, Pity, a little charity for the poor—for the blind, for the little servants of God, for the humble in heart!" The cries waver to you on the winds as the slope rises, and comes in faintly to the small chapel where is the reclining potent image of Guadalupe, second in power only to the Holy Tilma itself.

It is a more recent image, copied from the original picture, but now she is lying down, hands clasped, supported by a company of saints. There is a voluptuous softness in her face and pose—a later virgin, grown accustomed to homage and from the meek maiden receiving the announcement of the Angel Gabriel on her knees, she has progressed to the role of Powerful Intercessor. Her eyes are vague and a little indifferent, and she does not glance at the devout adorer who passionately clasps her knees and bows his head upon them.

A sheet of glass protects her, or she would be literally wiped away by the touches of her devotees. They crowd up to the case, and rub their hands on it, and cross themselves, then rub the afflicted parts of their bodies, hoping for a cure. A man reached up and rubbed the glass, then gently stroked the head of his sick and pallid wife, who could not get near enough to touch for herself. He rubbed his own forehead, knees, then stroked the woman's chest. A mother brought her baby and leaned his little toes against the glass for a long time, the tears rolling down her cheeks.

Twenty brown and work-stained hands are stretched up to touch the magic glass—they obscure the still face of the adored Lady, they blot out with their insistent supplications her remote eyes. They have parted a carved bit of wood and plaster, I see the awful hands of faith, the credulous and worn hands of believers; the humble and beseeching hands of the millions and millions who have only the anodyne of credulity. In my dreams I shall see those groping insatiable hands reaching, reaching, reaching, the eyes turned blinded away from the good earth which should fill them, to the vast and empty sky.

Cut upon the downward road again, I stop and look over the dark and brooding land, with its rim of mountains swathed in layer upon layer of filmy blue and gray and purple mists, the low empty valleys blackened with clumps of trees. The flat-topped houses of adobe drift away casting no shadows on the flooding blue, I seem to walk in a heavy, dolorous dream.

It is not Mary Guadalupe nor her son that touches me. It is Juan Diego I remember, and his people I see, kneeling in scattered ranks on the flagged floor of their church, fixing their eyes on mystic, speechless things. It is their ragged hands I see, and their wounded hearts that I feel beating under their work-stained clothes like a great volcano under the earth and I think to myself, hopefully, that men do not live in a deathly dream forever.

1923

The Mexican Trinity

(*Report from Mexico City,*
July, 1921)

Uneasiness grows here daily. We are having sudden deportations of foreign agitators, street riots and parades of workers carrying red flags. Plots
thicken, thin, disintegrate in the space of thirty-six hours. A general was
executed today for counterrevolutionary activities. There is fevered discussion in the newspapers as to the best means of stamping out Bolshevism, which is the inclusive term for all forms of radical work. Battles
occur almost daily between Catholics and Socialists in many parts of the
Republic: Morelia, Yucatán, Campeche, Jalisco. In brief, a clamor of
petty dissension almost drowns the complicated debate between Mexico
and the United States.

It is fascinating to watch, but singularly difficult to record because
events overlap, and the news of today may be stale before it reaches the
border. It is impossible to write fully of the situation unless one belongs
to that choice company of folk who can learn all about peoples and
countries in a couple of weeks. We have had a constant procession of
these strange people: they come dashing in, gather endless notes and
dash out again and three weeks later their expert, definitive opinions are
published. Marvelous! I have been here for seven months, and for quite
six of these I have not been sure of what the excitement is all about.
Indeed, I am not yet able to say whether my accumulated impression of
Mexico is justly proportioned; or that if I write with profound conviction
of what is going on I shall not be making a profoundly comical mistake.
The true story of a people is not to be had exclusively from official documents, or from guarded talks with diplomats. Nor is it to be gathered
entirely from the people themselves. The life of a great nation is too

399

widely scattered and complex and vast; too many opposing forces are at work, each with its own intensity of self-seeking.

Has any other country besides Mexico so many types of enemy within the gates? Here they are both foreign and native, hostile to each other by tradition, but mingling their ambitions in a common cause. The Mexican capitalist joins forces with the American against his revolutionary fellow-countryman. The Catholic Church enlists the help of Protestant strangers in the subjugation of the Indian, clamoring for his land. Reactionary Mexicans work faithfully with reactionary foreigners to achieve their ends by devious means. The Spanish, a scourge of Mexico, have plans of their own and are no better loved than they ever were. The British, Americans and French seek political and financial power, oil and mines; a splendid horde of invaders, they are distrustful of each other, but unable to disentangle their interests. Then there are the native bourgeoisie, much resembling the bourgeoisie elsewhere, who are opposed to all idea of revolution. "We want peace, and more business," they chant uniformly, but how these blessings are to be obtained they do not know. "More business, and no Bolshevism!" is their cry, and they are ready to support any man or group of men who can give them what they want. The professional politicians of Mexico likewise bear a strong family likeness to gentlemen engaged in this line of business in other parts of the world. Some of them have their prejudices; it may be against the Americans, or against the Church, or against the radicals, or against the other local political party, but whatever their prejudices may be they are pathetically unanimous in their belief that big business will save the country.

The extreme radical group includes a number of idealists, somewhat tragic figures these, for their cause is so hopeless. They are nationalists of a fanatical type, recalling the early Sinn Feiners. They are furious and emotional and reasonless and determined. They want, God pity them, a free Mexico at once. Any conservative newspaper editor will tell you what a hindrance they are to the "best minds" who are now trying to make the going easy for big business. If a reasonable government is to get any work done, such misguided enthusiasts can not be disposed of too quickly. A few cooler revolutionists have been working toward civilized alleviations of present distresses pending the coming of the perfect State. Such harmless institutions as free schools for the workers, including a course in social science, have been set going. Clinics, dispensaries, birth-control information for the appallingly fertile Mexican woman, playgrounds for children—it sounds almost like the routine program of any East Side social-service worker. But here in Mexico such things have become dangerous, bolshevistic. Among the revolutionists, the Communists have been a wildly disturbing element. This cult was composed mostly of discontented foreigners, lacking even the rudiments of the Russian theory, with not a working revolutionist among them. The Mexicans, when they are not good party-revolutionists, are simple syndicalists of an extreme type. By party-revolutionists I mean the followers of some leader who is not an adherent of any particular revolutionary formula, but who is bent on putting down whatever government happens to be in power and establishing his own, based on a purely nationalistic ideal of reform.

The present government of Mexico is made up of certain intensely radical people, combined with a cast-iron reactionary group which was added during the early days of the administration. In the Cabinet at the extreme left wing is Calles, the most radical public official in Mexico today, modified by de la Huerta at his elbow. At the extreme right wing is Alberto Pani, Minister of Foreign Relations, and Capmany, Minister of Labor. The other members are political gradations of these four minds. The pull-and-haul is intense and never ceases. Such a coalition government for Mexico is a great idea, and the theory is not unfamiliar to American minds: that all classes have the right to equal representation in the government. But it will not work. Quite naturally, all that any group of politicians wants is their own way in everything. They will fight to the last ditch to get it; coalition be hanged!

The revolution has not yet entered into the souls of the Mexican people. There can be no doubt of that. What is going on here is not the resistless upheaval of a great mass leavened by teaching and thinking and suffering. The Russian writers made the Russian Revolution, I verily believe, through a period of seventy-five years' preoccupation with the wrongs of the peasant, and the cruelties of life under the heel of the Tsar. Here in Mexico there is no conscience crying through the literature of the country. A small group of intellectuals still writes about romance and the stars, and roses and the shadowy eyes of ladies, touching no sorrow of the human heart other than the pain of unrequited love.

But then, the Indians cannot read. What good would a literature of revolt do them? Yet they are the very life of the country, this inert and slow-breathing mass, these lost people who move in the oblivion of sleepwalkers under their incredible burdens; these silent and reproachful figures in rags, bowed face to face with the earth; it is these who bind together all the accumulated and hostile elements of Mexican life. Leagued against the Indian are four centuries of servitude, the incoming foreigner who will take the last hectare of his land, and his own church that stands with the foreigners.

It is generally understood in Mexico that one of the conditions of recognition by the United States is that all radicals holding office in the Cabinet and in the lesser departments of government must go. That is what must be done if Mexico desires peace with the United States. This means, certainly, the dismissal of everyone who is doing constructive work in lines that ought to be far removed from the field of politics, such as education and welfare work among the Indians.

Everybody here theorizes endlessly. Each individual member of the smallest subdivision of the great triumvirate, Land, Oil, and the Church, has his own pet theory, fitting his prophecy to his desire. Everybody is in the confidence of somebody else who knows everything long before it happens. In this way one hears of revolutions to be started tomorrow or the next day or the day after that; but though the surface shifts and changes, one can readily deduce for oneself that one static combination remains, Land, Oil, and the Church. In principle these three are one. They do not take part in these petty national dissensions. Their battleground is the world. If the oil companies are to get oil, they need land. If the Church is to have wealth, it needs land. The partition of land in Mexico, therefore, menaces not only the *haciendados* (individual landholders), but foreign investors and the very foundations of the Church. Already, under the land-reform laws of Juárez, the Church cannot hold land; it evades this decree, however, by holding property in guardianship, but even this title will be destroyed by repartition.

The recent encounters between Catholics and Socialists in different parts of Mexico have been followed by a spectacular activity on the part of the Catholic clergy. They are pulling their old familiar wires, and all the bedraggled puppets are dancing with a great clatter. The clever ones indulge in skillful moves in the political game, and there are street brawls for the hot-heads. For the peons there is always the moldy, infallible device; a Virgin—this time of Guadalupe—has been seen to move, to shine miraculously in a darkened room! A poor woman in Puebla was favored by Almighty God with the sight of this miracle, just at the moment of the Church's greatest political uncertainty; and now this miraculous image is to be brought here to Mexico City. The priests are insisting on a severe investigation to be carried on by themselves, and the statue is to be placed in an *oratorio*, where it will be living proof to the faithful that the great patroness of Mexico has set her face against reform.

The peons are further assured by the priests that to accept the land given to them by the reform laws is to be guilty of simple stealing, and everyone taking such land will be excluded from holy communion—a very effective threat. The agents who come to survey the land for the purposes of partition are attacked by the very peons they have come to benefit. Priests who warn their congregations against the new land-laws have been arrested and imprisoned, and now and then a stick of dynamite has been hurled at a bishop's palace by a radical hot-head. But these things do not touch the mighty power of the Church, solidly entrenched as it is in its growing strength, and playing the intricate game of international politics with gusto and skill.

So far, I have not talked with a single member of the American colony here who does not eagerly watch for the show to begin. They want American troops in here, and want them quickly—they are apprehensive that the soldiers will not arrive soon enough, and that they will be left to the mercy of the Mexicans for several weeks, maybe. It is strange talk one hears. It is indulged in freely over café tables and on street-corners, at teas and at dances.

Meanwhile international finance goes on its own appointed way. The plans that were drawn up more than a year ago by certain individuals who manage these things in the United States, are going forward nicely, and are being hampered no more than normally by upstarts who have plans of their own. Inevitably certain things will have to be done when the time comes, with only a few necessary deviations due to the workings of the "imponderables." The whole program has been carefully worked out by Oil, Land, and the Church, the powers that hold this country securely in their grip.

Where Presidents Have
No Friends

Let me first repeat to you a story about Carranza told to me by a young Spaniard, Mexican born, who had identified his fortunes with that regime which ended with the sorry flight and death of its chief executive in the month of May, 1920.

A civilized creature was this Spaniard, suffering with a complication of spiritual disgusts. He maintained a nicely ironic tone of amusement in relating his adventure, wherein he had followed the high promptings of a fealty that led him into a situation gravely dubious, false, and pitiable. Because of this, he permitted himself an anodyne gesture of arrogance.

"Be as Anglo-Saxon, as American, as you like, madame, but try also to understand a little."

"I do not know whether this is understanding," I told him, "but whatever you may tell me, I promise you I shall not be amazed."

"That is good. I ask you to regard it as a *macabre* episode outside of all possible calculation of human events. I desire that you may be pleasantly amused at the picture I shall make for you. Here is a wide desert, harsh with cactus, the mountains glittering under the sun-rays like heaps of hewn brass. Hot! *O Dios!* our early summer! Many trains of coaches crowding upon one another in their gaudy and ridiculous colors, a little resembling the building-blocks for children, miles of them, you understand, attached to busy engines madly engaged in the ludicrous business of dragging a Government, equipped and encumbered, into exile.

404

"As Carranza goes, driven out by one of his own generals, he takes the *matériel* of government with him, and means to reestablish it in Vera Cruz. There are gold bars and coins, guns and ammunition, soldiers and women and horses, furnishing and silver from the castle, postage-stamps, champagne, jewels, a confusion of things seized in frantic emergency.

"His cabinet, his personal friends, were with him. I had the honor, having been recalled suddenly from Washington, to share this calamity with my chief. We numbered in all sixteen thousand people in those trains, officials, soldiers, friends—and enemies. How could a president fail to have enemies among sixteen thousand persons?

"Lupe Sánchez, general in the Federal Army, was waiting for us with his men along the way. Later there would be little Candido Aguilar, son-in-law of the chief. We were not without hope.

"If for a moment, madame, we thought escape possible, put it down, please, to that persistent naïveté of faith in the incredible which is in the heart of every Mexican. *La Suerte* will not fail forever! And still *la Suerte* betrays us, and still we are faithful to her. It is our happiest fidelity.

"Some one performed the simple feat of disconnecting the air-brakes of the first train. While we waited many hours on account of this, we smiled, for we had wondered what the first treachery would be, and it was this—trivial and potent, anonymous and certain. When we moved on slowly, revolutionary troops were stationed, waiting for us. We ran through a gantlet of bullets. We listened to the noise of firing, and drank champagne. The chief was silent, composed. We had nearly ten thousand effective soldiers. If he doubted them, no one knows to this day.

"The attacking forces were defeated, though our soldiers were disconcerted by rifle-shells refusing to explode. It was not surprising to discover that nearly half the shells were filled with sand and pepper. Who did it? It was convenient to blame it on the Japanese munition-makers.

"On the third day we met Lupe Sánchez, who had changed his mind, and had diverted his troops to the defense of the revolution. We had a battle with him all day, and in the morning he was joined by the troops of deserted little Candido, left armyless in some village to the south. Trevino came also with a fresh army. They attacked together.

"That was all. Now we were certain of failure, and we did what we could toward the destruction of the train we must leave with the enemy.

We dynamited and set fire to the coaches, and all of us gathered what gold we could for flight into the United States and Europe. My brother and I had each a satchel of gold, thirty thousand pesos, maybe; not much. Only for the moment, you see.

"All of us who had arms joined the soldiers for a while. Two little revolvers and a belt of shells do not go far. We were beaten, and the chief gave orders for each man to go for himself. He released them all from their loyalty to him. He knew how to value it, you see.

"I found a small horse, very lean, standing with his saddle on, a dead man hanging by one heel to the stirrup, head down. I rode with a group of soldiers. They were trying to desert to the enemy. I said to the leader:

" 'Why do you desert the chief? I shall kill you!'

" 'If you are not a fool, you will come with us,' he replied very amiably. 'This is a lost day.' I let him go. Well, it was his own affair. A man's honor is his own, no?

"The soldiers spread flat over the earth behind cactus and hillock, firing at one another, no man knowing whether the other was friend or enemy. Carranza was riding away on horseback, followed by several hundred of his men. I gave my brother place behind me in the saddle, and we set out after the party. Our bags of gold were too heavy for the little horse; so we buried them under a boulder (I could never find that place again!) and later we joined the old man.

"I remember him in this way, riding always ahead of us, without a word, his white beard blowing over his shoulder. I loathe all causes, madame, and all politics, but the man inspired admiration. At dark we stopped before a hut to buy tortillas, and mind what I say, the old man had not a centavo. One of us loaned him the few pennies needed. We made a dark camp that night, and all the next day we rode between hill and cactus.

"Men were falling away from the party. One or two at a time, they saluted and left him, or turned back with no sign at all, or pleaded fatigue and promised to overtake us. But not one came back.

"In the early evening we entered a friendly hacienda and there slept. At midnight I heard a continuous tramp of horses passing the outer wall under my window. I stood listening. I felt some one breathing beside me in the dark. One of the other men stood listening also.

" 'They are bandits hunting for the Old Man,' he whispered, 'on their way into the mountains.'

" 'We should wake the chief and tell him,' I said.

" 'Let him sleep,' said the man. 'What is the good of disturbing him now?'

"In the morning my brother and I decided to go no farther. The chief was a dead man; well, we would not be implicated in his death. So we saluted, and turned back also on our one little pony."

His eyes fixed themselves steadily upon me, a bitter regard of inquiry.

"Madame, it was a desperate little jest, played out. There are, no doubt, causes worth dying for, but that was not one of them."

"Who killed him?"

"It could have been any one of that group who went on with him. It could have been the bandits I heard passing in the night. Maybe an enemy who made this his special mission, or a friend who found himself in a situation he did not care for. He might, you see, go back to the new people in power and say: 'See, here I am, your servant. I have just escaped from the bandits of Carranza.' A poor chance, but an only one. Maybe the newest chief would believe him, maybe not. A President of Mexico can trust no one."

That final corroding phrase is the point of a cynical truth: a hundred years of revolutions have taught the President of Mexico that he can trust no one except his enemies. They may be depended upon to hate him infallibly; they will be faithful in contriving for his downfall.

In Mexican revolution the cause and the leader are interchangeable symbols. A man has his adherents, who follow him in the hope of arriving, through him, one step nearer to the thing they want, whatever that may be. Obregón is the leader, and his followers are the proletariat. The proletariat being for him, naturally the other classes and subdivisions of classes are opposed to him, acting on the curious theory that what is good for the laborer must logically be very bad for everybody else. Obregón's proletarian recalls that what was good for everybody else was very terrible for him, and he has set about evening up scores with more enthusiasm than justice, probably. Obregón has difficult work on hand. Himself a man of hardy good sense, an intellectually detached point of view, and civilized instincts, he must deal with the most conflicting welter of enmities and demands, surely, that ever harassed a holder of the executive office.

His Indians, his revolutionist mestizos, are filled with grievances and wrongs, suffering cruel exigencies; they turn the tragic, threatening eyes of their faith toward him, and wait for him to fulfill his promises to them. Those promises mean realities, immediate benefits, if they have any meaning at all: land, work, freedom. He must deal with these honestly and without delay.

As an Indian, exceedingly insular in his political views, he must deal in the subtleties of international finance and diplomacy with foreign politicians and capitalists who think in terms of continents and billions, and who are leagued powerfully with his chief enemies of his own country, the landholders, the church. These in turn may be divided again into delicate classifications: the aristocracy, the wealthy upper-class mestizo, the middle-class shopkeeping folk, and the great body of Indians who cling to their religion. For the sake of sufficient identification, they may call themselves reactionary or conservative or liberal. It does not signify. They have also a label for this present governing group. They call them bandits. It means nothing, and has a disreputable sound.

The chief complaint among the anti-Obregón factions is that the new Government is acting on the theory that the lands of Mexico belong to the Indian, and that it is to the interest of the country to care first for this prodigious majority of its population. This is true, and it is revolutionary enough, indeed. But all the men now concerned in the Government are frankly nationalists. Only three of them have ever had a glimpse of Europe or this country. They studied in text-books the forms of government in other countries. But when the time came, they went about their business with their eyes fixed on their native earth. Only afterward their international point of view, such as it is, was formed, when they had come into power.

For the first time they found themselves dealing not with the fervent episodes of battles fought out with personal minuteness of detail, where a general lay in ambush and fought beside his men, but with the gigantic and implacable facts: Mexico, a backward and menaced nation, dangerously rich in resource and weak in defenses, was in actual relation with a world of hostile, critical governments, all more powerful than Mexico herself, all more than a match for her in organized pillage, more nicely adjusted in a cynical freemasonry of finance, diplomacy, and war, the three Graces of civilization.

In selecting his cabinet Obregón announced his belief that de la Huerta, radical philosopher, would work harmoniously with Alberto Pani, friend of the American Senator Fall. That Calles, Sonora revolutionist, would somehow make his terms with Capmany, millionaire reactionary. That Vasconselos, radical minister of education, and Villareal, revolutionary minister of agriculture, could both be counted on not to be too extreme in moments of crisis. As an act of faith, this was magnificent. Faith in what? Watching Obregón's methods of disposing of his enemies each according to his degree, I believe his faith is in himself.

With this cabinet he set about the gigantic task of bringing order to a country in which order has been the least regarded of all laws. He had against him four tremendous opposing forces, the reactionaries against the radicals, the foreign against the native, an inextricably tangled mass of conflicting claims, any one of which he cannot afford to ignore. With a treasury virtually empty, he shouldered a national debt which, though not hopelessly large, is still enough to be a weapon in the hands of his opponents. And when he set about dividing the land, as he had promised, and collecting funds from the oil products to add to the national treasury, he cited Article Twenty-seven of the Mexican Constitution as amended by Carranza in 1917, and announced that it should now be made effective.

That has caused all, or nearly all, of his trouble. It delayed recognition from the United States. It has been the peg upon which to hang many promising little counter-revolutionary schemes. It may yet prove fatal to his Government.

Briefly, Article Twenty-seven gives to the Mexican Government full title to all the lands of Mexico, both surface and subsoil. It empowers the Department of Agriculture to break up unwieldy landholdings, and to divide the acreage among the Indians. It provides for a tax on all subsoil products, and thereby diverts to the national treasury and to the common life the fruit of the nation's labor and products.

This was the ideal which Obregón as President of Mexico designed to carry out. It had the noble simplicity of a hermit's vision of beauty, and it was about as sympathetically related to practical politics.

The oil interests were unanimous in opposing this article. Oil should be Mexico's greatest asset, but the Guggenheims and Dohenys have made of it a liability almost insupportable to the country. It is the fashion now to blame all the present difficulties between Mexico and the United States on the Obregón regime; but it was Carranza who redrafted the Mexican Constitution, aside from a detail or two, to its present form. It was his administration that set the tax of ten percent on the selling price of oil, with a fifteen-percent royalty payable in produce on all oil obtained. The land partition had been one of his political plans. He did not carry it out, it is true. It is one of the reasons why he is not now President of Mexico. But Obregón inherited all his problems, dead ripe.

El Aguila petroleum, a British company, and the Guffey interests made their peace, and announced their intention of complying with the national regulation of oil export. The Doheny interests, most implacable of all Mexico's interior enemies, together with other companies, have side-stepped the payment in this way: they admit that the tax is nominal; they will pay taxes cheerfully on the price paid them for oil by the boat companies, which they allege is about forty cents a barrel. The boat companies claim they buy the oil outright, and, once loaded into the tanks, Mexico has no further claim of interest. The price they sell for in foreign markets is their own affair.

This would be quite simple if the oil-producing companies and the oil-transportation companies were separate interests. But the case being what it is, the Government says pipelines shall have meters, the oil shall be measured as it flows into the tank-boats, and the amount shall be taxed at the selling price of oil, which fluctuates with the market. And there the matter sticks.

The Doheny interests are the source of eternal unrest. They want Obregón out, and nothing less will please them. A man of the old guard, say Esteban Cantu, is the choice of the Doheny faction. A good man, Cantu. Enormously wealthy, mixed upper-class blood, interested in oil. "Emperor of Lower California" they used to call him. When Obregón became president, Cantu was required to disband his standing army, was given to understand his vast estates would be repartitioned when the time came for it. Now, sporadically, he makes counterrevolution, designed to keep the oil and land question prominently before the eyes of the American public, or, I should say, the American politician.

That much for the subsoil controversy. The surface lands are needed for agricultural purposes. The country must be fed on its own fruits. The drain of import is too heavy. The farming lands are held almost exclusively by Spaniards who have held the grants for centuries, by oil companies, and by the church. These three are in effect one. If the Government continues to carry out its drastic plan, it means that the old haciendas will be destroyed, church lands confiscated, and every foot of earth will be subject to government control. The entire question of recognition hangs on this one sword's point.

In the meantime, so far as the oil people are concerned, they cheerfully admit it is cheaper to keep a few minor revolutions going than to pay taxes. So Pablo Gonzales and Esteban Cantu and all that restless body of Mexicans with political ambitions and no love of country can be sure of a measure of support and aid in their operations.

You see what Obregón has in the way of organized opposition. Even in the Chamber of Deputies he has a minority. In his own cabinet he can with difficulty strike a balance in his favor at moments of crisis. Yet he has held the Government together for two years, and appears to be growing steadily in strength. The currency exchange is at par; gold is the circulating medium; business is good; banks are steady. What is the source of his power?

He has, as I have said, the organized proletariat, the labor-unions. They are for him exactly as long as he is for them. He encounters no obscurities of motive there. His influence has wavered precariously at moments when he was threatened from foreign sources. His followers watch him, and criticize him savagely when he decides on compromise as preferable to extermination.

The unorganized proletariat follows, as a rule, the organized. There are his federal troops, a loose body of men not given to loyalties. As soldiers they follow the leader. They followed him at a time when they were theoretically loyal to Carranza. He has them—maybe.

There are the Yaqui Indians, a fierce and evil tribe who fight like demons lately unchained from hell. Obregón is the only man who has ever succeeded in taming them to regular warfare. His humanizing mediums were land and food and decent treatment. He has them—maybe.

The socialist bandits of Morelia are his. They are the most promising of all the radical groups, a fantastic mixture of doctors and lawyers and poets and teachers who took to the high roads against Carranza, soldiers who detached themselves from the army without leave and engaged in a personal pursuit of glory, plain road-pillagers converted to the revolutionary ideal. They were the remnants of Zapata's horde, those fanatic highwaymen who used to make speeches to their victims after this manner, poking them in the ribs with revolvers to emphasize the moral points of their discourse:

"In giving up your gold to us you are honored in contributing to the cause of freedom. These funds shall be used to further the revolution, to bring to our downtrodden brothers justice and peace and liberty. Be happy, brother, that we do not blow out your capitalistic brains."

These men are now engaged in running the state of Morelia on an outright socialist program. The state is at peace except for May-day battles between Catholics and Socialists and an occasional riot on feast days.

Yucatán, also a revolutionary state, is loyal to Obregón. It is a nation by itself, removed by language, by tradition, and custom from the rest of the country. The last of the Mayas are there, a spectacular, insular people, up to the eyes in social and economic grievances, who make their state a battle-ground. Felipe Carillo, a Maya, was elected governor by sixty thousand majority, and if he lives to take the chair, we shall see revolutionary theory practised freely in Yucatán.

From high to low, this is the strength of Obregón. He works quietly, slowly, holding his ground as he gains it with a tenacity that cannot be stampeded into action even with his mob of revolutionists growling at his heels, demanding that he ignore the claims of foreign capital and politics.

He gives personal interviews to all manner of strange persons who track him down indefatigably: reporters and magazine-writers from the United States; delegations from chambers of commerce; representatives of every type of promotion scheme under heaven, all designed to benefit Mexico; walking delegates from the labor-unions; unofficial diplomats and businessmen who wish to establish some sort of trades relation with Mexico.

Take this sort of thing to illustrate: Mexico has a body of lawmakers known as the Chamber of Deputies, which functions somewhat in the manner of our House of Congress. On one occasion the conservative faction went openly to war with Carillo, then deputy from Yucatán. The disturbances became a riot. For three days the lawmakers went on a debauch of dissension. A committee of deputies appealed to the president to put an end to the disgraceful episode. Acting through the governor of the district, Obregón ordered that the riot be quelled after the ordinary procedure against disturbances of the peace. Whereupon the city fire department went down to the white-pillared Chamber of Deputies, turned on high-pressure hose through the open windows, and the disorderly deputies were drenched to the bone. The disturbances stopped.

It would be absurd, comic, if death were not in it. The role of dictator is strangely associated with a civilized perception of government. Wherever generals playing the counterrevolutionary game are captured, there they are executed, usually within twelve hours. Pablo Gonzales has escaped so far, but only one of his numerous small forays recently resulted in the execution of five men, two of them being generals in the president's army.

If the revolutionists were all Mexicans, it would be, possibly, a local business. But Mexico has been hospitable to political refugees from all parts of the world. They have come making mischief each after his own taste, arrogantly bringing their diverse doctrines to a land already overborne with doctrines. A sudden flurry of antiradical sentiment resulted in a few of the more obviously annoying of the aliens being set gently over the borders of their native lands, in accordance with Article Thirty-three of the Mexican Constitution, which provides that a too impossible guest may be thrown out.

The foreign radicals, bereft of the security of government toleration, declared the Mexican Government was betraying its highest revolutionary ideals by way of currying favor with the United States. They accused the cabinet of taking orders from the American chargés d'affaires. Maybe so. Oddly enough, it did happen that most of the deportees were received hospitably by the American jails on their return from exile. But one might believe also that the long-suffering Mexican Government had grown humanly sick of gnat-stings, and had rid itself of a few minor curses in order to concentrate on greater ones.

Every foreign opportunist with a point to make can find the support of other opportunists in Mexico. The result is a hotbed of petty plotting, cross purposes between natives and foreigners, from the diplomats down to the unwashed grumbler who sits in the Alameda and complains about the sorrows of the proletariat. In all this the men in present power are struggling toward practicable economic and political relations with the world.

Psychologically, we are as alien to them as we are to the French, and in much the same way; for the Mexican upper class social and business customs are to-day more French than Spanish.

The hope of the Labor party is to establish an interdependent union with the South American states, leading naturally to clear avenues of trade and communication with Europe. It is the logical sequence of events, and would be a tremendous source of strength to Mexico. But if the union is established, it will be an achievement of finesse which Mexico may take pride in; for the idea is rankest treason to our high financial rights in that country.

Luis Morones, present chief of munitions for the Government, is the leader of this Labor party. He is wholly Indian, a leader by temperament, executive, and powerful. His pride is in his factories and plants, where the working conditions are ideal, and the wage is the highest paid in the republic.

In the educational work Vasconcelos, minister of education and president of the National University, has begun an intensive program of school founding among the Indians, with special attention to industrial and agricultural schools, his intention being not to oppress the Indian with an education he cannot use, but to fit him for his natural work, which is on the land.

Vasconcelos is, despite what we would call radical tendencies, a believer in applied Christianity. He might be called a Tolstoyan, except that he is Mexican, and the doctrine of nonresistance does not engage his faith. He claims in his calm way that the true purpose of higher education is to lift the souls of men above this calamitous civilization. We cannot outwear it until we have fixed the aspirations of our souls on something better. He publishes a magazine of religion, philosophy, and literature in Mexico City, giving translations from the works of Tolstoy, Rolland, Anatole France, and Shaw.

Other men, in no wise connected with politics, are each in his own individual manner deeply concerned with the rebuilding of his country. Widely separated as they are in caste and political sympathies, they are strangely of one mind with the others in their will to be of service to their shattered nation. There is Manuel Gamio, archaeologist and writer, wholly Spanish, but born in Mexico, whose research work and restoration of the Teotihuacán pyramids is sponsored and financed by the present Government. Mr. Gamio is studying race sources in Mexico with the sole aim of discovering the genuine needs of the Indian, and the most natural method of supplying them.

Jorge Enciso, also Spanish, is an authority on early Aztec art and design, and is making a comparative study of motives used by the early and widely separated tribes. Adolfo Best-Maugard, a painter, has spent eight years in creating a new manner of design, using as a foundation the Aztec motives. He has done valuable work in reviving among the Indian schoolchildren the native instinct for drawing and designing. His belief is that a renascence of the older Aztec arts and handicrafts among these people will aid immeasurably in their redemption.

Redemption—it is a hopeful, responsible word one hears often among these men. Strangely assorted are the true patriots of Mexico, and few as numbers go. But what country has many faithful sons? These men are divided as only social castes can divide persons from one another in a Latin-minded country, and yet they share convictions which, separately arrived at, are almost indivisible in effect.

They all are convinced, quite simply, that twelve millions of their fifteen millions of peoples cannot live in poverty, illiteracy, a most complete spiritual and mental darkness, without constituting a disgraceful menace to the state. They have a civilized conviction that the laborer is worthy of his hire, a practical perception of the waste entailed in millions of acres of untilled lands while the working people go hungry. And with this belief goes an esthetic appreciation of the necessity of beauty in the national life, the cultivation of racial forms of art, and the creation of substantial and lasting unity in national politics.

As a nation, we love phrases. How do you like this one? "Land and liberty for all, forever!" If we needed a fine ringing phrase to fight a war on, could we possibly improve on that one? The tragic, the incredible thing about this phrase is that the men who made it, meant it. Just this: land, liberty, for all, forever!

They fought a long, dreary, expensive revolution on it. As soon as they had it fought, they began to translate the phrase into action. Their situation today is as I have described it to you.

1922

La Conquistadora

Rosalie Caden Evans was an American woman, born in Galveston, Texas. She married a British subject, Harry Evans, who became owner of several haciendas in Mexico during the Díaz regime. They lost their property in the Madero revolution, and for several years lived in the United States and in Europe. In 1917 Mr. Evans died while in Mexico, after an unsuccessful attempt to regain his property under the Carranza administration. Mrs. Evans returned to Mexico, and for more than six years she proved a tough enemy to the successive revolutionary governments, holding her hacienda under almost continuous fire. This contest required a great deal of attention from three governments, Mexico, Great Britain, and the United States, and furnished a ready bone of contention in the long-drawn argument between Mexico and foreign powers respecting the famous Article 27 of the new Mexican Constitution, which provides among other things that the large landholdings of Mexico shall be repartitioned among the Indians, subject to proper indemnification to the former owner.

H. A. C. Cummins, of the British legation, was expelled from Mexico for his championship of Mrs. Evans, and a fair amount of trouble ensued between Mexico and Great Britain about it. The case of Mrs. Evans was cited in the United States as an argument against our recognition of the Obregón government. An impressive volume of diplomatic correspondence was exchanged between the three governments concerning the inflexible lady, who held her ground, nevertheless, saying that she could be removed from her holdings only as a prisoner or dead.

In August, 1924, the news came that Mrs. Evans had been shot from ambush by a number of men while driving in a buckboard from the village of San Martín to her hacienda, San Pedro Coxtocan.

Reading the letters Rosalie Evans wrote her sister, Mrs. Daisy Caden Pettus, from Mexico, this adventure takes on all the colors of a lively temperament; the story is lighted for us like a torch. The aim in publishing the letters was to present Mrs. Evans to a presumably outraged Anglo-Saxon world as a martyr to the sacred principles of private ownership of property: to fix her as a symbol of devotion to a holy cause. "Some Americans," says Mrs. Pettus in a foreward to the volume, "in ignorance of Mexican conditions, have said the fight carried on by Mrs. Evans was unwise, if not unworthy, in that it is charged that she was resisting the duly established laws and principles of the Mexican people. This is very far from true."

It is true, however, that she opposed, and to her death, the attempts of the Mexican people to establish those laws and principles which were the foundation of their revolution, and on which their national future depends. She cast her individual weight against the march of an enormous social movement, and though her fight was gallant, brilliant and wholehearted, admirable as a mere exhibition of daring, energy and spirit, still I cannot see how she merits the title of martyr. She was out for blood, and she had a glorious time while the fight lasted.

Her letters are a swift-moving account of a life as full of thrills and action as any novel of adventure you may find. They are written at odd moments, dashed off in the midst of a dozen things all going at once: the episodes are struck off white-hot. The result is a collection of letters that could scarcely be equaled for speed, for clarity, for self-revelation, for wit and charm. We are shown the most fantastic blend of a woman: fanaticism, physical courage, avarice, mystical exaltation and witch-wife superstition; social poise and financial shrewdness, a timeless feminine coquetry tempered by that curious innocence which is the special gift of the American woman: all driven mercilessly by a tautness of the nerves, a deep-lying hysteria that urges her to self-hypnosis. Toward the last she had almost lost her natural reactions. Anger, fear, delight, hope—no more of these. She was a Will.

Mrs. Evans returned to Mexico to take up her husband's fight when he had wearied to death of it. Belief in private property had not yet become a religion. She was animated by sentiment for her dead husband. All feminine, she insisted that his shade still guarded and directed her.

The demon that possessed her was by no means of so spiritual a nature as she fancied: she was ruled by a single-minded love of money and power. She came into Mexico at harvest time, and after a short, sharp battle she got hold of the ripened wheat on her main hacienda. This victory fired her, and was the beginning of the end. Shortly afterward the shade of her husband left her. "I stand alone."

No single glimmer of understanding of the causes of revolution or the rights of the people involved ever touched her mind. She loved Spaniards, the British, the Americans of the foreign colony. She thought the Indians made good servants, though occasionally they betrayed her. She writes with annoyance of Obregón's taking Mexico City and creating a disturbance when she was on the point of wresting from the Indians her second crop of wheat—"gold in color, gold in reality!" She is most lyrical, most poetic when she contemplates this gold which shall be hers, though all Mexico go to waste around her. Carranza's flight interested her merely because it menaced her chances of getting the only threshing machine in the Puebla Valley.

Of all the machinations, the crooked politics, the broken faiths, the orders and counter orders, the plots and counterplots that went on between literally thousands of people over this single holding, I have not time to tell. Mrs. Evans was passed from hand to hand, nobody wanted to be responsible for what must eventually happen to her. She pressed everybody into her service, from her maids to the high diplomats. Every man of any official note in Mexico, connected with the three governments, finally got into the business, and she shows them all up in turn.

The story of the double dealing here revealed is not pretty, showing as it does some of our eminent diplomats engaged in passing the buck and gossiping behind each other's backs. But sooner or later they all advised her to listen to reason, accept 100,000 pesos for her land and give way. At least they perceived what she could not; that here was a national movement that must be reckoned with.

At first she would not. And later, she could not. She loved the romantic danger of her situation, she admired herself in the role of heroine. Her appetite for excitement increased; she confessed herself jaded, and sought greater danger.

Speaking of a safe conduct she obtained in order to go over her hacienda and inspect the crops, she says: "You see it means a chance of gaining 80,000 pesos besides the adventure." After each hairbreadth encounter with sullen Indians armed with rope and scythe, with troops bearing bared arms, she was flushed with a tense joy. Later, when she came to open war, she would ride into armed groups with her pistol drawn, singing *"Nous sommes les enfants de Gasconne!"* She cracked an Indian agrarian over the head with her riding whip during an altercation over the watercourse and patrolled the fields during harvest with a small army.

Her love of the drama was getting the upper hand of principle. If at first her cry was all for law and justice, later she refers to herself merrily as an outlaw. "You have no idea how naturally one takes to the greenwood!" She became a female conquistador—victory was her aim, and she was as unscrupulous in her methods as any other invader.

There is not a line in her letters to show that she had any grasp of the true inward situation, but her keen eye and ready wit missed no surface play of event. She maintained peaceable relations first with one, then another of the many groups of rebels. Inexplicably the situation would shift and change, her allies would vanish, leaving her mystified. She had all Mexico divided into two classes: the Good, who were helping her hold her property, and the Bad, who were trying to take it from her.

She could be self-possessed in the grand manner, and seemed to have second-sight in everything immediately concerning herself. She sat for three days and fed her pigeons while serious persons advised her to pay the 300 pesos ransom demanded for her majordomo, kidnapped to the hills. She refused. It was too much to pay for a majordomo, and she felt they would not shoot him anyhow. They did not. When he returned she sent him back with a present of $80 to the kidnappers.

At another crisis she played chess. After a brilliant encounter with some hint of gunfire, she came in and washed her hair. At times she studied astronomy, other times she read Marcus Aurelius or poetry. At all times she played the great lady. Her love for her horses, her dogs, her servants, her workers and allies was all of a piece, grounded in her sense of possession. They were hers; almost by virtue of that added grace she loved them, and she looked after them in the feudal manner.

There was something wild and strange in her, a hint of madness that touches genius; she lived in a half-burned ranch house with her dogs, near a haunted chapel, hourly expecting attack, and longed to join the coyotes in their weird dances outside her door. She foretold the manner of her own death, and related for sober fact the most hair-raising ghost story I have ever read:

> The last night I was there I had been in bed an hour perhaps and was growing drowsy when I heard some one crying at my window. The most gentle attenuated sobbing; the most pitiful sounds you ever heard. I never for a minute thought of the spirits, but called the girl to light the candle. She heard it too—but the strange part is, *I* said it was at the back window and *she* heard it at the front, and neither did *she* think of spirits. As she opened to see who was there, IT came in sobbing—and we looked at each other and closed the windows. Perhaps you think we were frightened or horrified? I can only answer for myself—it filled me with an intense pity. I only wanted to comfort it and I said to the girl: "If it would *only* be quiet." I then promised to have the mass said and invite the people, and it left, sobbing. And we, of course, both went to our beds to sleep dreamlessly till morning.

Revolution is not gentle, either for those who make it or those who oppose it. This story has its own value as a record of one life lived very fully and consciously. I think the life and death of Mrs. Evans were her own private adventures, most gladly sought and enviably carried through. As a personality, she is worth attention, being beautiful, daring and attractive. As a human being she was avaricious, with an extraordinary hardness of heart and ruthlessness of will; and she died in a grotesque cause.

1926

Quetzalcoatl

The Plumed Serpent is a confession of faith, a summing up of the mystical philosophy of D. H. Lawrence. Mexico, the Indians, the cult of the Aztec god Quetzalcoatl—the Plumed Serpent—all these are pretexts, symbols made to the measure of his preoccupations. It seems only incidentally a novel, in spite of the perfection of its form; it is a record of a pilgrimage that was, that must have been, a devastating experience. Lawrence went to Mexico in the hope of finding there, among alien people and their mysterious cult, what he had failed to find in his own race or within himself: a center and a meaning to life. He went to the Indians with the hope of clinching once for all his argument that blood-nodality is the source of communion between man and man, and between man and the implacable gods. He desired to share this nodality, to wring from it the secret of the "second strength" which gives magic powers to a man. But blood itself stood between him and his desire.

"She had noticed that usually, when an Indian looked at a white man, both stood back from actual contact, from actual meeting of each other's eyes. They left a wide space of neutral territory between them. . . ." This acute flash of insight he gives to Kate Leslie, the Irish woman, the only white person among his chief characters. She carries all the burden of doubt and fear for the author, and is the most valid human being in the book. With all his will, his psychoanalytic equipment, and his curiosity, which is like a steel probe, Lawrence could not cross this neutral territory. These, and his poetic imagination touched to wonder drive him resistlessly within touching distance. His mind sniffs out delicately, the filaments of his thought are like living nerve-ends, they shudder and are repelled at the nearness of a secret steeped, for him, in cosmic possibilities. He remains a stranger gazing at a mystery he cannot share, but still hopes to ravish, and his fancy dilates it to monstrous proportions.

He has confessed somewhere that he was in a raging temper from the moment he passed over the line from the United States to Mexico. He blames this on the vibrations of cruelty and bloodshed in the country, the dark hopelessness that rises from the Indians and the very soil in an almost palpable vapor. He felt that the Mexican motive of existence is hatred. Lawrence is a good hater; he should know hate when he sees it. But it was not altogether an occult effluvium from the earth. His terror came halfway to meet it. A serpent lies coiled in the Indian vitals; their eyes are centerless. He cannot acknowledge blood-kin with them. He gives them a soul and takes it away again; they are dragon worshipers, only half-created; he surmises reptilian ichor in their veins. Yet he loves their beauty, and with all his soul he adores their phallic god; and so he remain a stranger, but makes his obeisance.

The genius of Lawrence lies in his power to create out of his own inner experience, his own sensitized fibers, a personal world which is also our world, peopled with human beings recognizably of our own time and place. His world is a place of complex despair, his tragedies are of the individual temperament in double conflict, against the inner nightmare and the outer unendurable fact. Terror of death and nausea of life, sexual egotism and fear, a bitter will-to-power and an aspiration after mystical apartness, an impotent desire for the act of faith, combine into a senseless widdershins; they spin dizzily on their own centers of sensation, with a sick void at the core.

Lawrence has turned away from this world, these persons, exhausted by their futility, unable to admit that their despairs and futilities are also his own. "Give me the mystery and let the world live again for me," Kate cried in her own soul. "And deliver me from man's automatism!" This woman is a perfect study of that last upsurge of romantic sex-hunger, disguised as a quest of the spirit, that comes with the grand climacteric. Lawrence identifies her purpose with his own, she represents his effort to touch the darkly burning Indian mystery. It could not happen: he is too involved in preconceptions and simple human prejudice. His artificial Western mysticism came in collision with the truly occult mind of the Indian, and he suffered an extraordinary shock. He turned soothsayer, and began to interpret by a formula: the result is a fresh myth of the Indian, a deeply emotional conception, but a myth none the less, and a debased one.

For sheer magnificence of writing, Lawrence has surpassed himself. His style has ripened, softened, there is a melancholy hint of the overrichness of autumn. Who looks for mere phrases from him? He writes by the passage, by the chapter, a prose flexible as a whiplash, uneven and harmonious as breakers rolling upon a beach, and the sound is music. His language rises from the page not in words but in a series of images before the eye: human beings move in vivid landscapes, wrapped in a physical remoteness, yet speaking with a ghostly intimacy, as if you were listening to the secret pulse of their veins.

All of Mexico that can be *seen* is here, evoked clearly with the fervor of things remembered out of impressions that filled the mind to bursting. There is no laborious building up of local color, but an immense and prodigal feeling for the background, for every minute detail seen with the eyes of a poet. He makes you a radiant gift of the place. It is no Rousseau-like jungle of patterned leaves and fruits half concealing impersonally savage beasts. The skies change, the lights and colors, the smells and feel of the air change with the time of day; the masses of the Indians move with purpose against this shifting landscape; the five chief characters live out a romantic drama of emotions, accompanied by all the commonplaces of every day, of dress, of food, of weather. A nation-wide political and religious movement provides the framework for a picture that does not omit a leaf, a hanging fruit, an animal, a cloud, a mood, of the visible Mexico. Lawrence puts in besides all his own accumulated protest against the things he hates: his grudge against women as opposed to his concept of woman, his loathing of the machine. His contempt for revolution and the poor is arrogant, not aristocratic: but he is plainly proud of his attitude. It is a part of his curiously squeamish disgust of human contact.

The triumph of this book as a work of art lies in this: that out of his confusions, the divisions of his mind, he has gained by sheer poetic power to a fine order, a mystical truth above his obsessions and debased occult dogma.

> Mexico pulls you down, the people pull you down like a great weight! But it may be they pull you down as the earth pull of gravitation does, that you can balance on your feet. Maybe they draw you down as the

earth draws down the roots of the tree so that it may be clenched deep in the soil. . . . Loose leaves and aeroplanes blow away on the wind, in what they call freedom. . . . All that matters to me are the roots that reach down beyond all destruction.

Thus Ramon, the Spanish-Indian scholar who has taken upon himself the role of the living Quetzalcoatl. "God must come to the Mexicans in a blanket and huaraches, else he is no god of the Mexican. . . . We live by manifestations." A full-blooded Indian joins him in the role of Huitzilopochtli, the god of war. Kate Leslie goes with them as Malintzi, wife of the war-god. They set about to restore the old phallic cult, based on an ancient religious tenet of the human race: that the male element is godhead, that man carries the unique secret of creation in his loins, that divinity originates in the potent germ. "I look . . . for my own manhood," says the living Quetzalcoatl. "It comes from the middle from God. . . . I have nothing but my manhood. The God gives it to me, and leaves me to do further." And again: "The universe is a nest of dragons, with a perfectly unfathomable life mystery at the center of it. . . . If I call the mystery the Morning Star, what does it matter? . . . And man is a creature who wins his own creation inch by inch from the nest of cosmic dragons." "Man is a column of blood, woman is a valley of blood." And man must be saved again by blood. Blood touches blood in the Morning Star, and thus the otherwise incommunicable secret will be shared.

And what, in fact, is the conclusion after all this grandiose preparation? The Indians must still be saved by a superior expert tribal Messiah and by means of the same worn-out devices. The living Quetzalcoatl works through the cumbrous machinery of drums, erotic-mystic ritual, ceremonial bloodshed. He is a marvelous study of the priestly pedagogue fired with a fanatic vision of a world saved and standing at his right hand praising his name forever. This is the answer we are given to a great quest for the meaning of life: man is not a god, and he must die. But he may hypnotize himself into momentary forgetfulness by means of ceremonial robes and a chorus of mystic mumblings, accompanied by synthesized gesture in praise of his own virility, that most variable and treacherous of all his powers.

The hymns of Quetzalcoatl form a broken cycle through the story, curious interruptions to the muscular power of the prose. There are many beautiful lines: "And say to thy sorrow, 'Ax, thou art cutting me down. Yet did a spark fly out of thy edge and my wound.' " Mostly they are booming, hollow phrases, involved as the high-sounding nonsense of a sixteenth-century Spanish mystic; their ecstasy follows the pattern of artificial raptures, self-conscious as a group of Gurdjieff's American disciples revolving in a dervish dance.

Altogether Lawrence cannot be freed from the charge of pretentiousness in having invaded a mystery that remained a mystery to him, and in having set down his own personal reactions to a whole race as if they were the inspired truth. His Indians are merely what the Indians might be if they were all D. H. Lawrences. The three characters who act as his mouthpieces are simply good Europeans at bottom—further variations of Lawrence's arch-type, the flayed and suffering human being in full flight from the horrors of a realistic mechanical society, and from the frustrations of sex.

When you have read this book read *Sons and Lovers* again. You will realize the catastrophe that has overtaken Lawrence.

1926

The Charmed Life

In 1921, he was nearly eighty years old, and he had lived in Mexico for about forty years. Every day of those years he had devoted exclusively to his one interest in life: discovering and digging up buried Indian cities all over the country. He had come there, an American, a stranger, with this one idea. I had heard of him as a fabulous, ancient eccentric completely wrapped up in his theory of the origins of the Mexican Indian. "He will talk your arm off," I was told.

His shop was on the top floor of a ramshackle old building on a side street in Mexico City, reached by an outside flight of steps, and it had the weathered, open look of a shed rather than a room. The rain came in, and the dust, and the sunlight. A few battered showcases and long rough tables were piled up carelessly with "artifacts," as the Old Man was careful to call them. There were skulls and whole skeletons, bushels of jade beads and obsidian knives and bronze bells and black clay whistles in the shape of birds.

I was immensely attracted by the air of authenticity, hard to define, but easy to breathe. He was tough and lean, and his face was burned to a good wrinkled leather. He greeted me with an air of imperfect recollection as if he must have known me somewhere. We struck up an easy acquaintance at once, and he talked with the fluency of true conviction.

Sure enough, within a quarter of an hour I had his whole theory of the origin of the ancient Mexicans. It was not new or original; it was one of the early theories since rejected by later scientists, but plainly the Old Man believed he had discovered it by himself, and perhaps he had. It was religion with him, a poetic, mystical, romantic concept. About the lost continent, and how the original Mexican tribes all came from China or Mongolia in little skiffs, dodging between hundreds of islands now sunk in the sea. He loved believing it and would listen to nothing that threatened to shake his faith.

At once he invited me to go with him on a Sunday to dig in his latest buried city, outside the capital. He explained his system to me. He had unearthed nearly a half-hundred ancient cities in all parts of Mexico. One by one, in his vague phrase, he "turned them over to the government." The government thanked him kindly and sent in a staff of expert scientists to take over, and the Old Man moved on, looking for something new.

Finally by way of reward, they had given him this small and not very important city for his own, to settle down with. He sold in his shop the objects he found in the city, and with the profits he supported the digging operations on Sunday.

He showed me photographs of himself in the early days, always surrounded by Indian guides and pack-mules against landscapes of cactus or jungle, a fine figure of a man with virile black whiskers and a level, fanatic eye. There were rifles strapped to the bales on the pack-mules, and the guards bristled with firearms. "I never carried a gun," he told me. "I never needed to. I trusted my guides, and they trusted me."

I enjoyed the company of the Old Man, his impassioned singleness of purpose, his fervid opinions on his one topic of conversation, and the curiously appealing unhumanness of his existence. He was the only person I ever saw who really seemed as independent and carefree as a bird on a bough.

He ate carelessly at odd hours, fried beans and tortillas from a basket left for him by the wife of his head digger, or he would broil a scrawny chicken on a stick, offer me half, and walk about directing his men, waving the other half. He had an outdoors sort of cleanliness and freshness; his clothes were clean, but very old and mended. Who washed and mended them I never knew. My own life was full of foolish and unnecessary complications, and I envied him his wholeness. I enjoyed my own sentimental notion of him as a dear, harmless, sweet old man of an appealing sociability, riding his hobby-horse in triumph to the grave, houseless but at home, completely free of family ties and not missing them, a happy, devoted man who had known his own mind, had got what he wanted in life, and was satisfied with it. Besides he was in perfect health and never bored.

Crowds of visitors came and bought things, and he dropped the money in a cigar-box behind a showcase. He invited almost everybody to come out and watch him dig on Sundays, and a great many came, week after week, always a new set. He received a good many letters, most of them with foreign postmarks, and after a few rapid glances he dropped them into the drawer of a long table. "I know a lot of people," he said, shuffling among the heap one day. "I ought to answer these. Big bugs, too, some of them."

One day, among a pile of slant-eyed clay faces, I found a dusty, dog-eared photograph of a young girl, which appeared to have been taken about fifty years before. She was elegant, fashionable, and so astonishingly beautiful I thought such perfection could belong only to a world-famous beauty. The Old Man noticed it in my hand. "My wife," he said in his impersonal, brisk tone. "Just before we were married. She was about eighteen then."

"She is unbelievably beautiful," I said.

"She was the most beautiful woman I ever saw," he said, matter-of-factly. "She is beautiful still." He dropped the photograph in the drawer with the letters and came back talking about something else.

After that, at odd moments, while he was polishing jade beads or brushing the dust off a clay bird, he dropped little phrases about his wife and children. "She was remarkable," he said. "She had five boys in eight years. She was just too proud to have anything but boys, I used to tell her."

Again, later: "She was a perfect wife, perfect. But she wouldn't come to Mexico with me. She said it was no place to bring up children."

One day, counting his money and laying it out in small heaps, one for each workman, he remarked absently: "She's well off, you know—she has means." He poured the heaps into a small sack and left the rest in the cigar-box. "I never wanted more money than I needed from one week to the next," he said. "I don't fool with banks. People say I'll be knocked in the head and robbed some night, but I haven't been, and I won't."

One day we were talking about a plot to overthrow the Government which had just been frustrated with a good deal of uproar. "I knew about that months ago," said the Old Man. "One of my politician friends wrote me. . . ." He motioned toward the table drawer containing the letters. "You're interested in those things," he said. "Would you like to read some of those letters? They aren't private."

Would I? I spent a long summer afternoon reading the Old Man's letters from his international big bugs, and I learned then and there that hair *can* rise and blood *can* run cold. There was enough political dynamite in those casually written letters to have blown sky-high any number of important diplomatic and financial negotiations then pending between several powerful governments. The writers were of all sorts, from the high-minded and religious to the hearty, horse-trading type to the worldly, the shrewd, the professional adventurer, down to the natural moral imbecile, but they were all written in simple language with almost boyish candor and an indiscretion so complete it seemed a kind of madness.

I asked him if he had ever shown them to anyone else. "Why, no," he said, surprised at my excitement.

I tried to tell him that if these letters fell into certain hands his life would be in danger. "Nonsense," he said vigorously. "Everybody knows what I think of that stuff. I've seen 'em come and go, making history. Bah!"

"Burn these letters," I told him. "Get rid of them. Don't even be caught dead with them."

"I need them," he said. "There's a lot about ancient Mexican culture in them you didn't notice." I gave up. Perhaps the brink of destruction was his natural habitat.

A few days later, I went up the dusty stairs and, there, in a broad square of sunlight, the Old Man was sitting in a cowhide chair with a towel around his neck, and a woman was trimming his moustache with a pair of nail scissors. She was as tall as he, attenuated, with white hair, and the beauty of an aged goddess. There was an extraordinary pinched, starved kind of sweetness in her face, and she had perfect simplicity of manner. She removed the towel, and the Old Man leaped up as if she had loosed a spring. Their son, a man in middle age, a masculine reincarnation of his mother, came in from the next room, and we talked a little, and the wife asked me with gentle pride if I did not find the shop improved.

It was indeed in order, clean, bare, with the show-windows and cases set out properly, and tall vases of flowers set about. They were all as polite and agreeable to one another as if they were well-disposed strangers, but I thought the Old Man looked a little hunched and wary, and his wife and son gazed at him almost constantly as if they were absorbed in some fixed thought. They were all very beautiful people, and I liked them, but they filled the room and were not thinking about what they were saying, and I went away very soon.

The Old Man told me later they had stayed only a few days; they dropped in every four or five years to see how he was getting on. He never mentioned them again.

Afterward when I remembered him it was always most clearly in that moment when the tall woman and her tall son searched the face of their mysterious Wild Man with baffled, resigned eyes, trying still to understand him years after words wouldn't work any more, years after everything had been said and done, years after love had worn itself thin with anxieties, without in the least explaining what he was, why he had done what he did. But they had forgiven him, that was clear, and they loved him.

I understood then why the Old Man never carried a gun, never locked up his money, sat on political dynamite and human volcanoes, and never bothered to answer his slanderers. He bore a charmed life. Nothing would ever happen to him.

1942

ON WRITING

My First Speech*

I have always had a fixed notion that a writer should lead a private life and keep silent in so far as writing is concerned and let published works speak for themselves, so, in trying to tell you something of what I think and believe about certain aspects of writing, I speak strictly as an individual and not as the spokesman for one school or the enemy of another.

Legend and memory is the title of the first section of a long novel I am now working on, and I called it that because it is from these two sources I am attempting to recreate a history of my family, which begins almost with the beginnings of the settlement of America. I have for this only legend, those things I have been told or that I read as a child; and I may say here that I consider most of our published history available to children quite as legendary as the siege of Troy: and my own memory of events taking place around me at the same time. And there is a third facet: my present memory and explanation to myself of my then personal life, the life of a child, which is in itself a mystery, while being living and legendary to that same child grown up. All this is working at once in my mind, in a confusion of dimensions. This may not sound so simple, and I believe it is less simple even than it sounds. But I feel that to give a true testimony it is necessary to know and remember what I was, what I felt, and what I knew then, and not confuse it with what I know or think I know now. So, I shall try to tell the truth, but the result will be fiction. I shall not be at all surprised at this result: it is what I mean to do; it is, to my way of thinking, the way fiction is made.

* These are short hand notes taken of a lecture I made before the American Women's Club in Paris, 1934.—K.A.P.

It is a curious long process, roundabout to the last degree, like a slow chemical change, and I believe it holds true as much when one is not recreating one's own life and past but the life-history of another person. I think there are very few living characters in fiction who were not founded on a real living original. I think of Anna Karenina, Madame Bovary, and the tragic characters in *The Possessed*. Thackeray, so fas as I know, never admitted that there had ever lived an Englishwoman like Becky Sharp. He was far too chivalrous for that. But that he did know, disapprove of, and admire such a person seems to me by the internal evidence fairly certain. I believe she could not have had so much vitality, if nature had not first created her for Thackeray to transmute into a work of art.

I should dare to say that none of these characters so living in fiction would have recognized their own portraits, for if the transformation is successful the character becomes something else in its own right, as alive as the person who posed for the portrait.

This is not a particularly easy thing to do, and I think of late a great many writers have found what they consider a way out, which leads really to an impasse. I mean the very thinly disguised autobiographical novel. It is an old saying that every human being possesses in his own life and experience the material for one novel. This may be true. It is one of those generalities hard to prove or disprove. It has been accepted a shade too literally, I think, by a great group of recent writers. This tendency is to make one's self the hero or heroine of one's own adventure, in literature as in life. It is only, I think, when the writer is adult enough to face the rather disheartening truth that he is not by any means always the hero of his own little history, much less the center of the universe, that we can begin to get near a human chronicle that could be worth reading. If writers, and not always professional writers, but anyone who really has a story to tell, could only tell the facts in such matters: the plain facts, it would be worth hearing. The novel is not really the vehicle for autobiography. It grows even more confusing when literary people live in such close-knitted groups that all of them have only one experience in common, and each one sits down to give his version of it, with himself as the hero and the others either pallid, minor figures, fools, or outright villains. For in the anxiety of each one to justify himself, he hardly takes care to disguise his characters other than in a kind of distortion.

Most certainly the artist is present in all he creates. He is his own work; and, if he were not, then there could be, I think, no true creation. But it is a confession of failure of what I shall call imaginative honesty to make one's self always the shining protagonist of one's own novels. It is true there do exist, I can't name one off hand, heroes who are the wish-fulfillment of the author. Everyone knows that Stendahl (Henri Beyle) was a short, lumpy, timid fellow, unattractive, and unlucky in love. He had a kind of minor official post under Napoleon, a dull job that he detested—we know from internal evidence that Stendahl was brilliant, witty, a great sober artist. He dreamed of himself and created to his heart's desire a hero whom I consider one of the most detestable in all fiction: Julien Sorel. But Julien Sorel is nonetheless a superb creation, a work of art beyond a doubt. Still, as I follow the adventures of Julien Sorel, the workings of his pretentious, disorderly, shallow mind and heart, I am beset by the uneasy feeling that Stendahl meant him to be an admirable, complicated, unusually sensitive young man: portrait of Stendahl, the handsome French mask of little Henri Beyle—in a word. Too many quite promising young writers have been misled by the same vanity, but with less adroitness, along this same path; and how many little books do I know written by rather drab young men whose experience has not been unusual but who make themselves always the golden hero, and how many young women of ordinary charm cannot resist being either the spangle-eyed heroine or much the brightest girl in the class.

In America there is a great deal of excitement about the importance of being American. Even the writers have taken it up. When I was in America, all my writing friends were here,* sending me word that Paris, or some city in Europe, was to be their final choice of a dwelling place; when I finally came here, it was only to begin receiving letters from them all, now back in America, telling me that I was wrong to expatriate myself. The discussion runs on and on about "typical" and "not typical" American writers. So far as I am able to remember, for such classifications mean little to me, Bret Harte, Mark Twain, Sara Orne Jewett, Ralph Waldo Emerson, and other such diverse personalities are mentioned most frequently as American; while such strangely different writers as Hemingway and Hergesheimer, let us say, are called "not typical."

This may seem a digression, yet it belongs to what I am trying to say.

What is a typical American? In any profession? or state of life? I believe that different periods produce a certain typical mode of thought, or

* In France.

habit of mind, and the causes for this habit of mind are so complicatec
so much a matter of the converging of a thousand influences to a give
point, that I, for one, could never attempt to account for them. I thin
that artists are quite often not prophets, and there is very little reaso
why they should be. They have a way of being formed by their epoch, a
other people are. Their code of morals, their religions, their mode c
dress, even their styles in writing, can usually be dated and placed witl
out much trouble. Now there was a time, or so legend insists, when ther
was a stable, settled world of society, when everybody thought, felt, an
believed the same thing. This was never true, but it has become th
fashion to say so; and in America we also had our golden age, whic
seems to have ended around 1910. Now, to a great many of us, and th
includes the larger number of our so-called modern writers, there hav
been varieties of experience, historical changes. For some of them, lil
dates from the great war.* Their independent life, if that after-war lil
could be said to have had any independence (it had revolt, and disill\
sion, and hardship, and the privilege of sinking or swimming); but th
is hardly independence, and above all there is nothing solid or comfoɪ
able about it. Also, with the new mixture of races, the breaking up ɑ
caste to some extent, economic upheavals, is it not possible that tl
author is merely again being the child of his time and is running ↑
variety instead of to type? But we have always had variety.

We have always had variety, and an American writer who, thirstir
for change, imitates Joyce is at least stating a point of view and a prefe
ence not likely to make his fortune; but he had better do that than ↑
write slick fiction for a slick weekly or attempt to return to an Americ
and an American mode of thought which no longer exists except po
sibly in a past which is too recent to be appropriately revived. What w
look upon now as typical may simply have been, once, one thing amor
many but was chosen as a type. You might say that Buffalo Bill was
typical American, or that Mark Twain was typical, or that Charles Fraɪ
cis Adams is, or that Nathan Hale was, or Jesse James. I believe tha
these men were not typical at all. They were individuals, who by th
mysterious workings of environment and education in blood and trad
tion became the finished products of a certain sort of society; more tha
that, a certain section or region of America. They became typical in tw
ways, by being distinguished enough to be imitated and by being so a

* 1914–1918.

nired or hated that their lives became symbols: but there was really, let
is remember, only one of each of these men; and, different as they are,
they were all Americans. Our blood has become pretty well mixed by
ow, and it was fairly well mixed before we came here. It is European or
Oriental blood, transplanted to a new Continent, our roots are here; and
ur types are as varied. I dare say there is no man living who can with
ertainty name *all* the bloods that flow in his veins.

Lately the mixing process has speeded up and is now going through a
ew phase. The changes that are taking place will end by giving us a new
et of features, so that I, for one, would be puzzled to say just what is a
ypical American. Think of our American writers. Let me name a few of
hem at random. They come on all levels of talent and achievement,
rom several periods, and from all parts of that tremendous country.
Herman Melville, Sherwood Anderson, Edgar Allan Poe, Henry Adams,
Steven Crane, Sinclair Lewis, Ralph Waldo Emerson, Henry James,
Walt Whitman, John Dos Passos, Ernest Hemingway, Washington Irv-
ng. Think of these last two together. But how can we say that they are
ot all Americans, and each one typically, oh quite typically, exactly him-
elf and nobody else. They are typical as Chekhov, Dostoievsky, and
Tolstoy are typical Russians, and each one a unique creature. I should
hink, one might very well say that Joyce is not a typical Irishman. No,
ut now that he has done it it is hard to imagine any other than an Irishman reacting in just such a way against his particular country, time, and
ociety. It is fairly easy to say that now, because it just happens that no
ne but this one Irishman has ever behaved in just that way. Whether
ou like him or not, I fancy he is here to stay for some time. He will be
here in the road: you may walk around him, climb over him, or dig
nder; but he will be there. I admire him immensely, but one of him is
nough. Indeed, that is all there *can* be of him. I know better than to try
o imitate him, and I wouldn't be influenced by him for the world; but I
hink he is going to begin a tradition, indeed has already. Now when one
peaks of tradition, even American tradition, which we are in the habit
f speaking of as new, it is better to remember that there are already a
reat many different traditions and most of them quite feasible. The
rtist, after having served his apprenticeship, may discover in what tradi-
ion he belongs. But the artist is usually too busy and too preoccupied
with his own undertaking to worry much about whether he has got into
he right tradition, or, indeed, into any at all. There have been more of

them lately worrying about how they were going to get out of the beaten track. I think they were mistaken. An artist does better to leave all such classifications to the critics. He had better follow the bent of his own mind, whether it is for the moment fashionable or not; and it isn't for him to worry about whether he is really great or a true genius: that throws him off most frightfully, and his audience too. I should say that a major work of art occurs in any medium when a first-rate creative intelligence gets hold of a great theme and does something hitherto unexampled with it. And if this happens in our time we had better bless our luck and not worry about whether this marks the beginning or the end of a tradition. The other day a young writing friend of mine burst out suddenly: "I am going to write like Racine!" Now this is an American boy, an Irish-American boy with a very good talent. He added, in a moment "I am Racine." Well, of course, the only possible answer to that was "You're nothing of the sort." And then he explained, and it wasn't so foolish as all that: he meant he admired the qualities of clearness and directness in the style of Racine, what he called Racine's coldness. He meant, after all, that he feels a sympathy in his mind for that kind of writing; and if he goes on writing and his mind goes on working that way he may develop a good measured spare style. But I feel pretty certain no one will even be reminded of Racine by it; above all, not if our American boy does a really good job.

It is my belief that the less typical a writer is the less you are able to catalogue him, the more apt he is to be a writer worth your attention. We don't need any more types. We need individuals. We always did need them. The value of a writer can be measured best, probably, by his capacity to express what he feels, knows, is, has been, has seen, and experienced, by means of this paraphrase which is art, this process of taking his own material and making what he wants to make of it. He cannot do this, indeed he is not an artist, if he allows himself to be hampered by any set of conventions outside of the severe laws and limitations of his own medium. No one else can tell him what life is like to him, in what colors he sees the world. He cannot sit down and say, Go to, I will be a writer because it's an interesting career! Even less can he say, I must be an American writer; or French, or whatever. He has already been born one kind of person or another, and taking thought about it cannot change much. He cannot even worry about whether the publishers are going to accept his work or not; if he does, he is as good as done for: he may as well never have begun. He may be interpreter, critic, rebel, prophet, conformist, devil, or angel, or he may be all these things in turn, or all of them a little at once; but he can be none of these things to order: nobody's order, not even his own.

Simply stated, maybe too simply, it is the writer's business first to have something of his own to say; second, to say it in his own language and style. You must have heard this many times before; but I think it is one of the primary rules to keep in mind. The great thing is to convey to you, in this saying, a sense of the reality and the truth of what he tells you, with some new light thrown upon it that gives you a glimpse into some wider world not built with hands. It is like the dizzying blue in the upper right-hand corner of some of Brueghel's paintings. I remember especially the two versions of the fall of Icarus. The lower left-hand corner is real, no doubt about it: we have all seen such fields, such figures of men, such furrows and animals; but the upper right-hand corner is true too, though it is this vast transfiguration of blue such as we may never have seen in the sky over us, but it exists for us because Brueghel has made it. Artists create monsters and many different sorts of landscapes; and they are true, if the artists are great enough to show you what they have seen. Matisse has said: the painter should paint the thing he knows. So far as it goes, this is good advice. The question is, how much more does any artist know imaginatively than factually? That is his test; for Dante knew both heaven and hell without ever having seen them; and described them for us so that we know them too: and Shakespeare, taking legends and his own great fertility, created for us countries which did not exist until then: but they exist now, and we may travel in them when we please. Only yesterday, I was looking again at some of Dürer's scenes representing St. John's revelations, and I am glad Dürer chose not to stick by the thing he knew with the eye of the flesh even though that was an exceptionally clear and magical eye too. But I have his view of the Apocalypse, and it is mine: I was there.

So the reader, whether with pleasure, pain, or even disgust (it is not necessary for you always to be pleased), must still find himself in the atmosphere created for him by the artists, and the artists do not always create a pleasant world, because that is not their business. If they do that, you will be right not to trust them in anything. We must leave all that to people whose affair it is, to smooth our daily existence a little. Great art is hardly ever agreeable; the artist should remind you that, for some, experience is a horror in this world, and that the human imagination also knows horror. He should direct you to points of view you have not examined before, or cause you to comprehend, even if you do not sympathize with predicaments not your own, ways of life, manners of speech, even of dress, above all of the unique human heart, outside of your normal experience. And this can better be done by presentation than by argument. This presentation must be real, with a truth beyond the artist's own prejudices, loves, hates; I mean his personal ones. The outright propagandist sets up in me such a fury of opposition I am not apt to care much whether he has got his facts straight or not. He is like someone standing on your toes, between you and an open window, describing the view to you. All I ask of him to do is to open the window, stand out of the way, and let me look at the view for myself. Now truth is a very tall word, and we are rather apt to tag our pet theories and beliefs with this abused word. Let me reconsider a moment and say, the writer must have honesty, he should not wilfully distort and obscure. Now I have said always that honesty in any case is not enough, but it is an indispensable element in the arts. No legend is ever true, but I believe all of them are founded on some germ of truth; and even these truths appear in different lights to every mind they are presented to, and the legend is that work of art which goes on in the human mind, adding to and arranging, harmonizing and rounding out, making larger or smaller than life, and holding the entire finished product in a good light and asking you to believe it. And it is true. No memory is really faithful. It has too far to go, too many changing landscapes of the human mind and heart, to bear any sort of really trustworthy witness, except in part. So the truth in art is got by change. In the work of art, nothing can be accidental: the sprawling, chaotic sense of that word as we use it in everyday life, where so many things happen to us that we by no means plan, it takes craftsmanship quite often beyond our powers to manage by plan even a short day for ourselves. The craftsmanship of the artist can make what he wishes of anything that excites his imagination. Craftsmanship is a homely, workaday thing. It is a little like making shoes, or weaving cloth. A writer may be inspired occasionally: that's his good luck; but he doesn't learn to write by inspiration: he works at it. In that sense the writer is a worker, a workingman, a workingwoman. Writing is not an elegant pastime, it is a sober and hardworked trade, which gives great joy to the worker. The artist is first a worker. He must roll up his sleeves and get to work like a bricklayer. The romantic notion of the artist—persons who live their romances, those who depend on the gestures, the dress, the habits, of what they hope is genius—hoping by presenting the appearance of genius, genius would be added to them.

It is not a career, it is a vocation; it is not a means to fame and glory—it is a discipline of living—and unless you think this, it is better not to take it up. It is not the sort of thing one "takes up" as one might take up knitting and put it down again.

All this you can learn about the mechanics, the technique, and it is all to the good for your education. It cannot make you an artist. But it will make of you a better reader, a cleverer critic, it will make of you some one the artist must look out for, and it will make for him an audience that he can't trifle with even if he would.

1934

Notes on Writing

(from the Journal of
Katherine Anne Porter)

Berlin, December, 1931
from a letter to G., in Madrid

My poem* as I look at it this morning is not so good as I hoped. It began well and may end well, but there is a long way to go. Sometimes I have regretted destroying all that poetry I worked on for so many years, but now I believe I was right.

The added notes on your Martin story help greatly, those very mysterious and personal allusions are better dredged up to the surface. It is all very well to be allusive and let your reader fill up the intervals with his own imagination, if you are writing that kind of story, or set out to write for that kind of reader. But this Martin is someone you should explain and make clear to the reader straight through. There is one thing I must say, please don't repeat words, phrases, as a device to increase intensity. This hardly ever works and it doesn't work here. Repetition can be extremely effective; it is as useful as the pause, as the change of rhythm, but it must be used carefully. Certainly not more than once in a long story and at a given exact point would I try it. I can't tell you what gives true intensity, but I know it when I find it, even in my own work—there perhaps first of all. It is not a matter of how you feel, at any one moment, certainly not at the moment of writing. A calculated coldness is the best mood for that, most often. Feeling is more than mood, it is a whole way of being, it is the nature you are born with, you cannot invent it. The question is, how to convey a sense of whatever is *there*, as feeling, within you, to the reader; and that is a problem of technical expertness. I can't tell you how to go about getting this technique either, for that also

* After a Long Journey, p. 493.

442

is an internal matter, if it is to have any value beyond a kind of juggling or tight rope walking. You'll know it when you have it, and you will finally be able to depend upon it somewhat. But for myself, unless my material, my feelings and my problem in each new piece of work are not well ahead of my technical skill at that moment, I should distrust the whole thing. When virtuosity gets the upper hand of your theme, or is better than your idea, it is time to quit. Be bold, and try not to fall in love with your faults. Don't be so afraid of giving yourself away either, for if you write, you must. And if you can't face that, better not write.

Berlin, December, 1931

A young poet here, asked me what I was reading, and when I told him I was working with my teacher on the *Elegies* of Rainer Maria Rilke, he made a sour little mouth, and said, "Oh, don't read Rilke. He belongs to the old romantic soft-headed Germany that has been our ruin. The new Germany is hard, strong, we will have a new race of poets, tough and quick, like your prize fighters."

He gave me some of his poems to read, and I worked them out with my teacher. The strangest thing: his words were tough and the rhythms harsh, the ideas all the most grossly brutal; and yet, it was vague weak stuff in the end. It was very embarrassing to give it back to him because I did not know what to say.

L. and von G. were talking about Nietzsche tonight in the Wiener Café, and after a while, I did not listen. Nietzsche is dangerous because his mind has power without intelligence; he is all will without enlightenment. His phrases are inflated, full of violence, a gross kind of cruel poetry—like Wagner's music. They both throw a hypnotic influence over their hearers. But I could always resist hypnotists. When I think of Nietzsche and Wagner, at once by simple association I find charlatans of all kinds and degrees—witch doctors, mountebanks, religious revivalists, shouting demagogues, snake charmers, fortune tellers, and sufferers from erotic religious hysteria. And madness. In Nietzsche's case, a real, clinical madness: his diseased brain gave his style the brilliancy of a rotting fish. L. and von G. worship them both with a religious awe.

When R. talks about religion, and he hovers around the subject almost continually, I am always restless because he is all malice, the most malicious man I ever knew, who speaks evil of everyone, and plays evil tricks with the most terrifying irresponsibility. I am distinctly unsympathetic when he tells me of his long search for God, and hints at his religious practices and exercises, which, if I know anything at all about religion, seem rather in the nature of suggestive magic. He tells me flatly that because I am a woman, the higher levels of religious experience are not for me. I can only tell him that I have heard that before. "Religious experience belongs exclusively to the masculine principle," he assures me. "Only ample, generous natures are capable of the love of God." This last is no doubt true. Saints and poets have proved it, but I am offended by the words in a mouth capable of such evil as I have heard from it.

R.'s talk for some reason reminded me of Gorky's estimate of Tolstoy —as a man who loved God and peasants, hated women and literature. This is perhaps too neat, but very sharp, too. Tolstoy was one of the purest egoists known to literature. He could love God, his invisible, unanswerable ally: and peasants, his humble inferiors waiting for him to teach them the truth. But women and literature have destinies of their own, and proved to be unconquerable antagonists. God and peasants: Tolstoy could look up, look down, but he could not look level. His self-love made him a prophet, his genius made him a great artist, but not God himself could make a saint of him. And yet in the ferocity of his pride, a saint he would be. . . .

Basel, Summer, 1932

Remember: The serious, bitterly humiliated little boy, about three years old, on the dusty country train in Central Texas, with a tin chamber pot wedged on his head; over his ears, down to the back of his neck almost, but not far enough over his face to hide the forlorn, hopeless shame in his eyes. Worried country mother taking him to the doctor in town. Other passengers stopped to gaze and inquire. She talked freely about the disaster as if it were a disease, and described the symptoms as they developed. "I seen he was restless," she said, "he wanted somethin to play with. I kep on givin him everythin I could think of, things I thought he couldn't break up or damage hisself with, but nothin satisfied him. He wouldn't go out and play in the yard, and he wouldn't be quiet in the house, so finally I gave him his potty to play with, and the last I seen of him he was fillin it with water from the hydrant and pourin it on the crepe myrtle, so I jus said to myself that don't do no harm; and I turned my back it wasn't more than a minute, I declare, and the next thing I knew there he was just like you see him now with it wedged down over his skull tight as wax. I tried everythin," she said, "soap and sweet oil and even a can opener, but I was too scared of hurtin him. It musta happened as quick as lightnin," she told the other passengers, "I can't think what got into him," as who should say, One moment he was in the best of health, and the next he was struck down before my eyes. "But the doctor, he'll know somethin to do, I hope. The funniest thing about it," she said mournfully, "is, this is the very first time he ever went to the doctor in his life." Her eyes, sweet and very blue, rested in fond bafflement on her prodigiously afflicted child. He gazed past her and the surrounding strangers with the solemn awful humiliation of one whose predicament is beyond pity, and so should never have been exposed to curious eyes.

Basel, November, 1932

Worked this afternoon on some notes for *Noon Wine*. The cold darkness is down once more, the beggar's grind-organ is still whining the same miserable tune over and over; it has been whining since early this morning with hardly a pause. The beggar is very fat, with a bald, scaly head; an ill-humored looking fellow. His flesh sags on him like dirty rags, and he has trespassed on that curve in the bridge (the Rheinbrücke), where the artist goes to repaint, by the changing lights and colors of weather and time of day and season, his one theme: the Münster. I have seen this painting change from lush greens and harrowing pinks to morbid purple, to pallid tans and mud tints and swooning grays in the course of these five months in Basel. Yesterday, he went as usual, to set up his easel, and there stood the fat beggar, scowling and twisting the mean tune out of his barrel organ. He did not give way an inch, so the painter edged around him, set up his canvas stool, seated himself, thumb in palette, raised his arm and began grandiosely to sweep the brush over the canvas. Every time the beggar's arm turned with the crank of the barrel organ, he would jog the painter, and the painter would squirm, but nothing more happened. I decided, then, the beggar should never have another pfennig from me if he loses a hundred pounds from starvation. The painter worked there patiently for an hour, shabby and thin and hungry looking—more than ever so, compared to the fat-jowled beggar. . . .

Next day. The painter is not there today, but the beggar is. And taking in money, too.

Paris, Summer, 1936
"Un Crime est Soupçonné"

Every day in the Paris newspapers there are wonderfully grim, comic stories; full of plot and action; with beginning, middle and end—everything the American correspondence schools for short-story writing furnish as a magic formula. "How do you know you can't write? If you will, you can." I know a dreary young man who takes all his plots from the newspaper stories, dresses them up a little, and sells them as fiction. Does fairly well, too. The French newspaper writers are all "literary" men. Apparently, the young man would find his work much easier here, where the style of the *roman policier* or of our own "True Confessions" has been brought to fine flower in the daily news column. The boy who killed his grandmother with a hatchet for her savings belt, the girl who poisoned her parents for their insurance, the man who strangled his mistress after she eloped with him and turned over her husband's savings: are made happy, reading about themselves the next day. There they are, their photographs retouched to bring out their secret characters, their speech garbled and high flown, appearing before the public at last as they had hoped—heroes and heroines in a pulp paper romance.

Memory translation from the infamous *Paris Soir:* "Last night in all Paris there was not a more unfortunate being than Pierre. . . . as, drawing his shabby coat collar about his ears to protect himself from the autumnal rain which beat upon his head with the insistent cruelty of his own thoughts, he found his way with the certitude of long habit and the trance-like stride of a sleepwalker to the door of his own apartment, number ——, rue ——. For months, who knows? perhaps for long dolorous years, he had been prey to the most humiliating suspicions that can afflict a husband; more, a husband who had devoted his heart to an idle and frivolous wife who, at his expense and without the slightest consideration, had cultivated insidiously a taste for the most perverse and exigent pleasures. Pierre . . . with the generosity of a noble nature, had long refused to entertain the ultimate, the darkest suspicion against his life companion, though for some time past he had been subjected to oblique glances from his neighbors, and remarks charged with double meanings from his friends dwelling in the same tenement. He had resolved at last to put an end to this situation. Having arrived at his own door an hour earlier than usual, he paused and applied his ear to the panel. Voices murmuring indistinctly proved that his wretched wife was not alone, and moreover, the accents of the intruder upon his domestic peace and honor were all too familiar to him. With a bold gesture he turned the knob, opened the door violently and stood upon the threshold of a small middle-class kitchen like any other, with the aroma of soup warming the air, the rain beating upon the window panes like the fingers of death. Face to face with his destiny he . . ."

Upshot was, he killed the intruder then and there. Unfamiliar and spicy twist: his wife's lover was a woman. This episode was good for a long series of similar narratives, with photographs, following the wronged hero through prison, his trial, his acquittal and triumphant return to freedom. Our own popular press, doing its very best, can't half come up to the French.

Other items: The Missing Persons Bureau report that though thousands of persons disappear annually in Paris, an astonishingly large number of them turn up again, good as new. Voluntary disappearance is what the Police always expect, though of course sometimes they are wrong, with very disastrous results. They refused to look for Jean de Koven because they took it for granted she had gone for a week-end of pleasure somewhere. Their over-sophisticated state of mind is based firmly on thousands of experiences like this: A wife reports that her husband has been away from home for three days, leaving no word. She fears he has been murdered. The police locate him in a small suburban hotel with a young woman, both in fine fettle. They report to the wife that her husband has been found, is in good health, will return soon, but they cannot tell her where he is because he does not wish her to know. The sequel to this story rarely becomes matter for the police, French wives being notably able to cope unaided with such crises.

Or: a young woman over twenty-one years of age disappears, to the natural horror of her parents. Police report they have found her, in pleasant company, in a safe place. She will return unharmed, if perhaps a little more mature. Father flies into a socially correct fury, shouting that it is quite impossible, she is a virtuous girl, let him lay hands on that hussy and her seducer, what he won't do to them both. Police warn him he must harm neither of them, it is not unusual nor a tragedy, and unless he promises to treat the girl well, he will not be allowed to see her at all.

Again: a rich South American living in Paris, wished to marry, but had destroyed his manhood by dissipation. A virile but poverty-cursed young Italian sold him one testicle for ten thousand lire. The operation was a success. But busy-bodies of the Italian's family, thinking to make more of the bargain, decided the operation was a crime in spite of his consent for payment, and brought the case into court. The Paris judge threw it out, with the decision that, since the South American had married and become a father, and since the young Italian was better off financially and still able, if he liked, to become a father also, all concerned were happier than if the transaction had never taken place.

Similar things may happen anywhere, but the decisions seem to me uniquely French, full of sound sense and the long view. As for the plots, they are of course most useful, if you still think plot is necessary, with only one disadvantage: they have been done already, and recently, and the only really important things in them are those you will *have to imagine for yourself*: all the internal circumstances that led up to the act, and led away from it, and if you undertake this, you may as well give up the comic aspects at once, or be able to put them in their proper proportions.

There are certain aspects of current life and certain kinds of people not worth writing about, but their stories are most often to be found in the newspapers. They belong to that level of realism which furnishes material for the newspaper reporters, who by their fictional, cinematographic treatment of human behavior and motives, furnish to gangsters, adultresses, delinquent boys and girls, politicians and other public figures, an ideal pattern of conduct. I once saw in New York a moving picture of a captured gunman's moll being conducted to jail by the police. Her head was thrown back at the angle which indicates ecstatic emotion, her waved hair was becomingly loosened, her eyes were half-closed. As she leaned upon the arm of her policeman, the long lines of her thin body assumed precisely the careful pose of her prototype in a motion picture play—not of the underworld, but of the romantic heroine of a love drama. She knew how to carry herself before the camera because she had seen herself in the films as she believed herself to be. Such characters do not belong to life in the least, but to a department of fiction.

Paris, Fall, 1936

Perhaps in time I shall learn to live more deeply and consistently in that undistracted center of being where the will does not intrude, and the sense of time passing is lost, or has no power over the imagination. Of the three dimensions of time, only the past is "real" in the absolute sense that it has occurred, the future is only a concept, and the present is that fateful split second in which all action takes place. One of the most disturbing habits of the human mind is its willful and destructive forgetting of whatever in its past does not flatter or confirm its present point of view. I must very often refer far back in time to seek the meaning or explanation of today's smallest event, and I have long since lost the power to be astonished at what I find there. This constant exercise of memory seems to be the chief occupation of my mind, and all my experience seems to be simply memory, with continuity, marginal notes, constant revision and comparison of one thing with another. Now and again thousands of memories converge, harmonize, arrange themselves around a central idea in a coherent form, and I write a story. I keep notes and journals only because I write a great deal, and the habit of writing helps me to arrange, annotate, stow away conveniently the references I may need later. Yet when I begin a story, I can never work in any of those promising paragraphs, those apt phrases, those small turns of anecdote I had believed would be so valuable. I must know a story "by heart" and I must write from memory. Certain writing friends whose judgments I admire, have told me I lack detail, exact observation of the physical world, my people hardly ever have features, or not enough—that they live in empty houses, et cetera. At one time, I was so impressed by this criticism, I used to sit on a camp stool before a landscape and note down literally every object, every color, form, stick and stone before my eyes. But when I remembered that landscape, it was quite simply not in those terms that I remembered it, and it was no good pretending I did, and no good attempting to describe it because it got in the way of what I was really trying to tell. I was brought up with horses, I have harnessed, saddled, driven and ridden many a horse, but to this day I do not know the names for the different parts of a harness. I have often thought I would learn them and write them down in a note book. But to what end? I have two large cabinets full of notes already.

1940

Three Statements
about Writing

Answers to Seven Questions

1. *Are you conscious, in your own writing, of the existence of a "usable past"? Is this mostly American? What figures would you designate as elements in it? Would you say, for example, that Henry James's work is more relevant to the present and future of American writing than Walt Whitman's?*

All my past is "usable," in the sense that my material consists of memory, legend, personal experience, and acquired knowledge. They combine in a constant process of re-creation. I am quite unable to separate the influence of literature or the history of literary figures from influences of background, upbringing, ancestry; or to say just what is American and what is not. On one level of experience and a very important one, I could write an autobiography based on my reading until I was twenty-five.

Henry James and Walt Whitman are relevant to the past and present of American literature or of any other literature. They are world figures, they are both artists, it is better not to mortgage the future by excluding either. Be certain that if the present forces and influences bury either of them, the future will dig him up again. The James-minded and the Whitman-minded people have both the right to their own kind of nourishment.

For myself I choose James, holding as I do with the conscious, disciplined artist, the serious expert against the expansive, indiscriminately "cosmic" sort. James, I believe, was the better workman, the more advanced craftsman, a better thinker, a man with a heavier load to carry than Whitman, His feelings are deeper and more complex than Whitman's; he had more confusing choices to make, he faced and labored over harder problems. I am always thrown off by arm-waving and shouting, I am never convinced by breast-beating or huge shapeless statements of generalized emotion. In particular, I think the influence of Whitman on certain American writers has been disastrous, for he encourages them in the vices or self-love (often disguised as love of humanity, or the working classes, or God), the assumption of prophetic powers, of romantic superiority to the limitations of craftsmanship, inflated feeling and slovenly expression.

Neither James nor Whitman is more relevant to the present and future of American literature than, say, Hawthorne or Melville, Stephen Crane or Emily Dickinson; or for that matter, any other first-rank poet or novelist or critic of any time or country. James or Whitman? The young writer will only confuse himself, neglect the natural sources of his education as artist, cramp the growth of his sympathies, by lining up in such a scrimmage. American literature belongs to the great body of world literature, it should be varied and free to flow into what channels the future shall open; all attempts to limit and exclude at this early day would be stupid, and I sincerely hope, futile. If a young artist must choose a master to admire and emulate, that choice should be made according to his own needs from the widest possible field and after a varied experience of study. By then perhaps he shall have seen the folly of choosing a master. One suggestion: artists are not political candidates; and art is not an arena for gladiatorial contests.

2. *Do you think of yourself as writing for a definite audience? If so, how would you describe this audience? Would you say that the audience for serious American writing has grown or contracted in the last ten years?*

In the beginning I was not writing for any audience, but spent a great while secretly and with great absorption trying to master a craft, to find a medium; my respect for this medium and the masters of it—no two of them alike—is very great. My search was all for the clearest and most arresting way to tell the things I wished to tell. I still do not write for any definite audience, though perhaps I have in mind a kind of composite reader.

It appears to me that the audience for serious American writing has grown in the past ten years. This opinion is based on my own observation of an extended reputation, a widening sphere of influence, an increasing number of readers, among poets, novelists, and critics of our first rank.

It is true that I place great value on certain kinds of perceptive criticism but neither praise nor blame affects my actual work, for I am under a compulsion to write as I do; when I am working I forget who approved and who dispraised, and why. The worker in an art is dyed in his own color, it is useless to ask him to change his faults or his virtues; he must, rather more literally than most men, work out his own salvation. No novelist or poet could possibly ask himself, while working: "What will a certain critic think of this? Will this be acceptable to my publisher? Will this do for a certain magazine? Will my family and friends approve of this?" Imagine what that would lead to. . . . And how much worse, if he must be thinking, "What will my political cell or block think of this? Am I hewing to the party line? Do I stand to lose my job, or head, on this?" This is really the road by which the artist perishes.

3. *Do you place much value on the criticism your work has received? Would you agree that the corruption of the literary supplements by advertising in the case of the newspapers—and political pressures—in the case of the liberal weeklies—has made serious literary criticism an isolated cult?*

As to criticism being an isolated cult, for the causes you suggest or any other, serious literary criticism was never a crowded field; it cannot be produced by a formula or in bulk any more than can good poetry or fiction. It is not, any more than it ever was, the impassioned concern of a huge public. Proportionately to number, both of readers and publishers, there are as many good critics who have a normal audience as ever. We are discussing the art of literature and the art of criticism, and this has nothing to do with the vast industry of copious publishing, and hasty reviewing, under pressure from the advertising departments, or political pressure. It is a pernicious system: but I surmise the same kind of threat to freedom in a recently organized group of revolutionary artists who are out to fight and suppress if they can, all "reactionary" artists—that is, all artists who do not subscribe to their particular political faith.

4. Have you found it possible to make a living by writing the sort of thing you want to, and without the aid of such crutches as teaching and editorial work? Do you think there is any place in our present economic system for literature as a profession?

No, there has not been a living in it, so far. The history of literature, musical composition, painting shows there has never been a living in art, except by flukes of fortune; by weight of long, cumulative reputation, or generosity of a patron; a prize, a subsidy, a commission of some kind; or (in the American style) anonymous and shamefaced hackwork; in the English style, a tradition of hackwork, openly acknowledged if deplored. The grand old English hack is a melancholy spectacle perhaps, but a figure not without dignity. He is a man who sticks by his trade, does the best he can with it on its own terms, and abides by the consequences of his choice, with a kind of confidence in his way of life that has some merit, certainly.

Literature as a profession? It *is* a profession, and the professional literary man is on his own as any other professional man is.

If you mean, is there any place in our present economic system for the practice of literature as a source of steady income and economic security, I should say, no. There never has been, in any system, any guarantee of economic security for the artist, unless he took a job and worked under orders as other men do for a steady living. In the arts, you simply cannot secure your bread and your freedom of action too. You cannot be a hostile critic of society and expect society to feed you regularly. The artist of the present day is demanding (I think childishly) that he be given, free, a great many irreconcilable rights and privileges. He wants as a right freedoms which the great spirits of all time have had to fight and often to die for. If he wants freedom, let him fight and die for it too, if he must, and not expect it to be handed to him on a silver plate.

5. Do you find, in retrospect, that your writing reveals any allegiance to any group, class, organization, region, religion, or system of thought, or do you conceive of it as mainly the expression of yourself as an individual?

I find my writing reveals all sorts of sympathies and interests which I had not formulated exactly to myself; "the expression of myself as an individual" has never been my aim. My whole attempt has been to discover and understand human motives, human feelings, to make a distillation of what human relations and experiences my mind has been able to absorb. I have never known an uninteresting human being, and I have never known two alike; there are broad classifications and deep similarities, but I am interested in the thumbprint. I am passionately involved with these individuals who populate all these enormous migrations, calamities; who fight wars and furnish life for the future; these beings without which, one by one, all the "broad movements of history" could never take place. One by one—as they were born.

6. *How would you describe the political tendency of American writing as a whole since 1930? How do you feel about it yourself? Are you sympathetic to the current tendency toward what may be called "literary nationalism"—a renewed emphasis, largely uncritical, on the specifically "American" elements in our culture?*

Political tendency since 1930 has been to the last degree a confused, struggling, drowning-man-and-straw sort of thing, stampede of panicked crowd, each man trying to save himself—one at a time trying to work out his horrible confusions. How do I feel about it? I suffer from it, and I try to work my way out to some firm ground of personal belief, as the others do. I have times of terror and doubt and indecision, I am confused in all the uproar of shouting maddened voices and the flourishing of death-giving weapons. . . . I should like to save myself, but I have no assurance that I can, for if the victory goes as it threatens, I am not on that side.* The third clause of this question I find biased. Let me not be led away by your phrase "largely uncritical" in regard to the "emphasis on specifically American" elements in our culture. If we become completely uncritical and nationalistic, it will be the most European state of mind we could have. I hope we may not. I hope we shall have balance enough to see ourselves plainly, and choose what we shall keep and what discard

* At the time this was written it was clear enough that I was opposed to every form of authoritarian, totalitarian government or religion, under whatever name in whatever country. I still am.

according to our own needs; not be rushed into fanatic self-love and self praise as a defensive measure against assaults from abroad. I think the "specifically American" things might not be the worst things for us to cultivate, since this is America, and we are Americans, and our history is not altogether disgraceful. The parent stock is European, but this climate has its own way with transplantations, and I see no cause for grievance in that.

7. *Have you considered the question of your attitude toward the pos sible entry of the United States into the next world war? What do you think the responsibilities of writers in general are when and if war comes?*

I am a pacifist. I should like to say now, while there is still time and place to speak, without inviting immediate disaster (for I love life), to my mind the responsibility of the artist toward society is the plain and simple responsibility of any other human being, for I refuse to separate the artist from the human race: his prime responsibility "when and if war comes" is not to go mad. Madness takes many subtle forms, it is the old deceiver. I would say, don't be betrayed into all the old outdated mistakes. If you are promised something new and blissful at the mere price of present violence under a new master, first examine these terms carefully. New ideas call for new methods, the old flaying, drawing, and quartering for the love of God and the King will not do. If the method is the same, trust yourself, the idea is old, too. If you are required to kill someone today, on the promise of a political leader that someone else shall live in peace tomorrow, believe me, you are not only a double murderer, you are a suicide, too.

1940*: INTRODUCTION TO
FLOWERING JUDAS

It is just ten years since this collection of short stories first appeared They are literally first fruits, for they were written and published in order of their present arrangement in this volume, which contains the first story I ever finished. Looking at them again, it is possible still to say that

* This was written on June 21, 1940, seven days after the fall of France.

I do not repent of them; if they were not yet written, I should have to write them still. They were done with intention and in firm faith, though I had no plan for their future and no notion of what their meaning might be to such readers as they would find. To any speculations from interested sources as to why there were not more of them, I can answer simply and truthfully that I was not one of those who could flourish in the conditions of the past two decades. They are fragments of a much larger plan which I am still engaged in carrying out, and they are what I was then able to achieve in the way of order and form and statement in a period of grotesque dislocations in a whole society when the world was heaving in the sickness of a millennial change. They were first published by what seems still merely a lucky accident, and their survival through this crowded and slowly darkening decade is the sort of fate no one, least of all myself, could be expected to predict or even to hope for.

We none of us flourished in those times, artists or not, for art, like the human life of which it is the truest voice, thrives best by daylight in a green and growing world. For myself, and I was not alone, all the conscious and recollected years of my life have been lived to this day under the heavy threat of world catastrophe, and most of the energies of my mind and spirit have been spent in the effort to grasp the meaning of those threats, to trace them to their sources and to understand the logic of this majestic and terrible failure of the life of man in the Western world. In the face of such shape and weight of present misfortune, the voice of the individual artist may seem perhaps of no more consequence than the whirring of a cricket in the grass; but the arts do live continuously, and they live literally by faith; their names and their shapes and their uses and their basic meanings survive unchanged in all that matters through times of interruption, diminishment, neglect; they outlive governments and creeds and the societies, even the very civilizations that produced them. They cannot be destroyed altogether because they represent the substance of faith and the only reality. They are what we find again when the ruins are cleared away. And even the smallest and most incomplete offering at this time can be a proud act in defense of that faith.

1942: TRANSPLANTED WRITERS

One of the most disquieting by-products of the world disorders of the past few years has been the displacement of the most influential writers. The ablest German authors and journalists, for example, are no longer in Berlin and Leipzig, but in London and New York. The most articulate of the Spanish intelligentsia are not in Madrid but in Mexico City and Buenos Aires. This paradoxical situation must have far-reaching consequences, not only for the intellectuals themselves but for Germany, England and the United States, Spain, Mexico, and the Argentine. What, in your opinion, may these consequences be, immediate and remote, desirable and unfortunate?

The deepest harm in forced flight lies in the incurable wound to human pride and self-respect, the complete dislocation of the spiritual center of gravity. To be beaten and driven out of one's own place is the gravest disaster that can occur to a human being, for in such an act he finds his very humanity denied, his person dismissed with contempt, and this is a shock very few natures can bear and recover any measure of equilibrium.

Artists and writers, I think, do not suffer more than other people under such treatment, but they are apt to be more aware of the causes of their sufferings, they are better able to perceive what is happening, not only to them, but to all their fellow beings. I would not attempt to prophesy what the consequences of all this world displacement by violence of so many people might be; but I can only hope they will have learned something by it, and will leave in the grave of Europe their old quarrels and the old prejudices that have brought this catastrophe upon all of us. We have here enough of those things to fight without that added weight.

Americans are not going anywhere, and I am glad of it. Here we stay, for good or ill, for life or death; and my hope is that all those articulate intelligences who have been driven here will consent to stand with us, and help us put an end to this stampede of human beings driven like sheep over one frontier after another; I hope they will make an effort to understand what this place means in terms of the final battlefield. For the present, they must live here or nowhere, and they must share the responsibility for helping to make this a place where man can live as man and not as victim, pawn, a lower order of animal driven out to die beside the road or to survive in stealth and cunning.

The force at work in the world now is the oldest evil with a new name and new mechanisms and more complicated strategies; if the intelligent do not help to clarify the issues, maintain at least internal order, understand themselves and help others to understand the nature of what is happening, they hardly deserve the name. I agree with Mr. E. M. Forster that there are only two possibilities for any real order: in art and in religion. All political history is a vile mess, varying only in degrees of vileness from one epoch to another, and only the work of saints and artists gives us any reason to believe that the human race is worth belonging to.

Let these scattered, uprooted men remember this, and remember that their one function is to labor at preserving the humanities and the dignity of the human spirit. Otherwise they are lost and we are lost with them and whether they stay here or go yonder will not much matter.

No Plot, My Dear, No Story

This is a fable, children, of our times. There was a great big little magazine with four and one half million subscribers, or readers, I forget which; and the editors sat up nights thinking of new ways to entertain these people who bought their magazine and made a magnificent argument to convince advertisers that $3,794.36 an inch space-rates was a mere gift at the price. Look at all the buying-power represented. Look at all the money these subscribers must have if they can afford to throw it away on a magazine like the one we are talking about. So the subscribers subscribed and the readers read and the advertisers bought space and everything went on ring-around-the-rosy like that for God knows how long. In fact, it is going on right now.

So the editors thought up something beautiful and sent out alarms to celebrated authors and the agents of celebrated authors, asking everybody to think hard and remember the best story he had ever read, anywhere, anytime, and tell it over again in his own words, and he would be paid a simply appalling price for this harmless pastime.

By some mistake a penniless and only semi-celebrated author got on this list, and as it happened, that was the day the government had threatened to move in and sell the author's typewriter for taxes overdue, and a dentist had threatened to sue for a false tooth in the very front of the author's face; and there was also a grocery bill. So this looked as if

Providence had decided to take a hand in the author's business, and he or she, it doesn't matter, sat down at once and remembered at least *one* of the most beautiful stories he or she had ever read anywhere.* It was all about three little country women finding a wounded man in a ditch, giving him cold water to drink out of his own cap, piling him into their cart and taking him off to a hospital, where the doctors said they might have saved their trouble for the man was as good as dead.

The little women were just silly enough to be happy anyway that they had found him, and he wasn't going to die by himself in a ditch, at any rate. So they went on to market.

A month later they went back to the hospital, each carrying a wreath to put on the grave of the man they had rescued and found him there still alive in a wheelchair; and they were so overcome with joy they couldn't think, but just dropped on their knees in gratitude that his life was saved; this in spite of the fact that he probably was not going to be of any use to himself or anybody else for a long time if ever. . . . It was a story about instinctive charity and selfless love. The style was fresh and clear as the living water of their tenderness.

You may say that's not much of a story, but I hope you don't for it would pain me to hear you agree with the editors of that magazine. They sent it back to the author's agent with a merry little note: "No plot, my dear—no *story*. Sorry."

So it looks as if the tax collector will get the author's typewriter, and the dentist the front tooth, and the crows may have the rest; and all because the poor creature was stupid enough to think that a short story needed *first* a *theme*, and then a point of view, a certain knowledge of human nature and strong feeling about it, and style—that is to say, his own special way of telling a thing that makes it precisely his own and no one else's. . . . The greater the theme and the better the style, the better the story, you might say.

You might say, and it would be nice to think you would. Especially if you are an author and write short stories. Now listen carefully: except in emergencies, when you are trying to manufacture a quick trick and make some easy money, you don't really need a plot. If you have one, all well and good, if you know what it means and what to do with it. If you are aiming to take up the writing *trade*, you need very different equipment

* "Living Water" by C. Sergeev-Tzensky, *The Dial*, July, 1929.

from that which you will need for the *art*, or even just the *profession* of writing. There are all sorts of schools that can teach you exactly how to handle the 197 variations on any one of the 37 basic plots; how to take a parcel of characters you never saw before and muddle them up in some difficulty and get the hero or heroine out again, and dispose of the bad uns; they can teach you the O. Henry twist; the trick of "slanting" your stuff toward this market and that; you will learn what goes over big, what not so big, what doesn't get by at all; and you will learn for yourself, if you stick to the job, *why* all this happens. Then you are all set, maybe. After that you have only to buy a pack of "Add-a-Plot" cards (free ad.) and go ahead. Frankly, I wish you the luck you deserve. You have richly earned it.

But there are other and surer and much more honest ways of making money, and Mama advises you to look about and investigate them before leaping into such a gamble as mercenary authorhood. Any plan to make money is a gamble, but grinding out "slanted" stuff takes a certain knack, a certain willingness to lose all, including honor; you will need a cold heart and a very thick skin and an allowance from your parents while you are getting started toward the big money. You stand to lose your youth, your eyesight, your self-respect, and whatever potentialities you may have had in other directions, and if the worst comes to the worst, remember, nobody promised you anything. . . . Well, if you are going to throw all that, except the self-respect, into the ash can, you may as well, if you wish to write, be as good a writer as you can, say what you think and feel, add a little something, even if it is the merest fraction of an atom, to the sum of human achievement.

First, have faith in your theme, then get so well acquainted with your characters that they live and grow in your imagination exactly as if you saw them in the flesh; and finally, tell their story with all the truth and tenderness and severity you are capable of; and if you have any character of your own, you will have a style of your own; it grows, as your ideas grow, and as your knowledge of your craft increases.

You will discover after a great while that you are probably a writer. You may even make some money at it.

One word more: I have heard it said, boldly and with complete sincer-
̱ ᵣ̱sons who should know better, that the only authors who do not
̱e high-paying magazines are those who have not been able to
̱grade; that any author who professes to despise or even disap

prove of such writing and such magazines is a hypocrite; that he would be too happy to appear in those pages if only he were invited.

To such effrontery I have only one answer, based on experience and certain knowledge. It is simply not true.

1942

On Writing

(recorded on tape)

In full summer, eighteen years ago, during a short return from Paris, where I was then living, I stood up before my first group of student writers at a Writers' Conference in a small midwestern college, Olivet College, Olivet, Michigan, 1936. The students, a mixed audience of all ages and sorts of persons, gazed at me with what I took to be challenging if not hostile expectancy; I gazed back, stricken. The full rather awful meaning of our gathering there, confronting each other, had just dawned upon me for I confess I had not taken the invitation to speak there to beginning writers very seriously. I still took it for granted that any writer worth taking seriously would naturally be at home where he belonged doing his work by himself under his own power. Why in this world should he be asking advice from me or any other writer, and what could he get from talk that he could not better find in the published books of those he wished to study? Yet, I told myself, it cannot possibly harm anyone to spend two weeks in a year reading and talking about great literature, even trying his hand at putting words and phrases together to discover what the work really is; at least it will help to do away with careless reading, as the study of music makes for good listening; whoever tries to paint never just glances carelessly at a canvas or a statue again. Or so I wish to believe. Lightheartedly I had come there, happy at the chance to see some of my old friends who were writers, to enjoy the human sociability, and to talk a little about writing, which I then liked ~~to~~ I don't anymore, and it is the Writers' Conferences which have

there frozen under the weight of a responsibility I had

assumed so easily it seems now, remembering, almost to have been frivolity on my part. These people sitting there were expecting something from me that I had been engaged to deliver without knowing what I had promised. They had come, many of them, from teaching jobs, from offices, from work of all kinds, using their vacation time and their savings and their few days of freedom for the whole year; and for this price and the price of their attention and hard trying, they expected to be taught how to write.

Whatever my carefully prepared opening line was to be, it disappeared. I said: "If you came here hoping for a miracle, there can be none. If you believe that you have paid to receive here a magic formula, a secret you may use at will, you have done no such thing. Writing, in any sense that matters, cannot be taught. It can only be learned, and learned by each separate one of us in his own way, by the use of his own powers of imagination and perception, the ability to learn the lessons he has set for himself. That is, if your intention is to try yourself out, to find whether or not you have the makings of an artist. If you have come to make this test on yourself, then this place might be a very good trial field for you—or better, a workshop, like a silversmith's or a cabinetmaker's. I mention these two because they are two of many fine crafts in which trickiness, dishonesty or just poor sense of form cannot be disguised, any more than they can be in writing; and you may properly expect here professional instruction in the working of what Henry James calls your 'soluble stuff.' The good artist is first a good workman, and yet you may become a very good workman without ever becoming a master. Nothing else is worth aspiring to, and we all run the risk of never arriving at it. If you have the vocation, it is very well worth spending a lifetime at it by living in the love of your work, you cannot be wasted. After all it is a lovely thing to live in the light and the presence of the great arts, and by this light and this presence to practice your own to the farthest reach of your own gift. So I am here to read your manuscripts and talk to you about them, so that in talking to me you may perhaps be able better to clear up your own doubts and difficulties. A working artist myself trying hopefully to do better someday, I shall show you as well as I can such technical devices as may have worked for me—eventually you must find your own. It is a good thing to know all the rules, but remember they are not the wings of Pegasus, but mere step-ladders, stilts, or even crutches, if you rely on them as such. The great works of literature come first, remember, and all rules, devices, techniques, forms, are founded on them, made out of their tissues, and every true genius creates new ones, or gives us imaginative (and workable) variations on the old. The familiar knowledge of this continuous, changing, bountiful life of the human imagination is something not to be missed, should be valued for its own sake, even if no one in this room ever writes another line."

Since then, the Writers' Conference has become a thriving domestic industry: sure enough, there have been no miracles. The effect has been to increase by the thousand the number of those who write, and there is almost no writer so bad (or so good!) that he cannot find a publisher. What the family magazines, regular publishers, literary reviews, cannot absorb, the paperback books and the anthologies can, and do. Processions of publishers' scouts visit the "creative writing" courses in hundreds of universities and colleges. Strolling bands of older critics, poets, novelists yearly ride circuit on writers' conferences in dozens of colleges and universities. I dare say prizes, grants, fellowships for every kind of writing there is number yearly into the hundreds. A brilliant young writer, William Styron, recently remarked in effect that this is not the Lost Generation, but the subsidized one. (There never was a lost generation of artists—that is only a cheerful myth, by the way.) I am happy to see four hundred and ninety-nine promising young writers comfortably provided for while they reach their level, for the sake of that one indispensable first-rater, even maybe a genius, we all look for and hope for. And don't worry, he will come, he always does. Usually only one or two in a century, now and then in a cluster or galaxy, in a well spring of richness, but he does not fail. In the present fevered rush to publish just anything and anybody, and all the critics hailing all writing on his own level of understanding as great, with books and poets of the year, of the month, of the hour, of the minute, we can get a little confused. Be calm. The real poet, the real novelist, will emerge out of the uproar. He will be here, he is even now on his way.

1954

"Noon Wine": The Sources

By the time a writer has reached the end of a story, he has lived it at least three times over—first in the series of actual events that, directly or indirectly, have combined to set up that commotion in his mind and senses that causes him to write the story; second, in memory; and third, in recreation of this chaotic stuff. One might think this is enough; but no, the writer now finds himself challenged to trace his clues to their sources and to expose the roots of his work in his own most secret and private life; and is asked to live again this sometimes exhausting experience for the fourth time! There was a time when critics of literature seemed quite happy to try digging out the author's meanings without help; or, failing to find any, to invent meanings of their own, often just as satisfactory to everybody—except perhaps to the author, whose feelings or opinion traditionally do not count much, anyway.

The private reader too has always been welcome to his own notions of what he is reading, free to remark upon it to his heart's content, with no cramping obligation to be "right" in his conclusions, such as weighs upon the professionals or paid critics; it is enough for him to be moved and stimulated to speak his thoughts freely; the author will not mind even harshness, if only he can be sure he is being read! But it is, I think, a relatively late thing for authors to be asked to explain themselves, though some have done it in self-defense against their hardier critics. Flaubert occurs to me as, if not the earliest, one of the most lucid and painstaking; Henry James as the most prodigally, triumphantly eloquent, and thorough. Yet they held closely to the work as a finished piece of literature, and made almost no attempt—perhaps they knew better—to trace its history to its sources in their blood and bones, the subterranean labyrinths of infancy and childhood, family histories, memories, visions, daydreams, and nightmares—or to connect these gauzy fantasies to the solid tissues of their adult professional lives.

Truth is, it is quite an impossible undertaking, or so I have found it; a little like attempting to tap one's spinal fluid—and if that is a gruesome and painful comparison, be sure that I meant it to be. For this incomplete account has cost me more work and trouble and presented me with more insoluble problems and unanswerable questions than the story itself ever did, in any phase of its growth. Indeed perhaps I have not succeeded in explaining anything at all, and this is a meditation rather than an exposition; for there are still, intact if somewhat disturbed by my agitating hand, all those same ancient areas of mystery and darkness in which all beginnings are hidden: I have confronted them before, and again, and again, only to return each time not altogether defeated, but with only a few tattered fragments of the human secret in my hand. Such as these mysteries are, or such as they reveal themselves in fragments to me, I love them, I do not fear them but I treat them with the respect I know they well deserve.

I chose to write about "Noon Wine" because among my stories it is at once the most remote and the most familiar, the most obscure in origin and the most clearly visible in meanings to me; or indeed, these are my reasons, but I do not know exactly why I chose it any more than I really know why I wrote it in the first place.

This short novel, "Noon Wine," exists so fully and wholly in its own right in my mind, that when I attempt to trace its growth from the beginning, to follow all the clues to their sources in my memory, I am dismayed; because I am confronted with my own life, the whole society in which I was born and brought up, and the facts of it. My aim is to find the truth in it, and to this end my imagination works and reworks its recollections in a constant search for meanings. Yet in this endless remembering which surely must be the main occupation of the writer, events are changed, reshaped, interpreted again and again in different ways, and this is right and natural because it is the intention of the writer to write fiction, after all—real fiction, not a *roman à clef*, or a ̣̣̣̣ disguised personal confession which better belongs to the psycho-
ance. By the time I wrote "Noon Wine" it had become
ιe almost in the sense that I felt not as if I had made that

tory out of my own memory and real events and imagined consequences, but as if I were quite simply reporting events I had heard or
witnessed. This is not in the least true: the story is fiction; but it is made
up of thousands of things that did happen to living human beings in a
certain part of the country, at a certain time of my life, things that are
till remembered by others as single incidents; not as I remembered
them, floating and moving with their separate life and reality, meeting
nd parting and mingling in my thoughts until they established their
elationship and meaning to me. I could see and feel very clearly that all
hese events, episodes—hardly that, sometimes, but just mere glimpses
nd flashes here and there of lives strange or moving or astonishing to
ne—were forming a story, almost of themselves, it seemed; out of their
pparent incoherence, unrelatedness, they grouped and clung in my
mind in a form that gave a meaning to the whole that the individual
parts had lacked. So I feel that this story is "true" in the way that a work
f fiction should be true, created out of all the scattered particles of life I
was able to absorb and combine and to shape into a living new being.

But why did this particular set of memories and early impressions
combine in just this way to make this particular story? I do not in the
east know. And though it is quite true that I intended to write fiction,
his story wove itself in my mind for years before I ever intended to write
t; there were many other stories going on in my head at once; some of
hem evolved and were written, more were not. Why? This to me is the
most interesting question, because I am sure there is an answer, but
nobody knows it yet.

When the moment came to write this story, I knew it; and I had to
make quite a number of practical arrangements to get the time free for
t, without fear of interruptions. I wrote it as it stands except for a few
pen corrections, in just seven days of trancelike absorption in a small
oom in an inn in rural Pennsylvania, from the early evening of November 7 to November 14, 1936. Yet I had written the central part, the
cene between Mr. Hatch and Mr. Thompson, which leads up to the
murder in Basel, Switzerland, in the summer of 1932.

I had returned from Europe only fifteen days before I went to the inn
n Pennsylvania: this was the end, as it turned out of my living abroad,
except for short visits back to Paris, Brittany, Rome, Belgium: but meantime I had, at a time of great awareness and active energy, spent nearly
fourteen years of my life out of this country: in Mexico, Bermuda, Spain,

Germany, Switzerland, but, happiest and best, nearly five years in Paris. Of my life in these places I felt then, and feel now, that it was all entirely right, timely, appropriate, exactly where I should have been and what doing at that very time. I did not feel exactly at home; I knew where home was; but the time had come for me to see the world for myself, and so I did, almost as naturally as a bird taking off on his new wing-feathers. In Europe, things were not so strange; sometimes I had a pleasant sense of having here and there touched home base; if I was not at home, I was sometimes with friends. And all the time, I was making notes on stories—stories of my own place, my South—for my part of Texas was peopled almost entirely by Southerners from Virginia, Tennessee, the Carolinas, Kentucky, where different branches of my own family were settled, and I was almost instinctively living in a sustained state of mind and feeling, quietly and secretly, comparing one thing with another, always remembering; and all sorts of things were falling into their proper places, taking on their natural shapes and sizes, and going back and back clearly into right perspective—right for me as artist, I simply mean to say; and it was like breathing—I did not have consciously to urge myself to think about it. So my time in Mexico and Europe served me in a way I had not dreamed of, even, besides its own charm and goodness: it gave me back my past and my own house and my own people—the native land of my heart.

This summer country of my childhood, this place of memory, is filled with landscapes shimmering in light and color, moving with sounds and shapes I hardly ever describe, or put in my stories in so many words; they form only the living background of what I am trying to tell, so familiar to my characters they would hardly notice them; the sound of mourning doves in the live oaks, the childish voices of parrots chattering on every back porch in the little towns, the hoverings of buzzards in the high blue air—all the life of that soft blackland farming country, full of fruits and flowers and birds, with good hunting and good fishing; with plenty of water, many little and big rivers. I shall name just a few of the rivers I remember—the San Antonio, the San Marcos, the Trinity, the Nueces, the Rio Grande, the Colorado, and the small clear branch of the Río Blanco, full of colored pebbles, Indian Creek, the place where I was born. The colors and tastes all had their smells, as the sounds have now their echoes: the bitter whiff of air over a sprawl of animal skeleton after the buzzards were gone; the smells and flavors of roses and melons, and peach bloom and ripe peaches, of cape jessamine in hedges blooming like popcorn, and the sickly sweetness of chinaberry florets; of honeysuckle in great swags on a trellised gallery; heavy tomatoes dead ripe and warm with the midday sun, eaten there, at the vine; the delicious milky green corn, savory hot corn bread eaten with still-warm sweet milk; and the clinging brackish smell of the muddy little ponds where we caught and boiled crawfish—in a discarded lard can—and ate them, then and there, we children, in the company of an old Negro who had once been my grandparent's slave, as I have told in another story. He was by our time only a servant, and a cantankerous old cuss very sure of his place in the household.

Uncle Jimbilly, for that was his name, was not the only one who knew exactly where he stood, and just about how far he could go in maintaining the rights, privileges, exemptions of his status so long as he performed its duties. At this point, I want to give a rather generalized view of the society of that time and place as I remember it, and as talks with my elders since confirm it. (Not long ago I planned to visit a very wonderful old lady who was a girlhood friend of my mother. I wrote to my sister that I could not think of being a burden to Miss Cora, and would therefore stop at the little hotel in town and call on her. And my sister wrote back air mail on the very day saying: "For God's sake, don't mention the word hotel to Miss Cora—she'll think you've lost your raising!") The elders all talked and behaved as if the final word had gone out long ago on manners, morality, religion, even politics: nothing was ever to change, they said, and even as they spoke, everything was changing, shifting, disappearing. This had been happening in fact ever since they were born; the greatest change, the fatal dividing change in this country, the War between the States, was taking place even as most of my father's generation were coming into the world. But it was the grandparents who still ruled in daily life; and they showed plainly in acts, words, and even looks (an enormously handsome generation they seemed to have been I remember—all those wonderful high noses with diamond-shaped bony structure in the bridge!) the presence of good society, very well based on traditional Christian beliefs. These beliefs were mainly Protestant but not yet petty middle-class puritanism: there remained still an element fairly high stepping and wide gestured in its personal conduct. The petty middle class of fundamentalists who saw no difference between wine-drinking, dancing, card-playing, and adultery, had not yet got altogether the upper hand in that part of the country—in fact, never did except in certain limited areas; but it was making a brave try. It was not really a democratic society; if everybody had his place, sometimes very narrowly defined, at least he knew where it was, and so did everybody else. So too, the higher laws of morality and religion were defined; if a man offended against the one, or sinned against the other, he knew it, and so did his neighbors, and they called everything by its right name.

This firm view applied also to social standing. A man who had humble ancestors had a hard time getting away from them and rising in the world. If he prospered and took to leisurely ways of living, he was merely "getting above his raising." If he managed to marry into one of the good old families, he had simply "outmarried himself." If he went away and made a success somewhere else, when he returned for a visit he was still only "that Jimmerson boy who went No'th." There is—was, perhaps I should say—a whole level of society of the South where it was common knowledge that the mother's family outranked the father's by half, at least. This might be based on nothing more tangible than that the mother's family came from Richmond or Charleston, while the father's may have started out somewhere from Pennsylvania, or have got bogged down one time or another in Arkansas. If they turned out well, the children of these matches were allowed their mother's status, for good family must never be denied, but father remained a member of the Plain People to the end. Yet there was nothing against anyone hinting at better lineage and a family past more dignified than the present, no matter how humble his present circumstances, nor how little proof he could offer for his claim. Aspiration to higher and better things was natural to all men, and a sign of proper respect for true blood and birth. Pride and hope may be denied to no one.

In this society of my childhood there were all sorts of tender ways of feeling and thinking, subtle understanding between people in matters of ritual and ceremony; I think in the main a civilized society, and yet, with the underlying, perpetual ominous presence of violence; violence potential that broke through the smooth surface almost without warning, or maybe just without warning to children, who learned later to know the signs. There were old cruel customs, the feud, for one, gradually dying out among the good families, never in fact prevalent among them—the men of that class fought duels, and abided, in theory at least, on the outcome; and country life, ranch life, was rough in Texas, at least. I remember tall bearded booted men striding about with clanking spurs, and carrying loaded pistols inside their shirts next to their ribs, even to church. It was quite matter of course that you opened a closet door in a bedroom and stared down into the cold eyes of shotguns and rifles, stacked there because there was no more room in the gun closet. In the summer, in that sweet-smelling flowery country, we children with our father or some grown-up in charge, spent long afternoons on a range, shooting at fixed targets or clay pigeons with the ordinary domestic fire arms, pistols, rifles of several calibers, shotguns to be fired single and double. I never fired a shotgun, but I knew the sounds and could name any round of fire I heard, even at great distances.

Someone asked me once where I had ever heard that conversation in "Noon Wine" between two men about chewing tobacco—that apparently aimless talk between Mr. Hatch and Mr. Thompson which barely masks hatred and is leading toward a murder. It seems that I *must* have heard something of the sort somewhere, sometime or another; I do not in the least remember it. But that whole countryside was full of tobacco-chewing men, whittling men, hard-working farming men perched on fences with their high heels caught on a rail, or squatting on their toes, gossiping idly and comfortably for hours at a time. I often wondered what they found to say to each other, day in day out year after year; but I should never have dared go near enough to listen profitably; yet I surely picked up something that came back whole and free as air that summer in Basel, Switzerland, when I thought I was studying only the life of Erasmus and the Reformation. And I have seen them many a time take out their razor-sharp long-bladed knives and slice a "chew" as delicately and precisely as if they were cutting a cake. These knives were so keen, often I have watched my father, shelling pecans for me, cut off the ends of the hard shells in a slow circular single gesture; then split them down the sides in four strips and bring out the nut meat whole. This fascinated me, but it did not occur to me to come near the knife, or offer to touch it. In our country life, in summers, we were surrounded by sharpened blades—hatchets, axes, plowshares, carving knives, Bowie knives, straight razors. We were taught so early to avoid all these, I do not remember ever being tempted to take one in my hand. Living as we did all our summers among loaded guns and dangerous cutting edges, four wild, adventurous children, always getting hurt in odd ways, we none of us were ever injured seriously. The worst thing that happened was, my elder sister got a broken collar bone from a fall, not as you might expect from a horse, for we almost lived on horseback, but from a three-foot fall off a fence where she had climbed to get a better view of a battle between two bulls. But these sharp blades slicing tobacco—did I remember it because it was an unusual sight? I think not. I must have seen it, as I remember it, dozens of times—but one day I really *saw* it: and it became part of Mr. Thompson's hallucinated vision when he killed Mr. Hatch, and afterward could not live without justifying himself.

There is an early memory, not the first, but certainly before my third year, always connected with this story, "Noon Wine"; it is the source, if there could be only one. I was a very small child. I know this by the remembered vastness of the world around me, the giant heights of grown-up people; a chair something to be scaled like a mountain; a table top to be peered over on tiptoe. It was late summer and near sunset, for the sky was a clear green-blue with long streaks of burning rose in it, and the air was full of the mournful sound of swooping bats. I was all alone in a wide grassy plain—it was the lawn on the east side of the house—and I was in that state of instinctive bliss which children only know, when there came like a blow of thunder echoing and rolling in that green sky, the explosion of a shotgun, not very far away, for it shook the air. There followed at once a high, thin, long-drawn scream, a sound I had never heard, but I knew what it was—it was the sound of death in the voice of a man. How did I know it was a shotgun? How should I not have known? How did I know it was death? We are born knowing death.

Let me examine this memory a little, which, though it is of an actual event, is like a remembered dream; but then all my childhood is that; and if in parts of this story I am trying to tell you, I use poetic terms, it is because in such terms do I remember many things and the feeling is valid, it cannot be left out, or denied.

In the first place, could I have been alone when this happened? It is most unlikely. I was one of four children, brought up in a houseful of adults of ripening age; a grandmother, a father, several Negro servants, among them two aged, former slaves; visiting relatives, uncles, aunts, cousins; grandmother's other grandchildren older than we, with always an ill-identified old soul or two, male or female, who seemed to be guests but helped out with stray chores. The house, which seemed so huge to me, was probably barely adequate to the population it accommodated;

but of one thing I am certain—nobody was ever alone except for the most necessary privacies, and certainly no child at any time. Children had no necessary privacies. We were watched and herded and monitored and followed and spied upon and corrected and lectured and scolded (and kissed, let's be just, loved tenderly, and prayed over!) all day, every day, through the endless years of childhood—endless, but where did they go? So the evidence all points to the fact that I was not, could not have been, bodily speaking, alone in that few seconds when for the first time I heard the sound of murder. Who was with me? What did she say—for it was certainly one of the caretaking women around the house. Could I have known by instinct, of which I am so certain now, or did someone speak words I cannot remember which nonetheless told me what had happened? There is nothing more to tell, all speculations are useless; this memory is a spot of clear light and color and sound, of immense, mysterious illumination of feeling against a horizon of total darkness.

Yet, was it the next day? next summer? In that same place, that grassy shady yard, in broad daylight I watched a poor little funeral procession creeping over the stony ridge of the near horizon, the dusty road out of town which led also to the cemetery. The hearse was just a spring wagon decently roofed and curtained with black oil cloth, poverty indeed, and some members of our household gathered on the front gallery to watch it pass, said, "Poor Pink Hodges—old man A— got him just like he said he would." Had it been Pink Hodges then, I had heard screaming death in the blissful sunset? And who was old man A—, whose name I do not remember, and what became of him, I wonder? I'll never know. I remember only that the air of our house was full of pity for Pink Hodges, for his harmlessness, his helplessness, "so pitiful, poor thing," they said; and, "It's just not right," they said. But what did they do to bring old man A— to justice, or at least to a sense of his evil? Nothing, I am afraid. I began to ask all sorts of questions and was silenced invariably by some elder who told me I was too young to understand such things.

Yet here I am coming to something quite clear, of which I am entirely certain. It happened in my ninth year, and again in that summer house in the little town near the farm, with the yard full of roses and irises and honeysuckle and hackberry trees, and the vegetable garden and the cow barn in back. It was already beginning to seem not so spacious to me; it went on dwindling year by year to the measure of my growing up.

One hot moist day after a great thunderstorm and heavy long rain, I saw a strange horse and buggy standing at the front gate. Neighbors and kin in the whole countryside knew each other's equipages as well as they did their own, and this outfit was not only strange, but not right; don't ask me why. It was not a good horse, and the buggy was not good, either. There was something wrong in the whole thing, and I went full of curiosity to see why such strangers as would drive such a horse and buggy would be calling on my grandmother. (At this point say anything you please about the snobbism of children and dogs. It is real. As real as the snobbism of their parents and owners, and much more keen and direct.)

I stood just outside the living-room door, unnoticed for a moment by my grandmother, who was sitting rather stiffly, with an odd expression on her face; a doubtful smiling mouth, brows knitted in painful inquiry. She was a woman called upon for decisions, many decisions every day, wielding justice among her unruly family. Once she struck, justly or unjustly, she dared not retract—the whole pack would have torn her to pieces. They did not want justice in any case, but revenge, each in his own favor. But this situation had nothing to do with her family, and there she sat, worried, undecided. I had never seen her so, and it dismayed me.

Then I saw first a poor sad pale beaten-looking woman in a faded cotton print dress and a wretched little straw hat with a wreath of wilted forgetmenots. She looked as if she had never eaten a good dinner, or slept in a comfortable bed, or felt a gentle touch; the mark of life-starvation was all over her. Her hands were twisted tight in her lap and she was looking down at them in shame. Her eyes were covered with dark glasses. While I stared at her, I heard the man sitting near her almost shouting in a coarse, roughened voice: "I swear, it was in self-defense! His life or mine! If you don't believe me, ask my wife here. She saw it. My wife won't lie!" Every time he repeated these words, without lifting her head or moving, she would say in a low voice, "Yes, that's right. I saw it."

In that moment, or in another moment later as this memory sank in and worked my feelings and understanding, it was quite clear to me, and seems now to have been clear from the first, that he expected her to lie, was indeed forcing her to tell a lie; that she did it unwillingly and unlovingly in bitter resignation to the double disgrace of her husband's crime and her own sin; and that he, stupid, dishonest, soiled as he was, was imploring her as his only hope, somehow to make his lie a truth.

I used this scene in "Noon Wine," but the man in real life was not lean and gaunt and blindly, foolishly proud like Mr. Thompson; no, he was just a great loose-faced, blabbing man full of guilt and fear, and he was bawling at my grandmother, his eyes bloodshot with drink and tears, "Lady, if you don't believe me, ask my wife! She won't lie!" At this point my grandmother noticed my presence and sent me away with a look we children knew well and never dreamed of disobeying. But I heard part of the story later, when my grandmother said to my father, with an unfamiliar coldness in her voice, for she had made her decision about this affair, too: "I was never asked to condone a murder before. Something new." My father said, "Yes, and a coldblooded murder too if there ever was one."

So, there was the dreary tale of violence again, this time with the killer out on bail, going the rounds of the countryside with his wretched wife, telling his side of it—whatever it was; I never knew the end. In the meantime, in one summer or another, certainly before my eleventh year, for that year we left that country for good, I had two memorable glimpses. My father and I were driving from the farm to town, when we met with a tall black-whiskered man on horseback, sitting so straight his chin was level with his Adam's apple, dressed in clean mended blue denims, shirt open at the throat, a big devil-may-care black felt hat on the side of his head. He gave us a lordly gesture of greeting, caused his fine black horse to curvet and prance a little, and rode on, grandly. I asked my father who that could be, and he said, "That's Ralph Thomas, the proudest man in seven counties." I said, "What's he proud of?" And my father said, "I suppose the horse. It's a very fine horse," in a good-humored, joking tone, which made the poor man quite ridiculous, and yet not funny, but sad in some way I could not quite understand.

On another of these journeys I saw a bony, awkward, tired-looking man, tilted in a kitchen chair against the wall of his comfortless shack, set back from the road under the thin shade of hackberry trees, a thatch of bleached-looking hair between his eyebrows, blowing away at a doleful tune on his harmonica, in the hot dull cricket-whirring summer day; the very living image of loneliness. I was struck with pity for this stranger, his eyes closed against the alien scene, consoling himself with such poor music. I was told he was someone's Swedish hired man.

In time—when? how?—Pink Hodges, whom I never knew except in the sound of his death-cry, merged with my glimpse of the Swedish hired man to become the eternal Victim; the fat bullying whining man in my grandmother's living room became the Killer. But nothing can remain so simple as that, this was only a beginning. Helton too, the Victim in my story, is also a murderer, with the dubious innocence of the madman; but no less a shedder of blood. Everyone in this story contributes, one way or another directly or indirectly, to murder, or death by violence; even the two young sons of Mr. Thompson who turn on him in their fright and ignorance and side with their mother, who does not need them; they are guiltless, for they meant no harm, and they do not know what they have contributed to; indeed in their innocence they believe they are doing, not only right, but the only thing they could possibly do in the situation as they understand it: they must defend their mother. . . .

Let me give you a glimpse of Mr. and Mrs. Thompson, not as they were in their real lives, for I never knew them, but as they have become in my story. Mr. Thompson is a member of the plain people who has, by a hair's breadth, outmarried himself. Mrs. Thompson's superiority is shown in her better speech, her care for the proprieties, her social sense; even her physical fragility has some quality of the "genteel" in it; but in the long run, her strength is in the unyielding chastity of her morals, at once her yoke and her crown, and the prime condition of her right to the respect of her society. Her great power is that, while both she and her husband believe that the moral law, once broken, is irreparable, she will still stand by her principles no matter what; and in the end he stands by too. They are both doomed by this belief in their own way: Mr. Thompson from the moment he swung the ax on Mr. Hatch; Mrs. Thompson from the moment she acted the lie which meant criminal collusion. That both law and society expect this collusion of women with their husbands, so that safeguards for and against it are provided both by custom and statute, means nothing to Mrs. Thompson. When Mr. Burleigh planned for her to sit in court, he was not being cynical, but only showing himself a lawyer who knew his business.

This Mrs. Thompson of "Noon Wine" I understand much better, of course, than I do that woman I saw once for five minutes when I was nine years old. She is a benign, tender, ignorant woman, in whom the desire for truthfulness is a habit of her whole being; she is the dupe of her misunderstanding of what virtue really is; a woman not meant for large emergencies. Confronted with pure disaster she responds with pure suffering, and yet will not consent to be merely the passive Victim, or as she thinks, the criminal instrument of her husband's self-justification. Mr. Thompson, of course, has not been able to explain anything to himself, nor to justify himself in the least. By his own standards of morality, he is a murderer, a fact he cannot face: he needs someone to tell him this is not so, not so by some law of higher truth he is incapable of grasping. Alas, his wife, whose judgment he respects out of his mystical faith in the potency of her virtue, agrees with him—he is indeed a murderer. He has been acquitted, in a way he is saved; but in making a liar of her he has in effect committed a double murder—one of the flesh, one of the spirit.

Mr. Thompson, having invented his account of the event out of his own hallucinations, would now like to believe in it: he cannot. The next best thing would be for his wife to believe it: she does not believe, and he knows it. As they drive about the countryside in that series of agonizing visits, she tells her lie again and again, steadfastly. But privately she withholds the last lie that would redeem him, or so he feels. He wants her to turn to him when they are alone sometime, maybe just driving along together, and say, "Of course, Mr. Thompson, it's as clear as day. I remember it now. It was all just as you said!"

This she will never say, and so he must accept his final self-condemnation. There is of course a good deal more to it than this, but this must do for the present—it is only meant to show how that unknown woman, sitting in my grandmother's parlor twisting her hands in shame all those years ago, got up one day from her chair and started her long journey through my remembering and transmuting mind, and brought her world with her.

And here I am brought to a pause, for almost without knowing it, I have begun to write about these characters in a story of mine as though they were real persons exactly as I have shown them. And these fragments of memory on which the story is based now seem to have a random look; they nowhere contain in themselves, together or separately, the story I finally wrote out of them; a story of the most painful moral and emotional confusions, in which everyone concerned, yes, in his crooked way, even Mr. Hatch, is trying to do right.

It is only in the varying levels of quality in the individual nature that we are able finally more or less to measure the degree of virtue in each man. Mr. Thompson's motives are most certainly mixed, yet not ignoble;

not the highest but the highest he is capable of; he helps someone who helps him in turn; while acting in defense of what he sees as the good in his own life, the thing worth trying to save at almost any cost, he is trying at the same time to defend another life—the life of Mr. Helton, who has proved himself the bringer of good, the present help, the true friend. Mr. Helton would have done as much for me, Mr. Thompson says, and he is right. Yet he hated Mr. Hatch on sight, wished to injure him before he had a reason: could it not be a sign of virtue in Mr. Thompson that he surmised and resisted at first glance the evil in Mr. Hatch? The whole countryside, let us remember (for this is most important, the relations of a man to his society), agrees with Mr. Burleigh the lawyer, and the jury and the judge, that Mr. Thompson's deed was justifiable homicide: but this did not, as his neighbors confirmed, make it any less a murder. Mr. Thompson was not an evil man, he was only a poor sinner doing his best according to his lights, lights somewhat dimmed by his natural aptitude for Pride and Sloth. He still had his virtues, even if he did not quite know what they were, and so gave himself credit for some few that he had not.

But Hatch was the doomed man, evil by nature, a lover and doer of evil, who did no good thing for anyone, not even, in the long run, for himself. He was evil in the most dangerous irremediable way: one who works safely within the law, and has reasoned himself into believing his motives, if not good, are at least no worse than anyone else's: for he believes quite simply and naturally that the motives of others are no better than his own; and putting aside all nonsense about good, he will always be found on the side of custom and common sense and the letter of the law. When challenged he has his defense pat and ready, and there is nothing much wrong with it—it only lacks human decency, of which he has no conception beyond a faint hearsay. Mr. Helton is, by his madness, beyond good and evil, his own victim as well as the victim of others. Mrs. Thompson is a woman of the sort produced in numbers in that time, that class, that place, that code: so trained to the practice of her prescribed womanly vocation of virtue as such—manifest, unrelenting, sacrificial, stupefying—she has almost lost her human qualities, and her spiritual courage and insight, to boot. She commits the, to her, dreadful unforgivable sin of lying; moreover, lying to shield a criminal, even if that criminal is her own husband. Having done this, to the infinite damage, as she sees it, of her own soul (as well as her self-respect which is founded on her feeling of irreproachability), she lacks the courage and the love to see her sin through to its final good purpose; to commit it with her whole heart and with perfect acceptance of her guilt; to say to her husband the words that might have saved them both, soul and body—might have, I say only. I do not know and shall never know. Mrs. Thompson was not that robust a character, and his story, given all, must end as it does end. . . . There is nothing in any of these beings tough enough to work the miracle of redemption in them.

Suppose I imagine now that I really saw all of these persons in the flesh at one time or another? I saw what I have told you, a few mere flashes of a glimpse here and there, one time or another; but I do know why I remembered them, and why in my memory they slowly took on their separate lives in a story. It is because there radiated from each one of those glimpses of strangers some element, some quality that arrested my attention at a vital moment of my own growth, and caused me, a child, to stop short and look outward, away from myself; to look at another human being with that attention and wonder and speculation which ordinarily, and very naturally, I think, a child lavishes only on himself. Is it not almost the sole end of civilized education of all sorts to teach us to be more and more highly, sensitively conscious of the reality of the existence, the essential being, of others, those around us so very like us and yet so bafflingly, so mysteriously different? I do not know whether my impressions were on the instant, as I now believe, or did they draw to their magnet gradually with time and confirming experience? That man on the fine horse, with his straight back, straight neck, shabby and unshaven, riding like a cavalry officer, "the proudest man in seven counties"—I saw him no doubt as my father saw him, absurd, fatuous, but with some final undeniable human claim on respect and not to be laughed at, except in passing, for all his simple vanity.

The woman I have called Mrs. Thompson—I never knew her name—showed me for the first time, I am certain, the face of pure shame; humiliation so nearly absolute it could not have been more frightening if she had groveled on the floor; and I knew that whatever the cause, it was mortal and beyond help. In that bawling sweating man with the loose mouth and staring eyes, I saw the fear that is moral cowardice and I knew he was lying. In that yellow-haired, long-legged man playing his harmonica I felt almost the first glimmer of understanding and sympathy for any suffering not physical. Most certainly I had already done my share of weeping over lost or dying pets, or beside someone I loved who was very sick, or my own pains and accidents; but *this* was a spiritual enlightenment, some tenderness, some first awakening of charity in my self-centered heart. I am using here some very old-fashioned noble words in their prime sense. They have perfect freshness and reality to me, they are the irreplaceable names of Realities. I know well what they mean, and I need them here to describe as well as I am able what happens to a child when the bodily senses and the moral sense and the sense of charity are unfolding, and are touched once for all in that first time when the soul is prepared for them; and I know that the all-important things in that way have all taken place long and long before we know the words for them.

1956

POEMS

Enchanted

On these familiar stones, this homely stair,
I set my feet as I am used to do;
I draw the curtains in my quiet house,
And feel the winds blow through.

Oh, tranquil roofs and muted drowsing bells,
Full of old secrets, marvel and be still
To see a wraith of fiery magic pass
Over my dark door sill.

Do not bewilder me, swift hunting moon,
With arrows of amazement in my eyes;
If these steep roofs should bloom, these stones should sing,
I would not know surprise!

1923

Two Songs from Mexico

I. IN TEPOZOTLAN

I should like to see again
That honey-colored girl
Dipping her arms shoulder-deep
In the hives of honey.
Who can tell me where she is gone,
That untroubled innocent
Whose hands were kissed by bees,
And whose fingers dripped honey?

II. FIESTA DE SANTIAGO

He moves in the subtle trance
Of a wild delicate dance.
Masked in a smile of death
He lifts his hand
In a gesture scrawled upon tombs.
The odour of silence
Is in his breath.
He turns his head
With the fatal repose
Of the indifferent dead.

1924

Little Requiem

She should have had the state
Of a king's daughter,
Or a hut of willow branch
Near running water.

Or a scaled silver armour
For a breast cover,
Or a sweet lie in her mouth
For a lying lover.

Since she had none of these,
But a song instead,
She has well hidden herself
With the beaten dead.

Since for lack of these things
She knew herself lost,
She has well chosen silence
With her hands crossed.

1924

Winter Burial

Now crunches down the frozen stalk
On sterile snow:
Chill core of winter fruit in the mouth
Is bitter as a blow.

Pluck out this seed and bury it
Under a rock:
Against the winter measure of thin days
Tapped out upon a clock.

1926

Anniversary in a Country Cemetery

This time of year, this year of all years, brought
The homeless one home again;
To the fallen house and the drowsing dust
There to sit at the door,
Welcomed, homeless no more.
Her dust remembers its dust
And calls again
Back to the fallen house this restless dust
This shape of her pain.
This shape of her love
Whose living dust reposes
Beside her dust,
Sweet as the dust of roses.

1940

November in Windham

These winds of Martinmas have stripped the trees
To cover the seeds of summer, and the limbs
Are rough as roots, and roots are cold as stone:
I catch my breath and shiver to the bone,
Blood-kinfolk to the crickets and the bees.

The deer have cut their trails in bedded leaves
Worm-bitter apples rot beside the wall,
The scanty crop is stored in loft and bin:
All day I feel the winter hurrying in,
All night the hunting owls cry at my eaves.

This is a country aching at the core,
Dead-tired of the year's labors, weary beyond sleep:
Seeded once more in stones against the yield
Of a forgotten scarecrow in a field
Set there to frighten birds that come no more.

[1924] 1955

After a Long Journey

(to Gene . . . Berlin, Fall, 1931)

This was never our season. We the spring-born, the May Children
Put on winter like a hair shirt, we dwell on death, we wait
For the turn of the year, the leap of the sun
Into the track of spring. Let us turn clasping mittened hands
Idly into the Puppen Allee of the Tiergarten.

This is not even a timely season for our love—
Kisses freeze in our mouths, our arms enfold by habit
Talking columns of stone; yet we do not talk of love,
Our love, or say again, once more, once and forever
As if it were for the first time and the last time, a long farewell
   "I love you."

Once and forever words are engraved on motionless objects:
On these monuments celebrating potbellied kings, high-bosomed
   ladies,
Philosophers, comedians, tyrants, saints, slender pages
With crossed ankles and sly ambiguous smiles;
Or knights in plate armor clasping with smooth fists the hilts
Of their long-blunted answerable arguments of heroics;
Above all, on the tombs of statesmen and handsome Somebodies
   on horseback.
Besides a few poets. Stone or not, we sweat salt grief
From every pore, and our eyes continually wandering
Continually seek each other's, and we smile with a grimace like
   weeping.

Our images of travel mingle, oh, what shall we remember?

These streets of burnished iron, tender winter grass
Neatly shaven to the gray lips of water;
Hotels, cinemas—those Russian films showing Russian workingmen
Living lives of the maddest sanity, taking showers under samovar
    spouts,
Tossing off bottles of milk with their lunches, working like mules,
Laughing their heads off the whole time as if they were full of
    vodka and red pepper—

—The loud cold shudders of our ship that sailed on sea and meadow
The Caribbean, the Atlantic, the river Weser;
The spouting of whales, the bitter trap-mouthed faces of friars
In Santa Cruz de Tenerife, or the slender girls with doll hats tied
    to their foreheads,
And water jars on their heads, running wildly sure-footed as deer
In the steep stony pathways; or the lonely music
Of the train wheels turning in the night with the lunatic tune
We never could follow?

All, all such memories are rayed metal, a star with a cutting edge,
That shears one moment from another. Must we lose them all
Or shall we do a montage of them, and frame it?

Landscapes such as the Flemish painted best are motionless
As if posing for their portraits, alive but asleep among the windmills,
Thick with the smell of warm milk-soaked hides, ruminant breath-
    ings,
Clean orderly hoofs, minute proprieties of doorways curtained with
    wood smoke,
Bowed under the clotted sky, bloated with winter-thick water,
Benumbed with humble certainties, snoring in a snowdrift.

If this frost stiffens our hair, we still have the taste
Of sun in our mouths, of Mexico and mangos and melons
And the feathery shade of the Peruano tree in our eyes.
The summer sea has hauled us by our shoulders down and over and
    under,

We have stretched our muscles and yawned like cats in the smell
    of cedar.

    Oh, let us remember!

    Catalogues of defeat, advantages, stratagems, warfares, successes,
Anticipations, dried glories under glass, a point of view
Petrified on its feet; medals, ribbons, citations, careers by appoint-
    ment,
Official status propped by protocol—all these
I would leave in my will if I could to those for whom
Such things are substance, who rub these stuffs between their fingers
    for pleasure.

    We will walk like ghosts of panthers in the Tiergarten: untamed,
    invisible
To the little pale eyes behind puffy lids buttoned up against the
    frail sunlight.
The swaying bellies rumble with beer. We will look at the garden,
Observe the dubious riches of decay, pity that fatal ripeness,
The agony of the year, the bereaved branches, the exhausted leaves
    falling
Like tears which nobody notices. O sorrow, sorrow!

    Shall we ever forget how once we traveled to a far country,
A strange land, ourselves strangers to all and to each other?
The morning country of love and we two still strangers—
Our land is in winter now and the dazzle is gone from the morning.

    Ah, this was never our season, the spring-born
Wear winter like a thorn wreath, sniff the winds with cold noses
For the earliest rumor of sap, the singing thaw of rivers,
Feel under their ribs the snap of locks when the earth
Turns the key to her wine vaults and the wines flow upward.

    We the May Children will be ready to drink, to unfold, to carouse,
We will dance on air and walk on water for joy!

    Remember?

Here on a marble bench in this winter city we are presently at
   peace
To mingle the ash of our cigarettes, and to exchange our tokens:
A peachstone for a pigeon feather, a grasshopper wing for a sea shell,
A thorn from your wreath for a scrap of my hair shirt—

The spring-born in November!

1957

Measures for Song and Dance

Eve gave Adam the apple;
Adam took the whole apple,
Gave Eve one bite of the apple,
And ate the rest with Lilith.

> Eve, burdened with numerous household cares,
> Abel at her breast, Cain at her knee,
> Found Adam and Lilith gorged to the ears,
> Asleep in the shade of the plundered tree.

Eve cried out upon Adam,
She seized the scruff of Adam,
Asked "Where's my apple, Adam?"
And Adam looked at Lilith.

> Lilith yawned deeply and braided her hair:
> "O, for some men of my own," said she,
> "O, for an effective leaf to wear,
> And novel fruit from a different tree!"

Eve then flew at Lilith,
She tore the braids of Lilith,

She smacked the hapless Lilith,
And Lilith screamed for Adam.

But Adam was taken with dreadful throes;
Holding his midriff, "Lilith!" he cried,
"You stole Eve's apples, but never suppose
That I can be tempted away from her side!"

The Lord gave one look at His garden,
Threw the three of them out of His garden,
Gave them a briar-patch for their garden,
And asked: "Where's that Serpent?"

In the midst of the briar-patch stood a tree
With nubbly apples of bitter flavor,
"Now this is strictly for you and me,"
Eve told Adam, "forever and ever."

Lilith cast her eyes on the young Cain,
Motioned hitherward the young Cain,
Said, "He's a likely lad, this young Cain,
And he'll find me apples."

Adam spoke to Eve: "Let's be reasonable, dear,
As an example to Cain and to Abel;
We'll have a few apples twice a year
As a special treat at the family table."

Eve frowned at Adam and Adam leered at Lilith,
Lilith smiled at Cain and Cain gazed at the tree:
His mouth watered and his eyes yearned, his stomach trembled:
"I like apples, too," said he.

1950